North Carolina Marriage Bonds
and Certificates Series

Caswell County, North Carolina Marriage Records

1778-1876

❧❧❧

Frances T. Ingmire

Heritage Books
2024

HERITAGE BOOKS
AN IMPRINT OF HERITAGE BOOKS, INC.

Books, CDs, and more—Worldwide

For our listing of thousands of titles see our website
at
www.HeritageBooks.com

Published 2024 by
HERITAGE BOOKS, INC.
Publishing Division
5810 Ruatan Street
Berwyn Heights, MD 20740

International Standard Book Number
Paperbound: 978-0-7884-8429-2

FOREWORD

This book contains a listing of Marriage bonds before 1851, after 1851 Marriage Certificates were issued. These are on file in the North Carolina State Archives. It is suggested that all records be examined for more information than is given herein. Bonds often will give the names of others such as family members the groom or the bride's family, bondsmen and person performing the ceremony.

Although entries have been proof read there will be mistakes. The records were very hard to read and some names were spelled several ways. There has been no attempt to correct spelling or change dates. Names may appear as many as four times. If there was a question, a question mark will follow. Dates may be date of application or date of filing, most are in a matter of days, but some are off as many as six or seven years. These are not in error, but as they appeared on records.

Please check all spellings.

Grooms are listed in alphabetical order with cross index for the brides.

MARRIAGE RECORDS OF CASWELL COUNTY, NORTH CAROLINA

GROOM	BRIDE	DATE
ABBOTT, Richard M.	BAINES, Martha	04/09/1867
ADAMS, Edmon	VADEN, Patsey	06/18/1818
ADAMS, Hannible A. H.	BIRD, Mary E.	04/13/1862
ADAMS, Joel T.	FEILDER, Sarah	10/16/1828
ADAMS, John W.	MCLAUGHLAN, Sally H.	11/21/1867
ADAMS, Philip	POWELL, Fanny	06/24/1800
ADAMS, Richard	RUCKER, Amelia Ann	03/30/1833
ADAMS, Sylvester P.	GUNN, Adaline A.	10/03/1846
ADAMS, William	HODGES, Julia	11/15/1845
ADAMS, William A.	PATTERSON, Pelina	09/02/1858
ADAMS, William C.	WILLIAMSON, Emily	11/13/1855
ADAMS, William W.	WOMACK, Mary P.	07/30/1842
ADKIN, William D.	RIGNEY, Talitha J.	09/08/1865
ADKINS, Akillis	GIPSON, Jemia A.	07/21/1864
ADKINS, Byrd	YANCEY, Anna	04/22/1866
ADKINS, Green	KIMBRO, Hannah	10/20/1866
ADKINS, Henry	KIMBROUGH, Charity	03/08/1867
ADKINS, Henry F.	OLIVER, Frances	12/09/1847
ADKINS, James	BROOKS, Polley	04/02/1814
ADKINS, William	FOSTER, Nancey	10/10/1815
ADKINS, William	FULLER, Polley	10/26/1815
ADKINS, William	CHANDLER, Mary	06/03/1828
AKIN, James	MURPHEY, Mary	07/09/1779
AKIN, John	WADDELL, Patience	08/03/1816
ALBART, William B.	STADLER, Nancy A.	11/21/1840
ALDERSON, James A.	WALTERS, Julia	11/23/1867
ALDRESS, William	SMITHEY, Elizabeth	10/14/1799
ALDRIDGE, Andrew	MELTON, Patsey	04/17/1834
ALDRIDGE, Joseph	GRAVES, Patsey	12/25/1815
ALDRIDGE, P. H.	DAMERON, E. H.	03/07/1860
ALDRIDGE, Richard	PLEASANT, Lucy	01/21/1822
ALDRIDGE, William J.	DONOHO, Elizabeth	02/06/1856
ALDRIGE, James	MOORE, Isbella G.	10/27/1824
ALEXANDER, Benjamin	-----, -----	08/24/1819
ALEXANDER, Wallace H.	ROBERTSON, Mary R.	10/21/1850
ALLEN, Bob	DENNY, America	01/06/1866
ALLEN, George W.	TURNER, Mary A.	12/26/1866
ALLEN, James M.	MOORE, Mary R.	11/10/1854
ALLEN, John	HAMLETT, Rebecca Ann	07/10/1864
ALLEN, John	FEAGINS, Elizabeth	01/29/1851
ALLEN, John W.	WOODS, Ann E.	10/03/1865
ALLEN, Moses	INGRAM, Priscilla	05/02/1795
ALLEN, Randolph J.	HOUSE, Mary J.	12/21/1859
ALLEN, Robert	SWANN, Lucrecia	01/11/1857
ALLEN, Thomas H.	SOMERS, Frances J.	03/13/1862
ALLEN, Thomas T.	PUGH, Martha	10/25/1837
ALLEN, William	HORTON, Mary	03/04/1866
ALLISON, John	JOHNSTON, Polly	12/02/1799
ALLISON, John J.	HINTON, Mary E.	04/13/1846
ALLRED, William B.	ALDRIDGE, Hannah	11/17/1845
ALVERSON, Azariah J.	FORD, Mary Ann	01/26/1849

MARRIAGE RECORDS OF CASWELL COUNTY, NORTH CAROLINA

GROOM	BRIDE	DATE
ALVERSON, Azariah J.	WHITE, Celia	12/11/1841
ALVERSON, Claiborn W.	SWANN, Matilda J.	11/30/1850
ALVERSON, Jesse	KINSEY, Salley	09/02/1818
ALVERSON, Jesse	WRIGHT, Henny	07/20/1816
ALVERSON, William L.	MCKINNEY, Mary	01/20/1853
AMOS, William T.	EVANS, Mary P.	09/27/1859
ANDERSON, Albert J. B.	KIRBY, Fanny H.	08/06/1860
ANDERSON, Dennis	WILLIAMSON, Margaret	12/25/1865
ANDERSON, James	FLOOD, Martha M.	02/02/1839
ANDERSON, James	CADAL, Margret	07/09/1782
ANDERSON, Jno. Q.	RICE, Minerva J.	12/16/1863
ANDERSON, Moses G.	SCOGGINS, Rachel	12/26/1867
ANDERSON, Nelson	BROWN, China	12/22/1865
ANDERSON, Nelson S.	JONES, Frances A.	01/18/1853
ANDERSON, Quintin A.	TAITE, Mary A.	03/06/1862
ANDERSON, Quinton T.	WALKER, Virginia A.	02/14/1866
ANDERSON, William	HIGHTOWER, Sarah L.	09/25/1834
ANDERSON, William	KEESEE, Paulina Ann	03/14/1836
ANDERSON, William A.	JONES, Elizabeth A.	01/18/1853
ANDERSON, William R.	JONES, Polly	11/19/1860
ANDERSON, Wm. B.	WILLIAMS, Sophia	12/14/1858
ANGLIN, Caleb	POWELL, Hannah	11/09/1809
ANGLIN, William	RICE, Kerin Happuch	11/15/1789
ANGLIN, Wright	RICE, Kerin Happuch	11/15/1789
ANTHONEY, James	CORDER, Elizabeth	02/07/1781
ANTHONY, Jonathan	BERRY, Rebecca	11/07/1781
ANTHONY, Joseph	CANTREL, Hannah	02/17/1802
ANTHONY, William	SIMONS, Sally	07/30/1794
APPLE, Samuel	SOMERS, Mary Ann	10/22/1851
APPLE, William	CARLEN, Sarah	02/14/1840
ARCHER, Richard F.	BROWN, Elizabeth	05/19/1819
ARNETT, Stephen	TRIGG, Teletha	04/17/1837
ARNN, George W.	WITCHER, Julina F.	03/26/1851
ARNOLD, James W.	RICE, Sarah M.	01/06/1840
ARNOLD, Luke	STADLER, Susannah	02/21/1810
ARNOLD, Richard	COCK, Betsey	09/30/1814
ARNOLD, Richard	MELTON, Mary	03/24/1818
ARNOLD, Thomas	SEWELL, Polley	12/16/1812
ARNOLD, Wiett	AUSTIN, Fannie	01/06/1836
ARTWELL, Richard	TENNESSON, Sarah	12/08/1803
ASHBURN, Lewis	HAMLETT, Elizabeth	12/05/1797
ASHFORD, Willis	MASSEY, Nancey	05/09/1812
ASHWELL, William A.	SHEON, Misura E.	02/18/1857
ASPIN, Thomas	STAFFRD, Sarh	03/14/1782
ASTIN, Wilson J.	HODGESX, Kesiah A.	01/24/1846
ATKINSON, James H.	PRATHER, Martha A.	11/14/1836
ATKINSON, Jessee T.	BURTON, Mary	02/13/1827
ATKINSON, John	LEA, Sarah	09/15/1782
ATKINSON, John	WAREN, Fanny	03/06/1816
ATKINSON, Johnson E.	INGRAM, Elizabeth	05/05/1832
ATKINSON, Le Roy	SNEED, Annis	03/02/1835

MARRIAGE RECORDS OF CASWELL COUNTY, NORTH CAROLINA

GROOM	BRIDE	DATE
ATKINSON, Thomas	SAMUEL, Betsey Pain	08/14/1822
ATWELL, John	SMITH, Beney	12/08/1810
ATWELL, John	-----, -----	12/20/1807
ATWELL, Lock	SMITH, Polley	12/05/1807
AUSTIN, John H.	RIGGS, Elizabeth	12/16/1863
AUSTIN, Ransom B.	SCOTT, Lucey	04/18/1854
AYNCEY, James M.	SHUEMAKER, Ann	06/05/1833
AYRES, William	HENDERSON, Julia Ann	10/11/1834
BADGETT, Henry	GLASS, Martha S.	01/02/1830
BADGETT, Jno.	HOWARD, Ann	01/16/1817
BADGETT, Peter	PINDEXTER, Nancy	09/16/1820
BADGETT, Ransom	CARLOSS, Nancy	01/15/1803
BADGETT, William	SERGANT, Polly	11/14/1801
BAGLEY, George	-----, -----	05/11/1808
BAILEY, Noah	RANSOM, Betsey	09/05/1809
BAINES, Willis	RUDD, Sabine	01/12/1867
BAINS, James	WILLIS, Ebby	12/29/1810
BAKER, General	JONES, Lucy	11/11/1819
BALDWIN, Henry S.	RAY, Mary	10/22/1824
BALDWIN, John C.	PINNICK, Sarah B.	12/27/1866
BALL, Alfred L.	SMITH, Elizabeth M.	02/05/1852
BALL, David	CLARK, Francis L.	07/20/1819
BALL, G. S.	TAYLOR, Margarett	09/27/1864
BALL, Rufus	LEA, Celestia	02/18/1866
BALLAD, Larkin	FERRELL, Polly	01/01/1846
BALLARD, Andrew	REED, Haley	12/23/1809
BALLARD, Larkin	LOAFMAN, Jincey	01/02/1812
BALLARD, Lewis	WARY, Sally	12/23/1812
BALLARD, Mourning	BUSH, Dilley	02/08/1802
BARBER, James	JOHNSTON, Jane	01/09/1802
BARBER, N. S.	DALTON, Annie	04/29/1848
BARKEDALE, Squire	WASHINGTON, Lucy	09/29/1867
BARKER, Burnley	-----, -----	04/25/1809
BARKER, David	COCHRAN, Sarah	04/20/1790
BARKER, Eaton B.	FARLEY, Mary C.	10/12/1865
BARKER, George	KERR, Frankey	10/18/1783
BARKER, James	JOHNSTON, Susana	01/26/1779
BARKER, James	TAYLOR, Nancey	12/14/1807
BARKER, James M.	HENSLEY, Dorithy	11/02/1846
BARKER, John	BARTON, Kezia	11/19/1806
BARKER, Josiah	DODSON, Mary F.	11/14/1865
BARKER, Minyard	WILKERSON, Marthy E.	11/14/1865
BARKER, Stephen Y.	SLAYTON, Martha J.	12/08/1864
BARKER, Tolbert	JACKSON, Margret J.	07/10/1864
BARKER, William	BRINCKLE, Nancey	01/11/1820
BARKSDALE, Armistead	LYDNAR, Ailcey	05/26/1824
BARLOW, Caloway	ADAMS, Mary	01/27/1846
BARNARD, William	HOLOWAY, Susan	02/15/1842
BARNARD, William L.	WITHERS, Jamima Jane	07/05/1857
BARNER, John	GARLAND, Amanda	12/27/1865
BARNET, Hugh	MCFARLAND, Margurete	01/26/1784

MARRIAGE RECORDS OF CASWELL COUNTY, NORTH CAROLINA

GROOM	BRIDE	DATE
BARNETT, Andrew	HARALSON, Agness	09/21/1791
BARNETT, Clifton R.	NICHOLS, Chainey	06/28/1851
BARNETT, John	JONES, Julia	07/01/1866
BARNETT, Thomas	HARGASS, Fanny	06/06/1803
BARNETT, William	BREEZE, Jane	02/18/1795
BARNETT, William	SANDERS, Betsey	10/27/1798
BARNWELL, Carter	PRENDERGAST, Caroline	08/02/1837
BARNWELL, David	ROBERTS, Judith	12/19/1804
BARNWELL, Edward	BEVILL, Lucy	02/21/1804
BARNWELL, John	MUZE, Sarah	12/31/1792
BARNWELL, Robert	LOVE, Rebeccah	05/28/1796
BARNWELL, Robert S.	SMITH, Mary F.	02/26/1850
BARNWELL, William	ENOCHS, ELizabeth	12/16/1812
BARNWELL, William H.	NELSON, Mary C. V.	09/21/1844
BARRICKS, David G.	BARRICKS, Mary J.	02/14/1843
BARROW, Henry	WARD, Letitia	11/09/1835
BARRY, Edward M.	GOODWIN, Mary Ann	01/20/1837
BARTLETT, Edward	MUZZALL, Elizabeth	02/24/1814
BARTLETT, Thompson M.	MOORE, Susan	06/19/1826
BARTON, Abraham	BURCH, Mary	06/20/1826
BARTON, Aquila	HENSLE, Sally	01/20/1842
BARTON, Aquilla	KENNEBREW, Elizabeth	02/10/1813
BARTON, Chesley L.	PAGE, Mary	05/15/1855
BARTON, Elisha	COCHRAN, Polley	01/09/1799
BARTON, Lewis	WILLSON, Margret	07/24/1804
BARTON, Lewis	HARRELSON, Sarah	03/08/1827
BARTON, Rice	BURCH, Elizabeth	10/31/1826
BARTON, Thomas	BURCH, Frances	01/20/1813
BARTS, Allen	SMITH, Alemdia	05/26/1866
BARTS, James H.	MANGUM, Margarett	01/13/1861
BARUTT, Jno. B.	DODSON, Rebeca H.	07/07/1846
BASS, Alex	FLINTOFF, Sally A.	07/08/1866
BASS, John B.	GALLION, Mary J.	04/08/1859
BASS, William	TOLBERT, Martha	05/31/1841
BASTIN, Henry	HOBBS, Kitty	07/10/1823
BASTIN, Thomas	HODGE, Judath	12/15/1823
BATEMAN, John	EVANS, Susannah	11/23/1807
BATES, Lemuel	CHAMBERLIN, Jane	12/30/1840
BATMAN, Bird H.	BARNHILL, Mary	11/14/1833
BAUGH, John J.	RODENHIZER, R. C.	01/23/1867
BAUGH, John J.	ATKINSON, Lucey Ann	06/20/1857
BAUGH, Peter	GORDON, Jane P.	01/15/1821
BAULDWIN, John	MURPHEY, Betsey	09/24/1808
BAULDWIN, John	MURPHEY, Frances	04/11/1825
BAXTER, James	STONE, Nancey	07/03/1804
BAXTER, John Jr.	WARE, Martha	08/15/1825
BAXTER, Thomas	DENNIS, Jenny	03/05/1793
BAYES, Robert J.	NANCE, Isabella G.	06/06/1866
BAYES, Thompson	-----, -----	10/09/1850
BAYNES, Archibald	MORTON, Barbary	02/22/1840
BAYNES, John	LEA, Sarah	09/10/1845

MARRIAGE RECORDS OF CASWELL COUNTY, NORTH CAROLINA

GROOM	BRIDE	DATE
BAYNES, Sidney Y.	FULLER, Mary L.	05/13/1855
BAYNES, Thornton Y.	PATILLO, Elizabeth B.	05/10/1854
BAYNS, Eaton	SHACFORD, Elizabeth	07/26/1810
BEADLES, John W.	SLAYDEN, Frances K.	03/27/1828
BEAVER, Humphrey	SANDERS, Jemima	11/24/1835
BEAVER, James P.	RICE, Nancy E.	08/23/1859
BEAVER, Jesse	RICHARDSON, Mary	02/13/1786
BEAVER, Jesse	WYNN, Jerusha	06/25/1810
BEAVER, Johnston	NUNNARY, Polly	07/03/1792
BEAVER, Joshua	CARROLL, Polly	10/05/1793
BEAVER, Solomon	BROWNING, Nancey	02/24/1809
BEEVERS, William T.	SMITHY, Sarah Jane	11/06/1854
BELEW, Daniel	HALL, Sally	11/01/1794
BELL, David	JONES, Agness	12/22/1812
BELLSIRE, Thomas	THOMPSON, Mary	08/25/1807
BENETT, Warren E.	SHACKELFORD, Ann A.	12/28/1855
BENNATT, Ambrose L.	DONOHO, Susannah	02/18/1804
BENNATT, Richard	BUCKINGHAM, Elizabeth	01/15/1830
BENNATT, Richard	PIRANT, Rebecca	02/18/1836
BENNATT, William T.	THORN, Kitty C.	07/16/1814
BENNETT, Ambrose L.	WATLINGTON, Frances	11/08/1822
BENNETT, Ambrose L.	RUDD, Vienna	11/30/1836
BENNETT, Ambrose L. Jr.	TAYLOR, Leathy	02/23/1830
BENNETT, Henry	HAMNER, Nancey	01/17/1828
BENNETT, James	PETERSON, Delilah	11/14/1833
BENNETT, James W.	PHELPS, Betty W.	02/20/1866
BENNETT, Jesse	PAUL, Patsey	11/25/1788
BENNETT, John	SHELTON, Eliza M.	12/24/1839
BENNETT, John A.	SMITH, Elizabeth A.	01/26/1854
BENNETT, John N.	BENNETT, Julia	11/11/1857
BENNETT, Mumford	LUMPKIN, Nancy	02/17/1821
BENNETT, Richard	ROPER, Rachel R.	01/21/1845
BENNETT, Thomas	SHACKLFORD, Anne	02/06/1813
BENNETT, Thomas	GIVINGS, Mildred	10/26/1826
BENNETT, William D.	SHACKLEFORD, Mary H.	12/29/1854
BENSON, Alexander	PLEASANT, Patty	02/10/1802
BENSON, John	LYON, Francis	12/24/1841
BENSON, John	PLEASANT, Nancey	02/25/1828
BENTON, Daniel	PRICE, Fannie	09/06/1867
BENTON, Joseph	FOSTER, Sarah	03/02/1798
BENTON, Richard	HOPPER, Winifred	12/28/1787
BENTON, Richard	KITCHEN, Salley	04/20/1819
BENTON, Robert	CATE, Nancey	10/25/1790
BENTON, Thomas	GROOM, Isabella	09/23/1828
BENTON, Titus	CATES, Mary	01/09/1789
BENTON, William	GROOM, Betsey	01/01/1820
BENTON, Zachariah	NUNN, Mary	01/11/1843
BERRY, Elisha	BOZWELL, Frances	01/03/1826
BETHELL, William	WILLIAMSON, Julia	01/12/1867
BETHELL, William P.	PRICE, Mary S.	06/15/1865
BEUSEY, John	BALDWIN, Nancey	07/03/1822

MARRIAGE RECORDS OF CASWELL COUNTY, NORTH CAROLINA

GROOM	BRIDE	DATE
BEVIL, Peter	BROWN, Margaret	09/23/1866
BEVILL, John	CHILDS, Salley	10/29/1815
BEVILL, Robert	SMITH, Nancey	11/28/1810
BEVINS, Grief	COATS, Sally	08/03/1816
BEWSEY, Charles	HODGE, Polley	06/09/1817
BIGELOW, Calvin	WILLIAMSON, Candice	06/01/1867
BIGELOW, Willis	BIGELOW, Harriet	12/30/1866
BINION, John	BURTON, Ann	01/17/1785
BINION, William	BURTON, Jane	11/19/1784
BIRD, Joel	HUBBARD, Mary	07/20/1867
BIRD, John	WALKER, Jane	12/05/1867
BIRD, Thomas	BOLDIN, Elizabeth	04/13/1824
BIRD, Wilie	JEFFREYS, Jane	12/08/1866
BIRD, William A.	ENOCK, Susan F.	08/29/1858
BIRK, Anderson	RICE, Nancy	11/20/1804
BIRK, Archibald R.	GRAVES, Isabella L.	10/18/1836
BIRK, Benjamin	VAUGHAN, Nancy	09/28/1800
BIRK, James	GOOCH, Cistey	07/31/1802
BIRK, James Jr.	PORTER, Polley	04/08/1809
BIRK, Matterson	ELLIS, Dolly	10/17/1804
BIRK, Tompson	MASSEY, Nancy	08/09/1805
BIRK, Wiley	COMPTON, Elizabeth	12/12/1826
BIRKS, James A.	SHEPARD, Susanna	01/22/1852
BIRKS, Johnson	WOODS, Betsey	08/24/1802
BLACK, Hardy	BASDALL, Francis	02/06/1821
BLACK, Robert	GILL, Lucy	02/08/1792
BLACK, Samuel	DELONE, Francis	12/24/1802
BLACKARD, Aaron C.	HARRISON, Mary	12/19/1836
BLACKARD, Charles	VERMILLION, Nancy	07/18/1780
BLACKARD, Jobe	HARGISS, Jean	01/31/1792
BLACKLOCK, John	PETERSON, Polly	12/15/1818
BLACKWELL, Carter	BRACKIN, Isabella	04/28/1797
BLACKWELL, Elias	WITHERS, Eliza	03/26/1867
BLACKWELL, Garland	SCOTT, Polly	12/02/1811
BLACKWELL, Garland	BROOKS, Sarah	02/22/1839
BLACKWELL, George	BOULDIN, Julia	12/13/1866
BLACKWELL, Henry	WEATHERFORD, Fannie	06/08/1866
BLACKWELL, James	HOOPER, Winnie	11/23/1867
BLACKWELL, James M.	WHITTEMORE, Aniva E.	09/16/1856
BLACKWELL, John N.	WITHERS, Nancy B.	10/07/1862
BLACKWELL, Levi	SMITH, Patsey	02/16/1799
BLACKWELL, Marshal	STRADOR, Betsey	08/25/1818
BLACKWELL, Milton	MITCHELL, Nancey	12/27/1820
BLACKWELL, Milton	MITCHELL, Nancy	04/26/1823
BLACKWELL, N. L.	SIDDLE, Martha E.	06/22/1859
BLACKWELL, Nathaniel L.	COBB, Ann E.	10/16/1847
BLACKWELL, Robert	NUNNALLY, Elmira J.	05/19/1838
BLACKWELL, Robert	SIMPSON, Matilda	01/11/1813
BLACKWELL, Robert A.	STUBBLEFIELD, Allice	10/12/1865
BLACKWELL, Samuel	KING, Frances	03/07/1868
BLACKWELL, Whitson G.	RICE, Sally	04/07/1853

MARRIAGE RECORDS OF CASWELL COUNTY, NORTH CAROLINA

GROOM	BRIDE	DATE
BLAIR, Thomas	FANNING, Letty	11/28/1791
BLAIR, William	RIGHT, Eliza A.	08/16/1834
BLAIR, William Thos.	HOOPER, Manerva A.	12/01/1858
BLAKE, Ellis G.	LEACHMOND, Elizabeth	02/19/1830
BLALOCK, Alfred	HARRISON, Harriet	02/03/1843
BLAND, Richard	DICKINS, Elisabeth	09/22/1790
BLANKENSHIP, Archa F.	CORBIN, Catherine C.	11/14/1866
BLANKS, Joseph	CLARK, Martha M.	02/06/1857
BOAZ, David R.	STUBBLEFIELD, Susanna	12/03/1816
BOHANAN, Ludwell	SPRATTEN, Elizabeth	11/25/1816
BOHANNAN, Ambrose	MARRIABLE, Elizabeth	07/09/1810
BOHANNAN, J. M.	BAINS, Elizabeth	10/08/1856
BOHANNAN, Nathaniel	AKIN, Betsey	05/07/1802
BOHANNAN, Thomas	HIGHTOWER, Martha	06/10/1867
BOHANNON, Maynard	BAYNES, Nancy	09/23/1841
BOHANNON, Yancey	COX, Martha	11/17/1823
BOLES, James M.	FULLER, Nisey L.	09/08/1830
BOLEY, Parham A.	FAIR, Esther D.	09/29/1854
BOLING, George	COLLINS, Syrena	06/11/1832
BOLING, George	COLLINS, Syrena	06/11/1832
BOLTON, Joel	WATLINGTON, Elizabeth	02/07/1820
BOLTON, Lewis	LANSDOWN, Elizabeth H.	09/18/1826
BOMAN, James W.	NICHOLSON, Nancy D.	01/07/1860
BOMAN, John	COOPER, Salley	04/29/1806
BOMAN, John	SOMERS, Nancy	12/28/1807
BOMAN, Joseph	DIXON, Elizabeth	03/01/1790
BOMAN, Samuel	CARLOSS, Betsey	06/30/1798
BOMAN, Siar	MORTON, Elizabeth	05/03/1793
BOMAN, Thomas P.	KENNON, Thursday Ann	12/23/1856
BOND, Balaam	COOK, Priciller	01/23/1819
BONDS, George	COLLINS, Syrena	06/11/1832
BONDS, George	COLLINS, Syrena	06/11/1832
BOOZ, Henry	HITE, Matilda	08/02/1820
BOSWELL, Abner	STAINBACK, Mary	11/22/1838
BOSWELL, Amza	HERNDON, Martha	10/14/1846
BOSWELL, Andrew J.	WATLINGTON, Malissa	09/07/1866
BOSWELL, Antiochus	SIDDLE, Mary	11/08/1836
BOSWELL, Bedford A.	BOSWELL, Nancy	11/71/1842
BOSWELL, Brown	GRAVES, Manilla	10/15/1829
BOSWELL, Calvin G.	BIRD, Lucinda	01/15/1844
BOSWELL, Craven	WINDSOR, Rebeccah	02/15/1812
BOSWELL, Howel	GOOCH, Susannah	12/22/1813
BOSWELL, Howell Jr.	THOMPSON, Ann E.	08/13/1856
BOSWELL, James	MERONY, Mary	10/21/1819
BOSWELL, James	SIMPSON, Nanny	12/11/1823
BOSWELL, James	BROOKES, Mary G.	12/03/1832
BOSWELL, James M.	BRANNOCK, Julia	04/03/1849
BOSWELL, John	SIMPSON, Citty	10/05/1805
BOSWELL, John	TURNER, Sarah	12/11/1826
BOSWELL, John A.	MILES, Elizabeth J.	01/24/1867
BOSWELL, Moses	MARTIN, Mary	12/01/1866

MARRIAGE RECORDS OF CASWELL COUNTY, NORTH CAROLINA

GROOM	BRIDE	DATE
BOSWELL, Romulus S.	WEST, Louisa J.	08/25/1856
BOSWELL, Thomas	SIMS, Mary	11/27/1802
BOSWELL, Thomas	BIRD, Eliza Ann	09/28/1861
BOSWELL, William	PAGE, Lucinda	12/19/1837
BOULDIN, Edward	PARKS, Hariet	07/03/1838
BOULDIN, George T.	LEATH, Susan	05/12/1840
BOULDIN, James	CONALLY, Sally	11/24/1802
BOULDIN, James O.	SIMPSON, Hannah Ann	02/07/1860
BOULDIN, John	CONNALLEY, Frances	09/20/1817
BOULDIN, John	GARNER, Catherine	02/28/1843
BOULDIN, Lewis P.	VINCENT, Sarah J.	10/08/1846
BOULDIN, W. L.	SIMPSON, J. T.	02/15/1866
BOULDIN, William J.	MONTGOMERY, Sarah L.	05/12/1837
BOULTON, Charles	FARLEY, Elizabeth	10/07/1791
BOULTON, George	RICHMOND, Mary	01/28/1867
BOULTON, William	DIXON, Polly	11/18/1799
BOWDEN, John	HARRIWAY, Kitty	11/26/1817
BOWE, Geo.	WILLIS, Malissa Rose	11/14/1867
BOWE, George	PHILLIPS, Mary	12/26/1866
BOWE, George	JACKSON, Huldah	03/09/1867
BOWE, William B.	JAMES, Amy	06/10/1858
BOWERS, John	EVANS, Mariann	06/15/1803
BOWERS, Lemual	LEA, Phebe	01/11/1810
BOWERS, William	CRISTENBURY, Nancy	07/26/1817
BOWLER, Ellis G.	SLAYTON, Mary	10/14/1850
BOWLES, Henry	DICKEY, Nancey	11/13/1813
BOWLES, Stephen	EUBANK, Mary	10/16/1818
BOWLES, Thomas	GWYN, Susen Y.	11/28/1853
BOWLS, John	BOSWELL, Maryann	10/21/1850
BOYD, Alexander Jr.	HARRISON, Nancey L.	12/09/1819
BOYD, David	GWYNN, Jane	12/01/1801
BOYD, Lindsey J.	GRAVETT, Elizabeth J.	11/24/1858
BOYD, Thomas	SHORT, Mavel	01/11/1813
BOYD, William	WILLIAMSON, Polley	02/13/1795
BOYKIN, Drury D.	CURRIE, Cornelia D.	05/20/1849
BOYLES, Abel	ROPER, Mary L.	11/06/1848
BOZES, Jno. Thos.	WEBSTER, Sallie Ann	07/26/1854
BOZWELL, Kindall	STOKES, Betsy	01/09/1817
BOZWELL, Thomas	YANCEY, ELizabeth	12/22/1819
BRACKIN, John H.	WOMACK, Martha	12/01/1835
BRACKIN, Joseph	DIXON, Jenny	06/10/1802
BRACKIN, Joseph	WOMACK, Sinna	01/28/1795
BRACKIN, Joseph	HOOPER, Nancey	01/05/1841
BRACKIN, Julius A.	HUBBARD, Martha J.	12/09/1867
BRACKIN, Samuel	REED, Rebecah	10/29/1799
BRADFORD, David	FAUCET, Elinor	06/03/1806
BRADLEY, James	BURTON, Dorrithy	09/18/1788
BRADLEY, Samuel	RAY, Sarah	12/26/1837
BRADSHAW, James M.	HODGES, Mary F.	01/17/1863
BRADSHER, Henderson	POTEAT, Martha	12/07/1867
BRADSHER, Henry	RAGSDALE, Leander	09/27/1867

MARRIAGE RECORDS OF CASWELL COUNTY, NORTH CAROLINA

GROOM	BRIDE	DATE
BRADSHER, John Jun.	STAFFORD, Cynthia	03/13/1830
BRADSHER, Moses	WALLIS, Elizabeth	01/11/1825
BRADSHER, Richard	NELLSON, Phebe	10/31/1817
BRADSHER, W. G.	BRADSHEAR, Mattie E.	07/08/1865
BRADSHER, Wilson A.	MARTIN, Martha	02/11/1858
BRADY, Thomas	NORTON, Marguret	12/21/1791
BRAGG, Cicero	PATTERSON, Mary	03/07/1855
BRAGG, John	STRADOR, Seluda	11/19/1866
BRANDON, David	CONLEY, Rebecca	12/15/1800
BRANDON, David G.	MCADIN, Mary J.	04/14/1821
BRANDON, Francis	SCOTT, Sarah	02/13/1786
BRANDON, Henry F.	NORFLETT, Fannie P.	10/22/1856
BRANDON, Irvin	FANNING, Judah	01/28/1788
BRANDON, Isaac	HUGHES, Elizabeth	11/21/1866
BRANDON, Jacob	CUNINGHAM, Harriett	12/22/1866
BRANDON, John	FOSTER, Peggy	12/20/1809
BRANDON, Joseph	FARMER, Sally	12/20/1867
BRANDON, Louis	WOODY, Nancy	02/17/1867
BRANDON, Reubin	STAMPS, July	11/18/1867
BRANDON, Thomas Jr.	PULLHAM, Jane Allin	01/08/1785
BRANDON, Thomas S. Jr.	ROPER, Frances C.	12/16/1846
BRANDON, William	WILEY, Esther	12/14/1811
BRANDON, William	SCOTT, Rebecah	08/15/1785
BRANDON, William	LANGLEY, Mary	01/12/1796
BRANDON, William L.	CONNALLY, Mary A.	04/11/1842
BRANN, John	FOSTER, Patsey	01/06/1800
BRANN, Peter D.	STANDFIELD, Martha T.	01/20/1859
BRANN, Vincent	JOHNSTON, Rebeca	08/26/1856
BRANNOCK, Samuel T.	BOSWELL, Francis	12/21/1850
BRAUGHTON, Jerremiah	FOLEY, Parrizetta	10/17/1809
BRECHEN, William Jr.	WHEELER, Elsey	01/12/1807
BREEZE, James	MCMULLIN, Rebeccah	11/01/1797
BREWER, James	BUTTERY, Elizabeth	04/28/1816
BRIGGS, Silas	GROGAN, Lucinda	06/01/184_
BRIGHTWELL, Wm. C.	ADAMS, Mary J.	09/02/1859
BRIGMAN, James	ANDERSON, Patsey	03/08/1816
BRINCEFIELD, A. J.	MATKINS, Martha E.	11/01/1865
BRINCFIELD, Bartlet Y.	GWYN, Jane	12/20/1858
BRINCFIELD, Colmon W.	HORTON, Francis	08/24/1858
BRINSFIELD, Anderson	DYE, Francis	12/13/1815
BRINSFIELD, Calvin	SHELTON, Mary	07/02/1847
BRINSFIELD, Dennard	-----, -----	10/13/1806
BRINTLE, Oliver	BROWN, Salley	02/24/1816
BRINTLE, Solomon	BELL, Sarah	05/29/1810
BRINTLE, William	MASSY, Aggy	05/13/1802
BRINTLE, William	HESTON, Lucy	11/15/1798
BRINTLE, William	CANTRELL, Elizabeth	06/30/1854
BRINTLE, Zachariah	SMITH, Eliza A.	01/01/1866
BROCHE, George	BURCH, Jenney	03/19/1803
BROCHE, George	BROACH, Jenney	03/19/1803
BRODIE, Thomas	MATHISON, Christian	05/13/1779

MARRIAGE RECORDS OF CASWELL COUNTY, NORTH CAROLINA

GROOM	BRIDE	DATE
BROOCKS, William M. Dr.	WORD, Virginia	12/01/1841
BROOKES, Christopher W.	KERR, Isbel	11/28/1812
BROOKES, Iverson I. W.	PASCHAL, Rebecca H.	02/05/1861
BROOKES, Jeremiah	THOMAS, Elisabeth	03/18/1795
BROOKES, John	WATLINGTON, Mary B.	11/17/1824
BROOKES, Robert H.	BOSWELL, Sinthy	12/06/1842
BROOKES, Samuel	WOOD, Betsey	11/10/1792
BROOKES, Thomas	ADKINS, Susanna	12/24/1816
BROOKES, Thomas	MITCHELL, Huldath	05/28/1823
BROOKES, Thomas Jr.	FLIPPING, Jane	02/26/1791
BROOKES, William 1.	PINNIX, Mary J.	02/03/1864
BROOKS, Andrew P.	WEDDING, Jereney	06/15/1850
BROOKS, Christopher	LEWIS, Eliza	09/16/1858
BROOKS, Christopher	MOORE, Melesia	05/09/1848
BROOKS, Christopher	HOLDERNESS, Salley	02/09/1810
BROOKS, David	TERRELL, Betsey	10/06/1816
BROOKS, James	TRAYLOR, Elisabeth	12/26/1782
BROOKS, John K.	SIMPSON, Celenis B.	11/03/1845
BROOKS, John K.	MALONE, ELiza	06/28/1847
BROOKS, William	GIPSON, Catharine	11/17/1816
BROUGHTON, Jeremiah	BIRD, Caty	09/21/1805
BROWDER, David A.	EUBALEY, Sarah	03/06/1820
BROWER, Lewis S.	STINSON, Lucy P.	03/25/1846
BROWN, Bedford	GLENN, Mary	07/06/1816
BROWN, Cicero	BOWES, Frances	09/12/1866
BROWN, Clark H.	FOURD, Wyeney B.	02/20/1834
BROWN, Edward	FLINN, Susanna	03/31/1798
BROWN, Franklin	WINDSOR, Susan	01/25/1866
BROWN, Green L.	SIMPSON, Nancey	01/01/1802
BROWN, Green W.	RICHMOND, Mary A.	03/15/1857
BROWN, Henry	STACY,(?) Elizabeth	11/27/1815
BROWN, Hudson	SIMMS, Henrietta	04/16/1796
BROWN, Isham	GUNN, Jinny	07/03/1866
BROWN, James	SHACKLEFORD, Salley	01/12/1815
BROWN, James	BROWN, Susanna	02/04/1808
BROWN, James	KERSEY, Juliann	08/11/1866
BROWN, James W.	CARTER, Mary A.C.	07/30/1818
BROWN, Jethro	WILLIAMSON, Lucey	05/28/1788
BROWN, John	TAIT, Lydia	11/02/1801
BROWN, John	JONES, Sally	12/29/1786
BROWN, John	BARKER, Mary	04/09/1814
BROWN, John E.	CARTER, Elizabeth B.	04/20/1827
BROWN, John T.	PURKINS, Julia A.	01/07/1861
BROWN, Jonathan	BUTLER, Eliza	01/01/1844
BROWN, Madison	BOSWELL, Ella	12/02/1866
BROWN, Michael	LEA, Mary H.	02/11/1840
BROWN, Nathan	WALKER, Mary	11/03/1842
BROWN, Ned	GRAVES, Edy	02/16/1867
BROWN, Obedih	ELINGTON, F.	01/22/1861
BROWN, Richard	BALLARD, Patsy	09/11/1810
BROWN, Richard H.	JOHNSON, Mary P.	09/25/1841

MARRIAGE RECORDS OF CASWELL COUNTY, NORTH CAROLINA

GROOM	BRIDE	DATE
BROWN, Robert	BRINTLE, Parthena	02/23/1818
BROWN, Robert	HARRIS, Lydia	12/19/1795
BROWN, Robert A.	FAULKS, Lucy A.	05/03/1830
BROWN, Samuel	FARLEY, Perthena	09/16/1813
BROWN, Stephen E.	LEA, Eliza G.	11/02/1846
BROWN, Tarlton W.	HILLIARD, Lucy	07/13/1830
BROWN, Thomas M.	STANLEY, Mary F.	12/18/1847
BROWN, William	JEFFREYS, Mary	03/02/1867
BROWN, William	STADLER, Elizabeth	03/19/1803
BROWN, William J.	HAILEY, Sarah	12/11/1857
BROWN, William V.	LYON, Frances	11/20/1812
BROWNING, Edmond	ALLEN, Sarah	02/13/1790
BROWNING, Edmund	MURPHEY, Marian	09/09/1800
BROWNING, Edmund E.	PITTS, Susan	10/13/1841
BROWNING, Elijah C.	STADLER, Mary S.	02/13/1859
BROWNING, Francis	MORTON, Mary	12/22/1838
BROWNING, James S.	PARKS, Drady	11/12/1826
BROWNING, John K.	SMITH, Mary	04/06/1825
BROWNING, John R.	DAMERON, S.W.	12/19/1860
BROWNING, Martin	HUBBARD, Nancy	12/22/1852
BROWNING, Martin	GOMER, Polly	02/20/1810
BROWNING, Nathan	MULLENS, Rilla	12/26/1810
BROWNING, Nimord	PARKS, Rachel	08/21/1789
BROWNING, Reubin	ROBINSON, Polly	02/09/1802
BROWNING, Richard	STREET, Polly	10/16/1798
BROWNING, Richard	CANTREL, Sophia	03/12/1816
BROWNING, Robert	BROWNING, Hannah	01/28/1786
BROWNING, Sanders	OAKLEY, Sarah	10/15/1857
BROWNING, Sanders	WARREN, Leatha	10/15/1823
BROWNING, Simeon	BROWN, Mary	12/23/1819
BROWNING, Thomas	LAY, Polly	11/09/1801
BROWNING, Thomas	ALLIN, Elizabeth	09/19/1795
BROWNING, William	ESTES, Jane	02/13/1837
BROWNING, William	NELSON, Permelia	11/12/1823
BROWNING, William	ANGLIN, Catherine	08/24/1797
BRUCE, David	ZACHARY Prudence	08/23/1795
BRUCE, James	COBB, Peggy	10/07/1808
BRUCE, John	BROWNING, Nelly	12/28/1796
BRUCE, Levi L.	BROOKS, Henrietta	01/29/1841
BRUCE, Robert	COCHRAN, Tabitha	02/02/1789
BRUCE, Robert	TURNER, Lottie	12/29/1801
BRUCE, Scott	REID, Milly	11/02/1867
BRUCE, Thomas	PERRY, Jenny	07/07/1792
BRUCE, William	HART, Betsy A.	09/04/1797
BRUCE, William	SAWYER, Mary	10/18/1806
BRUMIT, Pleasant	JONES, Barbara	01/11/1837
BRUMMIT, William	HIGHTOWER, Mary	11/30/1832
BRUMMITT, Anderson	EVANS, Eliza O.	11/07/1838
BRYAN, James	CARRELL, Sally	01/22/1783
BRYAN, John	FARLEY, Rebecca	08/11/1797
BRYANT, Fleming B.	SNODY, Elizabeth	12/21/1837

MARRIAGE RECORDS OF CASWELL COUNTY, NORTH CAROLINA

GROOM	BRIDE	DATE
BRYANT, Harrison	COOK, Betsy	03/17/1810
BRYANT, John	SHEARMAN, Heathy	10/31/1783
BRYANT, W. W. R.	POTEAT, V. E.	02/12/1867
BUCEY, Isaac F.	ASTIN, Margaret	10/25/1830
BUCHANAN, John	LEDFORD, Catherine	02/27/1799
BUCHANAN, Washington	MURPHEY, Mary M.	01/08/1857
BUCKINGHAM, Bird	ALLEN, Mary	08/10/1866
BUCKINGHAM, Bird	ELAM, Frances	03/24/1834
BUCKINGHAM, George	TALLAW, Joicy	11/26/1833
BUCKINGHAM, James	BASDELL, Mary	11/16/1819
BUCKLEY, John	SWAINEY, Margaret	11/26/1780
BUCKLEY, Nathan	POYNER, Sarah	01/04/1792
BUCKLEY, Peyton	MALLORY, Zebba	08/23/1811
BUCKLEY, Randolph	ROPER, Ann	11/15/1803
BUCKNER, James	PHELPS, Frances	02/03/1849
BUCKNER, John	KURSEY, Sarah	04/15/1830
BUCKNER, Thomas S.	BRANDON, Catherine A.	09/17/1854
BULL, Jacob	CHAMBERS, Judith	05/06/1781
BULL, Jacob	WALKER, Elizabeth	07/12/1784
BULLES, John	PEARCE, Philadelphia	04/30/1794
BULLOCK, John	BAXTER, Catherine	03/23/1791
BULLOCK, John C.	POINDEXTER, Eliza	12/20/1815
BURCH, A. J.	MOORE, Mary	03/05/1853
BURCH, Baylor	CRISP, Lucy	10/11/1790
BURCH, Ephraim	HENDSHAW, Francis	03/15/1825
BURCH, George	CRISP, Betsy	11/16/1789
BURCH, Henry	STUART, Aggy	12/21/1807
BURCH, James	BURCH, Mary	01/26/1829
BURCH, James S.	COLEMON, Nancy	02/17/1819
BURCH, Jesse	MOORE, Nancy	01/08/1834
BURCH, John	SHEARMON, Elizabeth	04/12/1791
BURCH, John W.	GOSNEY, Nanny J.	05/29/1862
BURCH, Larkin	PUTTERY, Sally	01/22/1812
BURCH, Peter L.	ADAMS, Martha A.	04/29/1842
BURCH, Richard	CRISP, Marian	02/23/1790
BURCH, Richard	MCKEE, Polly	01/02/1815
BURCH, Samuel	STOKES, Peggy	08/24/1802
BURCH, Squire	MOORE, Sarah	01/28/1826
BURCH, Thomas	BROWN, Polly	09/26/1798
BURCH, William	EUBANK, Betsy	06/21/1805
BURCH, William	DOBBIN, Nancy	10/10/1792
BURCH, William	WARREN, Mary A.	10/10/1850
BURGE, John	SMITH, Catherine	10/08/1787
BURGESS, William	PRICE, Elizabeth	08/20/1816
BURGISS, John	COX, Polly	03/28/1795
BURK, Granderson	WARREN, Agness	03/26/1840
BURK, William A.	DAMERON, Martha	10/04/1842
BURKE, James A.	SHEPPARD, Susan W.	01/20/1852
BURKE, John	RUSSELL, Elizabeth	03/05/1842
BURKE, Johnson	BIRD, Mary	12/17/1837
BURKE, William A.	WEST, Martha A.	09/23/1854

MARRIAGE RECORDS OF CASWELL COUNTY, NORTH CAROLINA

GROOM	BRIDE	DATE
BURKE, William A.	ALBRIDGE, Jane	01/04/1845
BURKE, William T.	BOSWELL, Nancy	05/04/1858
BURKE, Wyly M.	STANBACK, Mary F.	03/31/1832
BURKS, Joseph F.	HALL, Marthy J.	09/21/1866
BURKS, Richard H. Jr.	YUILLE, Susan S.	11/28/1852
BURNE, Thomas	COX, Sally	02/06/1813
BURRIS, Rawzel	KIRK, Pamela	01/16/1810
BURROUGHS, Bennett	RAIMEY, Sally	02/16/1820
BURTON, Absalom	JACKSON, Priscilla	10/02/1815
BURTON, Allen	CLETON, Nancy	01/19/1791
BURTON, Benjamin	GUNN, Rebecca	12/09/1801
BURTON, David	SIMPSON, Susanna	02/07/1780
BURTON, David S.	BURTON, Nancy J.	12/14/1842
BURTON, Drury	HUGHSTON, Jenny	10/04/1808
BURTON, Drury	BAYNES, Sally	04/07/1864
BURTON, Drury	RICHMOND, Peggy	12/03/1816
BURTON, Francis A.	BAYNES, Jane	02/02/1856
BURTON, Francis H.	LOVE, Zilphah	12/17/1810
BURTON, Franklin	WARE, Harriet	10/22/1847
BURTON, George M.	SMITH, F. E.	09/29/1866
BURTON, Henry	FARLEY, Keziah	11/20/1786
BURTON, Henry A.	SLADE, Nancy G.	12/21/1823
BURTON, Hutchens	MALONE, Eliza B.	11/02/1813
BURTON, Hutchens	BURTON, Louisa	12/22/1828
BURTON, Isaac	BURCH, Laney	08/08/1838
BURTON, James	DOSON, Phillisse B.	01/30/1838
BURTON, James	GUNN, Sarah	01/19/1800
BURTON, James	HORSEFORD, Elizabeth	01/01/1833
BURTON, James	WALKER, Mary	10/17/1861
BURTON, James M.	RICHMOND, Agness S.	10/20/1848
BURTON, John	DAMERON, Frances	11/14/1867
BURTON, John	RUSSELL, Judy	01/20/1867
BURTON, John A.	ROPER, Alice W.	10/22/1865
BURTON, John J.	KERNAL, Mary	11/13/1839
BURTON, Noel	DOBBINS, Nahcey	06/05/1817
BURTON, Noel	THOMPSON, Nanny	11/26/1857
BURTON, Noel	PAYNE, Priscilla	04/08/1822
BURTON, Richd.	-----, -----	--/--/1787
BURTON, Samuel	OLDHAM, Amy	05/19/1784
BURTON, Thomas	BRANDON, Jenny	12/28/1802
BURTON, Thomas	ENOCHS, Susan	10/21/1843
BURTON, Thomas W.	BRADSHER, Nancy E.	06/25/1845
BURTON, William	PINIX, Judeth	12/11/1827
BURTON, William	LOVE, Jane	11/17/1818
BUSBY, James	MANN, Elizabeth	06/01/1863
BUSEY, Samuel	TRIGG, Betsy	12/26/1823
BUSEY, William	HOLLOWAY, Patsy	02/06/1808
BUSH, Bennet	BRINTLE, Betsy	08/14/1809
BUSH, Ezenus	RICE, Liddey	06/14/1797
BUSH, Jeremiah	DICKINS, Rebecca	12/06/1794
BUSH, Zenas	BROOKS, Patsy	11/27/1805

MARRIAGE RECORDS OF CASWELL COUNTY, NORTH CAROLINA

GROOM	BRIDE	DATE
BUTCHER, George	DEBOE, Lucy	01/30/1828
BUTLER, Hudson	FARMER, Jincy	03/26/1795
BUTLER, J. H.	WALTON, Candis J.	09/23/1857
BUTLER, Moses M.	SUMMERS, Elizabeth	02/18/1855
BUTLER, Thomars	PASCHAEL, Susan	03/27/1839
BUTREY, John	FOLEY, Narcissia	11/09/1812
BUTT, Ambrose	CURLES, Sophia	07/01/1803
BUZWELL, John	RICE, Delphia	03/19/1799
BYRD, Albert G.	BOULDIN, Mary	01/23/1838
BYRD, James T.	CONNALLY, Caroline	02/11/1847
BYRD, John	BROOKES, Mary	07/21/1795
BYRD, Temple	MCMENEMY, Sally	05/28/1809
BYRD, Temple	FULLER, Nancy	07/14/1809
BYRD, Thomas	JOHNSTON, Rebecca	10/25/1816
BYRD, Thomas	BROWNING, Ann	10/11/1784
BYSOR, John	DIXON, Polly	01/28/1799
BYSOR, Peter	BENNETT, Betsy	02/22/1800
CABELL, P. B.	LANIER, Jane B.	09/03/1857
CALDWELL, Alexander	NICKLESON, Betsy	02/13/1811
CALDWELL, Jno. M. M.	LEVY, Caroline E.	06/07/1844
CAMEL,(?) Edley	JONES, Jincey	11/27/1812
CAMPBELL, Allen C.	BROWNING, Manerva E.	06/11/1855
CAMPBELL, Archibald	SHEPPARD, Joanna	09/22/1846
CAMPBELL, Banister	PINSON, Rhody	12/09/1815
CAMPBELL, Hugh	ROBINSON, Nelly	06/27/1812
CAMPBELL, James B.	HANCOCK, Susanna	07/22/1855
CAMPBELL, John	MOORE, Lucy	01/26/1785
CAMPBELL, William	HUNTER, Patsy	04/14/1816
CAMPBELL,(?) Edley	JONES, Jincey	11/27/1812
CANADAY, A. L.	GIBSON, Margaret	12/19/1865
CANADAY, James	WHALEBONE, Sina	03/27/1804
CANNADAY, John	BOSWELL, Elizabeth	12/16/1828
CANTRELL, Joseph	FLORENCE, Lettice	11/11/1814
CANTROLL, Alexander	FOSTER, Nancy	12/17/1834
CAPE, Thomas R.	LASHLY, Harriet J.	03/18/1865
CAPES, George	DOBBS, Mary	08/04/1863
CARDWELL, Richard M.	CROWDER, Sally	04/19/1817
CARDWELL, William	HUNT, Emily	07/23/1868
CARDWELL, William W.	RUSSELL, Martha J.	01/07/1868
CARLEN, Richard	MIDLETON, Mary	11/18/1780
CARMAN, Archibald	ROSE, Polly	02/11/1795
CARMAN, Elihjah	PONDS, Betsy	07/11/1797
CARMAN, Elijah	STANDSBURY, Rachel	09/19/1896
CARMAN, William	QUINE, Sarah	03/27/1792
CARMICHEL, William	WILLIAMS, Elizabeth	06/01/1818
CARMIKEL, William	SMITH, Sally	10/25/1799
CARNAL, Flemman	WARRIN, Frankey	10/22/1804
CARNAL, Hubbard	DIXON, Elizabeth	01/21/1797
CARNAL, Patrick	WARRIN, Anness	12/17/1790
CARNAL, Richard	VANHOOK, Sally	12/22/1789
CARNAL, Wm. Jr.	DUNN, Ellin	01/26/1818

MARRIAGE RECORDS OF CASWELL COUNTY, NORTH CAROLINA

GROOM	BRIDE	DATE
CARNEY, Joshua	MILES, Lucy	12/26/1786
CARNEY, Rhobartis	RICHMOND, Polly	10/29/1799
CARR, John	ZACHARY, Polly	03/15/1797
CARRAL, William	BRYANT, Sarah	01/05/1782
CARREL, Daniel	JONES, Suckey	01/05/1801
CARRELL, Ellis	WHITLOW, Caty	05/14/1817
CARROL, Edward	FERRELL, Polly	06/19/1826
CARROL, Edward	BAXTER, Delilah	01/09/1827
CARROL, Jackson	SHELTON, Martha	04/12/1838
CARROL, James	BRUCE, Sarah	11/29/1790
CARROLL, James R.	HUBBIRD, Polly	08/10/1827
CARROLL, Lemuel H.	HOOPER, Sally	09/11/1819
CARTER, Benjamin	CARTER, Sinai	08/10/1867
CARTER, Benjamin H.	COBB, Almedia A.	05/18/1859
CARTER, Braxston	FULLER, Polly	04/24/1832
CARTER, Iverson B.	GATEWOOD, Susan	11/27/1847
CARTER, James	WALTERS, Matilda	12/09/1832
CARTER, Jesse	BROWN, Sally	12/17/1809
CARTER, John	WILLIAMS, Sarah	09/12/1818
CARTER, John	BENNETT, Adeline	02/24/1849
CARTER, John	LEA, Betty	09/15/1784
CARTER, John B.	COX, Malinda	01/18/1847
CARTER, Joseph	MALLERY, Ann	12/18/1790
CARTER, Joseph G.	JOHNSON, Ann	06/25/1832
CARTER, Martin	SATERFIELD, Nancy	08/12/1863
CARTER, Patton	EUDALY, Elizabeth	12/09/1819
CARTER, Richard T.	SWAN, Arree	03/22/1854
CARTER, Robert H.	THOMAS, Martha J.	04/26/1843
CARTER, Theoderick	MALLARY, Diana	04/16/1793
CARTER, Thomas	WALKER, Martha	04/18/1846
CARTER, Thomas	POWELL, Anna	02/27/1816
CARTER, Thornton	WYNE, Carthrina	05/18/1814
CARVER, Benjamin F.	BASTIN, Ann W.	05/15/1830
CARVER, Lemuel	MOOR, Maria	01/02/1838
CARVER, William	DOOWNS, Fanny	07/07/1835
CASE, John L.	NELSON, Willy	06/22/1841
CASE, Luther A.	PERKINS, Lucy A.	02/13/1856
CASEY,(?) John	HIGHTOWER, Agniss	12/02/1794
CASEY,(?) John	HIGHTOWER, Agniss	12/02/1794
CASH, Moses	-----, -----	06/16/----
CASORT, John H.	GLASCO, Harriet	02/23/1843
CASORT, Wylie	CAMPBELL, Margaret	04/19/1847
CATES, John	FOSTER, Elizabeth	09/25/1804
CATES, Richard	GRANT, Lucy	03/26/1801
CAYNOR, John H.	HENSLEY, Artelia	04/27/1847
CAZORT, Squire	FOWLER, Maseniah	02/19/1833
CEARNAL, Robert V.	WOODS, Margaret A.	12/04/1837
CHALLES, John	RICE, Milly	11/25/1786
CHALMERS, John G.	HENDERSON, Mary W.	10/02/1827
CHALMERS, Joseph W.	HENDERSON, Frances M.	09/08/1829
CHAMBERLIN, Ebenezer	WELLS, Sarah	08/31/1819

MARRIAGE RECORDS OF CASWELL COUNTY, NORTH CAROLINA

GROOM	BRIDE	DATE
CHAMBERLIN, John	BURCH, Polly	09/16/1819
CHAMBERS, Abner	WALKER, Jemima	01/08/1789
CHAMBERS, Anthony	SWANN, Lucy	04/13/1867
CHAMBERS, James	CHAMERS, Nancy	04/08/1787
CHAMBERS, Joshua	POWELL, Nancy M.	02/17/1832
CHAMBERS, Josias	STANFIELD, Nanny	06/20/1780
CHAMBERS, William P.	PRICE, Mary J.	07/19/1843
CHANCE, David	LYON, Frances	06/24/1853
CHANCE, James	JACKSON, Frances	09/30/1848
CHANCE, Yancy	HORTON, Martha	01/08/1864
CHANDLER, Charles G.	CLEMPSON, Rachel	10/14/1837
CHANDLER, Daniel	GROOM, Polly	12/19/1821
CHANDLER, George W.	BOSWELL, Elizabeth	11/05/1857
CHANDLER, Hosea A.	BOSWELL, Judy	12/08/1847
CHANDLER, James C.	PRICE, Susan C.	07/11/1852
CHANDLER, James D.(?)	SMITH, Frances	10/26/1827
CHANDLER, John	KIMBRO, Mary J.	12/16/1822
CHANDLER, John J.	GOODSON, Sarah J.	12/01/1840
CHANDLER, Josiah	WILEY, Nancy	03/23/1810
CHANDLER, Pleasant	COBB, Jemima	10/28/1852
CHANDLER, Pleasant	JEFFREYS, Martha	08/26/1816
CHANDLER, Rufus W.	ALDRIDGE, Nancy	11/08/1843
CHANDLER, Stephen	INGRAM, Betsy	12/21/1805
CHANDLER, Stephen J.	PRENDERGAST, Nancy	12/28/1829
CHANDLER, Stephen J.(?)	SMITH, Frances	10/26/1827
CHANDLER, Thomas B.	HIGHTOWER, Sarah	11/28/1838
CHANDLER, Thomas J.	WALTERS, Louisanna	08/31/1852
CHANDLER, Thomas W.	WILEY, Julia	10/12/1830
CHANDLER, Thomas W.	RICHMOND, Sarah	10/24/1843
CHANDLER, Wilkins	WILLIS, Joicy	11/29/1818
CHANDLER, William	BOZWELL, Sally	05/14/1806
CHANDLER, William	WALTERS, Martha B.	11/23/1857
CHANDLER, William G.	COVINGTON, Virginia	01/31/1856
CHAPMAN, John	JOHNSTON, Betsy	07/26/1796
CHAPMAN, Nelson	MURPHEY, Jane	01/31/1849
CHAPMAN, Richard	GOING, Sally	06/21/1806
CHATHAM, John	DAVIS, Lucinda	02/07/1829
CHATHAM, John C.	SAUNDERS, Ann	06/15/1866
CHATHAM, Joseph	UNDERWOOD, Artelia	01/30/1847
CHATMAN, James	MURPHEY, Matilda A.	04/13/1866
CHATMAN, William	SOURTHERD, Matilda	01/01/1840
CHAVERS, Evans	JEFFREYS, Susan	12/22/1857
CHEANEY, William H.	HALCOMB, Elizabeth A.	05/27/1846
CHEEK, John W.	RUDD, Susan A.	11/14/1866
CHEEK, Robert	TERRELL, Tabitha	12/06/1838
CHEEK, Robert H.	SANDERS, Mary	07/24/1864
CHEEK, Robert H.	CATES, Martha E.	01/27/1867
CHILDRESS, James A.	FULLINTON, Susan J.	02/22/1856
CHILDRESS, Jeremiah	WELLS, Mary	07/07/1821
CHILDRESS, Solomon	BUSH, Susanna	09/--/1807
CHILES, William H.	FOSTER, Julia F.	05/01/1864

MARRIAGE RECORDS OF CASWELL COUNTY, NORTH CAROLINA

GROOM	BRIDE	DATE
CHILTON, Alfred	GROOM, Eliza	12/10/1842
CHILTON, James	KENNADAY, Joannah	01/09/1800
CHILTON, John	HAMILTON, Sally	01/31/1807
CHILTON, Joshua L.	FREMAN, Martha A.	11/23/1836
CHILTON, William	HOLLEWAY, Sally	10/04/1800
CHISSONBURY, John	BURCH, Elizabeth	11/24/1791
CHISUM, Joseph	DILLARD, Martha	08/17/1853
CHRESFIELD, James A.	DAY, Mary A.	02/28/1867
CHRISMAS, Thomas	UNDERWOOD, Margaret	04/13/1811
CHRISMUS, John	BRYANT, Mary	09/12/1783
CHUMBLY, Larkin	MONTGOMERY, Elizabeth	12/23/1835
CHUNING, Richard	RICE, Betsy	03/26/1802
CINKLER, James	HADDOCK, Elizabeth	02/01/1798
CLAIBORNE, William	STAMPS, Jane	12/20/1866
CLAPSADDLE, John H.	BAUGH, Louisa F.	09/24/1863
CLARDY, William H.	DAVIS, Martha A.	12/06/1866
CLARK, Benjamin	DODSON, Frances	12/21/1867
CLARK, John	HALL, Ann	04/18/1855
CLARK, Joseph	BRANDON, Amanda	12/26/1867
CLARK, Martin	SMITH, Susanna	10/04/1805
CLARK, Peter F.	MOORE, Mary A.	10/15/1856
CLARK, Richard H.	MANSFIELD, Amy J.	01/06/1853
CLARKE, Robert	ROBERTS, Hannah	05/26/1799
CLAY, Henry	LEWIS, Ellen	12/27/1867
CLAY, James	JOHNSTON, Phebe	10/22/1819
CLAYTON, Daniel	CLAYTON, Rebecca	01/15/1789
CLEMSON, William	DELGS, Polly	02/12/1800
CLENDENIN, James J.	HODGE, Susan A.	12/15/1857
CLIMER, Thomas	KERMICHAEL, Leminah	11/05/1799
CLOWDERS, Samuel	JOURDAN, Martha	12/26/1829
CLYBORNE, George	WILKES, Lucy A.	02/02/1836
CLYCE, James T.	MCCAMPBELL, Nancy J.	01/13/1850
CLYFT, John	LONG, Nancy	10/27/1780
COB, Maximin	GRANT, Pamelia D.	02/25/1837
COBB, Achy	WALKER, Martha F.	11/17/1863
COBB, Amsa	DENNY, Nancy	12/18/1822
COBB, Andrew J.	POWELL, Jemima	01/22/1846
COBB, Archy	CANNADY, Rebecca F.	07/20/1865
COBB, Ebenezar	EMONS, Hannah	03/05/1806
COBB, Ebenezear	HUMPHREYS, Nancy	12/04/1839
COBB, Henry	NUNNALY, Martha	12/07/1818
COBB, Henry Sr.	LOVELACE, Mary	06/14/1826
COBB, Hugh	MURPHEY, Elizabeth	09/20/1811
COBB, Hugh E.	RICE, Sarah	12/22/1832
COBB, James	COX, Frances	08/08/1854
COBB, James	BARKER, Louisa	12/04/1846
COBB, James N.	SIDDLE, Cloe	05/25/1830
COBB, Jesse	BOSWELL, Mary	12/05/1817
COBB, Jesse E.	COBB, Elizabeth	12/26/1838
COBB, John Jr.	SLADE, Elizabeth	12/09/1826
COBB, John Jr.	BRACKIN, Jane	12/18/1786

MARRIAGE RECORDS OF CASWELL COUNTY, NORTH CAROLINA

GROOM	BRIDE	DATE
COBB, John W.	KING, Elizabeth E.	12/14/1852
COBB, Joseph	GENNINGS, Nancy	11/09/1812
COBB, Joseph K.	HARRIS, Kitty	08/30/1825
COBB, Joseph P.	LIPSCOMB, Charlotte T.	11/02/1860
COBB, Levi	ELMORE, Rebecca	11/07/1808
COBB, Mastin H.	BUTLER, Malvina F.	02/04/1850
COBB, Mathew	NORTH, Polly	02/03/1809
COBB, Milton	SUTHARD, Elizabeth	10/25/1825
COBB, Neptha	COBB, Martha A.	09/13/1840
COBB, Noah	WALKER, Nancy	10/23/1812
COBB, Noah	LOVELACE, Phebe	01/29/1820
COBB, Noah Sr.	DILL, Jane	11/23/1833
COBB, Samuel B.	BURTON, Elizabeth C.	11/11/1851
COBB, Samuel C.	HARRIS, Sarah	12/07/1827
COBB, Samuel M.	POWELL, Matilda	01/05/1854
COBB, William	ELMORE, Mary A.	12/05/1821
COBB, William M.	GROOM, Dolpha	01/25/1830
COBBS, James S.	WILSON, Ann E.	10/05/1867
COCHRAN, Robert	SCOTT, Silvia	08/25/1800
COCHRON, Will	CATE, Elizabeth	10/24/1789
COCK, George	MILES, Bidsey	12/09/1822
COE, Joshua	PAUL, Rachael	10/26/1784
COE, William	ADKERSON, Susannah	02/05/1828
COIL, Ezariah	DUNNAVAN, Namcy	03/02/1826
COIL, Nicholas	ESKRIDGE, Sally	02/09/1796
COILE, Theopolas	LAMB, Martha	05/29/1828
COLE, Green W.	SMITH, Susan	11/18/1851
COLE, Harvie J.	WILLIAMS, Ann R.	01/16/1844
COLE, Theophilus M.	JERRILL, Willie L.	11/27/1843
COLE, Thomas	MCCOY, Unity	09/21/1780
COLE, Tilman	SMITH, Sarah Frances	10/22/1851
COLE, William T.	CRANE, Nancy T.	11/25/1866
COLEMAN, Alexander	HINTON, Mary	02/06/1837
COLEMAN, Alexander	BATEMAN, Martha B.	10/29/1855
COLEMAN, Archibald	PERKINS, Disey	02/13/1795
COLEMAN, Daniel	BUMPASS, Lucy	12/22/1789
COLEMAN, George A.	HAGEWOOD, Sarah F.	01/14/1858
COLEMAN, George J.	SWAN, Sarah W.	01/11/1847
COLEMAN, James	FLORENCE, Elizabeth	12/22/1832
COLEMAN, James E.	KING, Rebecca J.	10/14/1866
COLEMAN, James E.	HARRISON, Agness W.	01/05/1850
COLEMAN, Joshua	WRIGHT, Betsey	12/15/1809
COLEMAN, (?) Joshua (?)	WRIGHT, Betsy	12/15/1809
COLES, Willis	DAVIS, Letitia	05/19/1867
COLLEY, Bannister	BIRCH, Sarah	11/19/1848
COLLIER, Henry	ELLIS, Darky	12/03/1815
COLLIER, James	KIMBROUGH, Salley	09/05/1810
COLLIER, James H.	MIDKIFF, Mary J.	12/26/1866
COLLIER, Joseph	WHITE, Polley	07/06/1815
COLLIER, Joseph	KIMBRO, Isbel	09/17/1805
COLLIER, Thomas	PINSON, Susannah	12/21/1822

MARRIAGE RECORDS OF CASWELL COUNTY, NORTH CAROLINA

GROOM	BRIDE	DATE
COLLIER, Thomas	ROBERTSON, Dilly	12/20/1804
COLLIER, William	KIMBROUGH, Patsey	03/13/1814
COLLINS, Brice	TAIT, Huldah	12/17/1808
COLLINS, Josiah Jr.	DAVES, Ann Rebecca	12/17/1803
COLLINS, Theophilus J.	DEENS, Mary Ann	09/07/1840
COLQUHOUN, James	GATEWOOD, Patsey	12/19/1796
COMBES, James	SANDERS, Susan	05/01/1849
COMBES, Orrison G.	BRAUGHTON, Missouri S.	01/16/1837
COMBS, James	ROWLAND, Mary	08/23/1859
COMBS, Jesse	STEPHENS, Betsey	11/02/1799
COMER, John	MOORE, Matilda	01/04/1827
COMER, John	BROWN, Mary	10/26/1824
COMER, William G.	BOMAR, Ann W.	04/04/1836
COMPTON, Allen	COOPER, Lavinia	02/17/1835
COMPTON, Aquilla	COOPER, Salenia	02/04/1832
COMPTON, John L.	BURT, Nancy	10/24/1840
COMPTON, Samuel W.	BURT, Rebecca	12/02/1833
COMPTON, Thomas	GREER, Nancey	05/22/1811
CONALLY, William J.	MCCAIN, Nancy	07/23/1857
CONNALLY, Charles	SMITH, Kiziah	05/13/1794
CONNALLY, Charls.	SMITH, Nancy	03/02/1793
CONNALLY, George A.	WOMACK, Mary Jane	05/26/1830
CONNALLY, George O.	BALL, Polly	01/17/1811
CONNALLY, George R.	OWEN, Caroline	10/05/1854
CONNALLY, John S.	WALKER, Margaret	05/27/1826
CONNALLY, John Spencer	ROPER, Sarah	11/28/1844
CONNALLY, Solomon	CONNALLY, Emily	01/26/1867
CONNALLY, William T.	HOOPER, Mary W.	12/19/1854
CONNALLY, William T.	BRANDON, Mary E.	11/01/1858
CONNALY, William J.	BALL, Cary	03/23/1816
CONNER, William B.	GARRETT, Nancey	03/15/1855
CONOLEY, John	MOORE, Scecily	05/23/1788
COOK, Augustin	PAYNE, Clary	01/20/1789
COOK, Edmund	OBRIAN, Mary Ann	02/15/1830
COOK, George	HARDY, Lucy	07/19/1844
COOK, Henry	CHAPMAN, Elizabeth	12/23/1851
COOK, Johnston	STAFFORD, Delilah	07/25/1796
COOK, Lemuel	DOWNS, Margaret	03/10/1826
COOK, Owen	DUNERVENT, Jane	01/27/1855
COOK, Philip	RICHARDSON, Elizabeth	06/09/1792
COOKE, William	RICHARDSON, Unity	07/08/1793
COOPER, Allin	WARREN, Fanney	08/04/1800
COOPER, Hiram	SAWYER, Nancy	01/15/1805
COOPER, James	SIMPSON, Delilah	08/31/1811
COOPER, John	GIBSON, Mary	07/31/1782
COOPER, Martin	PARKER, Elizabeth	01/20/1790
COOPER, Plumer	PILES, Jane	03/24/1867
COOPER, Warren	CORBIT, Elizabeth A.	07/17/1851
COOPER, William	WARREN, Mary A.	02/06/1847
CORAM, William	CARMON, Abagail	04/10/1782
CORBET, John	RUSSELL, Emily T.	08/04/1840

MARRIAGE RECORDS OF CASWELL COUNTY, NORTH CAROLINA

GROOM	BRIDE	DATE
CORBET, Pleasant	BRACKIN, Sina	05/24/1839
CORBETT, Archer	WILLIAMSON, Littie	12/26/1867
CORBETT, B.H.	COOPER, Fannie	08/08/1860
CORBETT, Burel	MILES, Susan	12/16/1839
CORBETT, Burel	-----, -----	--/--/----
CORBETT, Solomon	RUSSEL, Judiah	04/20/1842
CORBETT, Solomon	HOOPER, Susan	12/10/1844
CORBIN, Thomas J.	RODENHIZER, Martha E.	03/21/1866
CORBITT, William	WARREN, Nancey	02/25/1830
CORDER, Joel	ANTHONEY, Jane	11/15/1784
CORHAM, Richard F.	ELLINGTON, Rachel T.	07/11/1865
CORLEY, Charles S.	BARKER, Sarah J.	12/20/1865
CORNWELL, Joseph	PRATHER, Margarett	12/31/1833
CORNWELL, Samuel	BOSWELL, Eliza	12/26/1839
CORUM, William J.	COLE, Frances	04/30/1857
COTHRAN, Elijah	CAMPBELL, Letecia	02/19/1822
COTHRAN, James H.	LOVELACE, Mary	01/11/1841
COTTON, Henry	BALLARD, Mary	08/28/1838
COURTS, Jennings H.	WILLIAMS, Eliza G.	07/12/1819
COURTS, William James	CARTER, Sarah Frances	01/04/1858
COUSINS, Alexander	JONES, Celia	03/29/1851
COUSINS, James	PARKS, Nancy	08/12/1820
COUSINS, Thomas	GOOD, Harriett	12/13/1859
COVEY, James G.	FOWLER, Elizabeth C.	04/27/1847
COVINGTON, Bird	KEY, Phoebe	05/25/1826
COVINGTON, Elisha J.	STEEL, Nancy E.	11/04/1866
COVINGTON, Henry	MALONE, Margaret	03/02/1867
COVINGTON, John	HOLDERNESS, Martha	06/09/1866
COVINGTON, John E.	ENOCKS, Nancy A.	02/05/1866
COVINGTON, John J.	FERGUSON, Sarah J.	12/30/1856
COWAN, Joseph	HART, Susannah	06/01/1808
COWARDIN, Francis C.	WILKERSON, Parthana F.	12/08/1836
COWMAN, William	COX, Sarah	12/13/1838
COX, Armstead	HUDSON, Ann	03/15/1834
COX, Gabriel	SMITH, Elizabeth	11/21/1846
COX, Gabriel	SHACKLFORD, Anna	12/10/1810
COX, Henry	SHACKLEFORD, Nancey	08/21/1827
COX, Henry	BRINSFIELD, Betsey	09/06/1845
COX, Nathaniel	GREEN, Nancey	10/16/1838
COX, Reuben	HOLCOMB, Mary	01/11/1792
COX, Thomas	BIRK, Mildred	01/09/1823
COX, Whitaker	SWANN, Pensey	11/04/1799
COX, William	LUMPKINS, Elizabeth	12/17/1853
COX, William	KENNON, Frances	03/23/1858
COX, William	SHACKLEFORD, Mildred	01/13/1821
COZENS, Tazwell	PHILIPS, Nancy	04/21/1851
COZZENS, Lewis	ELLIOTT, Frances	01/06/1855
CRAFT, Andrew J.	LOCKARD, Mary J.	09/28/1859
CRAWFORD, John	PETTIFORD, Frances	02/20/1868
CRAWFORD, William	WALKER, Rachiel	03/25/1833
CRENSHAW, John	DENNEY, Rebecca	04/01/1818

MARRIAGE RECORDS OF CASWELL COUNTY, NORTH CAROLINA

GROOM	BRIDE	DATE
CRENSHAW, Thomas E.	STACY, Fannie E.	05/03/1864
CRESWELL, John	LANDERS, Nancey	03/30/1810
CREWS, Abediah	COBB, Rebecca	11/10/1835
CREWS, Thomas	WILLIS, Joicey	01/21/1837
CREWS, Thomas	FORD, Elizabeth	04/23/1835
CRISP, Chesley	WARREN, Sarah	01/02/1827
CRISP, David H.	MITCHELL, Betty A.	08/31/1856
CRISP, John	BURCH, Janney	04/12/1791
CRISP, John H.	SMITH, Mary K.	08/31/1836
CRISP, Thomas	BURCH, Frances	10/14/1799
CRISP, William H.	BATTON, Sarah M.	06/09/1848
CRITINTON, Deveraux	PYRON, Elenor	07/03/1832
CRITTENDEN, Richard	MORTON, Elizabeth	06/29/1850
CRITTENTON, George	COX, Lucy	10/11/1800
CROCKETT, John H.	SNEED, Frances N.	12/07/1834
CROSET, James	JOHNSTON, Charlotte	02/15/1816
CROWDER, Godfrey	SHELTON, Susannah	02/23/1802
CROWDER, Richardson	SAMUEL, Anne	03/13/1821
CROWDER, Robert A.	ROBERTSON, Eleanor	06/23/1826
CROWDER, Thomas J.	DAVIS, Emily	07/29/1867
CROXTON, William R.	DANIEL, Elizabeth F.	06/02/1863
CRUMMELL, Charles	MCKNIGHT, Mary	03/19/1785
CRUMPTON, Robert T.	SLADE, Mary C.	03/23/1858
CRUTCHFIELD, George H.	GARROTT, Eliza A.	07/04/1838
CRUTCHFIELD, William B.	MATLOCK, Barbara	05/08/1837
CULBERSON, David	BROWNING, Clary	02/22/1782
CULBERSON, Joseph	CHITTELTON, Agnes	12/24/1787
CULBERSON, William	BROWNING, Mary	05/28/1800
CULBERTSON, Hiram	HIGHTOWER, Nancey	12/15/1806
CULBERTSON, James	GILLYON, Mary	12/13/1785
CUMMELL, William	COLESTON, Ann	03/08/1784
CUNINGHAM, Charles	HUNT, Mary	07/29/1866
CUNINGHAM, Glouster	CUNINGHAM, Sarah	07/27/1866
CUNNINGHAM, Moses	SCOTT, Nancy	10/05/1867
CUNNINGHAM, Nathaniel	SNEED, Elizabeth	09/24/1790
CUNNINGHAM, Thomas	BROWNING, Maryan	06/22/1808
CURL, John T.	HIGHTOWER, Susanah	08/29/1803
CURRIE, George	CHANDLER, Judith	09/09/1829
CURRIE, Isaac R.	JOHNSTON, Eliza	03/08/1824
CURRIE, James	MITCHELL, Julia Ann	02/24/1837
CURRIE, James	MITCHELL, Elizabeth A.	10/15/1822
CURRIE, Jesse	CHANDLER, Margarett	09/29/1830
CURRIE, Joseph	WILEY, Jincey	09/01/1802
CURRIE, Joseph M.	LEA, Mary J.	01/19/1858
CURRIE, Mitchell	CURRIE, Catharine	02/11/1832
CURRIE, William	CURRIE, Frances	12/28/1867
CURRIE, William	PATELLOR, Frances H.	12/28/1842
CURRIE, Young	BOLTON, Amanda	12/23/1867
CUTLER, Joshua	OLRIDG, Sally	07/18/1816
DABBS, Lemuel J.	CHANDLER, Nanny J.	11/05/1856
DABBS, William J.	DUNAWAY, Mary	09/24/1847

MARRIAGE RECORDS OF CASWELL COUNTY, NORTH CAROLINA

GROOM	BRIDE	DATE
DABNEY, Samuel	HARRISON, Jane	04/08/1817
DALTON, Claiborn	WEATHERFORD, Elizabeth	06/30/1810
DALTON, John	WEATHERFORD, Mary Ann	12/04/1838
DAMARON, James K.	MOORE, Olive Ann	11/30/1840
DAMERON, Alexander M.	DAMERON, Martha P.	07/21/1821
DAMERON, Bartholomew	MALONE, Rebeccah	08/27/1798
DAMERON, Benjamin	MATHEWS, Matilda	11/20/1820
DAMERON, Christopher	CAMRON, Martha A.	04/02/1851
DAMERON, Christopher	WARE, Salley	06/06/1815
DAMERON, Harrison	DAMERON, Martha P.	12/17/1822
DAMERON, James B.	CONNALLY, Elizabeth	12/12/1829
DAMERON, James H.	THOMAS, Sally	08/15/1846
DAMERON, James K.	BATEMAN,(?) Barsheba	11/28/1829
DAMERON, John	RICHMOND, Jane	08/14/1834
DAMERON, John	LOVE, Nancey	01/22/1828
DAMERON, John W.	EVANS, Catharine	11/27/1841
DAMERON, Joseph	BURTON, Mary	04/02/1790
DAMERON, Joseph C.	ROAN, Sarah	04/14/1841
DAMERON, Joseph C.	DAMERON, Salinda	09/20/1820
DAMERON, Samuel	HOLCOMB, Salley	01/10/1799
DAMERON, Samuel	SAMUELL, Fanney	07/11/1801
DAMERON, Samuel	BATEMAN, Susan	03/03/1828
DAMERON, William	DAMERON, Cathrine	12/05/1814
DAMERON, William	MALONE, Mary	08/26/1820
DAMERON, William J.	TRAVIS, Alcey S.	09/28/1841
DAMERON, William M.	BROWNING, Sarah F.	12/02/1852
DAMERON, Williamson	EVANS, Polley	12/21/1813
DAMERON, Willias A.	MURRY, Martha M.	12/22/1853
DAMERON, Zachariah E.	DAY, Martha	01/18/1847
DAMERRON, Azariah	BURCH, Lucretia	04/04/1848
DAMREON, Henry W.	RUSSELL, Sarah E.	01/13/1856
DANIEL, Alexander A.	BRANDON, Isabella	11/06/1866
DANIEL, Elias J.	TIRPIN, Susan R.	04/05/1843
DANIEL, James	STEWART, Jane	08/13/1830
DANIEL, Jno.	MURPHEY, Lucy	07/25/1805
DANIEL, John	HUSTON, Rebecca	12/21/1822
DANIEL, John	WALTERS, Lucy	03/29/1844
DANIEL, John	MANGUM, Martha	02/05/1860
DANIEL, John M.	CARTER, Carnelia A.	07/06/1836
DANIEL, John P.	HIGGASON, Jane C.	04/30/1857
DANIEL, Martin	MIMS, Charlotte	08/11/1834
DANIEL, Martin T.	CONALLY, Susan	12/19/1854
DANIEL, Robert	NORFLET, Julia A.	08/27/1842
DANIEL, Thomas	HARDIGE, Nancy	12/16/1814
DANIEL, William M.	WILLIAMSON, Adaline H.	08/14/1839
DARBY, Archibald L.	MOORE, Malinda	02/10/1830
DARBY, Daniel	GIBSON, Elizabeth	02/09/1791
DARBY, George	VANHOOK, Betsey	11/12/1800
DARBY, James	RONE, Anne	10/12/1802
DARBY, John	MCDANIEL, Elisabeth	09/15/1794
DAVIDSON, John A.	CHILTON, Mary A.	12/20/1828

MARRIAGE RECORDS OF CASWELL COUNTY, NORTH CAROLINA

GROOM	BRIDE	DATE
DAVIDSON, Leroy	MOORE, Adeline S.J.	03/14/1828
DAVIS, Alfred	WARF, Elizabeth	02/26/1840
DAVIS, Ashley	KENNON, Anney	09/08/1814
DAVIS, David	MONTGOMERY, Jane	03/23/1808
DAVIS, Elijah	WARRICK, Nancy	06/16/1823
DAVIS, Granville	HOGE, Louisa	11/10/1867
DAVIS, Henry J.	REID, Letetia J.	12/15/1852
DAVIS, James	QUINE, Nelly	10/23/1816
DAVIS, James	PARKES, Susanna	04/02/1822
DAVIS, James M.	KIMBROUGH, Elizabeth J.	09/01/1847
DAVIS, James M.	COX, Ann	12/15/1835
DAVIS, James T.	HILL, Virginia C.	02/15/1866
DAVIS, John	MATTHEWS, Martha	10/11/1817
DAVIS, John	LOGAN, Mecay	01/18/1859
DAVIS, Jonarthon	AUSTON, Mary	04/17/1781
DAVIS, Jonathan	WILKERSON, Rachel	10/--/1817
DAVIS, Lewis	WARF, Kezziah	12/18/1832
DAVIS, Thomas	MALLORY, Nancey	08/23/1805
DAVIS, Thomas W.	STANFIELD, Frances	09/02/1848
DAVIS, William	BAYNES, Polly	06/08/1812
DAVIS, William F.	EVANS, Mary C.	06/24/1854
DAVISE, James	HENDRICK, Crecy	12/25/1835
DAY, Henry	CATE, Margery	03/28/1788
DAY, Isaac	OAKLEY, Jeen	02/26/1791
DAY, Philip	SMITH, Jane	02/07/1815
DE NORDENDORF Charles Chak.	HOOPER, Elizabeth L.V.	04/24/1865
DE NORDENORF, Charles Chaky.	HOOPER, Elizabeth L.V.	04/24/1865
DEACON, Henry	ASLUM, Betsey	04/09/1857
DEBO, Benjamin	TUNKS, Frances	07/27/1790
DEBRULER, Charles	HARGRAVE, Betsey	02/03/1816
DEBRULER, Wesley	HARGREAVE, Lucy	11/04/1816
DEJARRATTE, James P.	PRICE, Martha A.	12/13/1856
DELPS, Michael	STARKEY, Elisabeth	01/29/1782
DENNEY, Azariah	MCKINNEY, Elizabeth	09/26/1823
DENNIS, Franklin J.	VERNON, Edith A.	04/07/1857
DENNIS, John	GRANT, Rachel	02/03/1796
DENNY, Lewis	SIMMONS, Levina	04/19/1830
DENNY, Simon	BARTON, Polly	04/26/1796
DENNY, William	CRANSHAW, Salley	04/--/1818
DENSON, Richard	PAUL, Elizabeth	08/28/1828
DENTON, John	PAYNE, Lucinda	07/08/1842
DEVINEY, Madison	POWELL, Ary W.	04/02/1838
DEWEESE, Samuel	WHITE, Rachel	04/08/1782
DEWESE, Isaiah	BARNETT, Rebeccah	12/06/1788
DICK, John W.	GRAVES, Martha W.	05/31/1822
DICKENS, Joseph W.	SADLER, Mary	09/27/1850
DICKERSON, Benjamin G.	WOOTSON, Bettie S.	03/24/1864
DICKEY, Jacob	PINNIX, Mary A.	12/17/1839
DICKIE, John	SMITHY, Nancy	10/10/1796

MARRIAGE RECORDS OF CASWELL COUNTY, NORTH CAROLINA

GROOM	BRIDE	DATE
DICKIE, Samuel	SHANKS, Elizabeth	12/11/1787
DICKIN, Beverly	SHELTON, Susan	12/05/1840
DICKINS, Henry	HEWS, Lydia	04/21/1791
DICKINS, Israel	DURHAM, Nancy J.	10/30/1844
DICKINS, Israel	WARE, Francis	03/04/1842
DICKINS, James	ESTRIDGE, Alley	03/28/1781
DICKINS, Jeremiah	DICKINS, Rebecah	10/12/1802
DICKINS, Jesse	MOORE, Frances	11/07/1791
DICKINS, William	POSTON, Priscilla	05/06/1794
DICKINS, William	DICKINS, Polly	03/30/1801
DICKINS, William	BRINTLE, Nancey	--/--/----
DILL, James	KENNON, Jane	05/20/1843
DILL, John H.	SAUNDERS, Susan	06/10/1841
DILL, Joseph	SANDERS, Elizabeth	01/09/1858
DILL, Reubin H.	SCOTT, Martha F.	03/09/1868
DILLARD, Richard	HOLT, Sarah	12/07/1796
DILLARD, William	CLAIBORNE, Sarah Ann	11/10/1866
DINWIDDIE, John	NEWTON, Rachel	11/01/1791
DISHOUGH, George F.	SAWYER, Mary	01/10/1835
DISHOUGH, Lewis	PLEASANT, Elizabeth	04/01/1845
DISHOUGH, Reddick	RAINEY, Elizabeth S.	12/12/1817
DISMUKES, James M.	MCADEN, Nancey G.	04/11/1838
DISMUKES, John	HUBBARD, Susan	07/13/1835
DISON, Thomas	HOOD, Lotty	09/17/1840
DIX, Geroge W.	COOK, Elizabeth	11/06/1834
DIX, Humphrey	DAVIS, Caroline	04/12/1832
DIX, JOhn M.	CRITTENTON, Nancey	08/15/1822
DIX, James	DIX, Lucinda	04/22/1846
DIX, John M.	TANNER, Patsey A.	12/13/1816
DIX, Tandy	SADDLER, Martha L.	02/17/1836
DIX, William	RAGSDALE, Mary E.	01/26/1862
DIX, William	PATTERSON, Jane	01/28/1836
DIXON, Henry	BOULTON, Nancy	03/08/1809
DIXON, Henry	BURNETT, Polly	05/28/1802
DIXON, Levi	BOULTON, Sarah W.	09/14/1823
DIXON, RObert	BRACKIN, Sinah	12/17/1823
DIXON, ROger	JOUETTE, Polley	12/16/1794
DIXON, Robert	BROOKS, Jenney	11/22/1796
DIXSON, Robert	BARNET, Mary	09/09/1779
DOBBIN, John	HINTON, Betsey	02/03/1796
DOBBINS, Azariah	TRIM, Frances	05/31/1828
DOBBINS, Hugh C.	DAMERON, Sarah	11/02/1824
DODSON, Carter	DODSON, Alcy	02/23/1818
DODSON, Hugh H.	MORRIS, Susannah	12/26/1816
DODSON, John F.	BAYNES, Isabella	07/04/1817
DODSON, Matthew	PENIX, Prudence	12/20/1819
DODSON, Thomas	FERRELL, Piety	02/26/1817
DODSON, Thomas C.	GRAVES, Isabella L.	10/23/1849
DODSON, William	WILLIAMSON, Louisa	12/25/1866
DODSON, William T.	YOUNG, Sally	09/28/1812
DODSON, Woodson	RICHMOND, Jane	12/26/1867

MARRIAGE RECORDS OF CASWELL COUNTY, NORTH CAROLINA

GROOM	BRIDE	DATE
DOLL, Archer	MEBANE, Sarah	09/28/1866
DOLLARHIDE, John	CHITTINGTON, Nancy	11/03/1784
DOLLARHIDE, William	DOLLARHIDE, Mary	09/28/1789
DOLTON, Isam	BINGHAM, Permela	06/03/1833
DONALDSON, James	JEFFREYS, Lydia	11/03/1866
DONALDSON, Robert	RICHMOND, Elizabeth	01/16/1799
DONALDSON, William	MOTEERAL, Margret	09/05/1793
DONELSON, Andrew	MOTHERAL, Mary	07/18/1791
DONOHO, Alexander	RAIMEY, Susan H.	08/06/1832
DONOHO, Charles D.	BOSWELL, Caroline	05/08/1861
DONOHO, James	TURNER, Susannah	04/22/1802
DONOHO, T.A.	GARLAND, Isabella	04/18/1854
DONOHO, William	HARALSON, Dorcass	04/06/1784
DONOHO, William	LEA, Nicey	11/08/1797
DONOHO, William A.	WILSON, Huldah G.	06/30/1859
DONOHO, William C.	MILES, Nancy R.	03/19/1833
DOOLEY, John	COLLEY, Sally	05/15/1806
DORIS, John	RUSSEL, Elizabeth	04/12/1804
DOSON, William H.	JONES, Ellin	12/13/1837
DOSS, Clark H.	HOLLOWAY, Joanna	01/02/1832
DOSS, Thomas	EDES, Betsy	03/06/1827
DOUGLASS, David	BENTON, Mary	11/05/1817
DOVE, William J.	STRADER, Susan	03/25/1853
DOWELL, James	FULLER, Sarah	03/14/1782
DOWELL, Walker	THOMPSON, Nancey	12/29/1806
DOWNEY, John A.	MARTIN, Lucinda S.	08/08/1846
DOWNS, Rolling L.	LANE, Mary E.	09/09/1842
DOWNS, William	MARR, Priscilla	03/09/1853
DOYLE, Edward	SARGENT, Ruth	04/17/1782
DOYLE, Simon	SARGENT, Elizabeth	08/26/1791
DRAKE, James M.	CHILDRES, Jane	12/22/1828
DRAKE, Thomas	PAGE, Rachel	06/27/1829
DRAPER, Joshua	NOWLES, Holly	04/01/1796
DRAPER, Solomon	TAYLOR, Joyce	07/04/1790
DRUSKILL, Samuel	DUDLEY, Ibby	04/20/1820
DUDLEY, Elisha	DILL, Joanna	12/14/1832
DUEST, Hezekiah	TRICKY, Anness	08/09/1784
DUKE, Buckner	DUNIVANT, Nancy	08/30/1825
DUNAVANT, Andy D.	HIX, Elizabeth	10/01/1854
DUNAVEN, John	DUKE, Betsey	07/13/1825
DUNAVENT, Edward	OVERBY, Susanah	10/19/1818
DUNAWAY, Allen	PASCHALL, Mary Ann	12/05/1841
DUNAWAY, James	FERRELL, Cathrine	12/29/1795
DUNAWAY, Samuel	BARSDALE, Kesiah	02/29/1792
DUNCAN, Jessee	PASCHELL, Hannah	07/14/1780
DUNCAN, Nathan	HUMPHREYS, Elizabeth	09/05/1818
DUNCAN, Nathan	TYRE, Martha	03/02/1827
DUNCAN, Nathaniel	RAINEY, Jane	11/06/1782
DUNERVANT, Abraham	HIX, Artemesia	08/03/1855
DUNEVANT, James	DUNEVANT, Virginia	12/31/1866
DUNEVANT, John H.	OVERBY, Virginia	10/02/1866

MARRIAGE RECORDS OF CASWELL COUNTY, NORTH CAROLINA

GROOM	BRIDE	DATE
DUNN, Jarrett	LOCKETT, Isabella R.	05/22/1852
DUNNAVANT, Jesse	OVERBY, Frances	10/25/1827
DUNNAVANT, Thomas	FUQUA, Elizabeth	04/07/1866
DUNNAVENT, Thomas	TOLER, Mary	08/26/1840
DUNNAWAY, Allen J.	HOOPER, Martha	04/12/1837
DUNNAWAY, James	HICKS, Frances	05/10/1822
DUPREY, John W.	WITHERS, Elizabeth A.	06/12/1843
DURHAM, Archibald	SHIRLY, Susanna P.	09/29/1830
DURHAM, Charles	HUGHS, Sarah	11/27/1862
DURHAM, George	DICKEN, Emily	09/11/1843
DURHAM, George	ROBERTSON, Ann S.	03/15/1841
DURHAM, James	STRADOR, Jane	12/14/1842
DURHAM, John	STRADER, Mary Ann	12/05/1861
DURHAM, John	FAIR, Catherihe	10/30/1848
DURHAM, Martin	STONE, Lucy	01/08/1847
DURHAM, Nathaniel	BUSEY, Eliza	11/05/1822
DURHAM, Newman	FARLY, Cathrine	04/07/1804
DURHAM, RIchard	STONE, Sarah	10/11/1844
DURHAM, Richard	HODGE, Hannah	12/06/1824
DURHAM, Richard	STRADOR, Martha	11/02/1838
DURHAM, Samuel	FREEMAN, Elizabeth	05/09/1836
DURHAM, William F.	WALKER, Eliza A.	12/24/1866
DURREM, Daniel	WILEY, Eleoner	02/22/1808
DURRETT, Francis	MOORE, Betsy	11/31/1807
DURRUM, Isaac	MATCH, Nancy	08/25/1789
DUTY, Joseph	FITCH, Polly	07/23/1826
DUTY, Richard	MCNEILL, Lois	07/21/1791
DUTY, William	WARREN, Rachel	02/13/1783
DYAR, Samuel	MATLOCK, Betsey	08/18/1796
DYE, Abraham	COLESTON, Lattis	02/03/1787
DYE, Benjamin B.	DODSON, Elizabeth W.	05/10/1823
DYE, Shadrach	WESTLY, Elionar	11/16/1802
DYE, William	GORDON, Sally	06/05/1799
EARP, Lawson	FOSTER, Sarah	08/04/1832
EARP, Smith L.	CHANCY, Rebecca	03/13/1845
EASELY, Charles	HUNT, Mary Jane	12/27/1866
EASLEY, John	HENDERSON, Harriott E.	09/27/1830
ECHOLS, Philip J.	JACKSON, Mary E.	01/20/1813
ECTOR, Hugh	MITCHELL, Elizabeth	10/19/1821
ECTOR, James	ANDERSON, Jenny	03/10/1808
ECTOR, Joseph	ANDERSON, Caty	10/15/1804
ECTOR, William S.	HODGES, Ellen T.	12/19/1855
EDDINGS, Joseph	HOLCOM, Elizabeth	07/17/1805
EDDINGS, William	JOHNSTON, Polly	03/18/1807
EDWARDS, Christopher B.	POWELL, Mary G.	11/16/1865
EDWARDS, Edward	GOOCH, Eliza	10/18/1859
EDWARDS, George R.	FIELDER, Jane	09/27/1834
EDWARDS, Gustavus A.	ALLEN, Sarah P.	02/22/1830
EDWARDS, James	BOLEY, Elvira B.	01/15/1829
EDWARDS, Joseph M.	SLADE, Martha L.	01/01/1854
EDWARDS, N.R.	ZIGLER, Martha Jane	03/02/1863

MARRIAGE RECORDS OF CASWELL COUNTY, NORTH CAROLINA

GROOM	BRIDE	DATE
EDWEL, Harrison	THOMAS, Celia A.	01/29/1842
EDWEL, Jim	GRIFFIS, Sally	04/10/1845
EDWELL, Harrison	COLE, Leaner	11/09/1847
EGMON, Lott	BURK, Polley	10/24/1812
ELAM, Robert	CARROL, Betsy	03/14/1804
ELDRIDGE, Daniel B.	EVANS, Amanda A.	02/19/1856
ELIOTT, George C.	PARRISH, S.T.	03/17/1860
ELLIOT, George	HAMLET, Julia	12/18/1824
ELLIOTT, Allen W.	TURNER, Mary F.	12/10/1855
ELLIOTT, David T.	CONALLY, Sarah L.	11/05/1855
ELLIOTT, Granderson	PULLIAM, Ann	04/15/1867
ELLIOTT, James	SLAYTON, Judith T.	10/09/1862
ELLIOTT, James A.	STONE, Ellen J.	08/07/1858
ELLIOTT, John	SIMS, Zilpah	08/20/1785
ELLIOTT, John	DONOHO, Polly	02/25/1808
ELLIOTT, Martin S.	TURNER, Nancey	10/12/1814
ELLIS, Andrew	TERRELL, Lucy	09/22/1819
ELLIS, John H.	ROLEN, Lucrasey F.	12/16/1856
ELLISON, David	EUBANK, Lucretia	12/24/1818
ELLMORE, Thomas	SMITH, Betsey	05/11/1801
ELMORE, Benjamin	COBB, Mary	01/23/1811
ELMORE, John	ELMORE, Lucy Ann	03/06/1830
ELMORE, John	LEA, Marianne	11/27/1798
ELMORE, John	TAYLOR, Polly	01/06/1829
ELMORE, John A.	ROPER, Ann E.	02/27/1833
ELMORE, William	PEARCE, Delilah	08/02/1819
ENGLISH, George C.	HUNLY, Mary H.	11/25/1856
ENOCH, Benjamin	SHY, Sally	10/08/1796
ENOCH, David	EVERET, Rachel	10/03/1803
ENOCH, John	WALKER, Nancy	12/03/1832
ENOCH, John	SHY, Nancey	06/30/1798
ENOCH, Rees H.	THOMPSON, Susan C.	01/06/1859
ENOCH, Samuel	SMITH, Betsey	08/13/1804
ENOCHS, Andrew	KING, Elisabeth	03/11/1787
ENOCK, Walker L.	EVERETT, Mildred A.	05/05/1864
EPPERSON, Branch	HUGHS, Martha	11/02/1842
EPPS, Lewis	BROWN, Nancy	05/20/1867
ERWIN, James	NASH, Nancy	10/10/1786
ESKRIDGE, Bird B.	JOHNSTON, Nancy R.	11/27/1821
ESKRIDGE, George	DOBBIN, Elisabeth	11/25/1790
ESKRIDGE, John	SMITH, Francis	11/22/1811
ESKRIDGE, Robert W.	GRAVES, Mary B.	08/25/1849
ESKRIDGE, Samuel	DOBBINS, Sarah	10/30/1829
ESKRIDGE, Thomas	STAFFORD, Phoebe	11/26/1827
ESKRIDGE, Walker	LEA, Matilda	08/04/1827
ESKRIDGE, William	JOHNSTON, Polly	01/04/1820
ESTERS, Daniel	MOTON, Pheby	03/03/1825
ESTES, Bartlet	REASE, Elizabeth	12/06/1819
ESTES, Bartlett	MUSICK, Pheby	12/28/1790
ESTES, Jonathan	SMITH, Sarah	03/26/1834
ESTES, Marcus E.	STONE, Sarah A.	06/23/1846

MARRIAGE RECORDS OF CASWELL COUNTY, NORTH CAROLINA

GROOM	BRIDE	DATE
ESTES, Micajah	PYRON, Margery	07/08/1801
ESTES, Nathaniel	SMITH, Isabella	11/16/1830
ESTES, Richard	SANDERS, Delpha	05/18/1822
ESTES, Samuel	HOLLES, Elenore	12/25/1815
ESTIS, Richard B.	PAGE, Susan M.	01/04/1855
EUBANK, George	MALONE, Dicey	09/03/1799
EUBANK, James	EUBANKS, Elisabeth	12/01/1791
EUBANK, Thomas	GRAVES, Nancey	12/16/1828
EUDALEY, David	BALDWIN, Salley	12/29/1817
EVANS, Allen W.	OWEN, Adeline A.	09/30/1850
EVANS, Barzallai A.	DAMERON, Phoebe W.	12/06/1845
EVANS, Berry	PAGE, Nancey	12/01/1830
EVANS, Bird	MATLOCK, Mary	12/23/1840
EVANS, Bird	SMITH, Betsey	12/11/1815
EVANS, Daniel	EVANS, Pherebe	03/06/1782
EVANS, David H.	MOORE, Mary	10/08/1851
EVANS, David H.	MURPHEY, Lilla	11/23/1860
EVANS, Edward	FITCH, Artelia	04/19/1848
EVANS, Elisha	LEA, Elisabeth	03/03/1789
EVANS, Ellis	MARTIN, Polly	04/25/1797
EVANS, Ellis	SCOTT, Martha R.	08/07/1838
EVANS, Francis	WALTERS, Sally	11/24/1842
EVANS, George	STEWARD, Elizabeth	05/16/1859
EVANS, Goodwin	KIMBROUGH, Nancey G.	01/05/1814
EVANS, Henry	FERREL, Nancy	02/28/1822
EVANS, James	WRIGHT, Nancey	08/02/1837
EVANS, James	FULLER, Nicey	11/09/1825
EVANS, James	CURRIE, Frances G.	12/26/1851
EVANS, Joel	HUBBARD, Mary	12/23/1846
EVANS, Madison	MATLOCK, Frances	10/07/1865
EVANS, Samuel J.	HOOPER, Barbara	10/08/1836
EVANS, Samuel J.W.	OWEN, Martha A.	12/05/1866
EVANS, Samuel W.	BOWE, Harriet A.	10/12/1862
EVANS, Thomas	WILLSON, Abbarillah	11/26/1821
EVANS, Walter	DAVIS, Cathrine	02/04/1804
EVANS, William	HENSHAW, Mary	03/30/1836
EVANS, William	THOMAS, Polley	12/17/1817
EVANS, Willis R.	EARP, Druzey	05/28/1862
EVANS, Zecheriah	GIBSON, Anne	01/03/1784
EVEHS, William A./G.	HALL, Elizabeth	11/13/1855
EVENS, Samuel	HENDERSON, Priscilla	12/01/1835
EVENS, William G./A.	HALL, Elizabeth	11/13/1855
EVERET, Samuel	SHY, Marthy	05/01/1786
EVERETT, Danl.	-----, Ann	07/04/1843
EVERETT, John	ATKINSON, Phebe R.	02/18/1813
EVINS, John	SWIFT, Nancey	03/15/1836
FACKLER, Abraham	SEATES, Harriett F.	10/23/1858
FADDIS, John	LEMORNS, Anne	01/31/1822
FALKNER, Franklin	MALONE, Mary J.	11/09/1867
FANNING, Hezekiah	JACKSON, Cloe	11/28/1796
FANNING, Midelton	MOORE, Delpha	12/13/1787

MARRIAGE RECORDS OF CASWELL COUNTY, NORTH CAROLINA

GROOM	BRIDE	DATE
FARELY, Abner B.	OWEN, Ann	09/15/1835
FARGUSSON, John	WRIGHT, Polley	02/01/1797
FARIS, Thomas D.	MCHANEY, Julia A.	03/10/1860
FARISH, Adam T.	PRATHER, Mary W.	03/16/1836
FARISH, G. James	TURNER, Elizabeth T.	11/22/1841
FARISH, Joseph	HARRIS, Gracie	12/27/1866
FARLEY, Abner B.	GORDON, Elizabeth	11/11/1848
FARLEY, Daniel S.	LOGAN, Cathrine	10/13/1785
FARLEY, Danl. S.	MCADEN, Cathrine	06/16/1800
FARLEY, Isehiah	BURTON, Martha	11/28/1786
FARLEY, James	LEA, Betsey	09/05/1793
FARLEY, John	DOBBIN, Peggy	--/--/1806
FARLEY, John	FLEMING, Nancy	02/21/1803
FARLEY, John B.	VAUGHN, Eliza	12/26/1816
FARLEY, John E.	LYON, Mary E.	02/10/1867
FARLEY, Kerr	COUSINS, Susan	03/17/1862
FARLEY, William A.	SMITHER, Julia C.	03/28/1849
FARLEY, William T.	POORE, Betty	08/29/1866
FARMER, Daniel	TAPLEY, Sarah M.	08/07/1781
FARMER, Evans	MARR, Lucy T.	05/01/1859
FARMER, Henry A.	FARMER, Elisabeth H.	12/24/1857
FARMER, James M.	RAGLAND, Martha S.	11/25/1849
FARMER, Joseph	STEWARD, Mildred C.	10/01/1865
FARMER, Samuel	STEWART, Lydia A.	12/26/1866
FARMER, Stephen	HARPER, Judy	03/17/1791
FARMER, William	POGUE, Hannar	12/30/1790
FARQUHAR, Abraham M.	LIPSCOMB, Mary	03/25/1823
FARRAR, Richard J.	KNIGHT, Sarah E.	09/14/1856
FARROW, John	MCNAB, Phebe	12/20/1813
FAUCETT, David L.	TERRY, Sarah A.	04/07/1849
FAUKNER, Osmund B.	ROBERTS, Eliza	12/24/1832
FAULKNER, Joseph T.	POOL, Matilda M.	10/16/1859
FAULKS, Abel	RUDD, Betsey	04/13/1815
FAULKS, Edwd J.R.	WINDSOR, Martha A.	04/24/1843
FAUSETT, James	DOUGLASS, Elizabeth	11/03/1827
FEATHERSTON, George A.	BOWE, Elizabeth J.	12/15/1858
FEATHERSTON, Thomas W.	RICHMOND, Virginia C.	11/14/1867
FEGANS, James W.	DUKE, Eliza J.	01/18/1847
FEGUSON, Thomas	BEAUCEY, Polley	12/15/1810
FENN, Gabriel	MARSHALL, Rebeccah	01/05/1796
FERGUSON, Albert G.	FARLEY, Sarah	11/23/1858
FERGUSON, Bethel	FITZGERALD, Ann	12/28/1867
FERGUSON, John	AKIN, Polly	04/10/1816
FERGUSON, Joseph	LAWSON, Silvey	11/17/1866
FERGUSON, Richard	HOOPER, Mary	05/20/1833
FERGUSON, Samuel D.	RAWLINS, Martha A.	01/06/1858
FERGUSSON, John J.	BROWN, Gerly G.	10/30/1853
FERRALL, John	CHRISTENBURY, Elizabeth	11/09/1781
FERRELL, Henry W.	PAGE, Sally A.	04/01/1858
FERRELL, Hutchings	GATEWOOD, Ann E.	10/11/1830
FERRELL, J.H.	FRETWELL, M.J.	10/18/1866

MARRIAGE RECORDS OF CASWELL COUNTY, NORTH CAROLINA

GROOM	BRIDE	DATE
FERRELL, James A.	JOHNSTON, Adaline M.	11/01/1859
FERRELL, John O.	PAGE, Rachael J.	02/03/1859
FERRELL, Moses	PANTON, Isabella	12/27/1867
FERRELL, William	PAGE, Martha	04/16/1825
FERRELL, William	WILLIAMS, Nancey	11/18/1789
FERRILL, George W.	LYNCH, Cynthia	11/10/1835
FIELDER, Alfred T.	TAIT, Isabell	11/28/1832
FIELDER, Benjamin T.	SWIFT, Susanna W.	10/02/1810
FIELDER, John	RICE, Willy	09/28/1842
FIELDER, Leonard L.	BOSWELL, Eliza	09/12/1829
FIELDER, Samuel C.	HENDERSON, Elizabeth	01/12/1833
FILLIPS, Joseph	WALTERS, Elizabeth	12/21/1812
FINCH, George A.	MCCORMICK, Catherine	05/19/1862
FINCH, Samuel	DODSON, Sarah	04/30/1859
FINLEY, Augustus C.	WILLIAMSON, Ann E.	06/09/1836
FINLEY, George	SAMUELL, Nancey	02/07/1816
FISHER, Anthony	TURNER, Nancey	09/06/1825
FISHER, Tressy	BAULDIN, Catherine	01/12/1801
FISHER, William	FARLEY, Polly H.	08/30/1814
FITCH, Anderson N.	PAGE, Susan	10/20/1860
FITCH, Empson	HIGHTOWER, Delilah	11/24/1834
FITCH, James	CLENDENING, Mary	03/13/1830
FITCH, William W.	NASH, Cornelia	11/20/1866
FITTS, Marcellus G.	HUDGINS, Susan A.	03/01/1865
FITZ, William	STADLER, Lidia	02/16/1805
FITZGERALD, Banister R.	BETTS, Maria H.	01/05/1829
FITZGERALD, James W.	SWANN, Elizabeth F.	04/23/1847
FITZGERALD, Jno. B.	LAND, Sophia A.	11/15/1867
FITZGERALD, Joseph M.	TERRY, Harriet	12/07/1843
FITZGERALD, Pleasant	GARRETT, Susan	10/06/1853
FITZGERALD, Richard	HOOPER, Martha	01/31/1822
FITZGERALD, William	WOODS, Sarah A.E.	03/14/1846
FITZGERALD, William	NANCE, Elizabeth	06/27/1848
FLACK, Elijah	TAIT, Fanny	05/08/1801
FLEMING, Jasper	STEGALL, Rebecca A.	01/22/1861
FLEMING, William	WINTERS, Elizabeth	12/14/1801
FLEMMING, Pleasant	RUSH, Betsey	07/25/1798
FLETCHER, James	REASON, Mary	11/28/1781
FLETCHER, Reubin	THOMPSON, Betsey	12/22/1802
FLINTOFF, John F.	PLEASANT, Mary M.	05/11/1850
FLIPPIN, Joseph W.	ATKINSON, Susan W.	06/04/1856
FLIPPO, Joseph	ELMORE, Sally	09/28/1801
FLORA, Melceger R.	DUNKLY, Lucy	11/18/1842
FLORANCE, Empson	BOSWELL, Eliza	12/07/1846
FLORENCE, Bennett	BIRD, Elizabeth A.	10/18/1837
FLORENCE, George W.	WOMBLE, SUsannah F.	09/21/1854
FLORENCE, James	BOULDIN, Sarah S.	09/21/1854
FLORENCE, James	DAMERON, Frances H.	11/22/1858
FLORENCE, William	PLEASANT, Patcey	11/06/1808
FLOYD, Samuel B.	SAILES, Permela F.	07/21/1833
FOARD, Francis	STEPHEN, Nancy	03/29/1798

MARRIAGE RECORDS OF CASWELL COUNTY, NORTH CAROLINA

GROOM	BRIDE	DATE
FORBES, William	POWELL, Virginia V.	05/09/1867
FORD, Alexander	FULLER, Pheby	08/19/1806
FORD, Amos	RUDD, Frances	09/24/1811
FORD, Eli	STADOR, Zeporiah	12/22/1827
FORD, George	TENNESSON, Elizabeth	12/13/1800
FORD, George	SCOTT, Mary	05/27/1852
FORD, John N.	STRADOR, Esther	12/22/1827
FORD, John R.	THORNTON, Susan E.	09/04/1851
FORD, Laban	GRIFFIN, Patsey	04/08/1813
FORD, Levi	PAYNE, Mary	01/04/1814
FORD, Lewis	GILL, Elizabeth	09/21/1841
FORD, Mumford	MCNEELY, Rachel	10/07/1806
FORD, Pleasant	SOUTHARD, Nancy M.	10/19/1833
FORD, Thomas	DOTSON, Elmina	05/01/1828
FORD, William	WRAY, Salley	12/05/1787
FORGERSON, Garrett	BAYS, Lucy	08/05/1841
FORGUSSON, James	DURHAM, Nancey	10/04/1816
FOROD, Elijah T.	CREWS, Martha	12/22/1834
FORRELL, Enoch	STONE, Lucy	11/03/1784
FORREST, Thomas	BURTON, Betsey	12/02/1809
FORSHEE, Joseph	STAFFORD, Nelley	02/15/1784
FORSTER, F. K.	TURNER, S. E.	10/14/1848
FOSSETT, Robert	HUGHES, Mary	02/07/1800
FOSTER, Anthony	PERKINS, Salley	10/01/1811
FOSTER, Colby	KING, Betsey	06/16/1808
FOSTER, Ezariah	KING, Nancey	06/30/1828
FOSTER, Franklin	MANLEY, Ibba	10/07/1841
FOSTER, Franklin	MANLEY, Lucy	01/28/1864
FOSTER, James	HARDEN, Nancey	09/04/1812
FOSTER, Jesse	ADKINS, Polley	11/03/1817
FOSTER, John	PULHIM, Agniss	12/31/1786
FOSTER, John	PIRKINS, Nancy	12/22/1783
FOSTER, John	PERKINS, Elizabeth	07/29/1816
FOSTER, John	BRANDON, Elizabeth	01/29/1820
FOSTER, Lewis,	MITCHEL, Cisily	09/02/1797
FOSTER, Madison P.	BLACKWELL, Nancy	01/17/1842
FOSTER, Richard	HOBBS, Lucy	02/28/1821
FOSTER, Robert	GRANT, Elizabet	09/05/1805
FOSTER, Samuel P.	GARROTT, Mary	12/04/1829
FOSTER, Thomas	HARRELSON, Polley	12/22/1814
FOSTER, Thomas T.	MITCHELL, Mary A.	11/12/1850
FOSTER, William A.	JONES, Ann P.	12/20/1860
FOSTER, William L.	TAYLOR, Lucinda	07/28/1846
FOSTER, Williamson P.	MONTGOMERY, Sally	01/27/1845
FOULKES, Edward M.	BROWN, Martha	12/16/1811
FOULKES, Thomas C.	MOORE, Pennelope	04/06/1811
FOULKS, Oliver	RUDD, Patience	10/11/1825
FOWLER, Elias	GLASGOW, Eliza	11/08/1834
FOWLER, Harrison,	BLAIR, Sallie	01/21/1866
FOWLER, John	FOWLER, Nancy	07/11/1853
FOWLER, William L.	CLAY, America F.	02/12/1853

MARRIAGE RECORDS OF CASWELL COUNTY, NORTH CAROLINA

GROOM	BRIDE	DATE
FOX, Nathan	REND, Mary J.	11/06/1848
FOX, Wm.	JACOB, Nancy	12/28/1820
FRAILEY, John	DALTON, Patience	04/01/1811
FRANKLIN, Ambrose	JONES, Elizabeth	03/18/1826
FRANKLIN, William C.	BURTON, Mary E.	11/10/1859
FRANKLIN, Zeary	BOSWELL, Sarah A.	05/07/1850
FRAZIER, Madison M.	HIGHTOWER, Nancey W.	08/18/1832
FREDERICK, Jesse	HICKS, Sophia	06/11/1833
FREELAND, Charles J.	BARTON, Margaret E.	08/30/1853
FREEMAN, John	MENDRICK, Rhody	01/10/1856
FREEMAN, John P.	HARDEN, Deborah	02/01/1815
FREEMAN, Moses	GOOD, Betsey	10/30/1811
FREEMAN, Wesley	GOOD, Vilet	01/29/1862
FREEMAN, Willis W.	PILES, Jane	05/06/1848
FRENCH, Benjamen	TURNER, Salley	11/10/1784
FRENCH, James	STRADOR, Mahala	05/14/1818
FRENCH, John	BRACKIN, Agripina	03/30/1833
FRETWELL, William A.	LOCKET, Caroline	05/23/1842
FRYER, William	WINDSOR, Elizabeth	04/14/1815
FULCHER, Henry	GREGORY, Mary	12/21/1786
FULCHER, William	ARCHDEACON, Alsey	09/04/1787
FULINGTON, John R.	MATHIS, Patience	11/17/1827
FULLAR, Peter	ROSEBROUGH, Jane	04/23/1781
FULLER, Abraham	SARGENT, Mary	02/06/1786
FULLER, Albert G.	POWELL, Ann Catharin	10/11/1847
FULLER, Henry	PASS, Jane	07/21/1867
FULLER, Jesse	MOORE, Sophronia	11/24/1846
FULLER, John	CLALYTON, Susannah	12/09/1778
FULLER, John H.	COOPER, Nancey	08/26/1836
FULLER, Levi	MCDANIEL, Susannah	02/03/1810
FULLER, Stephen	HIGHTOWER, Elizabeth	03/15/1825
FULLER, William	WALLIS, Elizabeth	03/09/1796
FULLINGTON, James	JOHNSTON, Anna	10/25/1825
FULLINGTON, James G.	CAMPBELL, Meranda	11/22/1856
FULLINGTON, William	PAGE, Milley	01/03/1825
FULTON, Jno K.	HARRISON, Louisa M.	01/10/1852
FULTON, Mathias	HUNTER, Jane L.	01/09/1822
FULTON, William J.	COLEMAN, Minerva	01/28/1842
FUQUA, Henry D.	FERRELL, Mary R.	08/03/1826
FUQUA, John	LEA, Rebecca V.	11/29/1851
FUQUA, William	FERRELL, Elizabeth	07/10/1833
FURGERSON, Alexander	HAILEY, Mary	10/06/1856
FURGERSON, Samuel	ARNETT, Mary L.	08/12/1822
FURGERSON, William G.	JEFFREYS, Elizabeth Jane	10/30/1848
FURGESON, Andrew J.	WILLIS, Judah F.	11/26/1856
FURGUSON, James T.	RUSSELL, Eliza J.	02/15/1866
FURGUSON, Robert F.	RICHARDSON, Harriet M.	09/14/1854
GADDIS, William	CONNOLLY, Anngelico	11/16/1795
GAFFARD, William	CLIMPSON, Nancey	10/30/1821
GALLANGHER, William	DOLLARHIDE, Sarah	11/26/1781
GALLOWAY, Robert	HILL, Fanny M.	03/10/1852

MARRIAGE RECORDS OF CASWELL COUNTY, NORTH CAROLINA

GROOM	BRIDE	DATE
GANN, William	PASS, Rebeccah	03/03/1798
GANNAWAY, G. T. F.	PASCHAL, Sally	02/12/1868
GANT, Jesse	ANDERSON, Minerva M.	06/20/1840
GARBER, A. M. Jr.	BALDWIN, A. C.	03/16/1864
GARDNER, Joseph C.	HOWARD, Martha E.	09/04/1867
GARDNER, Nathaniel W.	COBB, Martha H.	09/10/1832
GARDNER, Starke	HOLLADAY, Harriott	05/13/1835
GARLAND, Anderson	GUY, Rhoda	12/27/1867
GARLAND, Eustace	CLARK, Minerva	04/21/1867
GARLAND, Jacob	THOMAS, Allice	04/21/1867
GARLAND, Jno T.	GLENN, Christinia J.	05/15/1821
GARLAND, Nelson	GARLAND, Meldenna	06/16/1867
GARLAND, Oscar	GARLAND, Pheby Ann	05/19/1867
GARLAND, Peter	CLAY, Anna	12/06/1866
GARLAND, William	WILSON, Candis	10/08/1865
GARLAND, Wilson	JENINGS, Mary E.	07/16/1860
GARLINGTON, John L.	OLIVER, Mary E.	05/30/1857
GARNER, Archibald W.	YANCEY, Ann E.	01/09/1862
GARRETT, John W.	BLACKWELL, Martha	02/02/1835
GARRETT, R. J.	WALKER, Mary A.	02/27/1855
GARRISON, Daniel	SARTIN, Matilda P.	08/21/1867
GARRISON, George	HERNDON, Frances	11/29/1847
GARRISON, Hall	CANTREL, Catherine	05/20/1809
GARROD, John C.	REAVES, Mary E.	04/11/1867
GARROTT, Mansell	FRAZER, Ann	07/04/1790
GARROTT, Stephen	BRADSHER, Martha B.	01/18/1823
GATES, James M.	SMITH, Nancy B.	02/10/1824
GATES, John	RICHARDSON, Lucy	03/10/1821
GATES, Richard	WILLIAMS, Aggy	08/06/1798
GATES, Richard	FOWLER, Rebecca	11/12/1837
GATEWOOD, Lewis	STOKES, Salley	02/01/1811
GATEWOOD, Robert A.	HODGES, Eliza	11/18/1842
GATEWOOD, Thomas	FARLEY, Pamilia	09/23/1806
GATEWOOD, Thomas L.	BENNETT, Martha T.	05/31/1853
GATEWOOD, William D.	BADGETT, Mary W.	02/13/1856
GATEWOOD, William H.	HODGES, Mary	11/23/1847
GATLEY, John	MESSER, Mime	01/30/1787
GATTIS, Alexander Rev.	WOMBLE, Sarah E. F.	11/24/1857
GATTIS, W. A.	HAWKINS, Alice V.	12/17/1866
GATTIS, William	MONTGOMERY, Rebecca	03/18/1820
GATTY, Joseph	RAGSDALE, Elizabeth	12/22/1789
GEARY, Benjamin	CALDWELL, Appy	08/11/1817
GEORGE, Isaac	HENSLEE, Frankey	11/04/1805
GIBBS, John	MUCHMORE, Hannah	01/18/1783
GIBES, Shadrach	ROBINSON, Ester	05/11/1785
GIBSON, Benj.	TATE, Susannah	10/20/1795
GIBSON, Ivoson	COBB, Frances	02/03/1841
GIBSON, John	HOGG, Juda	06/08/1779
GIBSON, Samuel	DAVIS, Jane	11/11/1834
GIBSON, Thomas	BOSWELL, Margaret	12/28/1819
GILL, Richard D.	LAMPKIN, Sarah	11/18/1822

MARRIAGE RECORDS OF CASWELL COUNTY, NORTH CAROLINA

GROOM	BRIDE	DATE
GILL, Robert	DAVEY, Elisabeth	01/05/1784
GILLAM, Joseph	WALKER, Sarah	01/21/1839
GILLAM, Robert	WALKER, Martha	04/24/1837
GILLASPIE, Edward R.	AUSTIN, Mary F.	07/13/1855
GILLASPY, Gidel	PASS, Martha	11/24/1817
GILLASPY, James	HUBBARD, Rhody	02/18/1799
GILLASPY, William	JEFFRYS, Patty	10/26/1782
GILLESPIE, William	MANNEN, Susanah	06/13/1805
GILLIAM, R. C.	RUCKS, Virginia M.	11/30/1863
GILLIAM, Wm. M.	WATSON, J. B.	09/01/1860
GILLISPIE, David A.	POWELL, Rebecca F.	09/30/1848
GILLISPIE, David A.	COLLY, Mary F.	03/30/1852
GILLISPIE, Joseph M.	HENDRICK, Sophia J.	08/30/1865
GILLISPIE, William O.	WALTERS, Mary F.	12/02/1851
GLASGOW, William T.	HOWEL, Nancey	03/20/1815
GLASS, Iverson M.	FULLER, Sallie M.	10/08/1853
GLASS, John D.	POWELL, Margaret E.	02/14/1854
GLASS, Joshua S.	RICHARDSON, Elizabeth	11/24/1846
GLASS, Saml.	BLACKWELL, Huldah B.	04/28/1866
GLASS, Willison J.	DURHAM, Sally	04/20/1829
GLAZE, Ralph	SHELTON, Elizabeth	11.06.1823
GLENN, Sampson M.	INGRAM, Clary	02/--/1803
GOADGE, William	FERGUSON, Polly	07/01/1805
GODWIN, George W.	SHANKES, Sophia	11/13/1818
GOIN, John	HICKMAN, Betsey	11/24/1795
GOING, Goodrich	MATTHEWS, Betsey	09/06/1791
GOING, Jesse	BAIRDING, Seeley	06/09/1784
GOING, Jesse	DRAPER, Polly	11/12/1807
GOING, John	BAIRDING, Seeley	06/09/1784
GOING, Sherwood	COVENTON, Betsey	12/31/1804
GOING, Sherwood	RENNETT, Ruth	04/30/1793
GOLD, William	DAMERON, Mary	07/30/1806
GOMER, Barzillai	BEAVER, Judith	09/29/1814
GOMER, Benjamin	TARPLEY, Janey	11/04/1789
GOMER, James	GOMER, Dicey	12/17/1816
GOMER, James	HALL, Elizabeth	04/22/1819
GOMER, James J.	MITCHELL, Elizabeth	08/12/1845
GOMER, James J.	SANDERS, Anne	12/18/1838
GOMER, John	BEAVER, Ann	02/20/1810
GOMER, John	PARRISH, Polley	03/11/1816
GOMER, Pinckney	STRADER, Mary	10/02/1847
GOMER, Thomas	MASON, Salley	08/17/1829
GOMER, Wiley	BLACKWELL, Catharine	09/28/1846
GOMER, William	WATSON, Nancey	03/11/1807
GOOCH, David	WILLIAMS, Jenny	12/19/1788
GOOCH, Francis	KING, Alicey	12/30/1837
GOOCH, James	PORTER, Sally	11/29/1801
GOOCH, James	KELLEY, Elisabeth	08/03/1785
GOOCH, John	WALTERS, Polley	08/25/1807
GOOCH, Nathaniel	FERRELL, Louisa A.	07/19/1852
GOOCH, Nathaniel	BOZWELL, Jenney	01/23/1816

MARRIAGE RECORDS OF CASWELL COUNTY, NORTH CAROLINA

GROOM	BRIDE	DATE
GOOCH, Nathaniel	KING, Nancy	03/20/1864
GOOCH, Nathnl.	TATE, Patsey	11/30/1797
GOOCH, Thomas	MARTIN, Frances	10/06/1834
GOOCH, Thomas	ANTHONY, Elizabeth	08/12/1799
GOOCH, William	TURNER, Mary	06/10/1866
GOOCH, William Jr.	FANNING, Mary	12/05/1798
GOODMAN, Joseph	BROWN, Elioner	03/15/1781
GOODSON, George T.	BURTON, Sarah J.	10/09/1852
GOODSON, George T.	POWELL, M. E.	09/24/1865
GOODWIN, James H.	PHILIPS, Adeline	05/09/1837
GORDEN, William	NIPPER, Eliza	05/11/1802
GORDON, Alexander	JOHNSTON, Susannah	10/19/1807
GORDON, James	WALTERS, Elizabeth	11/19/1845
GORDON, Robert	TRAMMELL, Crosha	12/11/1845
GOSNE, Benjamin H.	WARE, Martha	09/19/1825
GOSSAGE, Danl.	HUDSON, Peggy	01/05/1801
GOSSAGE, Richard	GREENHAW, Rachel	04/12/1797
GOSSET, Joel	GORDON, Sarah	10/17/1827
GOSSETT, Thomas	PYRANT, Nelly	01/04/1808
GOULD, Benajmin	BRADY, Eliza	11/10/1838
GOWIN, Richard	BENNETT, Polly	07/04/1807
GOWING, Vincent	REED, Nancy	12/30/1806
GRAHAM, Albert	COOPER, Lillie J.	12/19/1867
GRAHAM, James	DAMERON, Susan	02/24/1853
GRAHAM, Thomas	WILLIAMSON, Emily G.	01/22/1857
GRAHAM, Travees	ROSE, Martha Stout	02/13/1786
GRAHAM, William P.	NASH, Farmesia	09/28/1819
GRAHAMS, James	DOUGLASS, Martha	01/09/1816
GRANT, James P.	DEAN, Virginia C.	05/31/1862
GRANT, John W.	COBB, Deborah	07/16/1812
GRANT, Neely	PERKINS, Lucy	09/23/1793
GRAVE, Charles I.	LEA, Maggie R.	11/08/1862
GRAVES, Alfred	GRAVES, Evelina	07/22/1867
GRAVES, Augustus	COMER, Elizabeth W.	11/13/1849
GRAVES, Azariah	SIMPSON, Penelope	05/16/1809
GRAVES, Azariah	HOWARD, Isabella S.	03/17/1858
GRAVES, Azariah Jr.	NEAL, Elizabeth	06/20/1846
GRAVES, Barzallai	WRIGHT, Ursley	04/09/1783
GRAVES, Benjiman	REID, Mary Ann	02/25/1867
GRAVES, Calvin	LEA, Elizabeth	06/02/1830
GRAVES, Cato	RUDD, Lizzie	10/20/1866
GRAVES, David S.	SANDERS, Ida V.	09/26/1852
GRAVES, Elijah Jr.	GUNN, Eliza A.	10/21/1828
GRAVES, Elijah Jr.	CRUMP, Mary J.	11/26/1849
GRAVES, Geo.	-----, -----	09/20/1866
GRAVES, George A.	WILLIAMSON, Isabella M.	04/04/1865
GRAVES, Henry L.	GRAVES, Rebecca W.	02/02/1836
GRAVES, Isaac	HUNLEY, Mary	09/21/1867
GRAVES, Iverson	PAYNE, Elizabeth B.	10/02/1828
GRAVES, Jacob M. Jr.	EUBANK, Polly	09/13/1827
GRAVES, James	SLADE, Polley	04/15/1800

MARRIAGE RECORDS OF CASWELL COUNTY, NORTH CAROLINA

GROOM	BRIDE	DATE
GRAVES, James	PLEASANT, Elizabeth	11/18/1824
GRAVES, James L.	KERR, Frances A.	11/07/1849
GRAVES, James L.	WOMACK, Elizabeth C.	03/12/1840
GRAVES, Jeremiah	LEA, Delilah	03/14/1816
GRAVES, Jeremiah Jr.	THORNTON, D. R.	06/13/1860
GRAVES, Jno. K.	WILLIS, Laura A.	01/20/1844
GRAVES, John	COLEMAN, Elizabeth	11/28/1808
GRAVES, John A.	WHITED, Catherine M.	05/31/1848
GRAVES, John Jr.	YANCEY, Polly	02/13/1794
GRAVES, John L.	DICK, Martha W.	05/20/1824
GRAVES, John S.	SIMPSON, Susan B.	04/04/1858
GRAVES, Lewis	GRAVES, Elizabeth	11/12/1818
GRAVES, Lewis Dixon	WILLIS, Nancey	09/20/1836
GRAVES, Lucien	BROWN, Matilda	10/27/1865
GRAVES, Morris	ADKINS, Susan	10/28/1866
GRAVES, Nathan	WOMACK, Adline	12/26/1865
GRAVES, Peter	PALMER, Hettie	11/19/1867
GRAVES, Solomon	GRAVES, Nancey S.	05/21/1836
GRAVES, Thomas	LAMPKIN, Nancey	07/26/1821
GRAVES, Thomas	BENNATT, Polley	05/05/1801
GRAVES, Thomas W.	GRAVES, Mary	07/17/1828
GRAVES, William	GRAVES, Isbell	11/25/1805
GRAVES, William	HESTER, Eliza	11/05/1833
GRAVES, William	GRAVES, Nancey	05/25/1815
GRAVES, William B.	LEA, Sarah H.	07/17/1863
GRAVES, William G.	LEA, Anna R.	12/11/1865
GRAVETT, Lodwick	MOSS, Susanah	12/07/1789
GRAY, Alexander	WILEY, Lucinda R.	11/10/1840
GRAY, James	STOKES, Elizabeth	11/29/1780
GRAY, John	WILEY, Margaret	12/16/1800
GRAY, Yancey	ROSE, Jane	03/25/1828
GREEN, Burwell	CADDEL, Phebe	07/04/1789
GREEN, Joseph G.	ALLEN, Amanda S.	10/12/1836
GREEN, Lewis	CADDELL, Elizabeth	12/26/1789
GREEN, Thomas C.	MCMULLEN, Jane	05/13/1844
GREENWOOD, Thomas	CARVER, Minerva J.	11/04/1843
GREGORY, John H.	SISSON, Mary	05/22/1841
GREGORY, Samuel	THARP, Patsey	12/05/1807
GREGORY, Thomas	PATTERSON, Cassindia Carol	04/04/1825
GREGORY, Thomas J.	WYNNE, Polly	12/01/1827
GRESHAM, Henry	LOOT, Mary	01/05/1788
GRIDER, Jacob	WASHBURN, Recey	04/22/1797
GRIFFIN, Alvis L.	FITCH, Malinda	02/23/1850
GRIFFIN, Ander J.	SAWYER, Martha Ann	09/20/1851
GRIFFIN, John	CRAWLEY, Elizabeth	07/21/1840
GRIFFIN, Owen	WISDOM, Catherine	04/17/1816
GRIFFIN, Vincent	EVENS, Salley	09/12/1820
GRIFFIN, William	PLEASANT, Lucy	04/13/1812
GRIFFIS, Alexander	ROAN, Anness	09/12/1809
GRIFFITH, James	ROE, Susanna	01/31/1822

MARRIAGE RECORDS OF CASWELL COUNTY, NORTH CAROLINA

GROOM	BRIDE	DATE
GRIFFITH, Jesse C.	VERNON, Mary J.	01/15/1845
GRIFFITH, Richard H.	STARKEY, Judith	12/10/1820
GROOM, Calvin	MARTIN, Elizabeth	11/08/1859
GROOM, Carter	BUTLER, Polley	10/27/1819
GROOM, John	RAINEY, Sarah A.	04/04/1858
GROOM, John	CHANDLER, Frances G.	08/03/1848
GROOM, Robert	PINSON, Elizabeth	12/04/1824
GROOM, Samuel	SCOTT, Frances	07/20/1824
GROOM, Thomas	CRAFTON, Welthy	12/28/1835
GROOM, Thomas	JEFFREYS, Mildred	10/17/1821
GROOM, William	PIERCE, Nancey	03/24/1813
GUDE, William Jr.	MITCHELL, Vilet	11/03/1850
GUERRANT, Peter M. C.	COBB, Mariah L.	01/19/1855
GUERRANT, T. D. F.	STANFIELD, Sarah J.	10/25/1858
GUINN, James	REW, Nannie	12/27/1866
GUNN, Allen Jr. Doct.	HENDERSON, Minerva Ann	10/07/1829
GUNN, Asa	HARRALSON, Nancey	11/22/1819
GUNN, Daniel	BURTON, Nancy	10/19/1818
GUNN, Daniel B.	BRANDON, Eliza H.	10/19/1839
GUNN, Geo. W. Dr.	BURTON, Jennie Hennie	10/21/1860
GUNN, George	HOOPER, Emily	01/12/1867
GUNN, Griffin	WOMACK, Vashti	09/18/1837
GUNN, James	WALKER, Barbary	04/21/1808
GUNN, James	HENDERSON, Frances A.	05/07/1835
GUNN, James M.	BATTON, Mary M.	03/13/1843
GUNN, John	WARE, Huldy	01/28/1807
GUNN, John	PHILLIPS, Eliza	04/04/1866
GUNN, John A.	HARALSON, Martha	04/02/1839
GUNN, John Jr.	PALMER, Elizabeth	07/05/1827
GUNN, Penny	WALKER, Catharine	12/24/1867
GUNN, Richard	FOSTER, Susannah	10/30/1810
GUNN, Samuel	JONES, Leanna	03/24/1866
GUNN, Sterling	JONES, Mary A.	01/14/1868
GUNN, Thomas	MILES, Patcey	09/20/1802
GUNN, Thomas	ALVERSON, Nelly	10/24/1797
GUNN, Thomas	GRAVES, Patsey	09/22/1792
GUNN, Thomas Junr.	MONTGOMERY, Anne	01/22/1811
GUNN, Wiley	LEA, Arrimenta	04/03/1867
GUNNELL, John	SMITH, Sally	01/04/1838
GURNES, Richard	TONEY, Mary	02/19/1855
GUTRY, John D.	MANLEY, Elacy	12/15/1838
GUTTEPY, William	SHEPPARD, Elisabeth	10/02/1782
GUY, Alvis	MITCHEL, Lavina	12/24/1867
GWYN, Augustus	CORBITT, Emily T.	06/21/1854
GWYN, Augustus	MADDING, Jane E.	06/02/1838
GWYN, Daniel	HATCHETT, Mary N.	08/30/1815
GWYN, James	WATLINGTON, Phillis	12/31/1866
GWYN, John	DUPREE, Permelia	08/02/1839
GWYN, John W.	HORNBUCKLE, Frances	09/14/1856
GWYN, Rice	RICE, Elizabeth B.	03/01/1842
GWYN, Robert Z.	CORBETT, Nancey	11/29/1859

MARRIAGE RECORDS OF CASWELL COUNTY, NORTH CAROLINA

GROOM	BRIDE	DATE
GWYN, Zeri	GOODSON, Temperance	12/21/1800
HACKNEY, Samuel	REYNOLDS, Sarah	09/23/1791
HADDOCK, Andrew	GREEN, Peggy	06/21/1806
HADDOCK, Bedford	HUGHS, Malinda	04/22/1829
HADDOCK, David	ROBERTS, Salley	05/13/1802
HADDOCK, Henry	BRUCE, Mary	02/17/1844
HADDOCK, Richard	WRIGHT, Providence	07/29/1796
HADDOCK, Stephen	PITTARD, Nancey	10/30/1820
HADDOCK, Stephen	DAVIS, Sarah	12/25/1834
HAGIE, Thomas	BROUGHTON, Luzella M.	10/19/1841
HAGUE, James	STREET, Martha	10/09/1784
HAGWOOD, James	HODGES, Nancey M.	11/23/1836
HAGWOOD, John	STEPHENS, Elizabeth	01/08/1835
HAGWOOD, John	STEPHENS, Catharine	10/24/1839
HAGWOOD, Lewis	JACKSON, Martha	04/07/1819
HAILEY, Henry B.	LYON, Polley	07/22/1812
HAILEY, Patrick C.	CRAWFORD, Bettie A.	07/12/1862
HAIRSTON, Charles	DIX, Lucy	12/29/1867
HAITHCOCK, Allen F.	BURCH, Lucinda	02/28/1821
HAITHCOCK, John	HAITH, Sarah J.	08/18/1867
HAITHCOCK, Martial	WILSON, Martha	12/07/1866
HAIZLIP, Haywood H.	HOOPER, Martha J.	09/25/1856
HALCOM, George	HENDERSON, Sarah	12/25/1788
HALCOM, George	MERRITT, Freelove	10/02/1786
HALCOMB, Warren	HOOPER, Elizabeth	01/20/1824
HALCOMB, William	THOMAS, Sarah	01/05/1824
HALCOMB, William	JEFFREYS, Nancy	08/16/1805
HALES, Samuel	JENNINGS, Elizabeth M.	07/01/1856
HALL, Alexander	BRINSFIELD, Patsey	03/25/1828
HALL, Anthony	HARVELL, Winney	09/22/1792
HALL, Anthony	BUTLER, Rithy	12/23/1794
HALL, Benjamin P.	YOUNG, Mary L.	06/16/1858
HALL, Berry	OWEN, Mary	03/28/1856
HALL, Beverly	OWEN, Lucy	08/21/1854
HALL, Charles	HARRISON, Cintha	03/24/1852
HALL, David	PETERSON, Blanche	03/07/1825
HALL, James	FERRELL, Eliza A.	12/29/1856
HALL, James H.	HANCOCK, Lucy Ann	09/07/1868
HALL, John	HARWELL, Nancey	10/18/1791
HALL, John	POTEAT, Sarah	07/03/1859
HALL, Lambert W.	BENNETT, Frances N.	03/25/1858
HALL, Pleasant	MCADEN, Cynthia	02/10/1807
HALL, Robert	SCOTT, Frances	12/11/1800
HALL, Solomon	INGROM, Morning	12/24/1817
HALL, William	ROBINSON, Peninah	11/18/1783
HALL, William J.	EARP, Lydia B.	02/01/1864
HALRESON, Calvin	MCDANIEL, Sally	02/16/1867
HAMBLETT, Bird	SIMPSON, Polley	01/04/1806
HAMLETON, Joseph	PRATHER, Elizabeth W.	12/18/1831
HAMLETT, Andrew J.	THOMAS, Catharine	05/11/1867
HAMLETT, James	CARROL, Rebechah	02/09/1793

MARRIAGE RECORDS OF CASWELL COUNTY, NORTH CAROLINA

GROOM	BRIDE	DATE
HAMLETT, James	TAYLOR, Patsey	10/07/1822
HAMLETT, Robert	GLIDEWELL, Mary	12/27/1843
HANCOCK, Farmer	TAYLOR, Frances	12/18/1852
HANCOCK, John J.	FOWLER, Rosa	10/10/1858
HANCOCK, Stephen	WARREN, Ann	07/03/1839
HANKS, Abraham	COMBS, Mary	01/12/1792
HANNER, James	CARTER, Mary	02/03/1817
HARALSON, Herndon	MURPHEY, Mary	10/04/1791
HARALSON, Major	BLACK, Elizabeth	07/16/1793
HARALSON, Thomas	BUSH, Anne	11/18/1787
HARALSON, William	KING, Sarah	11/07/1837
HARAWAY, William	WALTERS, Mary J.	01/29/1866
HARBEN, William	DILL, Maryann	12/04/1780
HARDEN, Henry	HONBUCKLE, Elisabeth	08/14/1795
HARDICREE, Jonathan	CAMERON, Patsey	07/05/1797
HARDING, Ephraim H.	RICHMOND, Mary D.	01/18/1859
HARDISON, Thomas	HOOPER, Sarah	08/02/1845
HARDY, George	DURHAM, Susannah	02/25/1850
HARDY, Green	WEEDEN, Mary A.	12/03/1844
HARDY, Robert	BRGG, Manerva	08/17/1854
HARDY, Robert T.	WRIGHT, Adaline W.	10/04/1865
HARDY, Samuel	TRU, Nancy	01/11/1851
HARGESS, Shadrach	JONES, Sally	12/18/1817
HARGIS, James O.	WEST, Martha T.	09/10/1825
HARGIS, John	PYRON, Jane	06/03/1778
HARGIS, Thomas	VANHOCK, Bridget	06/03/1778
HARGIS, William	HOWEL, Hannar	02/03/1791
HARLEY, Hiram	STAFFORD, Betsey	12/27/1815
HARPER, Jesse	COX, Anne	06/09/1813
HARPER, Thomas	NUNN, Nancey	12/25/1824
HARRALSON, Henderson	MORTON, Mary F.	03/31/1853
HARRALSON, Jonathan	HUSTON, Jane	03/12/1782
HARRALSON, Paul A.	GRAVES, Leannah H.	09/30/1824
HARRALSON, Sidney	MITCHELL, Lucy A.	04/09/1866
HARRAWAY, Daniel	HASKINS, Betty	10/04/1867
HARRAWAY, Richard	CLARK, Minerva	10/04/1867
HARRELSON, Benatt	VARSHEAR, Ammy	08/14/1815
HARRELSON, Forbes	HENDERSON, Betsey	11/19/1793
HARRELSON, Forbes	BUSH, Frances	11/24/1790
HARRELSON, James	POWELL, Polly	01/06/1834
HARRELSON, James C.	MANLEY, Ibby	02/10/1858
HARRELSON, James M.	GUNN, Betsey	05/23/1832
HARRELSON, Jeremiah	BRACKIN, Patcey	11/29/1803
HARRELSON, Madison	SLADE, Harriet	10/29/1866
HARRELSON, Nathaniel	TABER, Polly	08/09/1821
HARRELSON, Thomas	WILLIAMSON, Martha	07/10/1802
HARRELSON, Thomas W.	COLLINS, Euphrasia	01/23/1826
HARRELSON, Thomas W.	COLLINS, Martha	07/29/1839
HARRELSON, William E.	BOWE, Sarah V.	04/20/1853
HARRINGTON, J. B.	BURNS, J. F.	11/22/1860
HARRIS, Christopher	PAYNE, Polly	01/12/1801

MARRIAGE RECORDS OF CASWELL COUNTY, NORTH CAROLINA

GROOM	BRIDE	DATE
HARRIS, Gustin	IRVINE, Mary	01/19/1867
HARRIS, James	GUNN, Susannah	11/01/1819
HARRIS, James L.	ANTHONY, V. E.	02/04/1852
HARRIS, James M.	HAMLET, Elizabeth	12/04/1848
HARRIS, John	YANCEY, Elizabeth	05/28/1837
HARRIS, Reubin	RAIMEY, Catharine	01/16/1837
HARRIS, Robert	LAWSON, Elisabeth	10/18/1791
HARRIS, Robert S.	WILLIAMSON, Mary P.	08/31/1818
HARRIS, Tyree	SWIFT, Susanah	04/18/1785
HARRISON, Andrew	WILLIAMSON, Nancy	04/18/1785
HARRISON, Andrew W.	SHARPE, Matilda H.	09/30/1836
HARRISON, Calloway J.	RICHARDSON, Prudence	02/16/1839
HARRISON, Charles K.	STOKES, Martha	05/05/1818
HARRISON, Charles P.	PRICE, Susana B.	10/12/1820
HARRISON, Edmond R.	HARRISON, Eliza J.	09/13/1844
HARRISON, Headley	SHELTON, Sally	12/10/1803
HARRISON, James	KEY, Sarah	01/13/1825
HARRISON, James R.	BOLTON, Susan	02/03/1852
HARRISON, Jesse	BEWSEY, Eliza	06/13/1822
HARRISON, John L.	MURRAY, Mary Ann	12/15/1846
HARRISON, Martin	COBB, Bell	11/02/1867
HARRISON, Richard B.	EMERSON, Martha	12/12/1866
HARRISON, Robert L.	HARRISON, Mildred L.	02/19/1833
HARRISON, Samuel S.	MADANIEL, Louisa M.	09/11/1838
HARRISON, Thomas	JOHNSTON, Mildred	11/04/1807
HARRISON, Thomas D.	HARRISON, Virginia C.	04/30/1844
HARRISON, Thomas Jr.	BURTON, Jenny	03/09/1798
HARRISON, Thomas P.	ATKINSON, Mary F.	11/04/1852
HARRISON, Thomas S.	SLADE, Adeline H.	08/23/1863
HARRISON, William	YARBROUGH, Temperance D.	05/31/1833
HARRISON, William K.	VERSER, Martha	10/21/1839
HART, Ellick	GILLISPIE, Lucinda	12/09/1849
HART, Thomas	HART, Patsey	03/21/1792
HARTMAN, Frederig	CRAWFORD, Mahael S.	11/09/1852
HARVEL, Henry	GILLASPIE, Elizabeth	11/18/1814
HARVELL, Littleton Taz.	HARVELL, Levina	09/11/1826
HARVELL, Pati	BELEW, Jamima	09/17/1788
HARVELL, Peyton	BELEW, Jamima	09/17/1788
HARVELL, William	COX, Sarah	06/10/1825
HARVEY, Charles L.	GORDON, Nora W.	03/26/1867
HARVEY, David	STORKS, Salley	11/14/1809
HARVEY, John C.	HODGES, Susan M.	01/12/1864
HARVEY, John C.	GUNN, Dorothy M.	03/21/1827
HASKINS, John	BROWN, Salley	10/26/1799
HASTIN, Eldridge	MITCHELL, Susannah	01/02/1802
HASTIN, James	KING, Minerva	05/25/1830
HATCHETT, Allen L.	WOMACK, Elizer A.	03/30/1859
HATCHETT, Jack	JOHNSTON, Milissa	11/03/1867
HATCHETT, John W.	GWYN, Martha A.	02/18/1858
HATCHETT, Rufus	FOSTER, Sarah	12/24/1866
HATCHETT, William H.	MONTGOMERY, Harriett E.	12/04/1866

MARRIAGE RECORDS OF CASWELL COUNTY, NORTH CAROLINA

GROOM	BRIDE	DATE
HATLER, James R.	MCMULLIN, Margret	02/05/1825
HAWKER, James W.	HALL, Rebecca J.	02/01/1864
HAWKINS, Ephrem	FARMER, Ann	05/01/1788
HAWKINS, Harbird	WEBSTER, Nancey	11/28/1833
HAWKINS, John	MALONE, Margaret J.	12/13/1854
HAWKINS, Robert	WEBSTER, Mary	08/10/1844
HAWKINS, Stephen	ROBERTS, Martha J.	01/07/1857
HAWKINS, Thomas	ROARK, Dolly	12/21/1852
HAWKS, Randal	REAR, Lucy R.	12/24/1827
HAYES, James	BRUCE, Nancy	12/30/1788
HAYES, Richard H.	LEA, Barbara	11/04/1813
HAYMES, John B.	RICE, Marthy E.	07/12/1865
HAYMES, Richard W.	CHILDES, Mary M.	11/06/1827
HEGGIE, Archibald	LOVE, Nancey	09/24/1835
HEISLEEP, F. C.	SNIPES, Nici	07/03/1865
HENDERSON, Albert G.	HOOPER, Martha A.	02/19/1856
HENDERSON, Benjamin H.	COMPTON, Margarett	11/14/1840
HENDERSON, Bryon	NEAL, Emeline	09/08/1866
HENDERSON, Hiram Jr.	FOSTER, Martha	02/18/1837
HENDERSON, Jacob	HARALSON, Fanney	12/08/1807
HENDERSON, Jacob	HATCHETT, Sarah	12/31/1829
HENDERSON, James A.	JOHNSTON, Rebecca L.	05/23/1866
HENDERSON, James S.	SLADE, Hannah M.	11/26/1832
HENDERSON, John N.	KING, Elvira J.	01/18/1839
HENDERSON, Ludolphus B.	SIMPSON, Annie	08/10/1862
HENDERSON, Rufus	HOLDBERY, Ann	08/11/1866
HENDERSON, Rufus R.	WHITE, Sarah	09/06/1834
HENDERSON, Samuel	WARE, Rody	12/03/1804
HENDERSON, Thomas	VOSS, Kitty	07/05/1813
HENDERSON, William	SIMPSON, Elizabeth	12/19/1829
HENDERSON, William	BENNATT, Nancey	01/05/1807
HENDERSON, William	MIMS, Frances	09/18/1844
HENDERSON, William Jr.	HARRELSON, Elizabeth J.	10/29/1838
HENDRICK, A. J.	WORSHAM, Mary R.	10/15/1866
HENDRICK, C. M.	SMITH, E. M.	10/15/1866
HENDRICK, James	BROUGHTON, Hobsey A.	12/20/1836
HENDRICK, James	WORSHAM, Lucy	07/23/1814
HENDRICK, Thomas W.	BURTON, Aderlaid V.	12/13/1859
HENDRICK, William H.	BENNETT, Susan	03/19/1841
HENDRIX, John	STONER, Polly	11/11/1785
HENDRIX, William	BRADSHER, Nancey	12/23/1786
HENRY, James W.	GRAVES, Laura A.	10/12/1850
HENSLEE, Addison	PARKS, Eliza	09/15/1843
HENSLEE, Bedford W.	STAMPS, Lucinda	02/12/1833
HENSLEE, Benjamin	BRUCE, Elizabeth	01/04/1812
HENSLEE, Buford B.	UNDERWOOD, Annis	11/10/1853
HENSLEE, Enoch	HASTEN, Amy	10/27/1806
HENSLEE, John Jr.	KEMP, Matilda	04/02/1816
HENSLEE, Masfield	JONES, Frances	09/22/1801
HENSLEE, Micajah	HARRISON, Nancey	12/06/1836
HENSLEE, Thomas	BUSH, Lois	11/18/1805

MARRIAGE RECORDS OF CASWELL COUNTY, NORTH CAROLINA

GROOM	BRIDE	DATE
HENSLEE, William	PLEASANT, Mary Milberey	01/23/1811
HENSLEY, Addison	MUSTING, Rachel	11/25/1847
HENSLEY, Azariah	VAUGHAN, Frances	10/17/1824
HENSLEY, Henry T.	POWELL, Elizabeth A.	02/22/1866
HENSLEY, John	PARKS, Artilia	12/24/1840
HENSLEY, Sidney	BOWLS, Selia	05/03/1855
HENSLEY, Thomas	MILTON, Elizabeth B.	03/16/1842
HERITAGE, William	WILLIS, Polly	12/19/1809
HERNDON, Edmund	BOSWELL, Mary	08/26/1851
HERNDON, George	WELLS, Prisilla	12/20/1805
HERNDON, George	ALDRIDGE, Martha	01/18/1866
HERNDON, Larkin	JOHNSTON, Sophia	08/22/1802
HERNDON, Larkin	TERRILL, Elizabeth	02/13/1790
HERRING, James A.	ROBERTS, Elizabeth	12/07/1833
HESSE, Archibald U.	HEWELT, Susannah	05/06/1818
HESTER, Elijah	MCMULLIN, Polley	11/30/1813
HESTER, Elijah Col.	SNIPES, Nancey	09/06/1828
HESTER, Hamilton	BADGET, Recey H.	03/27/1837
HESTER, J. R.	RUSSEL, Mary N.	02/22/1866
HESTER, Robert H.	COLLINS, Mary	01/15/1834
HESTER, Wilson	WARREN, Pemelia	01/07/1833
HEYDON, John H.	MITCHELL, Catherine	09/16/1825
HEYDON, Leachman	MANLEY, Henrietta	02/01/1825
HEYDON, Samuel F.	SIMMONS, Rebeca H.	06/06/1840
HICKMAN, William	MAN, Jenny	12/07/1796
HICKS, John P.	HITOWER, A. L.	02/07/1867
HICKS, Larkin W.	PHELPS, Rebeckah	10/08/1818
HICKS, Luke	RASBERRY, Betsey	05/14/1810
HICKS, Maryland	WATKINS, Jane	09/12/1842
HICKS, Simon	ECHOLS, Lucy	12/27/1867
HICKS, Thomas D.	JOHNSTON, Malinda	10/21/1837
HICKS, William	DUNNAWAY, Elizabeth	02/07/1825
HICKS, William T.	LEA, Virginia E.	09/06/1865
HIGHTOWER, Allen	HATCHER, Elizabeth	01/27/1808
HIGHTOWER, Charnel	CORDER, Winneyford	01/17/1798
HIGHTOWER, Daniel	STEPHENS, Catey	10/14/1806
HIGHTOWER, Devereux	GOOCH, Cesley	01/13/1816
HIGHTOWER, Francis	BOSWELL, Martha	09/28/1850
HIGHTOWER, James	SMITH, Nancy	12/14/1812
HIGHTOWER, John	MATLOCK, Agness	03/22/1790
HIGHTOWER, John A.	JACKSON, Mary	11/09/1843
HIGHTOWER, John W.	HESTER, Margarett	01/27/1836
HIGHTOWER, Joshua	LEA, Enicey	03/31/1800
HIGHTOWER, Joshua	SLADE, Delitah	11/24/1792
HIGHTOWER, Joshua	JACKSON, Susan	10/18/1833
HIGHTOWER, Joshua	WALL, Jincy	04/15/1817
HIGHTOWER, Joshua	CHANDLER, Francis G.	11/17/1843
HIGHTOWER, Robert	LOWELL, Margarett	04/24/1830
HIGHTOWER, Thomas	THOMAS, Polley	11/23/1803
HIGHTOWER, Vinson	WEST, Margarett	04/22/1867
HIGHTOWER, William	STAMPS, Mary	12/16/1844

MARRIAGE RECORDS OF CASWELL COUNTY, NORTH CAROLINA

GROOM	BRIDE	DATE
HIGHTOWER, William	BARTLETT, Elizabeth	05/04/1824
HIGHTOWER, William	JOHNSTON, Vina	07/09/1847
HIGHTOWER, William S.	SWIFT, Margaret	09/25/1848
HILL, Anderson G.	RAGSDALE, Martha A.	11/07/1853
HILL, Garland	WAID, Betsey	09/14/1801
HILL, Henry	JAMES, Nancy	12/29/1866
HILL, John R.	SLATEN, Eliza F.	01/09/1866
HILL, Joseph W.	SHIELDS, Susan P.	04/20/1835
HILL, Levi	MERRICKS, Polly	01/18/1817
HILL, Lewis	HART, Lucy	05/21/1851
HILL, Richard	ROYAL, Betsey	10/15/1799
HILLYER, James	HART, Polley	11/08/1808
HINES, Benjamin	HLDER, Sarah P.	03/17/1834
HINES, Frank	DURHAM, Frances	05/19/1866
HINTON, Alexander	HOOPER, Elizabeth J.	07/15/1848
HINTON, Allen	NELSON, Mary A.	11/28/1843
HINTON, Christopher	OVERBY, Elizabith	09/01/1830
HINTON, Henry	WRAY, Milly	01/29/1801
HINTON, James	OVERBY, Rebecca	05/09/1833
HINTON, James N.	LYON, Margarett	09/09/1866
HINTON, John	WILSON, Keziah	10/05/1801
HINTON, Nathaniel	HOOPER, Frances	06/11/1848
HINTON, Richard	COCHRAN, Judith	12/07/1791
HINTON, Samuel	GUNN, Barbara	12/27/1825
HINTON, Wesley	WILLIS, Margaret	08/11/1866
HINTON, William	WATTSON, Anny	08/14/1805
HINTON, William	SMITH, Virginia	11/20/1867
HIPWORTH, Jno.	WINTERS, Mary	02/18/1782
HIX, Reubin	SIMPSON, Delphia	05/21/1792
HIX, William	MOORE, Tabitha	03/09/1784
HOBBS, Isaac	KNIGHTEN, Mary	09/02/1823
HOBSON, William	WARRIN, Betsey	06/10/1788
HODGE, David	KILE, Betcey	11/29/1819
HODGE, David	WALL, Nancy	02/07/1801
HODGE, Henry L.	GOODE, Amanda	10/10/1867
HODGE, Isaac	DAMERON, Nancey	11/17/1792
HODGE, John	LONG, Sally	03/28/1812
HODGE, John	ABLES, Sally	11/10/1822
HODGE, Samuel	ROBERTS, Mary	05/19/1790
HODGE, Thmas	HIGHTOWER, Jane	11/04/1828
HODGE, William	HODGE, Sina	11/16/1867
HODGES, Coleman	CHATTIN, Elizabeth	05/16/1837
HODGES, Fealding L.	JONES, Georgiana	02/01/1867
HODGES, Fielding L.	HARRALSON, Henriatta	02/04/1865
HODGES, Harrison L.	WARE, Aryann	11/15/1845
HODGES, Henry E.	KNIGHT, Margaret	01/14/1863
HODGES, Henry E.	MCDANIEL, Elvira A.	01/19/1853
HODGES, Henry E.	GUNN, Mary C.	12/10/1842
HODGES, James M.	WILSON, Martha	11/08/1865
HODGES, John T.	SLADE, Virginia E.	11/18/1867
HODGES, Nathan	EDMONDS, Bettie	04/24/1867

MARRIAGE RECORDS OF CASWELL COUNTY, NORTH CAROLINA

GROOM	BRIDE	DATE
HODGES, Washington T.	PRICE, Sarepta W.	07/27/1858
HODNETT, James M.	NOWLIN, Frances A.	11/23/1841
HODNETT, Philip	HARALSON, Parthena	04/26/1827
HOGE, Winston	HUNT, Lucinda	11/09/1867
HOITH, Alex	CORN, Martha	02/09/1864
HOLCOMB, Martha M.	HOLCOLMB, Martha N.	11/17/1820
HOLCOMB, Samuel	HENDERSON, Hannah	12/29/1789
HOLDEN, E. B.	CURRIE, Bettie R.	10/04/1855
HOLDEN, James	JOHNSTON, Sally	01/17/1805
HOLDERBY, James D.	KNIGHT, Martha	06/30/1832
HOLDERNESS, John	ROAN, Eliza	12/27/1865
HOLDERNESS, Robert	BROOKS, Elizabeth	02/20/1819
HOLLAN, James	WATSON, Polley	08/01/1816
HOLLAND, John	RUNNALDS, Patsey	05/04/1805
HOLLIS, Jesse	BROWN, Frances	09/27/1798
HOLLOWAY, James	PULLIAM, Susannah	01/19/1796
HOLLOWAY, Richard	STEWART, Rachel	02/13/1792
HOLLOWAY, Robert	SCOTT, Betsey	08/06/1799
HOLT, Clabin	DOBBIN, Elizabeth	05/22/1786
HOLT, Dibden	ALISON, Mary	04/03/1787
HOLT, James G.	BURTON, Lucy A.	02/04/1840
HOLT, Joseph R.	WYATT, Manerva J.	06/21/1865
HOLT, Pleasant A.	WILLIAMSON, Emily A.	09/09/1850
HOLT, Robert T.	LOCKETT, Laura A.	07/25/1858
HOLT, Washington	MITCHELL, Lucinda	06/05/1858
HOLYCROSS, Robert	ADAMS, Eliza A.	02/18/1841
HOOD, Jesse	SAWYERS, Polly	05/18/1807
HOOD, Martin	RAON, Nancey	12/25/1821
HOOD, Stephen	BOWERS, Henrietta	09/10/1823
HOOD, Thomas	THORNTON, Adaline	06/19/1867
HOOD, Wiley	FOX, Mary	12/10/1823
HOOPER, Benjamin	HENDERSON, Nancey	09/22/1800
HOOPER, Charles H.	MOORE, Amanda	12/10/1851
HOOPER, George J. N.	RAINY, Fannie	11/30/1857
HOOPER, Henry	BENNETT, Elizabeth	09/23/1854
HOOPER, Henry Jr.	KIMBROUGH, Tabitha	12/13/1830
HOOPER, John C.	WILLIAMSON, Mary	11/20/1856
HOOPER, John J.	WATLINGTON, Mildred	12/15/1825
HOOPER, N. C.	MCDANIELS, Jane	02/25/1867
HOOPER, Spencer	WILEY, Mary	10/06/1832
HOOPER, Squire	CRUMPTON, Rachal	09/08/1866
HOOPER, Thomas	BENNATT, Polley	05/28/1814
HOOPER, Thomas	HALL, Sally	11/08/1849
HOOPER, William	RAIMEY, Delilah L.	11/07/1833
HOOPER, William	JONES, Mary	12/21/1854
HOOPER, William Y.	HARRELSON, Elizabeth	01/25/1830
HOOPER, Woodlief	HENDERSON, Pirzilla	04/12/1802
HOOPER, Woodlieff	FOSTER, Virginia	01/24/1860
HOOPER, Z.	PATITE, Adaline	06/07/1854
HOOPER, Zachariah	HUBBARD, Mary	05/11/1860
HOOPER, Zachariah Jr.	LOVE, Mary	08/12/1825

MARRIAGE RECORDS OF CASWELL COUNTY, NORTH CAROLINA

GROOM	BRIDE	DATE
HOOPER, Zachariah Sr.	RAIMEY, Elizabeth	05/16/1825
HOOPER. Zachariah Jr.	WARE, Louisa	06/12/1836
HOOPPER, Samuel	ALFORD, Susanna	01/07/1817
HOPE, George N.	TAYLOR, Martha	08/18/1846
HOPPER, Samuel	MURPHEY, Elizabeth	03/24/1801
HORN, Abel	WALLACE, Nancey	11/07/1803
HORN, Edward M.	WHITTROW, Susan C.	10/06/1855
HORNBUCKLE, Franklin	BROOKS, Frances	01/15/1825
HORNBUCKLE, Richard	SMITH, Elisabeth	01/09/1792
HORNBUCKLE, Thomas	HORNBUCKLE, Nancey	07/22/1800
HORSFORD, John C.	COBB, Jane	02/17/1832
HORTON, George	GRIER, Margret	02/08/1809
HORTON, George	GRAY, Susannah	02/03/1813
HORTON, James G.	WILLIAMS, Elizabeth	11/03/1826
HORTON, John	POWEL, Eliza A.	01/28/1835
HORTON, John	GILASPYU, Milly	11/20/1797
HORTON, Sally	DOBBIN, Mary	02/09/1791
HORTON, Thomas J.	BRYANT, Eliza A.	08/21/1859
HORTON, William J.	POWELL, Mary C.	01/26/1862
HORTON, Willis	HOWARD, Mary	11/13/1835
HOSLER, Richard	BRANDON, Margret	04/02/1782
HOUSE, Henderson	OLIVER, Ann C.	11/13/1839
HOW, William	CHAMBERS, Permintia	12/29/1835
HOWARD, Alanson	SHELTON, Susan S.	12/10/1833
HOWARD, Alexis	-----, -----	12/01/1842
HOWARD, Baalam	NORMAN, Maria	02/29/1868
HOWARD, Braodie	HOWARD, Nancy	04/07/1813
HOWARD, Cary A.	BLACKWELL, Elizabeth S.	02/25/1828
HOWARD, Charles	WILLIAMSON, Maria	07/06/1867
HOWARD, Daniel	WATKINS, Mollie	01/12/1867
HOWARD, Francis	MONTGOMERY, Polly	11/11/1801
HOWARD, George Jr.	STAMPS, Anna	12/03/1861
HOWARD, Henry	MCADEN, Mary	12/19/1787
HOWARD, Henry	BETTS, Eliza	03/20/1820
HOWARD, Henry A.	SETTLE, Elizabeth G.	05/22/1847
HOWARD, Henry O.	WEMPLE, Laura	12/18/1867
HOWARD, Horac	LYIN, July	03/20/1841
HOWARD, Hugh	BRACKIN, Elizabeth	11/03/1815
HOWARD, JOhn	YANCEY, Pricilla	12/26/1814
HOWARD, John	MEREDITH, Elisabeth	11/28/1785
HOWARD, John W.	KEEN, Mary E.	09/08/1866
HOWARD, Woodson	FINLEY, Abigail	07/24/1824
HOWELL, Leroy	NOWELL, Elizabeth	12/29/1795
HUBBARD, Archibald D.	COBB, Malinda G.	11/26/1837
HUBBARD, Charles	STEPHENS, Nancey	09/27/1819
HUBBARD, Charles	HUSTON, Betsey	01/31/1804
HUBBARD, Freeman	SCOTT, Mary	06/08/1844
HUBBARD, Freeman	HINTON, Nancy	06/09/1803
HUBBARD, Freeman	WILLIAMS, Martha	12/09/1793
HUBBARD, Henry	WARE, Elizabeth	10/17/1842
HUBBARD, James	GRANT, Artimesia B.	01/02/1838

MARRIAGE RECORDS OF CASWELL COUNTY, NORTH CAROLINA

GROOM	BRIDE	DATE
HUBBARD, James	KENNON, Eveline	09/18/1849
HUBBARD, James	HARRIS, Mary E.	02/26/1862
HUBBARD, John S.	PETTY, Mariah A.	12/11/1838
HUBBARD, Phenias	INGRAM, Elizabeth	04/05/1839
HUBBARD, Ralph	GUNNELL, Patcey	08/10/1809
HUBBARD, Ralph	RICHARDSON, Frances	03/06/1821
HUBBARD, Rufis	LEA, Virginia	06/29/1857
HUBBARD, Sebulon B.	GILLGORE, Jane	01/19/1785
HUBBARD, Thomas	PURKINS, Mary J.	09/13/1856
HUBBARD, William	QUARLES, Nancey	09/14/1807
HUBBARD, William	PERKINS, Elizabeth	03/18/1852
HUDDLESTON, Rowland	DAWSON, Henrietta	10/05/1833
HUDGING, Thos.	HARGIS, Nancy	--/--/----
HUDSON, David P.	OWEN, Mary P.	01/15/1833
HUDSON, Ezekiel	COLEMAN, Judith	11/27/1811
HUDSON, George	FOSTER, Milly	01/22/1798
HUDSON, J. M.	WINN, Sarah F.	01/27/1859
HUDSON, Shadrach	BRANDON, Mary	09/25/1784
HUDSON, Shelton	WADE, Ann R.	11/08/1843
HUDSON, William F.	FOWLKS, Susan A.	12/13/1858
HUDSON, William F.	ROPER, Isabella C.	12/11/1865
HUGHES, Andrew	TATE, Lucinda	01/26/1818
HUGHES, B. G.	NEWBELL, Martha	01/13/1851
HUGHES, George	ELLIOTT, Ellen	06/10/1867
HUGHES, James	BARKER, Ann E.	01/15/1856
HUGHES, John D.	WOODS, Poley	08/14/1809
HUGHES, Milton T.	HUGHES, Lucy	01/10/1853
HUGHES, Thomas H.	MITCHELL, Cornelia	01/20/1844
HUGHES, William	HOBSON, Rachel	05/18/1855
HUGHES, Willliam	FITCH, Catherine	09/21/1844
HUGHS, Henry	SQUIRE, Sina	03/26/1828
HUGHS, John	JACKSON, Nancey	09/12/1810
HUGINS, Jacob	WARD, Susanna	10/28/1817
HUGLE, John	ARNETT, Sally	06/20/1814
HULGIN, John R.	OVERBY, Nancy	01/02/1856
HUMFRES, Alfred	PASKILL, Nancy	01/11/1825
HUMPHREYS, Henry	PASCHALL, Susanna	09/24/1824
HUMPHREYS, Henry A.	NORMAN, Nancey	07/19/1841
HUMPHREYS, John H.	KEEN, Susannah	01/11/1817
HUMPHREYS, Thomas	COBB, Celia	01/25/1826
HUMPHREYS, William	HOLLAWAY, Polley	12/27/1799
HUMPHRY, Colmore	ORR, Nellet	02/28/1809
HUNDLY, Henry W.	HOOPER, Eliza L.	12/14/1837
HUNT, Algernon	WILSON, Ellen	03/04/1867
HUNT, Charles	HUNT, Louisa	12/08/1866
HUNT, Eustance	WATKINS, Anna S.	09/30/1863
HUNT, Garland	JEFFREYS, Isabella	12/25/1865
HUNT, James	MARABLE, Fannie	03/23/1867
HUNT, L. J.	THORNTON, Susan J.	12/11/1856
HUNT, Littleton T.	JEFFREYS, Mary E.	06/14/1854
HUNT, Samuel	HUNT, Precilla	01/12/1867

MARRIAGE RECORDS OF CASWELL COUNTY, NORTH CAROLINA

GROOM	BRIDE	DATE
HUNT, Steven	BROADNAX, Chainy	06/15/1867
HUNTER, Solomon G.	HUBBARD, Malinda	04/16/1835
HUNTINGTON, Martin P.	DONOHO, Mary A.	09/29/1834
HUNTINGTON, Martin P.	HOLDER, Susan	04/30/1822
HURDLE, B. F.	WALKER, M. C.	12/23/1866
HURDLE, Jacob O.	BOSWELL, Eunice	09/27/1836
HURDLE, James	WLKER, Catherine	10/26/1840
HURDLE, James M.	WALKER, Margaret F.	12/09/1858
HURDLE, James M.	WALKER, Malinda	01/22/1856
HUSTON, Jonathan	SMITH, Joannah	10/21/1817
HUSTON, William	ALLEN, Susannah	01/26/1785
HUSTON, William	WALLACE, Sarah	11/18/1826
HUTCHERSON, Wm. W.	DUDLEY, Rebecca	04/03/1821
HUTSON, Moses	RANDOLPH, Betsey	10/09/1784
HYDE Joseph	COLLEY, Elizabeth H.	07/15/1851
INGRAHAM, T. E.	BANE, Anne	11/05/1851
INGRAM Yancey W,	TERRY, Lettice W.	07/28/1834
INGRAM, Benjamin	WOMACK, Nancey	05/09/1786
INGRAM, Benjamin	WRIGHT, Priscilla	04/21/1814
INGRAM, Charton	WAMACK, Lucy	11/02/1778
INGRAM, Elisha	TAYLOR, Peggy	--/--/1808
INGRAM, James	WYNN, Sarah C.	11/02/1841
INGRAM, James	EVANS, Betsey	10/18/1808
INGRAM, James	REID, Mary E.	05/13/1858
INGRAM, James J.	LUNSFORDM Mary A.	01/22/1858
INGRAM, Martin	HOWARD, Anne	11/06/1827
INGRAM, Stephen	BUSH, Mira	12/10/1808
INGRAM, Thomas E.	ECHOLS, Frances T.	11/13/1856
INGRAM, Vench	CAMMICHAL, Mary	03/18/1805
INGRAM, William R.	NEAL, Harret A. E.	11/10/1857
INGRUM, Jordan L.	SPARROW, Eliza C.	02/06/1860
INMAN, Henry	SMITH, Polly	12/16/1836
IPOCK, William	GASKINS, Eunice	10/02/1856
IRVIN, Robert	SAWYER, Nancey	04/04/1822
IRVINE, John	GARLAND, Mary	01/01/1867
IRVINE, John Sr,	STANFIELD, Anna	04/11/1811
IRVINE, Richmond	IRVINE, Jennie	04/20/1867
IRVINE, William C.	LEWIS, Mary A.	08/14/1843
IRVINE, William Jr.	JEFFREYS, Virginia A.	10/31/1857
IRWIN, James C.	HOOFMAN, Sarah E.	03/28/1840
ISELEY, Asa	SAWYERS, Jane	12/18/1849
JACKSON, Abel	HALL, Emily G.	09/04/1847
JACKSON, Andrew P.	FULLING, Agness	03/28/1821
JACKSON, Daniel	DAMERON, Patience	11/20/1805
JACKSON, Daniel	WARD, Salley	08/31/1807
JACKSON, Epaphroditus	HIGHTOWER, Nancey	08/23/1834
JACKSON, George	SPENCER, Francis	10/10/1785
JACKSON, J.R.	BURCH, Mary	06/16/1860
JACKSON, James	MATTHEWS, Ann M.	12/31/1824
JACKSON, John	EVANS, Ednea	06/05/1816
JACKSON, Richard W.	GREGORY, Julietta W.	10/17/1836

MARRIAGE RECORDS OF CASWELL COUNTY, NORTH CAROLINA

GROOM	BRIDE	DATE
JACKSON, Robert	DAMERON, Polley	09/27/1808
JACKSON, Robert	GUNN, Amy	01/02/1866
JACKSON, Robert Jr.	CARNEY, Rachel	06/01/1811
JACKSON, Shadrach	CORAM, Clorey	10/01/1782
JACKSON, Spencer	BRINTLE, Rainey	12/20/1815
JACKSON, Thomas	HUNTER, Marey	12/--/1818
JACKSON, Thomas	SMITH, Jenney	12/05/1798
JACKSON, William	LEWIS, Elizabeth	11/15/1828
JACKSON, William P.	DAMERON, Elizabeth	12/24/1811
JACKSON, Williams	TATE, Sarah	03/25/1786
JACOB, Lewis	FULLER, Amy	12/27/1866
JAMES, David	RICHARDSON, Lucy	07/18/1848
JAMES, Henry	BURTON, Susan	06/14/1866
JAMES, John	BOHANNAN, Rutha	04/22/1867
JARNAGIN, Jeremiah	HIGHTOWER, Elizabeth	12/24/1808
JAY, James	-----, -----	01/24/1798
JAY, James	WISDOM, Sally	02/04/1804
JEAN, Jessy	WYATT, Polly	11/23/1789
JEAN, Sherwood	LEA, Rosannah	02/20/1785
JEFFERS, John	CREWS, Mary A.	10/21/1833
JEFFRES, Newell	JONES, Cyntha	08/01/1828
JEFFRES, Walton	BALLARD, Silvy	08/08/1818
JEFFRESS, Newton B.	HATCHETT, Elizabeth A.	03/14/1855
JEFFRESS, Wm. C.	THORNTON, Sallie F.	06/11/1866
JEFFREYS, Adkinson	MARTIN, Sarah J.	02/03/1862
JEFFREYS, Archible W.	TAYLOR, Mary W.	05/12/1858
JEFFREYS, Atkinson	GILLASPIE, Mary	12/29/1837
JEFFREYS, Franklin	ENOCKS, Delphia	11/26/1867
JEFFREYS, Isaac	SWIFT, Frances	10/10/1827
JEFFREYS, Iverson	WILSON, Ann	12/21/1854
JEFFREYS, Jackson	JEFFREYS, Melissa	12/14/1848
JEFFREYS, James	HARPER, Louisa	12/23/1822
JEFFREYS, John	TAYLOR, Ruth	12/18/1843
JEFFREYS, John	EDWYN, Jincey	03/09/1795
JEFFREYS, John	MOSS, Nancey	11/29/1823
JEFFREYS, Joshua	WALTERS, Cloe	07/31/1804
JEFFREYS, Osborn	TAYLOR, Salley	06/03/1778
JEFFREYS, Reubin	HAWLY, Kissiah	05/30/1808
JEFFREYS, Thomas	WATLINGTON, KIziah B.	10/22/1824
JEFFREYS, Thomas Jr.	DONALDSON, Sarah	06/09/1866
JEFFREYS, Washington	STEPHENS, Betsy	02/03/1830
JEFFREYS, Washington	TAPP, Sophia	08/17/1866
JEFFREYS, William	HARTON, Basheba	04/24/1822
JENNINGS, Byrd T.	BRIGHTWELL, Martha S.	10/09/1839
JENNINGS, Joseph	GLASS, Patience E.	08/27/1842
JETER, Joseph H.	HARRISON, Araminta	10/10/1837
JINKINS, Edward	WILLIAMS, Sally	01/02/1796
JOHNSON, Hampton	ROYSTER, Elizabeth	08/25/1866
JOHNSON, Isaac	YANCEY, Nancy	12/10/1795
JOHNSON, James	HUSTON, Agness	10/04/1813
JOHNSON, James	POSTON, Rebeccah	06/19/1781

MARRIAGE RECORDS OF CASWELL COUNTY, NORTH CAROLINA

GROOM	BRIDE	DATE
JOHNSON, James	ELLIS, Rebeckah	10/03/1810
JOHNSON, John	LEATH, Rebecah	09/16/1796
JOHNSON, John Jr.	BASTIN, Margarett	10/26/1830
JOHNSON, Thomas	TERRY, Martha	11/06/1827
JOHNSON, William	BROWN, Nancey	12/18/1838
JOHNSTON, Caleb A.	GRAVES, Nancey	02/17/1866
JOHNSTON, Daniel	GRAVES, Catharine	12/12/1865
JOHNSTON, George	COBB, Elizabeth	10/11/1830
JOHNSTON, John	DONOHO, Fanney	01/04/1800
JOHNSTON, John	BRATCHER, Dicey	01/31/1792
JOHNSTON, John	HODGE, Sally	11/29/1819
JOHNSTON, Joseph	MAHAN, Mary	05/28/1831
JOHNSTON, Moses	GRAHAM, Lucinda	11/30/1867
JOHNSTON, Peter	WYATT, Hannah	02/21/1782
JOHNSTON, Peter	WALKER, Nancey	12/21/1835
JOHNSTON, Pleasant	JACKSON, Susanah	08/22/1804
JOHNSTON, Remus	JOHNSTON, Catherine	03/03/1866
JOHNSTON, Thomas	CARMON, Hannah	09/10/1783
JOHNSTON, Thomas D.	MCADEN, Sarah G.	02/23/1825
JOHNSTON, Thomas M.	RICHMOND, Sarah	11/20/1839
JOHNSTON, Warren	GARLAND, Cornelia	12/27/1867
JOHNSTON, William	RAINEY, Elizabeth	03/20/1783
JOHNSTON, William	CHAMBERLAIN, Catharine	12/10/1819
JOHNSTON, William H.	HIGHTOWER, Frances T.	11/29/1836
JONES, Allen	KIERSEY, Polley	07/29/1818
JONES, Allen	BURTON, Martha W.	06/26/1833
JONES, Allen	MCNEELEY, Polley	08/09/1811
JONES, Andrew	PHILLIPS, Celly	11/30/1843
JONES, Benjamin	ROBERTS, Faithey	11/30/1788
JONES, Benjamin B.	ROPER, Arreminta	11/09/1827
JONES, Beverly	PARTEE, Marshaw	06/17/1817
JONES, Calvin	ROBERTSON, Amy	06/10/1867
JONES, Calvin	HESTER, Mary C.	11/09/1841
JONES, David	WILLIAMSON, Rachael	08/16/1866
JONES, David	DIXON, Martha	11/23/1819
JONES, David A.	HURDLE, Ann	02/27/1856
JONES, Edward D.	RAINEY, Elizabeth H.	10/10/1811
JONES, Edward M.	BLACKWELL, Matilda	12/23/1817
JONES, Eli	WARREN, Frances	09/25/1837
JONES, Erasmus K.	LOVELACE, Lucind	09/13/1827
JONES, Ezekiel	MALLORY, Rebeccah	01/10/1799
JONES, Henry	COX, Susan	01/14/1833
JONES, Henry	JONES, Ellen	11/19/1865
JONES, Henry	COBB, Jennett	10/18/1866
JONES, J. Riley	GWYNN, Sarah	12/15/1865
JONES, James	THOMAS, Susan V.	02/17/1867
JONES, James	JONES, Jane	12/19/1850
JONES, James	VAUGHN, Eddy	08/31/1783
JONES, James B.	HALL, Judith B.	09/29/1814
JONES, James M.	CHANDLER, Elizabeth	08/30/1848
JONES, James W.	MIMS, Martha J.	09/24/1844

MARRIAGE RECORDS OF CASWELL COUNTY, NORTH CAROLINA

GROOM	BRIDE	DATE
JONES, Jeremiah	WALDROPE, Ann	06/03/1806
JONES, Jno. G.	MCCAIN, Elizabeth S.	12/10/1834
JONES, John E.	WATLINGTON, Mary	10/05/1847
JONES, Keen	SMITH, Mary W.	08/13/1862
JONES, Lawson	ROAN, Martha J.	10/11/1842
JONES, Matt	THOMAS, Margaret	02/24/1846
JONES, Mintus	BOWE, Susan	01/26/1867
JONES, Moses	KELLEY, Elizabeth	02/14/1809
JONES, Phillip	BOHAN, Katey	12/05/1815
JONES, Randolph	JONES, Maria	12/10/1828
JONES, Reuben	VANHOOK, Susannah	06/11/1801
JONES, Reuben	BOSWELL, Susan	01/02/1843
JONES, Richard	HOLCOMB, Perry	10/30/1804
JONES, Richard	BRUCE, Martha	12/25/1792
JONES, Richard	FULLER, Eliza	12/05/1866
JONES, Richard	FOSTER, Polley	12/09/1811
JONES, Richard H.	BLACKWELL, Martha A.	02/26/1848
JONES, Richard Jr.	SWIFT, Frances M.	12/08/1844
JONES, Robert	WARREN, Mary C.	12/13/1857
JONES, Robert	CHANDLER, Maria	12/26/1866
JONES, Simon	COBB, Bell	09/14/1867
JONES, Thomas	BULLARD, Darkus	10/16/1819
JONES, Thomas	LOCKHART, Nancy	01/24/1829
JONES, Thomas J.	CONNOLLY, Margaret A.	02/01/1845
JONES, Thompson	DICE, Martha A.	01/03/1856
JONES, Wilie	KIRSEY, Dicy	05/27/1797
JONES, William	LANDERS, Rachel	11/20/1816
JONES, William	DAY, Mary	12/04/1848
JONES, William	TRAVIS, Polley	06/20/1820
JONES, Willie Dr.	HENDERSON, Priscilla J.	05/05/1836
JONES, Yancey	MILES, Martha R.	07/20/1850
JONES, Zalman	BATEMAN, Mary	10/20/1846
JORDAN, Thomas N.	GUNN, Minerva A.	11/23/1865
JOUETT, Thomas	TATE, Hannah	01/26/1801
JUDKINS, Edmund	RICE, Zilpah	11/19/1832
JUSTICE, Benjamin W.	WOMACK, ELizabeth S.	11/08/1824
JUSTICE, Julas	STUART, Hannah	--/--/178-
KANON, Bartlet	KENNON, Janey	01/20/1794
KEARSON, Charles R.	CURTIS, Elizabeth	10/21/1841
KEEN, John	BALDIN, Mary	10/17/1800
KEEN, William	COBB, Elizabeth	02/23/1811
KEENER, Jackson	CHILDRESS, Sarah	05/13/1843
KEESEE, Charles	GATEWOOD, Elizabeth	07/26/1815
KEESEE, Jno. D.	JOHNSTON, Jane E.	01/26/1854
KEIRSEY, Wm.H.	HADOCK, Emiline	01/06/1858
KEIRSEY, (?) John	HIGHTOWER, Agniss	12/02/1794
KELLEY, George	WARREN, Catharine A.	11/05/1823
KELLEY, George	BRUER, Nancy	08/12/1805
KELLEY, George	HUNT, Salley	08/08/1820
KELLEY, James	MCCALIPS, Jane	01/23/1802
KELLY, Aaron	LEWIS, Pheby A.	08/24/1867

MARRIAGE RECORDS OF CASWELL COUNTY, NORTH CAROLINA

GROOM	BRIDE	DATE
KELLY, William	HATCHET, Harriet	06/16/1866
KEMP, Barnett	MCKEE, Mary	02/23/1810
KENNON, Abel K.	MORTON, Martha	01/28/1843
KENNON, Elijah	BUSH, Mary	06/11/1813
KENNON, James	ALVERSON, Mary A.	12/01/1821
KENNON, John	PYRON, Frances	08/28/1840
KENNON, John	CARROL, Hannah	11/01/1812
KENNON, John	PHILIPS, Mahala	02/02/1826
KENNON, Joseph B.	WHITE, Louisa D.	02/26/1851
KENNON, Ricahrd	HENDERSON, Polley	05/08/1813
KENNON, Richard	NORWOOD, Parthena	09/18/1850
KENNON, Thomas	HOOPER, Susanna	02/12/1814
KENNON, Thomas	BROWN, Mary	03/02/1839
KENNON, William	WILLIS, Mary	01/31/1827
KENT, S.S.	MITCHELL, Jane	--/--/1843
KENT, Smith F.	SADLER, Sally	02/21/1807
KENT, William S.	EPPERSON, Elizabeth C.	12/11/1855
KERBY, Richard	ANDERSON, Rachel	01/21/1802
KERNODLE, Richard	LEATH, mary E.	08/11/1843
KERR, Barzillai	CANTREL, Polley	03/22/1806
KERR, James	MCNIEL, Frances	09/29/1835
KERR, John Jr.	CAMPBELL, Evelina B.	12/23/1835
KERR, William	KYLE, Jane	01/19/1824
KERR, William	TAIT, Polly	07/14/1800
KERSEY, Alexander Jr.	BUCKNER, Elizabeth	06/23/1828
KERSEY, Clark A.	PAGE, Sarah A.	12/12/1860
KERSEY, James L.	ROBERTS, Bettie	05/20/1866
KERSEY, Ricahrd	FREDERICK, Jane	08/29/1829
KERSEY, Samuel	MATLOCK, Mary	12/23/1790
KERSEY, William	THOMAS, Nancey	12/07/1816
KIDD, Lewis	GRANT, Frances	03/26/1815
KIERSEY, Drury	MCFARLAND, Polly	02/09/1826
KIERSEY, Franklin	CURLS, Sarah A.	11/02/1849
KIERSEY,(?) John	HIGHTOWER, Agniss	12/02/1794
KILLGORE, Charles	LEA, Unice	09/24/1796
KILLGORE, Thomas	LEA, Pheby	01/02/1786
KIMBELL, Thomas M.	PATTILLO, Ann E.	11/19/1837
KIMBRO, Andrew J.	HOOPER, Mary	03/18/1858
KIMBRO, James	TURNER, Nancey	12/27/1787
KIMBRO, James B.	KIMBRO, Susannah	01/09/1823
KIMBRO, Miles	BURTON, Dianah	11/20/1822
KIMBRO, Thomas	JOHNAGAIN, Faithey	08/18/1781
KIMBRO, William	BARKER, Susannah	11/09/1797
KIMBRO, William N.	BALDWIN, Sarah A.	09/28/1847
KIMBROU, Thomas R.	EVANS, Elizabeth A.	01/30/1835
KIMBROU, William	MILES, Elizabeth	12/09/1799
KIMBROUGH, Elijah	FURY, Polly	09/05/1803
KIMBROUGH, John	WARWICK, Polley	10/19/1809
KIMBROUGH, John	LINK, Betsey	09/06/1804
KIMBROUGH, John M.	TURNER, Nancy	05/05/1825
KIMBROUGH, John T.	HENSLEY, Mary J.	08/19/1866

MARRIAGE RECORDS OF CASWELL COUNTY, NORTH CAROLINA

GROOM	BRIDE	DATE
KIMBROUGH, M.Duke	LOVE, Salley	11/30/1818
KIMBROUGH, Thomas	GRAVES, Elizabeth	03/29/1792
KIMBROUGH, William C.	KIMBROUGH, Nancy	08/26/1852
KIMBROUGH, Wm. T.	DAVIS, Lucinda	12/31/1853
KING, Daniel	MILTON, Nancy	10/19/1820
KING, Edmund	LEGRAND, Nancy	08/11/1800
KING, Harvey	NICHOLS, Polly	04/25/1822
KING, Henry	CAMPBELL, Delilah	12/08/1840
KING, Henry	JONES, Leana	12/07/1867
KING, Isaac	PERKINS, Rachel	11/07/1808
KING, J.W.	VAUGHAN, Elizabeth	10/15/1849
KING, James	ARVIN, Patsey	01/27/1817
KING, James	ROBERTS, Henrietta	11/17/1849
KING, James P.	BURTON, Sarah	10/27/1830
KING, Joseph	PAGE, Pamelia F.	06/26/1850
KING, Joseph	BULL, Fanny	05/19/1815
KING, Newton	KING, Lucy	12/25/1866
KING, Robert J.	BADGET, Salley	12/24/1821
KING, Samuel J.	BADGETT, Drusilla	06/28/1834
KING, William	PERKINS, Polley	10/30/1804
KING, William D.	HOWARD, Ann	02/17/1859
KIRK, Samuel	BERRY, Jane	06/17/1822
KIRK, William	BURROUGHS, Salley	01/25/1816
KITCHEN, John	MONTGOMRY, Elizabeth	12/23/1820
KITCHEN, Joseph	VAUGHAN, Betsey	11/08/1815
KITCHEN, Moses	STEPHENS, Polley	10/09/1815
KITCHEN, Stephen	FINLEY, Polly	12/23/1822
KNIGHT, Evans	ADAMS, Mary	12/27/1841
KNIGHT, Evans	BURTON, Sally	12/17/1800
KNIGHT, Jesse	COBBS, Rhoda	08/10/1867
KNIGHT, Joseph	DAMERON, Judith	12/08/1801
KNIGHT, Joseph D.	CLEMPSON, Magara	04/28/1830
KNIGHT, Robert	BURTON, Elizabeth	09/15/1832
KNIGHT, William	LYON, Rebeccah	03/30/1809
KNIGHT, William W.	HARRISON, Susan	01/08/1836
KNIGHTEN, James	TRAVIS, Purlina	08/09/1841
KNOTT, James	WILLIAMSON, Mary	06/13/1810
LACKEY, Robert	MITCHELL, Sarah	02/14/1795
LAIN, Beverly	DAWSON, Jane	12/30/1843
LAMB, John	RINES, Jane	12/23/1829
LAMBERT, Clayton	BRINCEFIELD, Isabella	04/14/1854
LAMBETH, John	WALKER, Frances	09/11/1828
LAMBETH, John J.	WALKER, Jane E.	12/16/1855
LAMBETH, Lovick L.	WINDSOR, Eliza J.	11/25/1848
LAMON, Alexander	GRANT, Sarah	03/11/1786
LAND, Williamson H.	ANDERSON, Ann P.	09/29/1858
LANDERS, Abraham	NELSON, Nancy	11/08/1809
LANDERS, John	PARKS, Mary	10/15/1833
LANDRUM, James A.	DAVIS, Emaline	07/02/1857
LANE, Joseph	RICE, Sally	10/10/1809
LANE, William N.	ROBERTS, Elizabeth M.	12/24/1834

MARRIAGE RECORDS OF CASWELL COUNTY, NORTH CAROLINA

GROOM	BRIDE	DATE
LANGHORNE, Maurice M.	FARLEY, Eliza M.	05/15/1837
LANGLEY, Thomas	KITCHEN, Ester	10/25/1813
LANIER, C.V.	JEFFERS, Isabella	01/14/1839
LANIER, James	JOHNS, Polly	10/23/1809
LANIER, James	JOHNS, Elizabeth	02/11/1804
LANNOM, Joseph	BROWNING, Delila	09/21/1799
LAOFMAN, Benjamin	PERKINS, Nancey	09/07/1813
LASHLEY, Powell	PRENDERGAST, Elizabeth	09/21/1844
LATTA, James G.	HOWARD, Caty F.	10/26/1867
LATTA, Jas. C.	HOWARD, Jane S.	10/26/1867
LAUSON, John B.	WHITEMORE, Jemima J.	09/29/1827
LAW, Butler	SOUTHARLAND, Patsy	12/28/1812
LAW, James T.	BADGETT, Pocahontas A.	02/24/1859
LAW, John	GRAVES, Sylvia	04/19/1867
LAWRENCE, James	SNEED, Catherine	12/29/1836
LAWSON, John	ROBERTSON, Dolly	12/28/1866
LAWSON, John Jr.	ALLEN, Elizabeth	03/25/1790
LAWSON, Moses	BRADLEY, Betsy	12/06/1788
LAWSON, Robert W.	BROWN, Nancy	11/20/1827
LAYN, Garret C.	PRYOR, Elizabeth W.	12/11/1834
LEA, Aaron V.	CURRIE, Sarah	08/13/1830
LEA, Absalom	MUZLE, Frances	04/30/1794
LEA, Alanson M.	HIGHTOWER, Rebecca S.	12/09/1834
LEA, Alexander	-----, -----	--/--/----
LEA, Alvis	KERR, Nancy	03/29/1832
LEA, Ambrose	WHEALER, Frances	08/10/1779
LEA, Archibald	HENDRICK, Lucinda	07/11/1821
LEA, Barnett	ROAN, Mourning	12/21/1782
LEA, Barzillia G.	HENDERSON, Elizabeth	12/08/1829
LEA, Bedford	WINSTEAD, Dianah	10/20/1866
LEA, Benjamin	KERR, Nancy	02/09/1796
LEA, Carter	MCNEILL, Patty H.	02/26/1782
LEA, Edmund	WRIGHT, Nancy	10/01/1784
LEA, George	DOUGLASS, Jane	02/24/1785
LEA, George G.	WRIGHT, Sarah E.	05/05/1835
LEA, Hearndon	HIGHTOWER, Fanny	06/22/1791
LEA, Henry	COE, Fanny	03/21/1846
LEA, Henry	ROAN, Virginia	12/26/1866
LEA, Isaac	STEPHENS, Malinda	11/10/1866
LEA, J.A.	LINDSEY, Mollie E.	02/15/1867
LEA, Jack	OLIVER, Lovina	12/21/1867
LEA, Jake	SWIFT, Caroline	11/25/1865
LEA, James	-----, -----	04/11/1821
LEA, James	MORGAN, Elizabeth	12/20/1819
LEA, James	HIGHTOWER, Nancy	11/15/1796
LEA, James	RICE, Elizabeth	03/09/1841
LEA, James K	SERGENT, Margaret D.	12/16/1848
LEA, James W.	HARRISON, Virginia S.	02/03/1858
LEA, James W.	DURHAM, Caroline N.	09/29/1858
LEA, James jR.	GRAVES, Betsy	04/15/1815
LEA, Jeremiah	KERR, Mary P.	11/09/1830

MARRIAGE RECORDS OF CASWELL COUNTY, NORTH CAROLINA

GROOM	BRIDE	DATE
LEA, Jeremiah	KERR, Polly	12/20/1797
LEA, John	WRIGHT, Susanna	09/10/1825
LEA, John	STEPHENS, Mary	12/30/1786
LEA, John	SLADE, Hannah	01/22/1793
LEA, John	CRIDER, Mary	03/04/1786
LEA, John	BRADLEY, Elizabeth	04/23/1780
LEA, John	SWIFT, Polly	03/30/1816
LEA, John	VAUGHAN, Elizabeth	05/08/1809
LEA, John B.	DOLLARHIDE, Frankey	11/24/1802
LEA, John W.	WILLIAMSON, Isabella	06/15/1861
LEA, Jonathan	HIGHTOUER, Mary	10/16/1786
LEA, Lawrence	SARGENT, Phebe	09/23/1793
LEA, Lemuel	CATES, Rebecca	11/14/1839
LEA, Louis	JONES, Hester	12/25/1866
LEA, Major	FARLEY, Sally	08/29/1790
LEA, Nelson	DAVIS, Mary	09/01/1867
LEA, Simeon	WESTBROOK, Peggy	03/28/1822
LEA, Thomas	LEA, Sally	10/13/1801
LEA, Thomas A.	WARE, Mary	10/11/1843
LEA, Thomas L.	WRIGHT, Ann B.	04/16/1833
LEA, Tinsley	FULLOE, Frances	09/18/1820
LEA, Westley	CATES, Caroline	10/29/1842
LEA, William	GOLD, Sarah	11/03/1790
LEA, William	GRAVES, Betsy B.	06/24/1836
LEA, William	WILLSON, Mary L.	10/07/1834
LEA, William	LONG, Leah	08/31/1816
LEA, William	BROOKS, Barbara	05/12/1848
LEA, William A.	WEASTBROOK, Jane	11/10/1824
LEA, William A.	HARGIS, Lucy A.	10/02/1851
LEA, William A.	CARTER, Martha B.	02/13/1862
LEA, William G.	LEA, Susan J.	03/19/1848
LEA, William M.	CHEEK, Mary	11/11/1851
LEAK, William Jr.	SIMMONS, Martha	03/24/1782
LEATH, Colman	SIMMONS, Hannah	03/14/1808
LEATH, Joel	JONES, Betsy	12/21/1798
LEATH, John F.	NUTT, Cornelia A.	04/03/1847
LEAVELL, Alfred R.	WILLIAMS, Phebe O.	04/22/1839
LECOUNT, John	HUBBARD, Mildred	04/06/1850
LEE, Alexander	FERGUSON, Elizabeth	10/24/1797
LEE, James	BURCH, Nancy	08/17/1795
LEGRAND, Herbert W.	MERRITT, Mary	04/04/1836
LEIGH, David G.	WILSON, Mary	12/16/1822
LEIGH, William	MCDANIEL, Mary	09/01/1814
LEMMON, Alexander	SOMERS, Catherine	09/12/1808
LEMMON, H.S.	PAYNE, Missouri F.	07/26/1846
LESLEY, John	WALLIS, Rachel	05/15/1799
LESTER, Robert	MOORE, Alcey	05/02/1832
LEWIS, A. S.	THOMPSON, Sarah S.	12/08/1846
LEWIS, Anderson	DABNEY, Martha A.	05/15/1852
LEWIS, Anderson	CHILDIRS, Isabella H.	01/26/1830
LEWIS, Burrell G.	TURNER, Fanney	08/24/1813

MARRIAGE RECORDS OF CASWELL COUNTY, NORTH CAROLINA

GROOM	BRIDE	DATE
LEWIS, Charles	BOULTON, Lucy	01/08/1795
LEWIS, Charles	WILLIAMSON, Winny	06/22/1804
LEWIS, Charles A.	LEWIS, Elizabeth	12/15/1853
LEWIS, Edward	KENDRICK, Elizabeth	02/09/1815
LEWIS, Feilding	EVANS, Betsey	10/06/1810
LEWIS, Fielding B.	JENNINGS, Samuella	12/07/1859
LEWIS, George W.	OWEN, Nannie W.	12/08/1863
LEWIS, Henry H.	FORD, Celia	12/28/1825
LEWIS, Hiram	CEARNEY, Agness	03/03/1806
LEWIS, J. T.	CORBIN, Sallie A.	03/05/1864
LEWIS, James	ROBERTS, Jane	12/19/1853
LEWIS, James H.	ROBERTS Mary A.	12/17/1857
LEWIS, Pleasant	CHILDRESS, Martha	01/29/1848
LEWIS, Pleasant	HIGHTOWER, Sally	12/31/1816
LEWIS, Shadras	LENOX, Elizabeth	10/10/1826
LEWIS, Thomas J.	GUNN, Harriet	02/16/1867
LEWIS, Wade W.	CARMICAL, Elizabeth C.	04/16/1860
LEWIS, William	MATLOCK, Nancy	01/31/1805
LEWIS, William	SHELTON, Elizbeth	08/06/1847
LEWIS, Zachariah	FERGUSON, Jemima	03/03/1866
LEWIS. Charles	MURPHY, Elizabeth	04/02/1865
LIGGON, John	HUGHES, Margaret	01/19/1867
LIGON, Richard F.	HAYES, Elizabeth C.	07/19/1837
LILLARD, Thomas M.	WRIGHT, Laura V.	10/06/1866
LINDSAY, Isaac N.	NUNNALLY, Hesteran	11/15/1865
LINDSEY, A. C.	GRAVES, Elizabeth L.	06/14/1843
LINDSEY, George R.	POTEAT, Sallie E.	02/05/1861
LINDSEY, Henry	STAMPS, Lucinda	04/20/1867
LINDSEY, William	COLEMAN, Rosy	09/17/1800
LINK, Byrd	MORTON, Avey	03/12/1799
LINK, John	MORTON, Betsey	01/12/1802
LINTHICUM, Henry	BOLOCK, Nancy	11/24/1827
LINTON, Michael	JONES, Sidney	06/09/1847
LIPFORD, John J.	MOSELEY, Agnes	11/01/1855
LIPSCOMB, J. H.	DRAIN, Sarah E.	02/03/1857
LIPSCOMB, John	RICHMOND, Phebe	12/14/1808
LIPSCOMB, John	GWYN, Elizabeth	01/26/1807
LIPSCOMB, Joseph R. E.	GRAVES, Margaret	05/29/1833
LIPSCOMB, Joseph R. E.	HARRALSON, Eliza	03/11/1830
LIPSCOMB, Thomas	ESKRIDGE, Martha	04/29/1828
LIPSCOMB, Thomas	TURNER, Elizabeth	10/14/1799
LIPSCOMB, Thomas	ESKERIDGE, Rebecah	10/13/1829
LIPSCOMB, Thomas W.	DODSON, Mary A. C.	01/30/1847
LITTLE, David	SNEED, Sarah	03/02/1789
LLOYD, Thomas	MAUGHAN, Jane	08/23/1804
LOAFMAN, Edward	PERKINS, Salley	07/24/1810
LOCARD, Hiram	MCKISSOCK, Priscilla	04/--/1819
LOCHER, Henry S.	ORRIH, Lucy A.	07/28/1852
LOCKETT, David S.	HAWKINS, Mary A.	02/27/1854
LOCKETT, Zachariah	MILLS, Ann	07/11/1825
LOCKHART, William	MCALPIN, Caroline	05/12/1841

MARRIAGE RECORDS OF CASWELL COUNTY, NORTH CAROLINA

GROOM	BRIDE	DATE
LOGAN, William	DICKS, Martha	02/10/1859
LONDON, Joseph	NUNN, Nancy	08/11/1835
LONG, Alexander M.	MONTGOMERY, Mary M.	07/19/1824
LONG, Baszeley M.	HODGE, Mary	07/05/1828
LONG, Benjamin	GOMER, Judith	06/03/1830
LONG, Benjamin	MOORE, Rachel	05/24/1780
LONG, Edmond	BOWE, Cilla	05/19/1866
LONG, James	TODD, Priscilla	02/16/1782
LONG, John	COMER, Elizabeth	04/21/1800
LONG, John	LONG, Sally	02/16/1866
LONG, John	EDWELL, Kizzia	12/09/1835
LONG, John D.	PENICK, Elizabeth A.	02/08/1854
LONG, Joseph	PHILIPS, Susan	05/31/1838
LONG, Robin E.	HARRIS, Sally	09/29/1830
LONG, Samuel	FEATHERSTON, Polly	06/17/1867
LONG, William	EDWELL, Eady	12/22/1807
LONG, William	TONEY, Nancy	01/26/1842
LONG, William	JOHNSTON, Sarah	10/02/1828
LONG, William	SKEEN, Hannah	11/05/1788
LONGWELL, David	GORDON, Cornelia A.	10/08/1857
LONGWELL, Timothy	RUARK, Polley	11/27/1811
LORENTZ, Joseph	DIX, Elizabeth	02/08/1865
LOUGHIN, David	GOING, Lithe	11/18/1783
LOVE, John C.	MORTON, Maranda R.	05/15/1839
LOVE, Lewis H.	VAUGHAN, Lucy	01/21/1851
LOVE, Robert	MOORE, Sarah	12/12/1833
LOVE, Samuel	MALONE, Frances	05/03/1791
LOVE, Samuel Jr.	LOVE, Mary	07/18/1828
LOVE, Snelson	BROWNING, Frances	12/18/1823
LOVELACE, Barnett	ORR, Betsy	05/23/1821
LOVELACE, Henry R.	BEAVER, Jemima	04/08/1858
LOVELACE, John	CARVER, Nancy	01/09/1826
LOVELACE, Joseph	LOVELACE, Matilda	07/02/1850
LOVELACE, Nicholas	LOVELACE, Matilda	12/26/1822
LOVELACE, Nicholas	WALKER, Celie	08/17/1864
LOVELACE, Pickney	SOUTHARD, Lithy	02/11/1840
LOVELACE, William	PASCHALL, Slema	01/24/1842
LOVELACE, William	LOVELACE, Libba	12/15/1828
LOVELESS, Benjamin C.	HALL, Nancey	11/01/1837
LOVELESS, Brewis W.	JONES, Martha	05/06/1824
LOVELESS, Joseph	WALKER, Martha	11/26/1857
LOVELESS, Pryor	PAGE, Salley	08/29/1809
LOWERY, Henry	OVERBY, Saluda	10/21/1850
LOYD, Alexander G.	MARTIN, Nancy	11/02/1825
LOYD, John	WALKER, Nancy	03/10/1823
LUMPKIN, George	GILLASPIE, -----	02/11/1815
LUNCEFORD, William	BEVIELL, Thursey	05/27/1833
LUNSFORD, Paten L.	FUQUA, Margaret	07/31/1866
LUNSFORD, Warner J.	CAMPBELL, Rusalinda	02/02/1850
LUNSFORD, Weldon H.	FOARD, Martha A.	05/17/1866
LUNSFROD, Walter H.	CAMPBELL, Lucitta A.	12/01/1836

MARRIAGE RECORDS OF CASWELL COUNTY, NORTH CAROLINA

GROOM	BRIDE	DATE
LUNSFURD, Colley W.	LEA, Elizabeth	09/17/1839
LUNSFURD, Rushea H.	SPARROW, Nancey	01/12/1835
LUSTER, Jacob W.	STEPHENS, Ann	07/14/1842
LUSTER, Robert	STEVENS, Matilda	10/28/1860
LYNCH, Thomas	BYRD, Mary	12/10/1827
LYNCH, William B.	NEAL, Rebecca M.	04/04/1861
LYNN, Bayless	BENTON, Lucinda	10/10/1820
LYNN, Patrick H.	NEAL, Virginia E.	03/08/1857
LYON, James N,	TRYWIG, Jane	11/21/1866
LYON, John	STEPHENS, Patsey	02/23/1813
LYON, Nicholas	JONES, Mildred	02/15/1853
LYON, Noel W.	HARF, Mary	12/26/1837
LYON, Noel W.	GODSON, Mildred	01/20/1852
LYON, Richard	NICKELS, Sarah	10/13/1791
LYON, Robert	SREPHENS, Elizabeth	12/30/1821
MAAYHON, William	GRANT, Sarah	12/19/1781
MABANE, David	YANCY, Elizabeth	10/28/1817
MABE, William P.	LOVE, Mary	07/17/1856
MABRY, Lewis	WOODEY, Judith	09/01/1784
MADDEN, Samuel Q.	PLEASANTS, Artelia S.	10/08/1861
MADDIN, Champness	DUNCAN, Francis	01/17/1792
MADDING, Robert	COBB, Martha	10/09/1818
MADREN, Amos	HICKS, Ellenor	09/09/1840
MAHON, Henery	EPPYSON, Patsey	12/16/1808
MALLERY, Thomas	SIMMS, Frances	12/29/1789
MALLORY, James	JONES, Salley	01/16/1798
MALLORY, Stephen	SOMMS, Lornah	12/18/1790
MALLORY, Thomas	FITZGERALD, Rosey	10/16/1802
MALONE, Alfred	SMITH, Polley	12/08/1813
MALONE, Bartlett Y.	CRUMPTON, Mary F.	11/15/1866
MALONE, Bennet	CHANDLER, Nancy	12/10/1817
MALONE, Daniel Jr.	LEA, Betsey	12/11/1801
MALONE, Henry	WILKERSON, Jane	11/05/1820
MALONE, James	YANCEY, Mildred A.	01/02/1849
MALONE, James T.	BATEMAN, V. W.	09/20/1857
MALONE, John	PITTARD, Rebecca	11/05/1816
MALONE, Lewis	BLACKWELL, Betsy	12/02/1811
MALONE, Lewis	BLACKWELL, Nancy	10/18/1792
MALONE, Lewis	RICHMOND, Margarett C.	03/11/1836
MALONE, Loney	EUBANK, Nancey	03/27/1811
MALONE, Mark	HAMLETT, Hannah	09/04/1796
MALONE, Staples	EVANS, Phebe	02/16/1789
MALONE, Stephen	PARKS, Celey	10/01/1804
MALONE, Thomas	MUZZLE, Jane	10/20/1739
MALONE, Thomas	DAMERON, Elizabeth	09/25/1819
MALONE, William	JOHNSTON, Frances	09/02/1829
MANLEY, John	PAGE, Lucy	11/14/1815
MANLEY, Samuel	COBB, Henrietta	02/01/1821
MANLY, George W.	PAGE, Mary	03/25/1852
MANLY, Rufus	THACKER, Martha A.	02/05/1849
MANLY, Thomas M.	COBB, Malina S.	12/20/1860

MARRIAGE RECORDS OF CASWELL COUNTY, NORTH CAROLINA

GROOM	BRIDE	DATE
MANLY, William	NUNN, Martha	01/20/1830
MANLY, William S.	MOORE, Rebecca H.	12/16/1858
MANN, Forgis	RICHARDSON, Rachel	02/21/1797
MANN, Henry	MOSS, Polly	01/11/1826
MANN, James	WARREN, Betsey	01/08/1810
MANN, Thomas	CROSSETT, Margret	01/10/1800
MANN, William Jr.	WARREN, Lucy	04/19/1800
MANSFIELD, James	GILLASPIE, Eliza	12/21/1849
MANSFIELD, James L.	WESTBROOKS, Malinda	12/19/1845
MANSFIELD, James L.	FERGASON, Lucy C.	10/10/1858
MANSFIELD, John	TERRELL, Salley	03/16/1814
MANSFIELD, Thomas	MORRIS, Mary	01/04/1853
MARAIN, Thomas	HUGHS, Mary	10/20/1800
MARKES, John	DOTSON, Paggey M.	01/26/1815
MARR, Ambrose R.	WILLIAMS, Judith C.	08/17/1837
MARR, David J.	TERRY, Mary A/	04/04/1862
MARR, George W.	SWANN, Huldah	02/03/1834
MARSHALL, Charles	ALLEN, Elizabeth	04/17/1833
MARSHALL, D. P.	DOOLY, Martha J.	09/12/1865
MARSHALL, G. W.	TALLY, Mary C.	05/25/1867
MARSHALL, Willis L.	ROBERTS, Sarah	12/23/1859
MARTIN, Claiborn R.	SWAIN, Martha A.	08/12/1867
MARTIN, Elijah	CANTRILLE, Sally	04/19/1815
MARTIN, George Jr.	MURPHEY, Mary	12/27/1824
MARTIN, George W.	SWIFT, Mary	10/21/1845
MARTIN, Goerge	CANTREL, Rachel	10/26/1813
MARTIN, Henry T.	DOWNS, Mary A.	05/09/1836
MARTIN, James	CANTRELL, Sarah	02/05/1816
MARTIN, James	CANTRILL, Nancey	03/08/1827
MARTIN, John	STEPHENS, Rebeccca	05/28/1809
MARTIN, John	BURTON, Lucy	11/19/1796
MARTIN, Lewis	MORTON, Polley	01/02/1811
MARTIN, Richard	TURNER, Frances	10/25/1783
MARTIN, Richard	BROWN, Sarah	03/16/1816
MARTIN, Robert	BROWNING, Nancy	03/21/1812
MARTIN, Robert	BALLARD, Betsy	01/02/1798
MARTIN, Robert	RICHARDSON, Susan	11/30/1781
MARTIN, Samuel F.	JEFFREYS, Harriett A.	11/06/1857
MARTIN, Thomas	RICHMOND, Catherine A.	10/17/1842
MARTIN, William	SANDERS, Elizabeth	07/18/1814
MARTIN, Zenes	LOVE, Kitty	12/11/1816
MASON, David	MAYO, Hannah	12/--/1800
MASON, Henry	PETTIFOOT, Eliza	08/06/1859
MASON, John	TONEY, Sarah	10/16/1843
MASON, John	HUGHES, Betsy	01/31/1814
MASON, Patrick	GOING, Patsey	12/03/1790
MASON, Patrick	DELANEY, Catherine	11/16/1836
MASON, Stephen	POINOR, Sally	07/29/1794
MASON, Stephen	PITTARD, Frances	05/02/1820
MASON, Wiley	SIMS, Nancy	12/16/1825
MASON, Willey	BEUSEY, Nancy	10/17/1809

MARRIAGE RECORDS OF CASWELL COUNTY, NORTH CAROLINA

GROOM	BRIDE	DATE
MASSEY, Benjamin	HENSLEY, Frances	02/10/1835
MASSEY, Eli	GOOCH, Frances	01/21/1833
MASSEY, John	HASTIN, Nanny	11/18/1801
MASSEY, Joseph	NICHOLS, Betsey	11/30/1815
MASSEY, Levi	STADLER, Polly	08/23/1836
MASSEY, Levi P.	BOSWELL, Sarah	12/12/1861
MASSEY, Mark	WARD, Louisa	06/28/1838
MASSEY, Nathan	BROWN, Mary	09/10/1828
MASSEY, Nathan	CANTRILL, Jemima	10/20/1826
MASSEY, Nathan T.	GOOCH, Artelia	11/09/1858
MASSEY, Nathan T.	BURKE, Elizabeth	09/25/1866
MASSEY, Pleasant C.	BOSWELL, Elizabeth	01/06/1853
MASSEY, Rainey	HENSLEY, Mary	11/02/1846
MASSEY, Raney	HENSLEE, Elizabeth	11/12/1850
MASSEY, Thomas	MASSEY, Margaret	08/29/1832
MASSEY, William	BURCH, Jane	11/17/1818
MASSEY, William	COLLIR, Judith	03/30/1814
MASSEY, William H.	MCKINNY, Martha A.	01/09/1844
MASSEY, William Sr.	REDDEN, Catherine	06/09/1835
MASSIE, Albert A.	FREDERICK, Emily L.	04/14/1867
MASSIE, Joseph W.	GARRISON, Margaret A.	08/21/1867
MASTERS, Enoch	GILBERT, Sally	04/19/1818
MATHEWS, Christopher	LOVE, Elizabeth	01/20/1814
MATHEWS, Drury	JACKSON, Delilah	07/21/1821
MATHEWS, Ezekiel	CUMBO, Sarah	05/07/1793
MATHEWS, Isaac	JACKSON, Sarah	09/19/1827
MATHEWS, Joel	MASON, Patsy	04/24/1822
MATHEWS, Luke	BURTON, Lucy	10/21/1822
MATHIS, Charles	DAMERON, Sally	09/21/1795
MATHIS, John	JACKSON, Elizabeth D.	12/03/1823
MATHIS, Samuel	HORSLEY, Susan	08/02/1784
MATHIS, William	LACKSON, Sarah	12/03/1823
MATKINS, Dennis	WALKER, Rebecca J.	01/29/1867
MATKINS, John C.	BOULDIN, Mary J.	02/28/1861
MATKINS, John H,	GWYN, Elizabeth	04/17/1843
MATKINS, Joseph	SIMPSON, Louisa	01/14/1834
MATKINS, Silas	BOULDIN, Susan	07/10/1862
MATKINS, William	WALKER, Sarah A.	12/18/1866
MATLOCK, B. L.	RICHMOND, Anne	01/18/1843
MATLOCK, Benjamin	LEE, Polly	01/21/1806
MATLOCK, Benjamin L.	HEYGOOD, Mary	08/26/1850
MATLOCK, James	GUNN, Patsy H.	01/13/1810
MATLOCK, John	BURTON, Mary J.	11/05/1860
MATLOCK, William	PCOL, Anniss	11/20/1848
MATTHEWS, Albert M.	LAMPKIN, Sophia W.	07/17/1833
MATTHIS, James	GOLDSBY, Elizabeth	11/30/1791
MATTHIS, Thomas	CHILDS, Betsy	11/29/1810
MAUGHAN, James	STADLER, Polley	07/29/1809
MAURY, Philip	CUNNINGHAM, Betsy A.	12/04/1793
MAXWELL, Bezl	LONG, Agness	06/30/1798
MAY, W. H.	BARNARD, Sarah F.	02/19/1850

MARRIAGE RECORDS OF CASWELL COUNTY, NORTH CAROLINA

GROOM	BRIDE	DATE
MAYHAN, William	COX, Mary	09/18/1822
MAYHAN, William	FITCH, Minerva	12/02/1847
MAYHOE, Vernell W.	SCHAVERS, Sally	06/07/1858
MAYNARD, Richard	MOORE, Margaret	10/23/1844
MAYNARD, Wagstaff	RICE, Julia A.	04/21/1859
MAYNARD, Wagstaff	PENICK, Barbara J.	12/04/1841
MAYO, Richard	BEAVOR, Nancy	12/23/1795
MAYS, Samuel	SOMERS, Sarah	09/30/1837
MCADAM, David	COLLINS, Elixena	03/02/1839
MCADEN, Henry	BRADLEY, Mary	11/06/1792
MCADEN, Henry	YANCEY, Frances W.	11/04/1829
MCADEN, James	DOWDWELL, Betsy	12/28/1815
MCADEN, John	MURPHEY, Betsey	11/30/1797
MCALISTER, John	PIKE, Nancy	01/26/1801
MCALPIN, Alexander	FARLEY, Charlotte	07/26/1818
MCALPIN, Alexander	BADGETT, Mary M.	01/19/1841
MCALPIN, Alexander	JONES, Jane W.	10/31/1857
MCBRIDE, Andrew	BORAN, Phebe	10/11/1784
MCCADEN, Atkinson	RICHMOND, Ann	06/30/1866
MCCAIN, Alexander	FOSTER, Hannah	01/29/1790
MCCAIN, Alfred P.	APPLE, Mary J. E.	09/07/1864
MCCAIN, Benjamin C.	SHELTON, Caroline M.	04/29/1842
MCCAIN, Edmund	MEBANE, Harriet	01/13/1867
MCCAIN, James A.	LOCKHART, Julia C.	11/20/1866
MCCAIN, John	WARRIN, Elizabeth	06/23/1790
MCCAIN, John	MORGAN, Nancy	12/20/1842
MCCAIN, John W.	BALL, Mary M.	11/08/1849
MCCAIN, Jospeh N.	BOULTON, Emily F.	05/15/1858
MCCAIN, Louis	MOORE, Roxey	12/20/1867
MCCAIN, Robert	WARE, Charlotte	03/15/1842
MCCAIN, Samuel D.	ROWELL, Arminta A.	09/25/1865
MCCAIN, Tillotson	ELMORE, Betsy	01/11/1825
MCCAIN, Tollotson	ROPER, Patsy	11/19/1839
MCCALLAM, William	WARE, Martha	11/02/1787
MCCAULEY, John	MOORE, Polly	09/14/1796
MCCAULEY, John W.	WALKER, Nancy J.	12/20/1845
MCCAULY, John	WALKER, Frances	01/10/1843
MCCLAIN, George	KEEN, Polly	11/02/1804
MCCLAIN, Joseph	POTEAT, Tempa	03/17/1806
MCCLARNEY, Holt	TYREE, Mary	12/30/1830
MCCORD, William	BARNWELL, Peggy	03/03/1801
MCCORD, William	BARNWELL, Temperance A.	09/25/1824
MCCORMACK, Aaron F.	CAMPBELL, Ann	08/16/1849
MCCRAY, James	DICKEY, Leannah	10/11/1806
MCCROREY, David	ALBERT, Frances	01/02/1838
MCCUBBINS, William	FAREBANKS, Rachel	02/17/1784
MCCUBINS, Alfred	WATSON, Sarah	12/05/1827
MCCULLOCH, Joseph	WALKER, Nancy	04/09/1814
MCDADE, John A.	WOODS, Nancy M.	08/21/1830
MCDADE, John M.	MURPHEY, Elizabeth F.	12/08/1853
MCDANIEL, Joel A.	CHAMBERS, Jane N.	10/10/1854

MARRIAGE RECORDS OF CASWELL COUNTY, NORTH CAROLINA

GROOM	BRIDE	DATE
MCDANIEL, John	PRICE, Mary M.	04/08/1828
MCDANIEL, William	DAMERON, Patsy	11/24/1802
MCDANIEL, William J.	HEWEANK, Priscilla	05/23/1832
MCDANIEL, William P.	HARRISON, Nancy	07/15/1817
MCDONALD, Alexander	JENNINGS, Mary	12/27/1818
MCDONALD, William R.	GRAVES, Virginia Y.	01/13/1864
MCDOWEL, James	ELLIOTT, Polly	10/20/1801
MCDOWELL, Joseph M.	TAYLOR, Margaret C.	10/24/1854
MCFARLAND, Daniel	BAZWELL, Mary	09/10/1789
MCFARLAND, James H.	WOMACK, Cisley	01/22/1787
MCFARLAND, Jno.	LEA, Dicey	07/15/1779
MCFARLAND, John	LEA, Frances	02/24/1804
MCFARLAND, Thomas	WINTERS, Rachel	03/15/1797
MCFARLAND, William	KIERSEY, Ritta	04/19/1832
MCFARLING, Zechariah	PITMAN, Emsey H.	12/10/1835
MCGEHEE, Albert G.	PAYNE, Ann V.	10/17/1834
MCGEHEE, Henderson	STANFIELD, Susan	12/29/1865
MCGEHEE, Jeremaih	LISBERGER, Lucinda	01/11/1868
MCGEHEE, Paul	JEFFREYS, Cornelia	04/20/1867
MCGEHEE, Thomas	JEFFREYS, Elizabeth M.	12/07/1812
MCGINNIS, James	WILLIAMS, Elizabeth	01/15/1790
MCGONNIGIL, Samuel	YATES, Celia	12/29/1832
MCGRUDER, Albert	GORDON, Mary A.	11/21/1860
MCHANEY, William R.	BLACKSTOCK, Lucy S.	12/26/1860
MCINTOSH, Nimrod	MURPHEY, Nancy	12/15/1788
MCKEE, James L.	GRAVES, Frances M.	06/15/1852
MCKEE, Robert	WILKERSON, Polly	07/23/1814
MCKEEN, Alexander	BIZWELL, Betsy	12/12/1799
MCKINEY, Thomas W.	CHANDLER, Judith	01/02/1814
MCKINNEY, Brooks	SARTIN, Elizabeth	02/04/1843
MCKINNEY, D.W.	RUDD, Elizabeth F.	10/31/1860
MCKINNEY, Drury	RICHARDSON, Susanna	09/19/1820
MCKINNEY, George C.	SARTIN, Emma C.	01/22/1866
MCKINNEY, Henry	SANDERS, Manerva	10/13/1829
MCKINNEY, Isaac	CARTER, Bettie	12/25/1867
MCKINNEY, James A.	STADLER, Martha F.	01/12/1854
MCKINNEY, Nathaniel	HENSLEY, Rachel	07/04/1833
MCKINNEY, Robert	ALVERSON, Martha G.	06/15/1852
MCKINNEY, William	PIERSON, Jane	02/20/1820
MCKINNEY, William T.	REID, Isabella V.	12/15/1858
MCKINSEY, John A.	PENNIX, Sallie A.P.O.	02/22/1864
MCKINSEY, John W.	WALTERS, Martha	03/24/1841
MCKISSACK, John	LOVE, Elizabeth	08/23/1830
MCKNIGHT, Andrew	NASH, Eliza	01/07/1783
MCKNIGHT, Anthony	WEST, Mary	03/11/1794
MCLAUGHLAN, Rawley	PHILIPS, Mar	10/16/1847
MCLEAN, Jesse R.	JENNINGS, Emma J.	01/18/1859
MCMENAMY, James	BOULDIN, Susan	01/09/1832
MCMULLEN, John	CURRIE, Margaret	01/11/1787
MCMULLIN, James M.M.	ALLEN, Sarah A.	08/06/1852
MCMURREY, James	GOULD, Jemima	12/22/1787

MARRIAGE RECORDS OF CASWELL COUNTY, NORTH CAROLINA

GROOM	BRIDE	DATE
MCMURRY, Charles	DOUGLASS, Janet	12/22/1789
MCMURRY, Samuel	OWENS, Parthena	11/07/1818
MCNEAL, M.	COMER, Amy	01/11/1866
MCNEELEY, Addom	PARKER, Ann	12/20/1791
MCNEELEY, George W.	HOWARD, Elizabeth	11/16/1834
MCNEELY, James	YATES, Polly	09/06/1804
MCNEILL, Hosea	GRAVES, Isabell	03/16/1807
MCNEILL, John H.	DARBY, Ann	06/25/1810
MCNIEL, Benjamin	MOORE, Elizabeth	12/18/1787
MCNIEL, John	LEA, Anniss	09/08/1780
MCNIELL, George	DILLARD, Minerva	11/29/1823
MCREYNOLDS, James	FLEMING, Lucy	12/02/1790
MEACHAN, Banks	LOVELASS, Louisa	11/24/1829
MEADERS, Major	VADEN, Amanda	11/05/1841
MEADOS, Samuel A.	DAVIS, Martha J.	11/19/1841
MEADOWS, Gabriel	MORTON, Polly	05/14/1818
MEBANE, Alexander	MITCHELL, Frances	09/26/1818
MEBANE, Benjamin F.	KERR, Fanny L.	09/08/1857
MEBANE, Edward	HARRIS, Tempy	12/04/1867
MEBANE, Giles	SMITH, Malissa	12/16/1865
MEBANE, Giles	YANCEY, Mary C.	03/08/1837
MEBANE, Henry	WILLIS, Malissa	01/01/1867
MEBANE, James	GRAVES, Polly	01/17/1833
MEBANE, Jno. H.	GRAVES, Ann S.	02/09/1837
MEBANE, Lemuel H.	YANCEY, Caroline L.	11/01/1841
MEBANE, William G.	MEBANE, Emma C.	12/14/1865
MEDLIN, Harrison	JONES, Susan	12/30/1819
MEEKS, John	DANIEL, Catharine	08/30/1833
MEGONEGAL, George W.	YATES, Mary B.	12/21/1839
MELEAR, John	BAGGETT, Rachel	01/12/1801
MELLETT, J.Y.Dr.	TERRY, Julia A.	03/27/1865
MELTON, Albert	MORRIS, Eliza	03/04/1841
MELTON, David	ALDRIDG, Susanna	12/30/1816
MELTON, James	COOK, Fanny	11/24/1818
MERIDETH, James	PATTERSON, Elizabeth	10/31/1780
MERRITT, Daniel	DUNCAN, Nancy	01/27/1784
MERRITT, Daniel T.	GAN, Frances	05/28/1820
MERRITT, George H.	GORDON, Narcissa R.	02/14/1850
MERRITT, James	CLIFT, Lettie	11/17/1795
MERRITT, Levi	HARVEL, Jincy	04/21/1825
MERRITT, Solomon	DUNAVANT, Sarah	09/09/1863
MERRITT, Solomon	STONE, Priscilla	08/30/186-
MERRITT, Solomon	POTEATE, Elizabeth	12/10/1789
MEUX, Thomas W.	NASH, Eliza E.	10/01/1819
MIDDLEBROOKS, John	LYON, Mary	07/16/1781
MIDDLEBROOKS, John	HUMPHRIES, Nancy	01/18/1781
MILAM, John	SHEPHERD, Martha	04/20/1854
MILES, Abner	WOMMACK, Delila	11/24/1819
MILES, Abner	SMITH, Sarah J.	04/10/1856
MILES, Abner Jr.	FOSTER, Mary A.	04/13/1849
MILES, Elijah H.	LUNSFORD, Mary	01/14/1840

MARRIAGE RECORDS OF CASWELL COUNTY, NORTH CAROLINA

GROOM	BRIDE	DATE
MILES, Henry	MALONE, Polly	05/06/1830
MILES, Jacob Jr.	RICE, Nancy	10/07/1783
MILES, James	GUNN, Betsy B.	02/03/1807
MILES, James Jr.	ROWLETT, Saludia(?)	11/20/1834
MILES, James Jr.	RUDD, Malinda	12/10/1834
MILES, John	LUNSFORD, Martha	12/30/1840
MILES, John Jr.	EVANS, Nancy	12/08/1828
MILES, John K.	MURRY, Sarah C.	12/23/1858
MILES, John S.	MURRAY, Eliza	01/25/1849
MILES, Richard	HOOPER, Martha J.	10/09/1850
MILES, Richard	WALKER, Mary C.	12/18/1860
MILES, Thomas	TOLBERT, Elizabeth	12/15/1784
MILES, Thomas C.	JACKSON, Catharine	09/17/1846
MILES, Thomas H.	PALMER, Lucy L.	11/18/1863
MILES, Uriah	RODD, Irena	09/11/1834
MILES, William	PLEASANT, Dolly	09/10/1821
MILES, William	WARREN, Viney(?)	09/29/1818
MILES, William	STUBBLEFIELD, Rebecca H.	03/10/1859
MILES, William W.	VAUGHN, Sarah J.	07/05/1859
MILLER, Charles	MITCHELL, Penny	04/07/1826
MILLER, Henry	GROOM, Nancy	07/16/1818
MILLER, James	HORTON, Leanah	11/29/1785
MILLER, James	COLEMAN, Polly	05/17/1814
MILLER, Jn.	SMITH, Ellen	10/15/1823
MILLER, John	DAVIS, Mary A.	04/11/1838
MILLER, Tho.	PANE, Polly	05/12/----
MILLER, William D.	BALDWIN, Frances	12/06/1845
MILLS, Samuel	SMITH, Ellen	05/15/1847
MILLS, Thomas J.	BRACKIN, Sarah H.	05/29/1841
MILNER, Jackson C.	HENDERSON, Susan P.	12/20/1837
MILUM, James L.	BURTON, Virginia	02/21/1867
MIMMS, Drury A.	SAWYERS, Martha	07/18/1836
MIMMS, Pinkney	HODNETT, Caroline	06/09/1866
MIMS, John W.Jr.	BURNS, Martha A.	06/11/1852
MIMS, John W.Jr.	HATCHITT, Martha N.	03/26/1850
MIMS, Martin M.	BROOKS, Susanna W.	01/29/1824
MINOR, Richard	MILES, Hulda	09/01/1844
MITCHALL, Gilliam D.	FRANKLIN, Sarah F.	10/13/1855
MITCHEL, Charles	DUTY, Ann	01/05/1829
MITCHEL, David	LOVE, Martha	01/30/1788
MITCHEL, Robert	LOVE, Ester	02/04/1787
MITCHELL, Alfred	BADGETT, Eunice	07/12/1836
MITCHELL, Charles	SMITH, Sarah	12/08/1803
MITCHELL, Charles	WEATHERFORD, Nancy	04/12/1828
MITCHELL, Charles G.	BLACKWELL, Martha	09/23/1843
MITCHELL, David	HUGHS, Joyce	02/20/1823
MITCHELL, David	HUGHS, Joyce	01/30/1823
MITCHELL, David Jr.	ANDERSON, Ann	06/24/1782
MITCHELL, David Jr.	MUZZALL, Nancy	02/12/1817
MITCHELL, James	FOSTER, Sarah	10/03/1826
MITCHELL, James E.	MURPHEY, Margaret	11/18/1819

MARRIAGE RECORDS OF CASWELL COUNTY, NORTH CAROLINA

GROOM	BRIDE	DATE
MITCHELL, James E.	JONES, Fanny	02/08/1833
MITCHELL, James T.	JEFFREYS, Mildred W.	03/19/1849
MITCHELL, Jefferson	MITCHELL, Martha	07/20/1867
MITCHELL, John	ANDERSON, Polly	01/02/1796
MITCHELL, John	SCOTT, Fanny	05/14/1800
MITCHELL, John	NEAL, Mary A.	11/18/1850
MITCHELL, John	MOORE, Manerva	06/09/1858
MITCHELL, John	CHAVOS, Charlotte	08/22/1857
MITCHELL, John B.	MONTGOMERY, Eliza C.	12/18/1856
MITCHELL, Milton P.	SIMPSON, Mary W.	11/20/1856
MITCHELL, Randolph	TERRELL, Margaret	10/04/1819
MITCHELL, Richard	BRACKIN, Arkey(?)	12/18/1821
MITCHELL, William	EPPERSON, Jane	01/03/1857
MITCHELL, William	FOSTER, Susanna	10/02/1826
MITCHELL, William	CHANDLER, Sally	10/23/1803
MITCHELL, William M.	MALONE, Minerva	01/29/1842
MITCHELL, Willy	FREEMAN, Rachel	02/25/1839
MIZE, Thomas	GILLAM, Fanny	12/22/1812
MONROE, Frederick	BRANDON, Frances	08/02/1867
MONROE, John	SHEPERD, Sally	02/08/1787
MONTGOMERY, Abraham B.	HATCHITT, Nancy M.	06/16/1821
MONTGOMERY, Alexander	MATLOCK, Lucy	12/03/1801
MONTGOMERY, David G.	DAVIS, Mary F.	06/30/1840
MONTGOMERY, David G.	DAVIS, Mary F.	02/04/1842
MONTGOMERY, Edward	PINIX, Tabitha F.	02/22/1825
MONTGOMERY, Frank	SANDERS, Patsy	10/11/1866
MONTGOMERY, James	CONWAY, Emeline	08/18/1867
MONTGOMERY, James	CONNALLY, Kitty	10/27/1807
MONTGOMERY, Michael Jr.	DAVIS, Lucy	02/26/1816
MONTGOMERY, William	MATLOCK, Sarah	02/28/1804
MONTGOMERY, William J.	FOSTER, Mary A.	11/25/1852
MOOR, Robert	FOSTER, Mary	12/20/1784
MOORE, Albert	ALLEN, Martha A.	08/07/1827
MOORE, Armistead	TURNER, Sally	12/14/1795
MOORE, Austin T.	COLMAN, Catherine	04/22/1837
MOORE, Brittain	TYRRELL, Isabell	01/02/1808
MOORE, Charles W.	SMITH, Martha	10/30/1858
MOORE, Charles W.	SMITH, Martha	11/21/1854
MOORE, Eps	DAMERON, Elizabeth	09/24/1811
MOORE, Jesse	PASS, Sally	01/07/1785
MOORE, John	REA, Sarah	04/11/1821
MOORE, John	FULLER, Hester A.	01/09/1867
MOORE, Joseph E.	EVANS, Sarah H.	10/05/1854
MOORE, Lawrence H.	OAKLEY, Cornelia F.	04/01/1854
MOORE, Lawrence H.	OAKLEY, Arrena	10/30/1865
MOORE, Leonadas B.	MCNEIL, Margaret J.	10/21/1844
MOORE, Matthew P.	GWYNN, Huldah	02/20/1843
MOORE, Robert	MCGEHEE, Elizabeth	08/24/1784
MOORE, Robert	DRUREY, Mary	05/24/1780
MOORE, Robert A.	HINES, Elizabeth B.	05/04/1859
MOORE, Rufus	SLADE, Lucinda	06/02/1866

MARRIAGE RECORDS OF CASWELL COUNTY, NORTH CAROLINA

GROOM	BRIDE	DATE
MOORE, Samuel	WILLIAMSON, Elizabeth	09/29/1783
MOORE, Solomon	GWYN, Frances	12/27/1867
MOORE, Spencer	CLARK Sarah	12/18/1856
MOORE, Stephen J.	BURTON, Sarah J.	08/13/1859
MOORE, T.Jefferson	WADLETON, Sina	10/20/1860
MOORE, Terrell	TERRELL, Ann	04/02/1834
MOORE, Thomas	SCOGGINS, Ann	08/06/1850
MOORE, Thomas A.	STEWART, Mary R.	09/18/1851
MOORE, Thomas E.	EVANS, Nancy A.	10/24/1842
MOORE, Thomas J.	MAYO, Dorothy C.	08/22/1837
MOORE, Thompson	WESTBROOKS, Caroline	09/07/1835
MOORE, William	HAMLETT, Belle	09/28/1867
MOORE, William	GRAVES, Nancy	11/25/1799
MOORE, William	ROAN, Patsy	09/10/1828
MOORE, William C.	JACKSON, Mildred	04/04/1856
MOORE, William D.	SPAIN, Elizabeth	11/22/1851
MOORE, William G.	NELSON, Martha B.	10/29/1842
MOORE, William J.	MCNEEL, Mary E.	12/21/1840
MOORE, William W.	MCKINNEY, Sarah	10/28/1826
MOOREFIELD, John H.	MILAM, Elizabeth	03/02/1865
MOORFIELD, James	POWELL, Polly	09/13/1816
MOREFIELD, Paul H.	CHANEY, Eliza E.	05/24/1860
MORGAN, Addison	RICHMOND, Mary	12/02/1839
MORGAN, Benjamin F.	WOODS, Mary J.	11/28/1848
MORGAN, Daniel	WRIGHT, Nancy	04/15/1806
MORGAN, George W.	DILLARD, Mary A.	07/23/1850
MORGAN, John	STENSON, Nancy	09/27/1796
MORGAN, John C.	WATERFIELD, Elizabeth	06/27/1827
MORGAN, L.D.	EVANS, Sarah A.	12/22/1857
MORGAN, Lafayette	FARMER, Catherine	01/19/1843
MORGAN, Warren	WOODS, Mary	12/19/1838
MORGAN, William	WILLSON, Betsy	09/07/1812
MORGAN, William	PASCHELL, Reliance	01/17/1806
MORGAN, William H.	WEDDING, Sarah	10/11/1838
MORGAN, William M.	MATLOCK, Judah	07/14/1847
MORRIS, Edward J.	VANHOOK, Araminta D.	07/18/1842
MORRIS, Edwin S.	FOWLER, Ann E.	01/23/1856
MORRIS, James	BARNWELL, Eliza	11/10/1841
MORRIS, John H.	FREEMAN, Mary A.E.	09/09/1832
MORRIS, John R.	BOWLES, Nancy	02/15/1830
MORRIS, Richard A.	BLARTLETT, Caroline	09/25/1836
MORRIS, Samuel	KINDRICK, Sally	01/10/1807
MORRIS, William	MCGINNIS, Betsy	03/12/1786
MORROW, Benjamin	LOVE, Margaret	01/29/1828
MORROW, Daniel	HALL, Fanny	10/08/1790
MORROW, John	DAVIS, Betsy	12/23/1835
MORROW, Robert	HURLEY, Ann	10/15/1732
MORROW, William	JAY, Sally	01/05/1789
MORROW, William	BURNS, Mary	07/10/1793
MORSE, Edward G.	CARROW, Julia A.	06/01/1860
MORTON, Alexander B.	-----, -----	06/16/1837

MARRIAGE RECORDS OF CASWELL COUNTY, NORTH CAROLINA

GROOM	BRIDE	DATE
MORTON, Alexander B.	CANTRIL, Henrietta	11/04/1819
MORTON, Anderson	SAMUEL, Letty	12/09/1803
MORTON, Azariah G.	MARTIN, Hetta C.	06/08/1837
MORTON, Bedford B.	TRAVIS, Maryann	05/30/1848
MORTON, Edward Z.	PETERSON, Susanna	07/03/1825
MORTON, Elijah	LEA, Polly	11/05/1811
MORTON, George	MCGHEE, Martha	02/18/1788
MORTON, Jesse	BURTON, Betsy	10/28/1802
MORTON, John	ZACHORY, Judah	04/04/1804
MORTON, John	MANLY, Matilda	07/04/1843
MORTON, John	HARRISON, Elizabeth	07/22/1846
MORTON, John	POTEET, Nancy	01/03/1820
MORTON, Martin	FULLER, Mary	03/14/1818
MORTON, Step(?)	RICHMOND, Nancy	01/02/1809
MORTON, William	SAMUEL, Milly	05/31/1803
MORTON, Williamson	COLLIER, Rebecca	12/23/1822
MOSELEY, John R.	JOHNSON, Frances	12/26/1866
MOSS, Daniel B.	WILLIAMSON, Sarah	08/14/1827
MOSS, John P.	SHELTON, Drucilla	09/12/1827
MOTHERAL, Samuel	MCMINAMY, Sarah	12/26/1782
MOTLEY, Alfred H.	WRIGHT, Mary J.	07/10/1856
MOTLEY, Booker	HUNT, Ellen	10/13/1867
MOTLEY, Hartwell	HOOPER, Martha	03/22/1824
MOTLEY, Joel	WHITEMORE, Eliza K.	10/24/1823
MOTLEY, Nathaniel C.	HATCHETT, Clarender F.(?)	10/26/1853
MOTLEY, Thomas J.	JOHNSTON, Mary S.	09/27/1855
MOTZ, Andrew	DODSON, Frances A.	09/23/1840
MUIRHEAD, Claud	WADE, Elizabeth	06/13/1781
MULLINS, Jerry	BETHELL, Ann	01/19/1867
MULLINS, Thomas	STUBLEFIELD, Patsy	07/26/1797
MULLINS, Thomas	MIMS, Matilda B.	10/10/1836
MURPHEY, Abraham	WALKER, Mary	03/07/1839
MURPHEY, Alexander	SMITH, Polly	08/29/1815
MURPHEY, Alexander	GRAVES, Sarah	09/11/1822
MURPHEY, Barzel	FURY, ELizabeht	09/21/1803
MURPHEY, Bazel	WARREN, Nancy	12/23/1846
MURPHEY, James	LOVELACE, Sarah	03/02/1843
MURPHEY, James	MOOR, Frances	08/11/1825
MURPHEY, James	NUNN, Ary	12/14/1824
MURPHEY, James	TERRELL, Patsy	03/21/1795
MURPHEY, Jno.	CORDER, Polly	02/11/1803
MURPHEY, John	TERRELL, Sarah	04/10/1804
MURPHEY, John C.	MURPHEY, Permilia A.	05/15/1851
MURPHEY, Jospeh	KENNON, Sally	10/27/1800
MURPHEY, Stephen	MALONE, Nancy	11/05/1827
MURPHEY, Thomas	LOVELACE, Nancy	02/--/1852
MURPHEY, Wiley	RICHMOND, Sarah	10/14/1866
MURPHEY, William	KENDIRCK, Mildred	10/07/1830
MURPHEY, William	PLEASANT, Artesia	02/06/1839
MURPHEY, William	TERREL, Lucy	03/02/1798
MURPHEY, William M.	SOUTHARD, Mary	12/28/1852

MARRIAGE RECORDS OF CASWELL COUNTY, NORTH CAROLINA

GROOM	BRIDE	DATE
MURPHY, Gabriel Jr.	HEARNDON, Clara	02/04/1788
MURPHY, Lewis	THORP, Louisa	09/10/1866
MURPHY, William	WYNNE, Charity	04/17/1832
MURPHY, William H.	SMITH, Susan A.L.	10/12/1858
MURRAY, David R.	MCCAIN, Sarah A.	07/06/1847
MURRAY, Eli	OLIVER, Nancy	07/28/1845
MURRAY, Hector	MURRAY, Frances T.	01/07/1843
MURRAY, Mark S.	FARLEY, Isabella	10/24/1849
MURRAY, Thomas	MONTGOMERY, Rebecca	03/12/1850
MURRAY, Walter	WARRIN, Frances	03/04/1825
MURRAY, William J.	CARTER, Isabella P.	04/18/1861
MURREY, William J.	BROOKS, Mary A.	08/25/1867
MURRIE, James	BROWNING, Tabitha	09/26/1818
MURRY, Walter	BRYANT, Eleanor	07/18/1797
MUSTAIN, Clark	DODD, Louisa	08/28/1828
MUSTAIN, James W.	SHELTON, Sally	03/11/1814
MUZZALL, Joseph W.	NORFLEET, Jean	05/02/1815
MUZZALL, William	MALONE, Mary	08/22/1789
MUZZALL, William A.	ANDERSON, Sarah	09/04/1838
NABERS, William J.	HENSLEY, Elizabeth Y.	02/12/1867
NANCE, Clemmons	BERRY, Frances	12/08/1819
NANCE, Frederick	BERRY, Polly	01/09/1809
NANCE, Joseph W.	BUTLER, Emeline D.	06/04/1853
NANCE, Thomas	CLARK, Elizabeth	12/20/1853
NANCE, William M.	HOWARD, Caroline M.T.	01/09/1844
NASH, Alfred M.	SNIPES, Cornelia	03/30/1841
NASH, Thomas	ERWIN, Rebecca	07/06/1784
NEAL, Abram T.	OWEN, Mary A.F.	09/16/1865
NEAL, James M.	MUNNALLY, Martha E.	05/18/1846
NEAL, Jno. T.	HOWARD, Lucy A.	12/11/1859
NEAL, John	LAWSON, Nancy	01/22/1788
NEAL, Philemon	SIMPSON, Nancy	12/08/1804
NEAL, Philemon H.	GWYN, Zippora J.	09/05/1861
NEAL, Stephen	HAMLETT, Aggy	05/19/1866
NEAL, Stephen	TURNER, Frances A.	12/26/1838
NEAL, William R.	HOOPER, Martha J.	11/11/1846
NEAL, Zachariah	RICE, Rebecca	12/16/1811
NEALY, John	DURHAM, Peggy	05/06/1819
NEBLETT, Colin	GARLAND, Victoria C.	10/24/1855
NEELEY, Garnett	DOLLERHIDE, Ann	06/07/1801
NELSON, Ambrose	BRADSHER, Frances	07/10/1822
NELSON, Ambrose	BRACHER, Nama	09/09/1817
NELSON, Azariah	EVANS, Eliza	12/10/1842
NELSON, Barzillai	OWENS, Margaret	08/26/1822
NELSON, Iverson	HIGHTOWER, Mary	04/12/1841
NELSON, James	TERREL, Mercy	02/01/1816
NELSON, James	STAMPS, Jane	08/18/1867
NELSON, Joel H.	COX, Tameran	12/19/1842
NELSON, John B.	MARR, Elizabeth	12/20/1852
NELSON, John H.	JONES, Elizabeth	07/28/1848
NELSON, Samuel	PRENDERGAST, Harriet	11/14/1820

MARRIAGE RECORDS OF CASWELL COUNTY, NORTH CAROLINA

GROOM	BRIDE	DATE
NEW, John D.	PERKINS, Malinda C.	11/13/1866
NEWBELL, John	SEAL, Rebecca	09/19/1828
NEWBY, Asa R.	ANGLES, Sophia	05/11/1859
NEWMAN, A.B.	CHANDLER, Mary F.	05/01/1867
NEWMAN, Aaron	RICHMON, Susan	08/02/1866
NEWMAN, Anderson B.	MOORE, Elizabeth E.	12/17/1851
NEWMAN, Remus	RICHMOND, Sarah	01/14/1866
NEWMAN, Robert	STEWART, Adeline T.	11/16/1849
NEWMAN, Washington	WALKER, Leticia	12/05/1838
NEWMAN, Wm.	WILLIAMS, Sarah	11/17/1866
NEWTON, Henry	WHITE, Mildred	03/23/1791
NEWTON, John G.	CRIDER, Judith	10/14/1818
NICHOLLS, Isaac	LONDON, Sarah	10/27/1825
NICHOLS, David A.	TAYLOR, Martha	12/13/1849
NICHOLS, James E.	PARRISH, Martha	07/18/1867
NICHOLS, John W.	FURGERSON, Jane M.	11/27/1866
NICHOLS, Wright	BURCH, Sarah	01/11/1791
NICHOLSON, Joseph	FIELDER, Margaret	02/03/1829
NICKOLS, Isaac	NORMAN, Ann	12/25/1818
NIGHTIN, James	WALKER, Peggy	01/07/1814
NIGHTON, Turner	GLAZE, Sarah	01/02/1849
NIPPER, James	PLERRA, Susan	08/05/1809
NIPPER, Samuel	GORDON, Tabitha	11/23/1816
NOBLE, Andrew	MOORE, Louisa A. E.	12/04/1857
NOBLE, John	PAYNES, Frances	04/06/1807
NOEL, Ephraim	BOMAN, Nancy	12/13/1803
NORFLEET, James S.	MCNEEL, Ursula G.	02/11/1826
NORFLEET, M. W.	KIRKPATRICK, M. E.	12/15/1864
NORFLEET, Marmaduke	ROAN, Mary	12/05/1833
NORMAN, Charles H.	NORMAN, Mary S.	02/26/1856
NORMAN, Henry J.	CAHAL, Louisa S.	03/11/1852
NORMAN, James B.	CAHAL, Martha E.	03/11/1852
NORMAN, Wesley	BARNETT, Elizabeth	05/24/1816
NORMAN, William	WEST, Milcey	01/14/1812
NORMAN, William	HARRIS, Betsy	10/09/1850
NORMAN, William	BAYS, Nancy	12/01/1858
NORMAN, William	YATES, Nancy	07/03/1845
NORMOND, William	COOK, Priscilla	05/28/1825
NORRIS, William	OWEN, Sally K.	10/01/1840
NORTHERN, T. H.	SMITH, S----	06/29/1854
NORVELL, Braxton	PHILIPS, Mildred A.	12/28/1830
NOWEL, Ephraim	SIDDEL, Sarah	12/27/1787
NOWLES, William	HAILEY, Rebecca	07/01/1812
NOWLS, John	DAWSON, Mileah	09/29/1807
NUNN, Admiral N.	SARTIN, Ann	01/26/1836
NUNN, Carlton	STANBACK, Martha	01/25/1820
NUNN, James	WATERS, Mary J.	12/27/1860
NUNN, Miller	SWANN, Susan B.	10/10/1859
NUNN, William	BASTINE, Hannah	10/26/1830
NUNNALLY, Archelaus (?)	SPENCE, Caroline	09/14/1835
NUNNALLY, Archelaus (?)	GATEWOOD, Pamela	03/04/1822

MARRIAGE RECORDS OF CASWELL COUNTY, NORTH CAROLINA

GROOM	BRIDE	DATE
NUNNALLY, Hartwell	PINNIX, Jane	11/09/1867
NUNNALLY, James S.	GILLASPY, Tabitha H.	01/21/1824
NUNNALLY, Jas	FARISH, Lucy	04/18/1866
NUNNALLY, John	WITHERS, Sytha A.	07/22/1817
NUNNALLY, John	FITZGERALD, Nancy	12/21/1865
NUNNALLY, John H.	WITERS, Susan L.	06/20/1854
NUNNALLY, William H.	PRICE, Nancy	05/06/1823
NUTT, Absalom	LEATH, Frances	08/04/1820
NUTT, David D.	JACKSON, Agness	04/18/1816
OAKELEY, Thos.	CROSSIX, Elizabeth	11/16/1820
OAKLEY, Alexander	BROUGHTON, Parthena	02/19/1833
OAKLEY, Archibald	SMITH, Jirilla (?)	03/13/1847
OAKLEY, F. L.	RUDD, Frances A.	10/25/1866
OAKLEY, William	ASHLEY, Nancy	12/04/1790
OAKLY, Thomas P.	COOPER, Susan J.	12/21/1856
OBRIANT, E. M.	COOPER, Eliza	12/10/1866
OGLESBY, John S.	ALLEN, Sarah P.	10/07/1834
OLD, William B.	TUCKER, Sally P.	04/21/1867
OLDHAM, George	STACEY, Henrietta	01/06/1807
OLDHAM, John	RICE, Ann	02/26/1783
OLDHAM, Richard	PEOPLES, Ursley D.	10/20/1786
OLIVER, Alva	HOLLOWAY, Betsy	02/13/1792
OLIVER, Bivin D.	BALL, Helen M.	12/02/1867
OLIVER, Charles J.	JONES, Amanda	09/22/1835
OLIVER, Creed T.	HARRISON, Jane D.	01/15/1830
OLIVER, Douglas	KERNALL, Milly	03/18/1783
OLIVER, Durrett	LEA, Matilda	11/02/1811
OLIVER, Ireson L.	COVERINGTON, Mary T.	11/13/1859
OLIVER, Jerry	WILLIAMSON, Silvy	12/22/1866
OLIVER, John M.	PAMPLIN, Virginia H.	11/15/1865
OLIVER, Josiah	PHELPS, Nicey N.	12/ 2/1834
OLIVER, Linsey	WILLIS, Martha A.	05/24/1842
OLIVER, Monroe	HOOPER, Ann L.	05/24/1860
OLIVER, Reuben	LEA, Nancy	01/17/1824
OLIVER, Yancy	LEA, Judith	12/22/1826
OLVIS, John	COCK, Addeline	05/20/1833
ONEILL, John	WARE, Hannah	12/20/1790
OODS, Andy M.	RICHMOND, Minerva	07/18/1834
ORR, Ezekiel J.	FORREST, Ann J.	10/15/1867
ORR, Robert	SWIFT, Frances	01/02/1811
ORR, Samuel	SWIFT, Nancy	03/16/1813
ORR, William	PASCHALL, Catherine	11/09/1804
OUTLAW, Samuel	PINNIX, Margaret	05/16/1867
OVERBY, Owen	WILKERSON, Puritha	04/19/1825
OVERBY, Samuel	COILE, Sarah	10/11/1830
OVERBY, Thomas	HICKS, Levina	08/13/1827
OVERBY, Thomas	WEST, Mahaley J.	02/05/1833
OVERSTREET, John	OVERSTREET, Mary	04/01/1779
OVERSTREET, Robert	WILKERSON, Rhody	10/27/1801
OWEN, Alfred	TUCKER, Perlina	06/25/1860
OWEN, Eliza W.	ROAN, Margaret A.	05/01/1847

MARRIAGE RECORDS OF CASWELL COUNTY, NORTH CAROLINA

GROOM	BRIDE	DATE
OWEN, Henry S.	NELSON, Rebecca	09/28/1842
OWEN, John	OWEN, Martha	01/25/1825
OWEN, John	MARTIN, Nancy	11/05/1788
OWEN, Peter	JONES, Lucy	12/22/1842
OWEN, Sharod	HARRIS, Martha	10/14/1815
OWEN, Thomas W.	THOMAS, Mildred	01/28/1834
OWEN, Thomas W.	VANHOOK, Penelope M.	10/28/1845
OWEN, William	ROWARK, Polly	11/11/1794
OWENS, Andrew J.	HINTON, Adaliade	08/23/1865
OWENS, William T.	EDGAR, Martha E. A. H.	01/09/1842
OWIN, David	MARTIN, Polly	09/21/1798
OXFORD, Jonathan	CANNON, Susan	12/12/1784
OYLER, James T.	MORGAN, Louisa J.	10/24/1867
PADGETT, Joseph M.	VERMILLION, Mary J.	10/08/1841
PADGETT, Tinsly	POWELL, Elizabeth	01/14/1833
PAGE, Albert M.	SIMPSON, Nanny L.	--/--/1867
PAGE, Benjamin	SCARLETT, Jane	04/10/1832
PAGE, Bently	TERRELL, Lucy	09/29/1843
PAGE, Daniel J.	PAGE, Elizabeth	01/26/1860
PAGE, Franklin B.	MCKINNY, Milly D.	08/04/1859
PAGE, James	HERNDON, Sally	10/25/1855
PAGE, James	ADKENS, Betsy	02/22/1802
PAGE, James	WILLIS, Mary	11/24/1830
PAGE, James B.	GUNN, Mary C.	10/15/1865
PAGE, James H.	ROBERTSON, Eady	12/23/1860
PAGE, James P.	BOSWELL, Margaret	12/16/1837
PAGE, John	PERKINS, Betsy	11/10/1806
PAGE, Joseph F.	BRINTLE, Amy	02/03/1832
PAGE, Josiah	PAGE, Henrietta	04/05/1827
PAGE, Levi C.	VERNON, Marinda C.	07/21/1841
PAGE, Milton	ADKINS, Ann R.	10/12/1839
PAGE, Noah	PETERSON, Susan	01/10/1820
PAGE, Samuel	PAGE, Delila	12/21/1819
PAGE, Stephen	SHEPARD, Elizabeth	01/11/1832
PAGE, Thomas	VAUGHN, Nancy	02/19/1800
PAGE, Whitehead	ATKINS, Jenny	12/23/1795
PAGE, Whitehead	KING, Rachel	03/20/1815
PAGE, William	BOWE, Lilly	11/19/1866
PAGE, William	COBB,(?) Nancy	12/31/1796
PAGE, William	WHITEHEAD,(?) Nancy	12/31/1796
PAGE, William	MANLEY, Mary	12/09/1854
PAGE, William A.	STAULCUP, Silvia	12/09/1833
PAGE, William C.	PLEASANT, Martha A.	12/28/1848
PAGE, William C.	GRANT, Jane E.	12/10/1844
PAGE, William M.	FOSTER, Celia	11/05/1839
PAGE, Zacharian	PINSON, Frances	10/01/1867
PAGE, Zenith	PAGE, Mary	04/06/1858
PAGE, Zenith	COBB, Martha	03/20/1837
PAGE, (?) Whitehead (?)	WRIGHT, Betsy	12/15/1809
PAISELY, John	CROSSETT, Jane	04/25/1828
PALMER, Clem	BLACKWELL, Mary B.	09/16/1867

MARRIAGE RECORDS OF CASWELL COUNTY, NORTH CAROLINA

GROOM	BRIDE	DATE
PALMER, Dabney	BARGE, Fanny	12/30/1848
PALMER, John	FREEMAN, Eliza A.	05/12/1862
PALMER, Joyner	HIGHTOWER, Susan	02/16/1850
PAMPLIN, James	CHILDRESS, Susan J.	12/20/1866
PANTON, Scott	HAIRSTON, Amanda	12/27/1867
PARISH, James	SAWYERS, Anthony	10/12/1826
PARISH, William T.	TOTTEN, Mary A.	10/28/1856
PARK, Jno. S.	MIMS, Mary J.	12/04/1856
PARK, M. A.	CRUTCHFIELD, Nanny L.	12/20/1866
PARKER, Byrd G.	SARGENT, Elizabeth	08/06/1807
PARKER, Jeptha	WHITE, Jincy	10/02/1813
PARKER, Powel	LUMKIN, Nancy	12/24/1787
PARKER, William	WILLIAMS, Betsy	12/15/1801
PARKER, William	KERSEY, Ursley	10/20/1798
PARKS, Alfred	NELSON, Polly	03/11/1806
PARKS, Alfred	SMITH, Polly	10/16/1825
PARKS, Hiram	VAUGHN, Lucy	01/02/1799
PARKS, James N.	WALKER, Malinda	10/20/1843
PARKS, Jeptha	CULBERSON, Libby	09/14/1800
PARKS, Robert	HENSLEE, Lucinda	06/19/1825
PARKS, Robert G.	MCCLARY, Polly	02/26/1803
PARKS, Samuel B.	CURRIE, Mary A.	06/02/1845
PARKS, Solomon	ATKINSON, Avey	12/20/1782
PARKS, William	CORDER, Hannah	03/09/1798
PARR, William	NORTON, Elizabeth	12/26/1788
PARRETT, Thomas	LONG, Margaret	01/10/1860
PARRISH, A. P.	FULKS, S. A.	12/04/1860
PARRISH, James	BLACKWELL, Zilla	05/29/1861
PARRISH, John J.	FORD, Emily N.	07/18/1867
PASCCHALL, William D.	DAVIS, Susan	11/17/1819
PASCHAL, Elisha	HORRELSON, Martha F.	02/17/1857
PASCHAL, Ezekiel D.	PARRISH, Eliza E.	10/09/1850
PASCHAL, Jesse D.	CANADAY, Eliza A.	03/06/1861
PASCHAL, John H.	TOTTEN, Parthena A.	10/18/1860
PASCHALL, Elisha	MCCALIN, Rachel	12/22/1819
PASCHALL, Isiah	SANDERS, Patsy	01/13/1813
PASCHALL, Jerry	HOWARD, Betsy	01/06/1866
PASCHELL, Thomas	PRICE, Nancy	02/11/1789
PASHAEL, William	PASCHAEL, Nancy	01/14/1840
PASKEL, John	JUSTICE, Martha J.	11/20/1854
PASS, Fantelleroy	PRUETT, Frances	03/10/1837
PASS, Holoway	ROBINSON, Kiziah	12/21/1785
PASS, James M.	CHAMBERS, Harriet A.	08/30/1851
PASS, John	BIRCH, Delany	05/28/1820
PASS, John A.	BUCKNER, Judith	01/07/1823
PASS, Nathaniel Jr.	TAPLEY, Milly	07/09/1794
PASS, Nathaniel W.	BUCKNER, Frances	02/22/1821
PASS, Seth W.	TATE, Elizabeth	10/07/1840
PASS, Thomas C.	SAMUELS, Nancy	11/03/1859
PASS, Thomas C.	ROPER, Jane N.	12/19/1837
PASS, Thomas Y.	RUDDER, Sally	11/26/1826

MARRIAGE RECORDS OF CASWELL COUNTY, NORTH CAROLINA

GROOM	BRIDE	DATE
PASS, William H.	CHAMBERS, Elizabeth	11/29/1847
PATE, Richard A.	WOODING, Susan T.	01/07/1848
PATERSON, John	TAYLOR, Mary A.	07/26/1838
PATTERSON, Turner	DURHAM, Sarah E.	06/06/1866
PATTERSON, Turner	TENNISSON, Celia	07/25/1808
PATTERSON, William B.	POWELL, Leah	05/19/1843
PATTILLO, Albert A.	DODSON, Eliza A.	05/21/1838
PATTILLO, Anderson H. W.	ADKINS, Mary E.	09/13/1866
PATTILLO, Lewis A.	BASWELL, Lucinda	01/22/1839
PATTILLO, William	GUNN, Margaret	12/29/1866
PATTILLO, Zachariah	JORDON, Mary	12/10/1814
PATTILLO, Zachariah A.	WILLIS, Elizabeth B.	05/22/1847
PATTON, John D.	MCALPIN, Mary J.	12/27/1853
PATTOSON, David	CHAMBERS, Sally	03/27/1781
PAUL, Asa	ANTHONY, Pembrook	08/27/1803
PAUL, James	FAWLING, Rebecca	09/25/1797
PAUL, James	HIGHTOWER, Lettice	02/13/1795
PAUL, Robert	BURTON, Priscilla	05/28/1781
PAUL, Samuel	LEA, Elizabeth	03/22/1819
PAUL, Samuel	BURTON, Judith	01/14/1784
PAXTON, William C.	BURTON, Harriet H.	05/19/1852
PAYLOR, James H.	PATTILLO, M. V.	03/14/1865
PAYLOR, Moses	REID, Laura	02/14/1867
PAYNE, Daniel	HARREL, Elizabeth	01/22/1806
PAYNE, John	GUNN, Priscilla	09/--/1802
PAYNE, John	CHANDLER, Betsy	11/10/1811
PAYNE, John	HENSLEY, Ann	03/05/1779
PAYNE, Robert	MCKENNEY, Eliz.	09/14/1807
PAYNE, Thomas W.	SHOCKLEE, Polly	09/16/1821
PAYNE, William	DABBS, Ann E.	11/24/1853
PEALE, Anderson N,	BUSHNELL, Sarah J.	04/28/1857
PEALE, Jonathan	BUSHNELL, Margaret	10/07/1845
PEARCE, James S.	STRADER, Sarah J.	02/07/1867
PEARCE, Obediah	WALLACE, Parthena	01/21/1829
PEARSON, Thomas	ENNET, Nancy	12/30/1815
PEMBERTON, William B.	STUBBLEFIELD, Nancy	07/01/1819
PENICK, Giles	MCGILL, A. B.	02/21/1866
PEOPLES, Reuben	WILLIAMS, Ursly D.	02/01/1783
PERKINS, Jesse	INGRAM, Susan	08/19/1795
PERKINS, John	POWELL, Mary A.	02/10/1846
PERKINS, John	SMITH, Virginia	11/29/1862
PERKINS, Logan	LANDRUM, Elgy	02/01/1845
PERKINS, Martin	SAWYER, Dicy	08/21/1787
PERKINS, Martin	SAWYER, Elizabeth	12/02/1833
PERKINS, Nathan	LOVELASS, Cloey A.	10/05/1832
PERKINS, William	YATES, Polly	12/26/1811
PERROW, Stephen W.	HENRICK, Virginia	05/16/1839
PERRY, William	JOHNSTON, Ann	11/19/1792
PERRYMAN, William	STOKES, Nancy	01.16.1782
PERYMAN, Richard	FLEEMING, Mary	04/07/1794
PETERSON, James O.	MURRAY, Mary F.	05/30/1858

MARRIAGE RECORDS OF CASWELL COUNTY, NORTH CAROLINA

GROOM	BRIDE	DATE
PETERSON, Joseph Jr.	STAFFORD, Cinthia	09/07/1790
PETERSON, Thomas	BROWN, Ann	--/--/----
PETERSON, Vincent	PETERSON, Polly	05/19/1821
PETERSON, William	NOWLES, Patsy	01/20/1814
PETERSON, Williamson	FERGIS, Nancy	12/22/1835
PETTERFORD, Levi T.	HART, Elizabeth	07/30/1861
PETTIGRUE, Charles L.	TATE, Adeline	12/28/1855
PHAROAH, John	-----, -----	10/21/1789
PHELPS, Ambrose	DYE, Sally	08/19/1796
PHELPS, Henry J.	WILSON, Lucy	10/13/1867
PHELPS, Hiram	PASS, Sarah	10/06/1818
PHELPS, James L.	STEVENS, Temperance	11/19/1866
PHELPS, Larking	DYE, Ann	08/19/1796
PHELPS, Levi	WALTERS, Leathy M.	07/25/1866
PHELPS, Obediah	DYE, Peggy	12/28/1796
PHELPS, Reuben	TAYLOR, Mary M.	05/16/1848
PHELPS, Robt. C.	FOSTER, Ann E.	02/24/1858
PHELPS, Thomas	PASS, Mary	12/17/1791
PHELPS, William	WARRIN, Jane	01/10/1786
PHILIPS, Frederick	BASS, Margaret	01/14/1846
PHILIPS, John	CAMPBELL, Emily A.	10/08/1840
PHILIPS, William	HUGHES, Elizabeth	12/25/1857
PHILLIPS, Ben	BRIGGS, J.	12/12/1860
PHILLIPS, Franklin	CAMPBELL, Evelina	01/04/1841
PHILLIPS, Hugh	WILSON, Catherine	01/22/1814
PHILLIPS, Joshua	GRIFFIN, Polly	11/01/1802
PHILLIPS, Paul C.	POWELL, Mary C.	10/17/1863
PHIPPS, James	PAUL, Charlotte	04/28/1848
PICKREL, Henry	BOSWELL, Elizabeth	10/06/1854
PIERCE, Gabriel	JAMES, Virginia	11/19/1865
PIKE, Joshua	MALLORY, Sally	03/01/1805
PIKE, Lewis	BERRY, Mary	01/10/1787
PIKE, Samuel R.	BARKER, Martha A.	01/01/1852
PILES, Albert	BASS, Mahala	10/08/1855
PILES, Henry	PHILIPS, Susan	07/01/1858
PILES, Henry	BRANNUM, Emily	05/27/1861
PILES, James	ASHFORD, Sally	10/23/1802
PINCHBACK, John W.	JEFFREYS, Helen E.	07/19/1841
PINNIX, Benjamin	SIMPSON, Almeda	02/12/1840
PINNIX, Frank	MILES, Sally	07/05/1867
PINNIX, George W.	GRAVES, Mary U.	09/19/1854
PINNIX, James	SNIPES, Frances	02/01/1868
PINNIX, Jerry	WALKER, Priscilla	0/11/1867
PINNIX, John	SPENCER, Barbara	12/08/1780
PINNIX, John	GUNN, Martha	06/10/1867
PINNIX, John C.	DAVIS, Barbara E.	03/27/1844
PINNIX, Joseph	KERR, Betsy	01/22/1816
PINNIX, Robert	PINNIX, Martha	09/02/1866
PINOX, Alexander K.	HARRISON, Harriet S.	04/28/1848
PINSON, Drury	SMITH, Susan	10/18/1816
PINSON, Isaac	PINSON, Rebecca	12/15/1810

MARRIAGE RECORDS OF CASWELL COUNTY, NORTH CAROLINA

GROOM	BRIDE	DATE
PINSON, Thomas	SMITH, Patsy	02/19/1823
PIPER, Robert P.	KENT, Ann	10/13/1858
PITMAN, John	COOK, Sarah	04/10/1794
PITMON, Moses	HIGHTOWER, Eliza	01/13/1846
PITTARD, Benjamin S.	RICHMOND, Agness S.	01/07/1839
PITTARD, Benjamin S.	RICHMOND, Susan A.	11/05/1859
PITTARD, Davis	TERRELL, Lucy	11/30/1840
PITTARD, Jno.	STANFIELD, Mary L.	12/19/1851
PITTARD, Martin	GARLAND, Malissa	05/19/1867
PITTARD, Samuel	SAMUEL, Elizabeth	12/21/1790
PITTARD, Samuel	DAMERON, Sarah F.	03/13/1866
PITTS, James S.	MCCULLOCH, Narsissus	01/26/1859
PLATS, Frank	LESTER, Mary C.	04/21/1864
PLEASANT, Beauford	HENSLEE, Elizabeth	10/31/1810
PLEASANT, Beaufort	HENSLEE, Sarah	01/21/1822
PLEASANT, John	FLORENCE, Frances H.	12/14/1860
PLEASANT, John J.	MILES, Martha E.	09/05/1838
PLEASANT, Micajah Jr.	MURRAY, Nancy	05/07/1827
PLEASANT, Pinkey J.	MILES, Elizabeth	10/06/1849
PLEASANT, Rufin	ENOCKS, Sarah	02/18/1823
PLEASANT, Stephen N.	LUNSFORD, Sarah E.	01/13/1868
POE, John	PARKS, Elizabeth	01/12/1793
POE, Jonathan	LANNOM, Tabitha	--/--/1804
POGUE, Daniel	TOMSON, Sally	08/10/1814
POGUE, Joshua	THOMAS, Jinsy	07/13/1804
POLLARD, Joseph B.	NORRIS, Catherine J.	11/17/1865
POND, James	STANDBURY, Elizabeth	01/16/1786
POND, Walter	HARDGEGREE, Ellenor	07/28/1795
PONDS, Benjamin	SWAN, Milly	01/19/1807
POOL, Isaac	POTEATE, Cindy	01/12/1867
POOL, Lea	SWIFT, Sally	06/09/1866
POORE, Thomas S.	COVINGTON, Mary E.	07/21/1852
POORE, Thomas S.	MCCAIN, Elizabeth	11/21/1842
POPE, Abraham	FARLEY, Elizabeth	01/24/1820
POSEY, Alexander	OLIVER, Patsy	08/09/1816
POSTON, Jeremiah	WARSON, Elizabeth	05/03/1779
POSTON, William	TAIT, Edy	01/29/1803
POTEAT, Alex	MORGAN, Mary	01/25/1867
POTEAT, Allen	SMITH, Isabella	08/30/1866
POTEAT, Charles	SMITH, Frances	12/27/1866
POTEAT, George	RICHMOND, Fanny	01/26/1867
POTEAT, James	ROBERTS, Isabella G.	10/14/1837
POTEAT, James	MCNEILL, Julia A.	11/17/1855
POTEAT, John Jr.	HORTON, Elizabeth	02/08/1859
POTEAT, Thomas	RUDD, Martha	12/22/1834
POTEAT, Thomas	SCOTT, Nanny	12/17/1855
POTEAT, William	PRYRANT, Subrina	03/23/1856
POTEET, James	LYON, Tempy	11/11/1801
POTEET, Miles	TAPLEY, Susan	05/12/1796
POTEET, Miles Jr.	HUNTER, Rebecca	07/10/1828
POTEET, William	HENDERSON, Martha	06/26/1828

MARRIAGE RECORDS OF CASWELL COUNTY, NORTH CAROLINA

GROOM	BRIDE	DATE
POTEET, William	CHRISTENBERY, Polly	03/03/1796
POUNDS, Shack	RUNNELLS, Sally	08/09/1847
POWEL, Thomas	KENNON, Ann	08/04/1820
POWELL, Barzilai	POTEET, Betsy	12/17/1825
POWELL, Barzilai	SPARROW, Willy	01/02/1834
POWELL, Edmund	MITCHEL, Jenny	11/09/1865
POWELL, Edward M.	WATLINGTON, Ann P.	01/08/1857
POWELL, George	ROBERTS, Jamima	03/08/1793
POWELL, Giles	CARTER, Susan	02/24/1853
POWELL, Henry	POTEET, Nancy	07/14/1826
POWELL, Henry A.	SHEPPARD, Mary	01/09/1840
POWELL, J. C.	MCKINNY, Susan	11/12/1866
POWELL, James	CHAMBERS, Mary A.	08/17/1864
POWELL, James B.	TERRY, Narcesia B.	10/06/1840
POWELL, James M.	MITCHELL, Betsy	01/10/1809
POWELL, John	HUMPHREYS, Margaret C.	03/18/1834
POWELL, Joshua	HOOPER, Martha	06/26/1849
POWELL, Mastin J.	GILLISPIE, Susan H.	06/20/1852
POWELL, Peter	CARROL, Patsy	08/31/1802
POWELL, Peter Jr.	PHILIPS, Frances	09/19/1832
POWELL, Richard M.	HOWARD, Margaret S.	12/18/1867
POWELL, Thomas B.	CARTER, Mary W.	04/22/1866
POWELL, Thomas J.	MORRISON, Malinda A.	10/14/1863
POWELL, William B.	GATEWOOD, Martha T.	01/01/1860
POWELL, William H.	YARBROUGH, Mary N.	01/05/1861
POYNOR, Jesse	PASCHALL, Nancy	01/03/1818
PRATHER, Leonard	WILLIAMSON, Frances	02/11/1799
PRATHER, Leonard D.	TAIT, Mary S.	01/01/1833
PRENDERGRAST, George W.	KIMBROUGH, Mary	09/14/1841
PRENDERGRAST, Thomas	HARRISON, Nancy	03/12/1799
PRESNELL, Gilbert	WATLINGTON, Nancy	07/14/1835
PRESTON, David	BRANDON, Rebecca	08/20/1787
PRICE, Abraham	MOORE, Betsy	07/18/1808
PRICE, Brunswick	SLADE, Josephine	05/20/1867
PRICE, Charles	WADLINGTON, Frances	02/20/1792
PRICE, Christopher M.	SUTHERLAND, Philena	05/10/1827
PRICE, Daniel S.	HARRISON, Agness R.	02/12/1833
PRICE, Daniel S.	STOKES, Eliza F.	12/14/1842
PRICE, George	PALMER, Mary	09/26/1823
PRICE, Grinville	PRICE, Louisa	05/27/1866
PRICE, Haskin	FISHER, Nancy	11/18/1799
PRICE, Hiram M.	FERRELL, Arminta	04/16/1852
PRICE, James A.	WRIGHT, Martha J.	06/26/1841
PRICE, John	BROWN, Mary	01/15/1781
PRICE, John Jr.	GARROTT, Susan	01/04/1808
PRICE, John P.	PRICE, Ann W.	11/10/1851
PRICE, John S.	RICHARDSON, Mary	12/22/1824
PRICE, Joshua	CULBERSON, Mary	12/28/1818
PRICE, Mathew	ESKRIDGE, Elizabeth	02/22/1796
PRICE, Meredith	MCDANIEL, Sarah	04/13/1819
PRICE, O. D.	MORTON, Ellen	01/20/1864

MARRIAGE RECORDS OF CASWELL COUNTY, NORTH CAROLINA

GROOM	BRIDE	DATE
PRICE, Peter	ARNETT, Nancy	09/01/1804
PRICE, Robert M.	STAMPS, Mary E.	12/13/1854
PRICE, Robert M.	MCDANIEL, Susan W.	11/10/1851
PRICE, Robert M.	KNIGHT, L.	12/12/1860
PRICE, Thomas L.	BOLTON, Lydia	09/21/1830
PRICE, William	PRICE, Matilda	12/18/1866
PRICE, William	CULBERSON, Edney	01/12/1807
PRICE, William W.	STOKES, Susan B.	09/24/1814
PRICE, Wm.	JONES, Martha	06/23/1866
PRIDE, Burton	BIZWELL, Sally	10/29/1780
PRIOR, Joseph	MANGRAM, Eliza	06/17/1859
PRIOR, Pinky C.	MARR, Margaret	02/19/1859
PRITCHETT, Edward	POWELL, Kesiah	06/09/1805
PROCTOR, Daniel R.	HAWKINS, Elizabeth	08/04/1852
PRUETT, Nathaniel	DRISKILL, Laura L.	12/30/1864
PRUIT, Griffin P.	LOVELACE, Jemima A. P.	05/21/1867
PRUIT, John A.	RAY, Rachel	10/10/1850
PRYOR, William	GOING, Heaty	07/19/1803
PUCKET, Goselin	REID, Mary	01/25/1808
PUCKET, Thomas	SOTHERLAND, Susan	12/24/1832
PUCKETT, James	ALDERIDGE, Nancy	12/27/1833
PUGH, Alfred M.	PUGH, Mary E.	03/01/1857
PUGH, E.L.	FOWLER, Nancy A.	11/28/1861
PULLIAM, Calvin	ELLIOTT, Caroline	03/10/1867
PULLIAM, Jack	CURRIE, Martha	10/16/1867
PULLIAM, James	PAYLOR, Manda	12/19/1867
PULLIAM, Thomas	CURRIE, Mary	01/19/1867
PURKINS, Robert	HOBBS, Edy	07/26/1820
PURKINS, Wm. N.	MARSHALL, Mary A.	10/24/1857
PUTNAM, Jeremiah	DEAN, Susanna	04/04/1823
PYRON, Charles	CHILDERS, Nancy	09/22/1836
PYRON, John	LEATH, Sarah	11/26/1799
PYRON, Westley	MANLY, Polly	07/02/1839
QUINE, Benjamin	CORAM, Ester	09/02/1780
QUINE, Goolsby	HUBBIRD, Patsy	01/07/1823
QUINE, Jacob	GUNN, Eleanor	11/09/1801
QUINE, William	BAXTER, Frances	11/12/1808
RAGGAN, John C.	MCFARLAND, Fanny	01/24/1861
RAGIN, William T.	MCFARLIN, Julia	12/31/1858
RAGSDALE, Benjamin	DUNCAN, Mary	--/--/1792
RAGSDALE, Clement	HAMBLETT, Nancy N.	11/12/1817
RAGSDALE, John	DOUGLASS, Nancy	10/14/1783
RAGSDALE, Peter	HAMLETT, Mary	12/09/1788
RAGSDALE, William	HAMLETT, Fanny M.	10/02/1788
RAILEY, C.H.	TANNER, Mary J.	11/09/1849
RAINEY, Dabney	CHELES, Nancy C.	05/05/1821
RAINEY, James G.	HENDRICK, Sophia	08/20/1823
RAINEY, Jno. P.	DURHAM, Martha	01/14/1836
RAINEY, John	MEELEY, Nelly	09/14/1798
RAINEY, John P.Jr.	RICHMOND, Elizabeth	05/12/1855
RAINEY, Sanford H.	FURGIS, Sarah L.	10/19/1859

MARRIAGE RECORDS OF CASWELL COUNTY, NORTH CAROLINA

GROOM	BRIDE	DATE
RAINEY, Thomas	SAMUEL, Jenny	09/17/1792
RAINEY, William	AKELS, Elizabeth	01/22/1782
RAINEY, William	MALONE, Chloe	09/28/1789
RAINEY, William	WRIGHT, Molly	10/01/1784
RAINEY, William T.	CARTER, Mary J.	12/25/1851
RALPH, Thomas	CORAM, Jane	04/12/1791
RAMEY, Albert W.	RIFFETOE, Lavinia E.	04/11/1848
RAMEY, Edward	RAMEY, Susan	12/05/1846
RAMEY, George	PASS, Lucy	12/30/1866
RAMSEUR, S.Dodson	RICHMOND, Ellen	10/27/1863
RAMSEY, Ambrose K.	YANCEY, Nancy	10/07/1817
RAMSOUR, Jacob A.	DODSON, Lucy M.	10/03/1833
RANDOLPH, George	HARP, Eleanor	07/06/1813
RANDOLPH, James	HARP, Jamima	10/11/1813
RANDOLPH, James	DYE, Mary	12/12/1781
RANDOLPH, John	CURLS, Sally	03/04/1806
RANDOLPH, William	HINTON, Mary	08/21/1808
RANDOLPH, William	WHITE, Sally	11/15/1783
RANSOM, Charles	MARSHALL, Elizabeth	01/03/1867
RASCO, Henry T.	LOYD, Elizabeth	01/19/1855
RASCO, John	COLEMAN, Sarah E.	09/24/1859
RASCO, W.M.	RASCO, Mrs. Nancy	10/19/1867
RASCO, William	PLEASANT, Harriet	07/05/1815
RASCOE, Ethelbert	KIMBROUGH, Nancy	10/20/1840
RASCOE, John	PLEASANT, Martha	12/05/1816
RAVENS, James	ALLREN, Nancy	10/19/1791
RAWLINS, James M.	GATEWOOD, Mary A.	01/10/1855
RAWLINS, James M.	SIMPSON, Martha G.	05/03/1865
RAY, Charles	FISHER, Jinsy	12/14/1804
RAY, Darling	REID, Mary	11/12/1794
RAY, David	ORR, Nancy	12/09/1820
RAY, James	HENSLEY, Eleanor	10/28/1794
RAY, Joseph	HENSLEE, Keziah	10/24/1798
RAY, Robert	WARNER, Mary	01/24/1843
RAY, Robert	JONES, Elizabeth	10/01/1840
RAYNER, Willie	RAGLAND, Orphie	08/11/1850
READ, Jackson	SCOTT, Amanda	04/30/1845
READ, James W.	THOMAS, Susan B.	05/10/1839
READ, Noel	HUBBARD, Nancy	04/15/1815
READ, Thomas	SMITH, Mary	10/11/1841
READ, Thomas	ROBERTS, Lucy	01/22/1823
REAGAN, John C.	ROYESTER, Lou F.	11/09/1865
REAGIN, John C.	MCFARLAND, Frances	03/27/1861
REANY, Isaac	MELONE, Sarah	03/06/1786
REDDIN, William	BURK, Milly	11/25/1812
REDMUN, William	ALLIN, Sarah	12/27/1791
REECE, John	STRINGER, Maryann	07/29/1780
REED, A.	RICHMOND, Sally J.	08/21/1860
REED, Anthony	OWEN, Tabitha	11/30/1824
REED, Blewford(?)	NOWLES, Nancy	06/25/1793
REED, James W.	LOCKET, Margaret	10/10/1844

MARRIAGE RECORDS OF CASWELL COUNTY, NORTH CAROLINA

GROOM	BRIDE	DATE
REED, John	BALLARD, Nancy	06/26/1807
REED, John	VAUGHAN, Nancy	07/01/1825
REED, Thomas	ROPER, Mary M.	11/06/1838
REESE, Josias	SHAW, Nancy	06/19/1779
REEVES, Asa	NICHOLS, Nancy J.	10/09/1867
REID, Anthony	OWEN, Martha	03/09/1833
REID, Hugh K.	GRAVES, Caroline H.	05/27/1857
REID, James	WILSON, Polly	02/12/1800
REID, Jno. W.	RICHMOND, Martha W.	11/21/1865
REID, John	BUCHANAN, Keziah	03/20/1784
REID, William B.	BROWN, Edy H.	11/15/1825
RENO, John P.T.Dr.	WATSON, Susan E.	10/27/1838
RHOADES, John	BURCH, Amy	06/18/1822
RHODES, Noah	MEDLIN, Sidney	04/06/1827
RICE, Archibald	BUSH, Zibba(?)	02/02/1803
RICE, Archibald	YANCEY, Sally	07/06/1811
RICE, Archibald	RICHMOND, Sarah	07/22/1813
RICE, Edmond	RICE, Henrietta	12/05/1795
RICE, Edmond B.	SIMMONS, Margaret	10/19/1844
RICE, Edmund	BROWN, Martha	11/30/1814
RICE, Henry	SHELTON, Margaret	12/20/1798
RICE, Ibzan	TOTTEN, Emeline	12/13/1849
RICE, Ibzan	CARLOSS, Dolly G.	02/27/1796
RICE, Ibzan	BROOKS, Ursley	05/05/1824
RICE, Ibzan	BROOKS, Polly	12/08/1818
RICE, Iverson	GOMER, Nancy	10/23/1845
RICE, James	BRUCE, Nancy	11/03/1825
RICE, Jepthah	JOVET, Nancy	08/19/1784
RICE, Jeremiah	HARDEN, Elizabeth	10/14/1816
RICE, Jeremiah	HARRISON, Nancy	10/20/1843
RICE, Jeremiah	PERKINS, Mary A.	06/03/1851
RICE, John	-----, -----	12/23/1806
RICE, John	STARKEY, Elizabeth	12/21/1805
RICE, John	COBB, Mary	11/19/1844
RICE, John H.	PAGE, Jane	12/30/1845
RICE, Joshua M.	GUNN, Susanna	10/01/1806
RICE, Nathan	KING, Polly	01/19/1825
RICE, Nathan Jr.	POYNER, Sally	12/23/1801
RICE, Nathaniel	BUTLER, Susanna	01/29/1781
RICE, Nathaniel L.	RICE, Henrietta	12/23/1812
RICE, Solomon	SWIFT, Sarah S.	11/18/1826
RICE, Thomas	PARISH, Harriet	12/22/1828
RICE, Thomas B.	HIGHTOWER, Isabella	02/20/1847
RICE, William	CHOUNAN, Ester	12/21/1793
RICE, William	BROOKS, Susanna	12/20/1784
RICE, William H.	WALKER, Eliza	11/23/1841
RICE, William H.	MOORE, Sally	11/11/1852
RICE, William H.	GOOCH, Sarah	09/07/1795
RICE, Williamson	SIMMS, Zuriah(?)	01/09/1797
RICE, Zadok	LYNCH, Celia	02/27/1821
RICE, Zeri	MITCHELL, Mary	09/03/1782

MARRIAGE RECORDS OF CASWELL COUNTY, NORTH CAROLINA

GROOM	BRIDE	DATE
RICE, Ziba	BROWNING, Fanny	05/17/1806
RICHARDS, Durritt	MOORE, Polly	07/12/1802
RICHARDSON, George	MIMMS, Fanny	02/12/1866
RICHARDSON, James	PASS, Elizabeth	04/04/1803
RICHARDSON, James N.	STANDFIELD, Elizabeth A.	04/01/1856
RICHARDSON, Josiah	HEWELL, Elizabeth A.	12/31/1834
RICHARDSON, Robert P.	WATLINGTON, Mary E.	12/30/1850
RICHARDSON, Thomas	GATES, Obediance	01/10/1819
RICHARDSON, William	BURTON, Polly	08/28/1802
RICHHOND, Caleb H.	RAINEY, Ann S.	04/11/1830
RICHMOND, Bethel	LEA, Caroline	12/27/1866
RICHMOND, Caleb H.	DODSON, Mary R.	09/28/1838
RICHMOND, Calvin J.	COLLINS, Frances	12/23/1837
RICHMOND, Daniel	COMER, Nancy	12/16/1805
RICHMOND, David	FLINTOFF, Sarah	10/03/1867
RICHMOND, David	MCNIEL, Elizabeth	12/09/1834
RICHMOND, Franklin	FREEMAN, Charlotte	02/06/1867
RICHMOND, George T.	MOORE, Martha	03/15/1840
RICHMOND, Henry A.	EVANS, Elizabeth	04/10/1851
RICHMOND, James	BOMAN, Betsy	11/10/1802
RICHMOND, James D.	RICHMOND, Susan T.	06/01/1865
RICHMOND, Jesse	HUGHSTON, Elizabeth	12/29/1817
RICHMOND, John	MORTON, Nancy	12/21/1805
RICHMOND, John	LEA, Sarah	12/21/1799
RICHMOND, John	CURRIE, Mary	02/15/1802
RICHMOND, John C.	STEPHENS, Betsy	07/31/1821
RICHMOND, John Jr.	ROSE, Elizabeth A.	10/10/1827
RICHMOND, John L.	DAVIS, Mary A.	07/28/1839
RICHMOND, Joseph	CONNALLY, Anna	02/06/1804
RICHMOND, Joshua	ROBERTS, Phebe	01/04/1800
RICHMOND, Leonidas	LEA, Annis(?)	04/04/1859
RICHMOND, Thomas B.	BURTON, Susan	11/18/1833
RICHMOND, Tinsley	RICHMOND, Violet	01/12/1866
RICHMOND, William	WOODS, Margaret	10/01/1802
RICHMOND, William A.	GOLD, Mary	10/08/1829
RICHMOND, William D.	MARTIN, Sue F.	05/15/1862
RICHMOND, Willis M.	RICHMOND, Maranda	10/06/1846
RICHMOND, Yancey	MURPHEY, Harriet A.	07/08/1866
RICKMAN, John	RICKMAN, Agnes	11/13/1794
RIGGS, Aderson	MORGAN, Susan	11/25/----
RIGGS, Drusis	LONG, Mary	02/04/1812
RIGGS, George W.	RICHARDSON, Louisa	12/03/1846
RIGGS, George W.	BURKE, Fanny G.	08/19/1862
RIGGS, John	STEPHENS, Rebecca	12/19/1866
RIGGS, John	PHILLIPS, Ann	04/01/1840
RIGGS, Thomas	BRADSHER, Martha A.	12/20/1838
RIGGS, Thomas	RIGGS, Polly	12/22/1812
RIGGS, Thomas	REID, Eliza W.	11/26/1849
RILEY, Thomas W.	WARD, Nancy	12/27/1855
RIMARE, James W.	HOLMES, Malinda	02/19/1822
ROACH, William	HILL, Leanna	04/26/1860

MARRIAGE RECORDS OF CASWELL COUNTY, NORTH CAROLINA

GROOM	BRIDE	DATE
ROALING, William P.	HILL, Sarah F.	03/22/1860
ROAN, George	PHELPS, Delphia	03/29/1788
ROAN, James	MCADEN, Caroline	04/22/1867
ROAN, James	BURCH, Rita	07/01/1809
ROAN, James P.	ROAN, Sarah	08/27/1825
ROAN, James T.	FULLINGTON, Elizabeth	08/31/1826
ROAN, John	COMER, Fanny	12/14/1802
ROAN, Justin	LONG, Elizabeth G.	10/26/1836
ROAN, Nathaniel M.	HENDERSON, Mary B.	11/18/1835
ROAN, Thomas	PHELPS, Nancy	11/14/1782
ROAN, Weldon	EVANS, Fanny	11/05/1867
ROARK, Benjamin	HESTER, Sarah C.	05/03/1854
ROBBINS, Thomas J.	MUSE, Frances E.	04/19/1850
ROBENHISER, Robert R.	ANNMONETT, Rose E.	07/04/1866
ROBERDS, David	HAWKINS, Nancy A.	12/16/1858
ROBERSON, Christopher	PAYNE, Caty	12/17/1835
ROBERSON, Christopher	MILES, Polly	04/15/1830
ROBERSON, Pinckney	MCKINNEY, Lucy	01/31/1839
ROBERSON, Pleasant	DUDLY, Lucinda	01/04/1825
ROBERSON, Thomas	MILES, Fanny	11/20/1832
ROBERSON, William	STRADER, Lydia M.	12/29/1824
ROBERTS, Arthur	HARGIS, Nancy	03/25/1789
ROBERTS, David	MOORE, Ann	07/20/1790
ROBERTS, Elijah	DAVIS, Rebecca B.	11/04/1826
ROBERTS, Geo. W.	ALLEN, Arenia M.	01/02/1840
ROBERTS, George	BLACKWELL, Martha	03/01/1827
ROBERTS, George	WARREN, Betsy	01/13/1811
ROBERTS, Henry	PILES, Eliza	12/22/1836
ROBERTS, Humphrey	BROWNING, Elizabeth	01/23/1793
ROBERTS, James	WISDOM, Sally	11/02/1818
ROBERTS, James L.	LYON, Elizabeth F.	08/19/1857
ROBERTS, James L.	HENDRICKS, Martha	10/15/1856
ROBERTS, John	TAPLEY, Sally	12/28/1802
ROBERTS, John	GRIFFIN, Martha	04/30/1843
ROBERTS, John	BENTON, Polly	01/19/1846
ROBERTS, John R.L.	PARISH, Mary J.	12/07/1849
ROBERTS, Joshua	STEPHENS, Nancy	01/29/1820
ROBERTS, Laton T.	HARRIS, Susan S.	12/17/1833
ROBERTS, Levin	CARRELL, Nancy	11/14/1798
ROBERTS, Roland	BRINTLE, Polly	04/06/1829
ROBERTS, Roland W.	GOMER, Mary	12/24/1818
ROBERTS, Simon	HUDSON, Betsy	09/01/1798
ROBERTS, Step	BURGESS, Eleanor	01/22/1814
ROBERTS, Stephen	MITCHEL, Eleanor	08/13/1791
ROBERTS, Thomas	CANTREL, Sophia	01/01/1859
ROBERTS, Thomas	SWANN, Peggy	10/14/1812
ROBERTS, William A.	WATLINGTON, Mary C.	02/01/1859
ROBERTS, William H.	WILLIS, Nancy E.	12/17/1865
ROBERTS, William R.	WARD, Elizabeth J.	05/19/1852
ROBERTS, Zephanieh(?)	SMITH, Betsy	08/29/1822
ROBERTSON, Aaron P.	BROWNING, Ann	11/15/1838

MARRIAGE RECORDS OF CASWELL COUNTY, NORTH CAROLINA

GROOM	BRIDE	DATE
ROBERTSON, Albert G.	RUDD, Sarah J.	07/01/1866
ROBERTSON, Alex	HUNT, Hannah	11/12/1866
ROBERTSON, Edward	IRBY, Sarah	07/12/1856
ROBERTSON, Edward S.	YOUNG, Susan A.	12/10/1844
ROBERTSON, George W.B.	ALLEN, Sarah S.	08/02/1826
ROBERTSON, Green	MCKINNEY, Mary J.	09/30/1857
ROBERTSON, Green	RUDD, Margaret	01/02/1849
ROBERTSON, James	SMITH, Amanda	07/27/1854
ROBERTSON, Jesse	BOYLES, Mahala A.	06/10/1867
ROBERTSON, John	BAILEY, Glasshey(?)	12/25/1794
ROBERTSON, John	MOORE, Mary	04/03/1782
ROBERTSON, John	STOKES, Nanny	12/25/1866
ROBERTSON, John E.	MEBANE, Henrietta V.	06/12/1867
ROBERTSON, John M.	BURK, Nancy	11/29/1866
ROBERTSON, Joseph	DARBY, Margaret	09/02/1780
ROBERTSON, Thompson G.	PATTERSON, Martha A.	11/09/1854
ROBERTSON, William	REID, Silvey	04/20/1867
ROBERTSON, William A.	TOLLOH, Frances	05/05/1821
ROBERTTSON, Christopher	RUDDER, Mildred	02/05/1830
ROBESON, John	BAZWELL, Fanny	10/12/1784
ROBINSON, Jesse	GRIFFY, Ann	04/19/1785
ROBINSON, John	CAVANIS, Nancy	10/08/1816
ROBIRSON, John H.	SCOTT, Susanna	12/30/1853
ROBSON, J.W.	WORD, M.C.	11/13/1863
ROBSON, William	MCCAIN, Nancy	08/25/1817
ROBSON, William G.	MCCAIN, America L.	09/14/1865
RODDEN, James W.	HUGHES, Ann T.	09/27/1853
RODDEN, Spencer	HILL, Elizabeth	12/27/1821
RODGERS, R.S.	GWYNN, Permelia A.	12/05/1865
RODGERS, William M.	HILL, Lucinda B.	11/20/1856
ROE, Robert	BOZWELL, Kitty F.	05/08/1822
ROE, Robert	HOOPER, Polly	01/01/1817
ROGERS, Armistead	JOUIT, Susanna D.	06/11/1781
ROGERS, Bird	CLAY, Sarah	02/04/1785
ROGERS, John C.	SAMUEL, Patsy	03/09/1810
ROGERS, John Jr.	HARALSON, Jane	01/02/1785
ROGERS, William A.	ADAMS, Sarah J.	04/29/1842
ROHR, William M.	WEST, Judith	05/26/1830
ROLAND, Fendul	WALKER, Rachel	01/18/1790
ROLAND, Fendul	ADAMS, Elizabeth	01/16/1815
ROPER, David	LEWIS, Nancy	07/13/1801
ROPER, Henry	ELMORE, Polly	11/09/1832
ROPER, Henry	FARLEY, Rachel	10/04/1810
ROPER, James	ONEILL, Mary	03/27/1792
ROPER, William	YATES, Keziah	08/31/1781
ROPER, William F.	GUNN, Emily N.	08/15/1836
ROSE, Alexander Jr.	VANHOOK, Polly	04/03/1805
ROSE, Duncan Jr.	MCADEN, Sally M.	08/19/1799
ROSE, Howel S.	DURHAM, Mary	11/19/1829
ROSSON, Abner	POGUE, Fanny	02/20/1790
ROWARK, Elisha	BARNETT, Elizabeth	09/18/1804

MARRIAGE RECORDS OF CASWELL COUNTY, NORTH CAROLINA

GROOM	BRIDE	DATE
ROWARK, John	COMPTON, Elizabeth	09/26/1817
ROWARK, Larkin	EUBANK, Frances	03/03/1816
ROWLAND, Micajah	LEE, Ann	11/19/1812
ROYESTER, Thomas	HUGHS, Louisa R.	02/05/1833
RUARK, Edward	ARNETT, Margaret	11/03/1802
RUARK, Henry	WALKER, Jane	02/24/1816
RUARK, John	SMITH, Mimi	07/22/1811
RUARK, Samuel	RHOADES, Mary	08/03/1815
RUCKER, George G.	POPE, Mary R.	12/30/1850
RUDD, Aldridge	MURPHEY, Nancy	08/28/1824
RUDD, Alexander	SAWYER, Zibby	08/31/1842
RUDD, Bethel	LOVE, Dicy	01/31/1867
RUDD, David	JACKSON, Nancy F.	01/26/1846
RUDD, David	SMITH, Teby	12/25/1853
RUDD, Franklin G.	EVANS, Mary	11/21/1838
RUDD, Hezekiah	SARTIN, Mary	07/25/1848
RUDD, James	SWIFT, Sarah	04/30/1845
RUDD, James	BALL, Nancy	03/27/1812
RUDD, James C.	MASSEY, Mary A.	02/12/1857
RUDD, Jeremiah	EVANS, Susanna	01/02/1811
RUDD, Jeremiah Jr.	SAWYERS, Sarah	07/10/1837
RUDD, Jesse	RUDD, Judy	08/18/1866
RUDD, John S.	CHEEK, Cornelia A.	12/25/1866
RUDD, Joseph	CULBERSON, Tabitha	01/19/1824
RUDD, Joshua	CULBERSON, Susanna	02/24/1819
RUDD, Lorenzo D.	CHAMBERS, Arabella C.	02/03/1854
RUDD, Luther	STEPHENS, Sarah	06/21/1855
RUDD, Pleasant	BROWNING, Annise(?)	02/21/1822
RUDD, Rufus A.	PAGE, Frances	06/15/1846
RUDD, Thomas	MONTGOMERY, Elvira	11/19/1844
RUDD, Thomas H.	ALRED, Louisa E.	01/16/1866
RUDD, William	GOODSON, Rebecca	03/08/1809
RUDD, William	MANNING, Susanna	06/10/1805
RUDD, William H.	WILLIAMSON, Isabella	09/02/1866
RUDDER, Edward V.	FARLEY, Martha J.	04/02/1866
RULING, William T.	DAVIS, Sally E.	11/21/1867
RUNNELS, William	ELLIOT, Susan	06/17/1848
RUSSEL, Edward	BLAIR, Polly	01/09/1808
RUSSEL, Joseph	PAYNE, Caty	04/07/1815
RUSSELL, James	TORIAN, Mandy	12/19/1866
RUSSELL, John	BOHANNON, Rebecca	01/05/1815
RUSSELL, John A.	STANFIELD, Sarah J.	09/21/1844
RUSSELL, John P.	WATSON, Nancy A.	08/10/1863
RUSSELL, Joseph M.	HODGE, Louisa	04/05/1854
RUSSELL, William	WOMACK, Martha J.	07/27/1861
RUSSELL, William	SLADE, Isabella	05/29/1828
RUSSELL, William	NEAL, Cynthia A.	03/29/1859
RUSSELL, William F.	CARREL, Tabitha T.	11/24/1825
RUTHERFORD, John	HUBBARD, Polly	02/16/1782
RYAN, Charles J.	HARRISON, Mary E.	07/29/1843
SADLER, Benjamin	DUNAWAY, Lucy	03/02/1811

MARRIAGE RECORDS OF CASWELL COUNTY, NORTH CAROLINA

GROOM	BRIDE	DATE
SALMAN, William T.	ROBERTS, Eliza F.	12/24/1865
SALMON, Henry	WINTERS, Elizabeth	08/23/1824
SAMMAN, John	COLMON, Sucky	02/11/1815
SAMMONS, Branch	WOMACK, Susan A.	06/04/1842
SAMUEL, Anthony	WATERS, Anna	12/25/1786
SAMUEL, James Jr.	FISHER, Polly	11/15/1803
SAMUEL, Jeremiah	SAMUEL, Sally	12/30/1782
SAMUEL, Walker	SAMUEL, Lucy	12/29/1829
SAMUELL, Archibald	SAMUEL, Mary	03/13/1782
SAMUELL, Benjamin	SANDERS, Aggy	01/24/1785
SAMUELL, Harnden	ROPER, Jane F.	11/04/1815
SAMUELL, Josiah	SANDERS, Ann P.	02/27/1804
SAMUELL, Walker	SAMUELL, Judith	01/10/1811
SANDERS, Alves	SANDERS, Susan	11/04/1856
SANDERS, Alves	SOMERS, Susan	01/06/1845
SANDERS, Andrew	HUMPHREYS, Nancy	03/22/1830
SANDERS, James	BURGES, Elizabeth A.	09/23/1860
SANDERS, James	DIX, Polly	09/22/1809
SANDERS, James	BALLAD, Priscilla	11/19/1822
SANDERS, James M.	POTEAT, Nancy	11/23/1865
SANDERS, Jesse	SANDERS, Omah(?)	01/13/1838
SANDERS, Leroy	ROBERTS, Lucy A.	10/25/1858
SANDERS, Leroy	SANDERS, Polly	09/05/1832
SANDERS, Obadiah	FARLEY, Elizabeth	01/24/1786
SANDERS, Ranson P.	BEAVER, Delila	03/08/1832
SANDERS, Richard P.	CHANDLER, Mary J.	01/30/1847
SANDERS, Robert	ELAM, Verlinchey W.	07/06/1801
SANDERS, Robert	MURPHY, Susan	12/23/1861
SANDERS, Romulus M.	CARTER, Rebecca	12/21/1812
SANDERS, William	CUNINGHAM, Nancy	01/13/1795
SANDERS, William	BOULAND, Elizabeth	10/24/1863
SANDERS, Zepheniah	PAYNOR, Eleanor	08/25/1822
SANDRES, Zephaniah	ROE, Susanna	12/28/1821
SARGENT, Daniel	CARNY, Delphy	01/03/1780
SARGENT, Demsy	-----, -----	--/--/1815
SARGENT, Ephraim	HODGE, Elizabeth	07/25/1792
SARGENT, James	PHELPS, Rachel	08/04/1791
SARGENT, James	LOVE, Jane	10/02/1792
SARGENT, Stephen	LONG, Fanny	11/11/1786
SARTIN, Anslum	BEAVER, Frances	10/22/1834
SARTIN, Anslum E.	GIPSON, Elizabeth	07/30/1855
SARTIN, Ellis	ROLAND, Susan H.	08/30/1864
SARTIN, Moses R.	PAGE, Mary C.	10/11/1865
SATERFIELD, Isaac	YARBROUGH, Sarah	09/03/1782
SATERFIELD, William	WHEELER, Susanna	10/01/1791
SATTERFIELD, Amos	SAMUEL, Susanna	02/04/1805
SATTERFIELD, Anthony	PETERSON, Martha	12/27/1825
SATTERFIELD, Jesse	ALLIN, Elizabeth	05/16/1789
SATTERFIELD, R.A.	TURNER, Elizabeth F.	08/17/1859
SAUNDERS, Charles W.	UNDERWOOD, Sarah E.	12/27/1866
SAUNDERS, John	ROE, Sally P.	10/23/1820

MARRIAGE RECORDS OF CASWELL COUNTY, NORTH CAROLINA

GROOM	BRIDE	DATE
SAUNDERS, Reason C.	WOMACK, Mary A.	03/18/1842
SAUNDERS, Robert D.	CARTER, Missouri A.	08/17/1841
SAUNDERS, William	MARTIN, Frances	01/15/1825
SAUNDERS, William F.	FOSTER, Nancy J.	12/20/1855
SAUNERS, Drewry W.	TURNER, Louisa	12/22/1864
SAWYARS, Isaac O.	RICKETTES, Nancy D.	11/20/1839
SAWYER, Cary	COX, Agnes	06/26/1805
SAWYER, John	PALMER, Lucy A.	05/12/1845
SAWYER, John	CARTER, Mary P.	02/08/1799
SAWYER, John	MICHEL, Nancy	12/15/1807
SAWYER, John	MALORY, Nancy	04/30/1820
SAWYER, Levi	FAUCETT, Martha	12/14/1842
SAWYER, Robert	SIMMS, Alletha	01/23/1798
SAWYER, Stephen	PARRISH, Elizabeth	01/09/1816
SAWYER, Stephen	WEEDEN, Louisa	12/01/1818
SAWYER, Thomas	FAUCETT, Fanny	12/26/1832
SAWYER, William	MALLORY, Sally	01/02/1805
SAWYER, William	BENNATT, Lucy	10/08/1804
SAWYERS, Absalom	LOAFMAN, Ann	02/08/1808
SAWYERS, Henry	POWELL, Maria A.	02/22/1843
SAWYERS, John	ALLEN, Sally	12/31/1825
SAWYERS, Solomon	FARLER, Nancy	07/19/1823
SAWYERS, Willam	MITCHELL, Mirine(?)	12/06/1824
SAWYERS, William	KITCHEN, Elizabeth	01/11/1814
SCALES, Joseph A.	SWANN, Louisa A.	01/07/1850
SCARLETT, William	SIDDLE, Sarah	09/07/1829
SCOGGIN, William	RICE, Patsy	06/20/1804
SCOGGIN, William D.	FULLER, Frances	01/25/1830
SCOGGINS, Milton G.	STEVENS, Marth J.	01/11/1837
SCOGGINS, William H.	DAMERON, Martha A.	09/18/1852
SCOOGIN, Johnson	FULLER, Mary	04/07/1827
SCOTT, Allen	BENNETT, America	03/30/1823
SCOTT, Asa	SHALTON, Patsy	12/--/1812
SCOTT, Azariah	PAGE, Deborah	05/03/1837
SCOTT, Bartlett	ROBERTS, Barshaba	01/14/1824
SCOTT, Daniel	CANNON, Darcas	12/21/1811
SCOTT, David	DODSON, Emily	06/09/1853
SCOTT, German	HOLLOWAY, Sally	06/08/1799
SCOTT, Harry	HARRISON, Sarah	05/23/1798
SCOTT, James	RICE, Polly	07/02/1806
SCOTT, James M.	COBB, Cinthia	12/07/1840
SCOTT, Jesse M.	MALONE, Senia	07/25/1833
SCOTT, John	WATLINGTON, Mary	12/17/1823
SCOTT, John	BEAVER, Mary	12/22/1789
SCOTT, John	JEFFREYS, Mary	10/28/1816
SCOTT, John H.	MARTIN, Malinda	07/08/1836
SCOTT, John J.	MCKINNEY, Martha J.	07/05/1860
SCOTT, John W.	BURNETT, Ann	05/01/1855
SCOTT, John W.	WATLINGTON, Mary A.	07/21/1849
SCOTT, Miles	MILES, Rody	06/08/1808
SCOTT, Pleasant	MCKINNEY, Susan	06/05/1851

MARRIAGE RECORDS OF CASWELL COUNTY, NORTH CAROLINA

GROOM	BRIDE	DATE
SCOTT, Richard	CORDER, Fanny	12/10/1797
SCOTT, Robert	VOWELL, Susan	01/25/1832
SCOTT, Robert	VAUGHN, Patsy	02/15/1800
SCOTT, William	SCOTT, Rachel	03/11/1786
SCOTT, William	HARPER, Rebecca	06/22/1814
SCOTT, William	MASON, Elizabeth	11/08/1824
SCOTT, William	PUCKETT, Polly	09/30/1826
SCOTT, William	MASON, Betsy	05/02/1827
SEAMORE, Singleton	SEAMORE, Susan	01/27/1820
SEARCY, Alexander M.	COOK, Elizabeth L.	06/13/1848
SEED, Thomas	JONES, Nancy	12/09/1818
SEEWELL, Robert W.	DONOHO, Cornelia A.	01/08/1838
SELLEARS, William	SWIFT, Nancy	08/19/1836
SERGANT, Stephen	RICHARDSON Nancy P.	01/01/1828
SERTAIN, Elisha	PASCHAEL, Frances	12/08/1840
SERTAIN, Johnston	BERRY, Nancy	07/20/1830
SETTLE, Joshua	GRAVES, Frances L.	06/03/1826
SETTLE, Thomas	GRAVES, Henrietta	09/18/1820
SEYMOUR, Robert	DUTY, Amy	01/28/1784
SHACKLEFORD, Abraham	GARLAND, Lucinda	08/25/1866
SHACKLEFORD, Armstead	HALCOMB, Nancy	10/24/1786
SHACKLEFORD, Francis	DAVIS, Ann	12/10/1819
SHACKLEFORD, Francis A.	HARRIS, Elizabeth A.	09/30/1857
SHACKLEFORD, John	KEEN, Nancy	12/08/1815
SHACKLEFORD, William	EDWARDS, Mary E.	09/21/1867
SHAMAN, William	EDWARDS, Fanny	03/08/1791
SHAMAN, (?) Charles	EDWYN, Milly	10/31/1794
SHAMAN, (?) Charles	EDWYN, Milly	10/31/1794
SHANKS, Charles	STREET, Sally	01/05/1798
SHANKS, Joseph	ROBERSON, Mary	01/18/1832
SHANKS, Thomas	MEANS, Poly	01/09/1799
SHANKS, Thomas Jr.	ROBERSON, Hannah	08/02/1828
SHANNON, William R.	INGRAM, Sarah E.	07/15/1858
SHANON, Marcus	SHAW, Letta	01/02/1837
SHAPARD, John J.	WATTS, Martha S.	02/11/1867
SHAPARD, Louisa	NICHOLSON, Martha	11/22/1796
SHAPPARD, James	BROOKS, Frances	08/30/1797
SHARMAN, William	EDWYN, Polly	08/17/1799
SHARP, George	HAMLETON, Polly	11/25/1811
SHARP, William T.	HARRISON, Ann S.	11/07/1837
SHAW, James	GIBSON, Elizabeth	05/28/1783
SHAW, James	PENDERGRASS, Mary	01/09/1786
SHAW, John S.	WOODS, Martha	02/15/1848
SHAW, John W.	VAUGHAN, Nancy	11/16/1847
SHAW, Joseph M.	HUGHS, Elizabeth A.	12/04/1857
SHAW, Nathaniel	COX, Suckey	10/11/1800
SHAW, Samuel	WALKER, Sarah	09/23/1867
SHEARMAN, Thomas	BURCH, Sarah	12/11/1800
SHEARMAN, (?) Charles	EDWYN, Milly	10/31/1794
SHEARMAN, (?) Charles	EDWYN, Milly	10/31/1794
SHELTON, David	VAUGHN, Susan	06/03/1784

MARRIAGE RECORDS OF CASWELL COUNTY, NORTH CAROLINA

GROOM	BRIDE	DATE
SHELTON, F. L. R.	THOMAS, Martha A. E.	11/17/1849
SHELTON, Henry	HARRIS, Temperance	08/02/1815
SHELTON, James F.	SHELTON, Mary A. M.	04/24/1843
SHELTON, James W.	JONES, Mary A.	02/09/1841
SHELTON, James W.	MARTIN, Martha C.	04/04/1848
SHELTON, John	BRADLEY, Susan	05/13/1780
SHELTON, Peter	MURPHEY, Sena	06/05/1838
SHELTON, Samuel E.	MCCAIN, Mary	08/04/1846
SHELTON, W. N.	JOHNSTON, Fanny	01/20/1863
SHELTON, William	SWIFT, Betsy	12/25/1809
SHELTON, William H.	GATEWOOD, Frances	11/27/1812
SHIELDS, Doctor P.	TALLY, Eliza E.	08/29/1864
SHIELDS, John	DUPREY, Christina	01/12/1820
SHIELDS, Johnson	SIKES, Mary	10/10/1826
SHIELDS, Thomas R.	HUBBARD, Martha	02/28/1867
SHORT, James	TENNESSON, Creasy	12/25/1800
SHREVE, Robert	SUMMERS, Elizabeth	02/14/1854
SHREVE, Robert D.	COX, Sally	12/19/1866
SHRYER, Jacob	BENNATT, Nancy	01/13/1810
SIBLEY, James W.	STANFIELD, Ann M.	05/28/1862
SIDDALL, Ira	SMITH, Polly	11/02/1802
SIDDALL, Job	HUDSON, Sarah	08/17/1791
SIDEBOTTOM, James H.	HENDERSON, Julia A.	07/02/1832
SIDEBOTTOM, James H.	MIMS, Mary A.	10/04/1832
SIMKINS, Nathan	SIMMONS, Lydia	08/13/1807
SIMMONS, Abraham	BARTON, Sally	03/06/1813
SIMMONS, Elisha	BIRKE, Frances	11/25/1845
SIMMONS, George	BARTON, Ann	12/16/1797
SIMMONS, James	BUSH, Avicey	03/08/1812
SIMMONS, James	ROBERTS, Stacy	09/05/1791
SIMMONS, John	THOMAS, Martha	12/19/1835
SIMMONS, John	BUSH, Rhody	11/15/1809
SIMMONS, John	SIMMONS, Nancy	12/15/1840
SIMMONS, Joseph B.	MCNUTT, Elizabeth L.	10/16/1854
SIMMONS, Levi	JACKSON, Elisha	12/16/1832
SIMMS, Buckner	WHITLOCK, Nancy	10/20/1784
SIMPKINS, Meldon	LAUGHINGHOUSE Melinda	02/07/1856
SIMPSON, Alvis	RICH, Nancy V.	12/20/1859
SIMPSON, Benjamin F.	HIGHTOWER, Martha P.	10/13/1843
SIMPSON, Charles	CANNON, Jemima	07/15/1841
SIMPSON, Dennis	BOULDEN, Jane	08/18/1866
SIMPSON, Enoch	CARTER, Elizabeth	12/29/1818
SIMPSON, Fracis L.	SIMPSON, Priscilla	12/16/1815
SIMPSON, George	BARKER, Elizabeth	12/11/1830
SIMPSON, James H.	SMITH, Martha A.	05/25/1858
SIMPSON, John C.	GATWOOD, Martha G.	10/03/1849
SIMPSON, John H.	SNIPES, Elizabeth L.	11/08/1853
SIMPSON, Joseph	ANDERSON, Susan B.	12/12/1843
SIMPSON, Moses	TRACEY, Jenny M.	11/23/1809
SIMPSON, Moses	SMITH, Jane	11/04/1833
SIMPSON, Moses S.	FLORENCE, Delphey	10/22/1804

MARRIAGE RECORDS OF CASWELL COUNTY, NORTH CAROLINA

GROOM	BRIDE	DATE
SIMPSON, Oliver	RICE, Betsy	03/10/1810
SIMPSON, Richard	DURHAM, Jane	12/19/1860
SIMPSON, Richard Jr.	SIMPSON, Susan	02/02/1807
SIMPSON, Roger	WILLIAMSON, Peggy	12/27/1808
SIMPSON, Silas	BOLEY, A. M. F. P.	05/08/1844
SIMPSON, Solomon	HUNTER, Elizabeth	11/17/1813
SIMPSON, Thomas T.	HODGES, Martha W.	11/21/1848
SIMPSON, Vinson	HUSKINS, Mary	02/16/1826
SIMS, John	WRIGHT, Polly	10/18/1791
SIMS, William B.	RICHMOND, Sally L.	05/20/1858
SIMSON, William	DOWELL, Nancy	07/17/1788
SINGLETON, Jerry	BENTON, Cary	04/11/1801
SINGLETON, Joseph	KITCHEN, Elizabeth	12/23/1824
SINGLETON, Robert	ROBERTS, Kitty	12/11/1816
SINGLETON, William A.	CATES, Nancy	03/26/1855
SKEEN, Jonathan	SARGENT, Elizabeth	01/14/1792
SKEEN, Peter	SARGANT, Sarah	10/15/1782
SLADE, Abisha	GRAVES, Mary	04/23/1846
SLADE, Abisha	HARRISON, Polly K.	01/05/1826
SLADE, Elias	TURNER, Elizabeth	04/11/1825
SLADE, Ezekiel	HUBBARD, Mary	01/17/1798
SLADE, James M.	JONES, Priscilla	01/16/1866
SLADE, John R.	MCCAIN, Betty A.	05/27/1863
SLADE, John T.	WALTERS, Martha A.	05/26/1866
SLADE, Joshua	GOMER, Jane	07/22/1815
SLADE, Lemuel	SMITH, Betsy	04/02/1867
SLADE, Nathan	YANCEY, Elizabeth	06/26/1792
SLADE, Robert	SLADE, Margaret	11/30/1867
SLADE, Thomas	TABER, Elizabeth	01/30/1823
SLADE, Thomas Jr.	GRAVES, Isabella	12/12/1782
SLADE, Thomas Jr.	WILLIAMS, Mary	11/22/1779
SLADE, Thomas T.	COBB, Emeline	05/09/1849
SLADE, William	REID, Sarah	12/23/1856
SLADE, William	KERR, Martha	12/22/1786
SLADE, William	TURNER, Mary	11/22/1820
SLADE, William G.	HENDRICK, Adelaide R.	11/22/1854
SLATE, Richard J.	NEWBELL, Parthena E.	11/03/1841
SLAYDON, William W.	ROWLAND, Mary R.	12/02/1833
SLAYTE, James H.	WELDON, Marthany	08/05/1829
SLAYTON, James	PARSONS, Mary	10/20/1849
SLAYTON, Richard	RUSSELL, Rebecca	12/10/1853
SLEDGE, Crawford D.	NEAL, Mary P.	02/03/1863
SLEDGE, John P.	CLAY, Elizabeth	11/17/1823
SLEDGE, Littleton	RAY, Susanna	11/24/1821
SMALES, Thomas	DEANE, Mary	11/06/1841
SMITH, Abenego	YARBROUGH, Matilda	04/22/1867
SMITH, Amasa	BAZWELL, Susanna	04/02/1811
SMITH, Andrew H.	MURPHY, Lucinda	12/19/1846
SMITH, Clement	COBB, Sarah	01/11/1850
SMITH, Daniel	POLSTON, Elizabeth	12/08/1804
SMITH, Daniel	HINTON, Polly	12/12/1842

MARRIAGE RECORDS OF CASWELL COUNTY, NORTH CAROLINA

GROOM	BRIDE	DATE
SMITH, Daniel	HUBBARD, Sally	01/09/1810
SMITH, Edmond	WILSON, Silvia	12/28/1866
SMITH, Elijah R.	THOMAS, Frances	12/14/1854
SMITH, Ewell	CRUISE, Elizabeth	11/06/1826
SMITH, Francis	WILLIS, Betsy	10/21/1802
SMITH, Gardner	JONES, Milly	11/02/1822
SMITH, Garnett	SAWYERS, Betsy	04/20/1810
SMITH, George	JACKSON, Sally	08/14/1807
SMITH, George	TAIT, Jenny	12/20/1800
SMITH, Green	BURCH, Parthenia	01/08/1820
SMITH, Green	THORNTON, Fanny	09/22/1866
SMITH, Green D.	BOLTON, Leony	09/01/1819
SMITH, Henderson	CHANDLER, Polly C.	11/24/1828
SMITH, Henry	CARTER, Martha	12/13/1818
SMITH, Henry	POWELL, Mary J.	03/17/1840
SMITH, James	WHITMORE, Sally	06/08/1825
SMITH, James	CULBERSON, Sarah	10/06/1778
SMITH, James	FAUCETT, Ann	02/18/1833
SMITH, James C.	HAWKINS, Sarah J.	07/25/1867
SMITH, James M.	POTEAT, Liley A.	08/07/1859
SMITH, James M.	FARMER, Mary J.	09/30/1848
SMITH, James T.	HERNDON, Elizabeth	12/21/1832
SMITH, James T.	WARREN, Mehala	05/23/1850
SMITH, Jeremiah	ROWE, Mary	11/13/1835
SMITH, Jerry	RUDD, Mary A.	12/27/1855
SMITH, Jesse S.	GRAVES, Margaret J.	03/15/1853
SMITH, John	HUBARD, Virginia	12/07/1854
SMITH, John	STARKY, Rebecca	11/09/1803
SMITH, John	MERRITT, Susanna	01/02/1824
SMITH, John	PERSONS, Helena	10/07/1826
SMITH, John C.	BROWNING, Ava P.	04/26/1845
SMITH, John H.	DAMERON, Nancy	04/24/1862
SMITH, John R.	CONNALLY, Priscilla H.	12/22/1852
SMITH, John W.	WADE, Elizabeth D.	02/21/1866
SMITH, Jonathan	WILLIS, Nancy	02/09/1822
SMITH, Joseph	PARKS, Celia	11/08/1827
SMITH, Lea A.	COLE, Sarah F.	08/10/1866
SMITH, Mace	BROWN, Constant	08/12/1782
SMITH, Mace	COLESTON, Margaret	11/18/1780
SMITH, Maurice	REED, Clarissa H.	04/27/1830
SMITH, Moses	KELLY, Margaret	07/30/1794
SMITH, Nicholas C.	SANDERS, Ann	11/02/1832
SMITH, Peter	APPLE, Mary F.	03/08/1865
SMITH, Reuben	KEMP, Elizabeth	03/01/1818
SMITH, Richard	ANGLIN, Sally	10/26/1804
SMITH, Richard	GIBSON, Sophia	11/03/1815
SMITH, Richard S.	MOORE, Blanche A.	12/26/1866
SMITH, Robert	COLE, Mary W.	08/06/1783
SMITH, Robert	DANIEL, Martha	05/29/1815
SMITH, Robert	MATLOCK, Leathy	11/17/1846
SMITH, Robert J.	WILLIAMSON, Corneila A.	04/15/1840

MARRIAGE RECORDS OF CASWELL COUNTY, NORTH CAROLINA

GROOM	BRIDE	DATE
SMITH, Robt. H.	DICKSON, Charlotte	03/04/1862
SMITH, Sam P.	LAWSON, Kate	10/22/1860
SMITH, Samuel	WILLIAMSON, Elizabeth	11/09/1812
SMITH, Samuel	BROWNING, Frances	11/13/1826
SMITH, Samuel Jr.	HARRISON, Elizabeth	04/23/1792
SMITH, Samuel R. Jr.	TUCK, Louisania C.	10/20/1836
SMITH, Solomon	HASTIN, Peggy	01/04/1816
SMITH, Starkey	BRINSFIELD, Sarah	12/19/1814
SMITH, Stephen	PAYNE, Martha	10/16/1827
SMITH, Stephen	JOHNSTON, Fanny	09/02/1812
SMITH, Thomas	ATKINS, Mildred	11/27/1804
SMITH, Thomas	JOPLING, Catherine	04/04/1815
SMITH, Thomas B.	RICHMOND, Hulday A.	06/02/1860
SMITH, Thomas H.	BURNETTE, Martha J.	01/20/1841
SMITH, Vincen M.	DAVIS, Elizabeth	01/01/1866
SMITH, William	WILSON, Betsy A.	06/28/1832
SMITH, William	WALKER, Elizabeth	10/20/1816
SMITH, William	POSTON, Betsy	06/28/1800
SMITH, William	MALONE, Tempy	09/07/1819
SMITH, William	FORD, Phebe	01/27/1814
SMITH, William	HIGHTOWER, Sarah	01/04/1800
SMITH, William A.	SMITH, Isabella	02/06/1833
SMITH, William B.	MILES, Nancy	12/22/1859
SMITH, William H.	DAMERON, Mary	02/15/1856
SMITH, William P.	BARNES, Fanny M.	11/07/1865
SMITH, Willis B.	PHELPS, Lucy	11/11/1794
SMITH, Zion	DOUGLASS, Mary	12/15/1840
SMITHEY, John	PAYNE, Betsy	08/13/1805
SMITHEY, John	KERMICHAEL, Sarah	11/18/1798
SMITHEY, Reuben	WALKER, Elizabeth	02/04/1840
SMITHEY, Reuben	ROBERTS, Polly	05/19/1802
SMITHEY, Samuel	GROOM, Martha	01/14/1841
SMITHEY, Thomas	PASCHALL, Polly	08/03/1837
SMITHEY, Thomas	GOMER, Amy	10/30/1838
SMITHY, John	PARSCHALL, Sarah	02/05/1842
SMYTHE, Samuel	WARRIN, Nancy	03/17/1787
SNEAD, Benjamin	HALL, Martha A.	02/24/1853
SNEAD, Micajah	BRANDON, Judith	10/24/1792
SNEAD, Wm. L.	RICHARDSON, Mary S.	12/08/1849
SNEED, Archibal	COVINGTON, Frances	12/23/1846
SNEED, John	LANGHORN, Elizabeth	04/26/1841
SNEED, William H.	CALLOWAY, Belverderrie F.	10/17/1832
SNEED, William M.	BETHEL, Louisa N.	06/28/1842
SNIPES, Cato	WALKER, Jane	01/30/1867
SNIPES, James C.	SWIFT, Emeline	05/27/1847
SNIPES, James L.	MCMULLIN, Margaret	12/20/1837
SNIPES, Nathaniel	KIMBROUGH, Tabitha	06/16/1801
SNOW, Richard	ADKINS, Caroline	08/11/1845
SNOW, Stephen T.	LOVELACE, Nancy F.	02/15/1866
SOMERS, Alfred	MIMS, Sarah F.	05/05/1858
SOMERS, Henry	POWELL, Susan	10/21/1866

MARRIAGE RECORDS OF CASWELL COUNTY, NORTH CAROLINA

GROOM	BRIDE	DATE
SOMERS, James	SMITHEY, Elizabeth	12/17/1846
SOMERS, James	GILLASPEY, Viney	01/30/1806
SOMERS, John	BEAVERS, Mildred	11/11/1843
SOMERS, John	WRIGHT, Rebecca	07/25/1804
SOMERS, Reuben T.	SMITHY, Martha E.	04/08/1867
SOMERS, William	SARTIN, Mary A.	11/12/1852
SOMERS, Zeary	BERREY, Nancy	07/20/1844
SOMERS, Zera	PASKELL, Sarah	02/22/1837
SOMMERS, William	BUTLER, Frances	01/11/1853
SOUTHARD, John	LOVELACE, Nelly	12/22/1840
SOUTHARD, William	DURHAM, Susan	04/14/1845
SOUTHARD, William	FULLER, Malinda	10/24/1840
SOUTHARD, William	CARTER, Mary	02/08/1848
SOWELL, Thomas L.	MITCHELL, Nancy S.	06/01/1830
SOWELL, Thomas L.	MUZZAL, Frances	01/21/1819
SPARKS, Milton	COOK, Martha	09/28/1847
SPARKS, Thomas	MCCULLEY, Nancy	07/08/1817
SPENCER, Daniel	DAVIS, Susanna	12/31/1804
SPENCER, John	KEER, Ann	07/26/1781
SPENCER, Thomas	MITCHELL, Polly	02/21/1796
SPRUCE, George	WHITE, Milly A.	05/08/1858
ST JOHN, Abraham	MURRY, Franky	09/26/1806
STACE, Malon	SPENCER, Mary	04/09/1787
STACEY, Eli	SPENCER, Elizabeth	12/23/1789
STACY, John	HIGHTOWER, Frances	05/19/1828
STACY, Thomas	BENTON, Deborah	07/30/1816
STADLER, John	ARNOLD, Nancy	12/13/1812
STADLER, John J.	CALDNOND, Susan A.	10/28/1860
STADLER, John T.	GOOCH, Arrena	01/02/1844
STADLER, Robert D.	BROWNING, Nancy M.	08/10/1862
STADLER, Robert D.	ARNOLD, Lydia F.	12/03/1838
STADLER, William B.	ALDRIDGE, Artila	10/20/1840
STAFFORD, Adam	RUDD, Boza	12/25/1809
STAFFORD, Adam	PETERSON, Nancy	09/07/1790
STAFFORD, Eli	MORGAN, Nancy	12/26/1807
STAFFORD, James	LEA, Sally	12/30/1817
STAFFORD, James	ESKRIDGE, Polly	05/08/1799
STAFFORD, John	JOHNSTON, Ann	07/29/1800
STAFFORD, John	QUINE, Betsy	06/13/1791
STAFFORD, Joseph	WHITLOW, Nancy	06/09/1809
STAFFORD, Samuel	CARMAN, Mary	08/02/1796
STAFFORD, Thomas	WHITLOW, Fanny	02/23/1791
STAFFORD, William	JOHNSTON, Sally	08/15/1793
STAINBACK, William H.	SIDDLE, Parthena	08/20/1841
STALCUP, William	LEA, Cornelia K.	07/06/1847
STALLCUP, Austin	PLEASENT, Betsy	09/24/1802
STALLCUP, John	PLEASENT, Sylvia	01/30/1801
STAMPS, James	LEWIS, Milly	05/18/1867
STAMPS, Jno.	SLADE, Nancy	01/13/1808
STAMPS, Rufus	MOORE, Martha F.	06/17/1845
STAMPS, Samuel	WILSON, Dafney	12/01/1866

MARRIAGE RECORDS OF CASWELL COUNTY, NORTH CAROLINA

GROOM	BRIDE	DATE
STAMPS, Thomas	WALKER, Eliza A.	03/16/1842
STAMPS, William	LINDSEY, Dorcas	12/27/1867
STAMPS, William	PINIX, Sarah	11/20/1825
STANDFIELD, Harrison	MCGHEE, Sarah	03/31/1789
STANDLEY, Allen	JONES, Selley	07/24/1838
STANDLEY, Will R.	TRAVIS, Eliza A.	07/04/1844
STANELY, James	BROWN, Tabitha J.	05/31/1852
STANFIELD, Benjamin F.	JOHNSTON, Sarah P.	09/05/1825
STANFIELD, David V.	BRADSHER, Frances C.	08/01/1850
STANFIELD, Durret	WARREN, Lucy	12/18/1797
STANFIELD, Jno.	ROBINSON, Patsy	03/24/1800
STANFIELD, Joseph M.	BARKETT, Ann	05/26/1836
STANFIELD, Mark M.	CARTER, Martha M.	04/24/1849
STANFIELD, Marmaduke	SAMUEL, Ann	08/26/1795
STANFIELD, William	BEADLES, Elizabeth	12/14/1789
STANFIELD, William A.	READ, Mary	05/04/1854
STANLEY, Alfred M.	DONOHO, Emily	09/18/1843
STANLEY, Alpheus	MCKINNEY, Mary F.	11/18/1858
STANLEY, James	SCOTT, Delila	06/09/1840
STANLEY, Joel	DUNCAN, Lucy	03/13/1824
STANSBERY, Samuel	HIX, Hannah	10/07/1786
STANSBURY, Luke	HADDOCK, Nancy	01/30/1791
STANSBURY, Luke	ROBERTS, Comfort	05/16/1788
STARKES, Chesley	HARRISON, Euphranier	11/24/1846
STARKEY, John	SAWYERS, Nancy	09/27/1790
STARKEY, Thomas	ROBERTS, Frances	01/22/1829
STAULCUP, Levi	JONES, Catherine L.	06/12/1843
STEGALL, Durell	NELSON, Harriet	12/18/1850
STEP, Joshua	DOLLERHIDE, Nice	02/06/1789
STEPHENS, Alfred	LONG, Hannah	11/10/1866
STEPHENS, Andrew W.	CHAMBERS, Ann	02/27/1840
STEPHENS, Anthony Jr.	THOMAS, Diana	09/22/1837
STEPHENS, Armstead	KIERSEY, Lucy	12/24/1835
STEPHENS, Benjamin	ROBERTS, Polly	01/25/1803
STEPHENS, Benjamin	MALONE, Sally	06/19/1822
STEPHENS, Benjamin A.	BRANDON, Mary	12/--/1858
STEPHENS, C.	WEIRE, Betty J.	01/06/1866
STEPHENS, George	GOING, Rhoda	07/28/1806
STEPHENS, George	EVANS, Ann	09/08/1866
STEPHENS, Henry	THOMAS, Dicy	08/03/1835
STEPHENS, Isaac	HARVILLE, Eliza	04/12/1838
STEPHENS, Isaac	MUSTION, Sinai(?)	02/22/1849
STEPHENS, Iverson G.	FRASIER, Jane	08/21/1834
STEPHENS, James	DRUMMOND, Joanna	01/31/1817
STEPHENS, John	STANLEY, Nancy	04/22/1830
STEPHENS, John Q.	MELONE, Mary A.	12/13/1837
STEPHENS, Matt	COMER, Jenett	09/08/1866
STEPHENS, Peter	GARLAND, Eliza A.	07/07/1846
STEPHENS, Peter	SCOTT, Frances	03/18/1850
STEPHENS, Thomas	LEGRAND, Mary	09/07/1838
STEPHENS, Thomas	WARWICK, Elizabeth	02/04/1788

MARRIAGE RECORDS OF CASWELL COUNTY, NORTH CAROLINA

GROOM	BRIDE	DATE
STEPHENS, William	SLADE, Nancy	12/01/1866
STEPHENS, William	WATTERFIELD, Polly	10/09/1816
STEPHENS, Williamson M.	STEPHENS, Barbara	11/16/1844
STEVENS, George	RICHARDSON, Susan	08/19/1830
STEVENS, Henry	HAMLETT, Caroline	04/06/1867
STEVENS, Thomas L.	FARLEY, Martha J.	07/23/1832
STEVENS, William	NOWEL, Mary	01/04/1789
STEVENS, William	HUGHS, Rosetta	06/11/1859
STEVENS, William	EVENS, Jane	07/26/1855
STEWARD, Littleton	STEWARD, Betsy	12/11/1838
STEWART, Anderson	FARMER, Martha	02/26/1865
STEWART, Barzillai	ROAN, Nancy	11/04/1833
STEWART, Mack	BOLTON, Candis	12/26/1866
STOANE, Thomas	GREER, Elizabeth	08/19/1793
STOCKES, Moore	BAXDALE, Nancy	10/22/1817
STOKES, Allen	STOKES, Mary	02/23/1829
STOKES, Jesse	MEADOWS, Betty	11/12/1866
STOKES, Joel A.	PAYNE, Elizabeth C.	10/07/1836
STOKES, John Y.	STONE, Susan A.C.	04/05/1866
STOKES, Sylvanus	GATEWOOD, Nancy	12/25/1809
STOKES, William Y.	HATCHETT, Lucy W.	10/28/1836
STOKES, William Y.	KEESEE, Louisa T.	12/18/1829
STONE, Eli C.	BURNS, Sarah A.	05/30/1840
STONE, John F.	FURGUSON, Mary E.	03/10/1853
STONE, Thomas R.	HENDERSON, Priscilla M.	04/24/1849
STONE, William M.	ESTES, Mary F.	11/23/1855
STOW, Henry C.	HART, Mildred A.	09/20/1855
STOWERS, John	BEAVER, Catherine	01/29/1810
STRADER, Christian	BURNS, Eveline	02/20/1844
STRADER, David	WALF, Lucy A.E.	12/14/1856
STRADER, Henry	SCOTT, Polly	03/16/1784
STRADER, James	STONE, Ann	05/27/1849
STRADER, Jeremiah	CHAPMAN, Ann	01/30/1845
STRADER, John	SCARLET, Mary A.	06/04/1863
STRADOR, Christian Jr.	LOVELACE, Lucinda	09/19/1827
STRADOR, David	DILL, Hannah	05/31/1841
STRADOR, John	ROLLEY, Martha	12/23/1822
STRADOR, Obediah	FULLER, Mary	01/29/1838
STRATEN, William	BALDEN, Delila	01/31/1825
STRATEN, William	KENNON, Polly	01/21/1824
STRATEN, William	BAWLDIN, Delia	12/23/1823
STRATTON, John C.	BURNS, Lenora E.	06/27/1855
STRATTON, John D.	WEST, Ann	12/04/1829
STREET, Anthony	GRAY, Polly	06/18/1803
STREET, John	VINCENT, Ann	12/15/1798
STRICKLAND, Edwin C.	SPARROW, C.G.	10/19/1856
STROTHER, Peter	BAXTER, Maryann	06/11/1788
STUART, Edward G.	CRUISE, Sarah	11/06/1826
STUART, John	ROAN, Asanath	07/15/1815
STUART, Stephen	HUGHSTON, Anna	09/12/1812
STUART, William	WISDOM, Rachel	07/23/1802

MARRIAGE RECORDS OF CASWELL COUNTY, NORTH CAROLINA

GROOM	BRIDE	DATE
STUBBLEFIELD, Beverly	WILLSON, Rebecca	10/07/1826
STUBBLEFIELD, George W.	LAWSON, Sally	08/12/1817
STUBBLEFIELD, Nathan	TODD, Elizabeth	11/06/1794
STUBBLEFIELD, Peyton T.	NUNNALLY, Mary P.	10/27/1832
STUBBLEFIELD, Richard C.	RICE, Eliza	06/08/1832
STUBBLEFIELD, William	MABREY, Mary	12/18/1778
STUBLEFIELD, Barnett	BROWN, Emily	11/27/1866
STUBLEFIELD, Solomon	MITCHELL, Caty	12/25/1867
SUIT, John	BOWLS, Sarah	12/22/1789
SUIT, William	WILSON, Rebecca	05/28/1787
SULLVENT, Jordan	GOMER, Polly	12/23/1805
SUMERS, John	WALKER, Jemima	09/02/1824
SUMERS, John	GIMBOE, Mary	07/02/1783
SUMERS, Pharo	PASCHALL, Eliza	11/05/1841
SUMMERS, Andrew	SWIFT, Mary H.	03/18/1833
SUMMERS, George	SMITH, Manerva	09/12/1855
SUTHEN, Zachariah	CHAPMAN, Nancy	12/18/1847
SWAN, Daniel W.	MARLOW, Nancy	12/14/1826
SWANN, Burch	YATES, Dolly	04/09/1808
SWANN, Edward	YATES, Joyce	04/20/1782
SWANN, Geo.	SWANN, Adaline	11/08/1866
SWANN, James	MARLER, Sally	04/08/1820
SWANN, James	DARBY, Elizabeth	08/17/1816
SWANN, John	WALKER, Polly	11/25/1803
SWANN, John M.	VOSS, Sarah E.	02/22/1852
SWANN, Joseph	WILLSON, Agnes	01/03/1787
SWANN, Joseph	HIGHTOWER, Betsy	10/20/1818
SWANN, Joseph	PATTERSON, Fanny	01/17/1811
SWANN, William	ATWELL, Peggy	12/24/1807
SWANN, William W.	PATTERSON, Cassandra	10/20/1843
SWAYNEY, James	BURFORD, Judith	10/02/1780
SWEPSON, Elijah	VERNON, Narcissa	02/24/1866
SWEPSON, George W.	YANCEY, Virginia B.	11/23/1842
SWIFT, Alex	GUNN, Bell	09/23/1867
SWIFT, Anthony	BROWN, Elizabeth	08/19/1784
SWIFT, George A.	RUDD, Elizabeth	12/14/1847
SWIFT, George R.	HOOPER, Elizabeth	03/18/1852
SWIFT, Harvy	ELMORE, Polly	10/09/1819
SWIFT, John	HAGGARD, Lydia	06/26/1792
SWIFT, John	MOTT, Phebe M.	05/04/1815
SWIFT, Joseph M.	LOWNS, Isabella C.	11/18/1856
SWIFT, Richard	MOSS, Catherine	11/02/1787
SWIFT, Robert	SIDDLE, Nancy	12/17/1825
SWIFT, Thomas	COX, Lucinda	08/09/1847
SWIFT, Washington	HARRISON, Hulda	06/12/1866
SWIFT, William	CHILDRESS, Nancy	04/11/1813
SWIFT, William B.	STOKES, Nancy	10/01/1821
TAIT, James M.	MILES, Peggy	10/29/1834
TAITE, Robert J.	MCFARLAND, Nancy	03/31/1859
TALLEY, Orren	FULLER, Barbara M.	10/15/1827
TALLEY, Peyton S.	BATTON, Jane	12/04/1850

MARRIAGE RECORDS OF CASWELL COUNTY, NORTH CAROLINA

GROOM	BRIDE	DATE
TALLEY, William S.	SELF, Sarah J.	01/20/1858
TALLEY, William S.	NUNN, Mary J.	01/02/1867
TALLMAN, James	GOOCH, Mary A.	03/04/1835
TALLY, D.H.	SHIELDS, Sally A.	01/27/1868
TALLY, P.F.	WALKER, Martha F.	01/23/1866
TANKERSLEY, James M.	ADAMS, Amanda	12/13/1866
TANKERSLEY, Pleasant	PETERSON, Nicy L.	08/05/1852
TANNER, Matthew	LANGELY, Alcy	01/20/1800
TAPSCOTT, Edney	WINDSOR, Sarah	05/23/1797
TAPSCOTT, John	SWIFT, Frances T.	01/29/1827
TAPSCOTT, Wesley	GRAVES, Martha	12/06/1866
TARPLEY, James	HIX, Nancy	07/03/1786
TARPLEY, James A.	AUSTIN, Sarah V.	11/16/1840
TATE, A.J.	MARTIN, Lucy F.	02/19/1868
TATE, Caswell	WILLIAMSON, Martha	02/24/1819
TATE, Caswell	SWIFT, Polly	12/29/1806
TATE, James	ROBERTSON, Emily	09/01/1842
TATE, Joseph	KIMBROUGH, Rebecca	01/11/1828
TATE, R.T.	BIRD, Sarah	09/25/1821
TATE, Robert	HARVELL, Elizabeth	09/09/1814
TATE, Samuel S.	JACKSON, Julia W.	11/19/1849
TATE, William S.	CORBETT, Mary F.	01/18/1857
TAYLOR, Abel	PASS, Fanny	12/22/1795
TAYLOR, Alfred G.	FOSTER, Geneva C.	11/28/1866
TAYLOR, Dorman	KENT, Sally	03/21/1808
TAYLOR, George	PASS, Ellis	12/22/1795
TAYLOR, Harrison	LEWIS, Henrietta	01/16/1867
TAYLOR, Hiram	HUGHS, Martha	12/23/1837
TAYLOR, James	BROWN, Rebecca	11/27/1802
TAYLOR, James	MOORE, Polly	02/18/1807
TAYLOR, James A.	BUCKINGHAM, Martha	12/11/1845
TAYLOR, John	REED, Lucy	11/01/1802
TAYLOR, John W.	RAYNOLDS, Lelia S.	05/29/1861
TAYLOR, Joshua	SIMMONS, Priscilla	09/06/1785
TAYLOR, Napolean B.	AUSTIN, Martha	09/07/1845
TAYLOR, Nathaniel M.	TAYLOR, Sarah L.	03/25/1843
TAYLOR, Phillip	LEWIS, Sally	08/06/1780
TAYLOR, Reuben	WOFF, Sally	08/12/1806
TAYLOR, Robert	CAMPBELL, Elizabeth	12/15/1857
TAYLOR, Samuel	BROWN, Sarah C.	01/30/1841
TAYLOR, Samuel	HARVEY, Sally	10/19/1841
TAYLOR, Septimus(?)	BRANDON, Elizabeth	02/13/1786
TAYLOR, Shadrach	MOORE, Jamima	04/24/1841
TAYLOR, William	HART, Polly	11/03/1808
TAYLOR, William	LEA, Prudence	01/07/1791
TAYLOR, William W.	BRADSHER, Sally B.	11/22/1856
TAYLOR, William W.	STEWART, Frances A.	06/08/1846
TEAGUE, Josiah	BURTON, Mary	05/22/1867
TENNISON, John	CHEATWOOD, Betsy	03/03/1798
TERILL, Thomas J.	JACKSON, S.C.	01/31/1866
TERREL, William	OWEN, Susanna	10/31/1814

MARRIAGE RECORDS OF CASWELL COUNTY, NORTH CAROLINA

GROOM	BRIDE	DATE
TERRELL, Harrison A.	AUSTIN, Elizabeth	10/20/1843
TERRELL, James	HANSHAW, Eliza	09/30/1852
TERRELL, James	CRISP, Elizabeth	03/19/1816
TERRELL, John H.	BRINCEFIELD, Letitia	06/29/1861
TERRELL, Jonathan H.	MATHEWS, Susan L.	12/11/1851
TERRELL, Joseph J.	PIPER, Catherine	09/18/1860
TERRELL, Julius B.	DAVIS, Mary	12/26/1818
TERRELL, Lewis	GRAVES, Hannah	10/31/1816
TERRELL, William E.	BURCH, Lucinda	11/16/1852
TERRY, Abner R.	YARBROUGH, Sally B.	07/04/1850
TERRY, Christopher G.	BURNS, Louisa G.	06/08/1840
TERRY, Christopher G.	BURNS, Julia F.	05/20/1844
TERRY, Dabney	YARBOROUGH, Martha	06/20/1846
TERRY, Dabney	JEFFREYS, Betsy	10/13/1825
TERRY, Enoch	WILKERSON, Edy	12/07/1832
TERRY, John	CARROL, Betsy	04/14/1804
TERRY, Matthew	ROBINSON, Chany	04/07/1800
TERRY, Wm. E.	YATES, Elizabeth	12/09/1867
THACKER, Charles	HAYS, Polly	08/12/1808
THACKER, Isaac	RICE, Mary F.	08/29/1849
THAXTON, Henry S.	CURRIE, Eugenia F.	09/05/1865
THAXTON, Thomas	COBB, Jamima	02/04/1782
THAXTON, William	GRAVITT, Sarah	08/16/1783
THOMAS, A.W.	HARRAWAY, Nancy W.	05/24/1865
THOMAS, Andrew	DICKEY, Elizabeth	09/27/1825
THOMAS, Archibald W.	WILLIAMS, Susan A.	04/03/1850
THOMAS, Christopher	BARTLETT, Patsy	11/19/1808
THOMAS, Daniel	ATKINS, Zilly	01/12/1808
THOMAS, Daniel C.	SMITH, Nancy	08/06/1827
THOMAS, David	KIMBROUGH, Patsy	04/14/1799
THOMAS, David	ELAM, Patience	04/21/1807
THOMAS, Henry	CHANDLER, Sally	01/03/1803
THOMAS, Henry Jr.	SIMMONS, Rita	12/10/1839
THOMAS, Hurt	MEBANE, Jane	06/16/1866
THOMAS, Jacob	ROAN, Fanny	01/29/1805
THOMAS, Jacob	HICKMAN, Mary	10/16/1819
THOMAS, James W.	HICKS, Rebecca C.	03/14/1857
THOMAS, Jesse H.	DOBBINS, Lethe E.	04/18/1821
THOMAS, Joel P.	WILLIAMS, Mary	12/16/1837
THOMAS, John	NELSON, Sally	08/15/1803
THOMAS, John	-----, -----	12/31/1811
THOMAS, Marcus C.	LEA, Henrietta	06/15/1858
THOMAS, Nelson	WARREN, Sarah	05/13/1834
THOMAS, Phillip	BOULTON, Judith	06/13/1781
THOMAS, Richard W.	RAGLAND, Ann W.	06/30/1832
THOMAS, Robert	WARWICK, Margaret	12/26/1787
THOMAS, Thomas	THOMAS, Margaret	06/29/1857
THOMAS, William	BOSWELL, Rebecca	12/29/1865
THOMAS, William	MCCAIN, Matilda	01/17/1867
THOMAS, William A.	GRAVES, Hannah S.	10/01/1844
THOMAS, Woodliff	REID, Frances	11/08/1834

MARRIAGE RECORDS OF CASWELL COUNTY, NORTH CAROLINA

GROOM	BRIDE	DATE
THOMASON, Fleming	GOMER, Sarah	12/25/1799
THOMPSON, Andrus J.	BOSWELL, Martha C.	11/16/1859
THOMPSON, George	STAMPS, Milly	12/19/1867
THOMPSON, George W.	HARRISON, Elizabeth J.	02/20/1838
THOMPSON, James	MORTON, Vina	09/15/1866
THOMPSON, James H.	LEA, Delila	03/17/1822
THOMPSON, John	LEA, Nancy	02/19/1823
THOMPSON, John	DAVIS, Elizabeth W.	02/01/1837
THOMPSON, Robert	THAXTON, Amanda	12/13/1866
THOMPSON, Thomas	GLASS, Sarah J.	08/10/1867
THOMPSON, Thomas A.	MURPHEY, Nancy S.	11/03/1820
THOMPSON, Thomas M.	SMITH, Arrela S.	11/02/1857
THORNTON, Francis F.	GUNN, Hulda M.	10/22/1834
THORNTON, Joseph	WRIGHT, Ester J.	12/25/1866
THORNTON, Presly L.W.	THOMPSON, Eveline	10/07/1859
THORNTON, Robert B.	SMITH, Susan F.	11/02/1833
THORP, John	TERY, Milly	07/03/1802
THORP, Richard	SMITH, Ann R.	10/30/1838
TILLINGTON, Barrington	HENSHAW, Sarah	12/10/1832
TOLLER, John	NASH, Viny	07/11/1854
TOMSON, Robert	BROWN, Usley	09/28/1781
TONEY, Arthur Jr.	EDWELL, Polly	10/16/1833
TONEY, Charles	DYSON, Martha	07/02/1835
TONEY, John	EDWIN, Lucy	12/19/1832
TONEY, Monroe	ROBARDS, Susan	12/26/1865
TONEY, Nat	PHILIPS, Polly	11/23/1837
TORIAN, Thomas	BETHELL, Agnes G.	06/17/1836
TOSH, Thomas	MCCLENEHAN, Lucy J.	04/06/1833
TOTTEN, John C.	HARALSON, Dorcas	06/05/1826
TOTTEN, Joseph H.	SARTIN, Nancy A.	10/20/1859
TOTTEN, Joseph S.	MCALPIN, C.A.	09/24/1840
TOTTEN, Richard W.	FOSTER, Nancy	09/13/1826
TOTTEN, Thomas R.	WATLINGTON, Sarah L.	12/21/1853
TOTTON, Sidney	MOTLEY, Virginia	05/15/1866
TOWLER, H.A.	KNIGHT, Margaret E.	05/07/1858
TOWLERMAN, Phillip	SHEMCY, Catherine	08/15/1820
TOWLES, James M.	CALLUM, Mary A.	02/19/1838
TOWNLEY, Alvah R.	WORSHAM, Emily	05/26/1830
TOWNS, William M.	LIPSCOMBE, Mary C.	08/06/1851
TRAMMEL, Elisha B.	GORDIN, Elizabeth F.	12/24/1856
TRASCO, Henry	LOYD, Elizabeth	01/21/1855
TRAVIS, Alfred R.	SWANN, Sarah C.	08/10/1851
TRAVIS, Ellis	INGRAM, Priscilla	02/27/1836
TRAVIS, Ellis	WHITE, Mary	04/10/1843
TRAVIS, Elzey	FUGERSON, Arey A.	09/28/1841
TRAVIS, George A.	HODGES, Susanna	07/03/1861
TRAVIS, Isaac	INGRAM, Mary N.	12/30/1836
TRAVIS, James	WARE, Nancy	07/19/1814
TRAVIS, James F.M.	GATEWOOD, Ann E.	10/25/1866
TRAVIS, James J.	STANLEY, Martha J.	10/23/1844
TRAVIS, John	COLEMAN, Elizabeth B.	01/14/1836

MARRIAGE RECORDS OF CASWELL COUNTY, NORTH CAROLINA

GROOM	BRIDE	DATE
TRAVIS, John	WEST, Mary B.	06/26/1843
TRAVIS, John C.	FORD, Elizabeth M.	12/21/1854
TRAVIS, John W. P.	BURTON, Mary A.	04/11/1854
TRAVIS, Stephen	INGRAM, Tirzah	11/21/1836
TRAVIS, Thomas	PINICK, Jane M.	08/20/1830
TRAVIS, William	CHILTON, Rachel	11/18/1816
TRAVISE, David	MOORE, Judith	02/04/1782
TRAYNHAM, David	WARSHAM, Mary	12/28/1825
TREW, Oza	WINTERS, Polly	09/11/1815
TRIGG, William B.	BUSEY, Sally	12/31/1822
TRUE, Benjamin H.	PRUITT, Emily	01/19/1853
TRUE, Lewis J.	BAYES, Lavina J.	04/12/1864
TUBERVILLE, Fountain M.	GRAVES, Fanny	12/10/1851
TUDER, Landon	FULLER, Mary	01/21/1832
TULLOCH, David	BRUCE, Betsy	03/26/1796
TULLOCH, James M.	SINGLETON, Ann	02/29/1808
TULLOCH, Thomas	TAYLOR, Jane	04/30/1822
TULLOH, William	PRICE, Mary	03/05/1800
TULLOH, William	GOIN, Alsey	01/03/1809
TUNSTALL, Green	PINNIX, Mary E.	06/07/1867
TURBEVILLE, Lewis W.	GRAVES, Cornelia W.	09/14/1852
TURBIVILLE, Charles P.	HOLDEN, Mary E.	10/24/1853
TURNER, Abraham R.	BLACK, Sarah	10/20/1784
TURNER, Berry	STRADOR, Susanna	11/18/1828
TURNER, C. F.	HODGES, Betty	10/16/1866
TURNER, Charles	RUDD, Polly	04/10/1805
TURNER, Chesley	HATCHETT, Mildred R.	04/19/1821
TURNER, Daniel	FISHER, Susanna	09/23/1805
TURNER, Dennis	RUDD, Julia	08/26/1866
TURNER, Edmund	SLADE, Mary A.	10/12/1824
TURNER, Ephraim	DAVIS, Frances	12/04/1857
TURNER, George W.	CARTER, Isabella	12/16/1866
TURNER, Gideon B.	DODSON, Permelia	02/27/1826
TURNER, Green	POWELL, Harriet E.	12/27/1849
TURNER, Henry	MCKINNEY, Patsy	11/23/1826
TURNER, Henry	WILLIAMSON, Lethe	11/02/1866
TURNER, Isham	ARNOLD, Mary	11/02/1832
TURNER, James	PLEASANT, Lucy	08/05/1793
TURNER, James B.	ARRINGTON, Adeline	06/10/1862
TURNER, James C.	BIGELOW, Mary	12/17/1823
TURNER, James H.	KIMBRO, Margaret	04/10/1847
TURNER, James H.	GIPSON, Mary	02/08/1855
TURNER, James R.	ROBERTS, Lucinda	10/21/1854
TURNER, James R.	ROBERTS, Lucinda	10/13/1854
TURNER, John	ATKINSON, Polly	11/22/1796
TURNER, John	MOORE, Mildred	08/27/1854
TURNER, John	KIMBRO, Sarah	02/14/1787
TURNER, John P.	TRAMMEL, Elizabeth	04/11/1867
TURNER, Jordon	TURNER, Matilda	05/06/1867
TURNER, Lewis	WILKINS, Patsy	09/27/1825
TURNER, Lewis P.	MOORE, Emily	09/21/1855

MARRIAGE RECORDS OF CASWELL COUNTY, NORTH CAROLINA

GROOM	BRIDE	DATE
TURNER, Marcus A.	MCNEIL, Millisa V.	09/25/1851
TURNER, Moses	MOORE, Martha	02/22/1780
TURNER, Stephen D.	HINTON, Henrietta M.	03/20/1854
TURNER, Stephen H.	TURNER, Mary A.	01/01/1850
TURNER, Thomas	FISHER, Elizabeth	11/08/1815
TURNER, Thomas	HARALSON, Betsy	10/28/1794
TURNER, Thomas	WARE, Celia	10/21/1819
TURNER, Thomas	PYRANT, Mary	11/17/1862
TURNER, Thomas	PUCKET, Agnes	12/18/1856
TURNER, Walter	EVERETT, Lucy	02/20/1868
TURNER, William	BARTLETT, Ann	12/04/1802
TURNER, William A.	EVANS, Sally A.	11/10/1858
TURNER, William B.	HOLYCROSS, Sarah	08/04/1864
TURNER, William W.	DODSON, Seignara M. (?)	06/26/1824
TURNER, William W.	YATES, Sarah	10/09/1860
TYLER, Zachariah	PARKER, Edey	04/08/1822
TYREE, David	OBRION, Hannah	04/06/1830
UNDERWOOD, Henry	EASLEY, Caroline	03/26/1866
UNDERWOOD, James	SAWYER, Elizabeth	12/14/1816
UNDERWOOD, James	SAWYER, Sally	09/13/1851
UNDERWOOD, John	ROBERTS, Sarah	10/06/1841
UNDERWOOD, Jonathan B.	BRINCEFIELD, Nancy	12/21/1860
UNDERWOOD, William	PLEASANT, Sarah A.	12/05/1843
UPTON, Edward	LONG, Jane	12/19/1781
UPTON, William	MATHIS, Susanna	11/03/1823
UPTON, William	DAMERON, Mildred	01/20/1820
USSERY, James G.	FLEET, Mary A.	10/25/1838
VALENTINE, Thomas J.	WILLIS, Martha A.	10/21/1850
VALENTINE, Thos. J.	MCALPIN, Narcissa G.	12/24/1842
VANHOOK, Aaron	LEONARD, Elizabeth	--/--/----
VANHOOK, Francis M.	CARTER, Elizabeth J.	01/18/1860
VANHOOK, Isaac	COMER, Peggy	01/27/1817
VANHOOK, Isaac D.	MCMULLIN, Elizabeth	12/02/1817
VANHOOK, Jacob T.	TOTTON, Nancy W.	07/19/1865
VANHOOK, John	GORDON, Betsy	12/14/1807
VANHOOK, John C.	LEA, Phebe	11/24/1819
VANHOOK, Kindal	BURTON, Diana	05/22/1813
VANHOOK, Kindle	DOBBIN, Ann	11/25/1800
VANHOOK, Laurance Jr.	SARGENT, Rachel	09/17/1785
VANHOOK, Laurence Sr.	RANKIN, Vottory	11/01/1787
VANHOOK, Loyd Jr.	AUSTIN, Sally	11/09/1804
VANHOOK, Reuben	ROBERTSON, Maria	04/20/1867
VANHOOK, Robert	DOBBIN, Rachel	12/10/1793
VANHOOK, Solomon	RICHMOND, Mary A.	04/29/1839
VANHOOK, Thomas	PALMER, Sarah	06/21/1779
VASS, Thomas Jr.	BADGETT, Elizabeth	11/19/1838
VAUGHAN, Bailey	MCCALRNEY, Polly	12/18/1827
VAUGHAN, Drury M.	TURNER, Martha M.	03/11/1830
VAUGHAN, James	MALONE, Henrietta	12/--/1803
VAUGHAN, James Jr.	PAGE, Betsy	02/14/1826
VAUGHAN, John	MILES, Elizabeth	11/18/1847

MARRIAGE RECORDS OF CASWELL COUNTY, NORTH CAROLINA

GROOM	BRIDE	DATE
VAUGHAN, John	GRAVES, Tabitha	10/30/1832
VAUGHAN, John	CIRLS, Betsy	01/15/1825
VAUGHAN, John Jr.	MILES, Leah	03/20/1827
VAUGHAN, Lewis	WILSON, Polly	08/01/1801
VAUGHAN, Nicholas	PLEASANT, Polly	03/06/1804
VAUGHAN, William	ALDRIDGE, Susan	10/03/1851
VAUGHN, A. B.	MILS, Caroline	12/21/1860
VAUGHN, Maurice	JONES, Ann	09/10/1825
VAUGHN, Richard	TURNER, Nancy	09/28/1803
VAUGHN, Thomas	FRENCH, Polly	08/31/1808
VAUGHN, Warren T.	MILES, Dolly	10/06/1859
VAUGHN, Wiatt	SIMPSON, Anice	03/28/1868
VAUGHN, William	LAMKIN, Susan	08/18/1820
VAUGHON, Gidon	LAY, Sarah	02/09/1780
VENABLE, Joseph	PRICE, Jenny	02/22/1866
VERNON, Calvin D.	WATLINGTON, Penelope	03/08/1855
VERNON, Robert T.	RICE, Elizabeth	12/21/1854
VERNON, Thomas	SIMPSON, Martha A.	01/05/1855
VERSER, Daniel	PONSONBY, Elizabeth	09/30/1837
VERTRES, James C.	LEA, Susan C. V.	07/28/1849
VINCENT, James	MARTIN, Mary	08/14/1841
VINSON, Henry	RICHMOND, Sina	01/17/1867
VIRMILLION, Wilson	MCNEIL, Nancy	07/18/1778
VISAGE, Thomas	SHY, Polly	10/01/1792
VOSS, Greenbery	SWANN, Betsy	10/30/1793
VOSS, Milton	STONE, Mary L.	12/14/1858
VOSS, Okelly	CARTER, Elizabeth E.	12/05/1825
VOSS, Paschall	SWAN, Mahaley	12/16/1833
VOSS, Pleasant	COOK, Unity	02/04/1829
WADDILL, Branch	ELMORE, Martha	02/08/1834
WADDILL, John C.	WIMBUS, Nancy	10/27/1817
WADE, Charles D.	SARGENT, Dready	04/18/1816
WADE, Lawson	DIXON, Nanny	12/28/1866
WADE, Robert D.	CURRIE, Mary	02/01/1828
WADE, Robert Jr.	WADE, Ann	09/16/1788
WADE, William	HAMLET, Jane	01/22/1864
WADKINS, Isaac	JONES, Jenny	02/23/1816
WAGSTAFF, John F.	OLIVER, Caroline	01/25/1851
WAID, Hampton	DURHAM, Ann	11/12/1796
WAITE, William	PRYOR, Tabitha	12/11/1778
WALKER, Abraham	JONES, Martha J.	12/17/1857
WALKER, Abraham	SMITH, Elizabeth	11/02/1833
WALKER, Ajax J.	LEWIS, Lucy M.	05/18/1820
WALKER, Alexader J.	DILL, Mary A.	12/26/1832
WALKER, Archibald J.	STRADER, Celia	10/13/1859
WALKER, Azariah	WALKER, Jane	12/18/1837
WALKER, Benjamin	HIGHTOWER, Sally	12/09/1800
WALKER, Benjamin	RICE, Susan	03/01/1833
WALKER, Charles H.	WALKER, Mary E.	04/29/1867
WALKER, Daniel	WALKER, Milly	06/23/1866
WALKER, David	DOLTON, Patsy	01/30/1806

MARRIAGE RECORDS OF CASWELL COUNTY, NORTH CAROLINA

GROOM	BRIDE	DATE
WALKER, David	BALDWIN, Frances	03/17/1827
WALKER, David	GROOM, Satiry	09/30/1845
WALKER, David	CARVER, Suffy	12/24/1825
WALKER, Empson	CURRIE, Martha	09/11/1825
WALKER, Fielding L.	WILSON, Pensy C.	11/28/1866
WALKER, Freeman	BAYNES, Perthena	11/25/1842
WALKER, Garrison	WALKER, Lucinda	10/12/1840
WALKER, George	WALKER, Mary	12/17/1822
WALKER, George	CURRIE, Catherine	02/16/1811
WALKER, James	PARKS, Milly	11/22/1843
WALKER, James	ELLIOT, Elizabeth	11/21/1781
WALKER, James	TAPSCOTT, Lucinda	12/21/1820
WALKER, James	MASON, Ann	12/16/1820
WALKER, James M.	WILLIAMS, Letitia F.	05/11/1853
WALKER, James M.	LEA, Martha A.	03/30/1835
WALKER, Jefferson M.	COOPER, Mary F.	10/22/1854
WALKER, Jere (?)	CROSS, Ruth	12/02/1805
WALKER, Jethro J.	GOMER, Ann	12/26/1839
WALKER, John	BEAVER, Betsy	12/18/1813
WALKER, John	LOYED, Margaret	11/23/1858
WALKER, John G.	CURRIE, Partheana	03/08/1824
WALKER, John H.	NEW, Susan	08/24/1838
WALKER, John H.	BROWN, Sarah F.	02/26/1862
WALKER, John M.	MCKINNEY, Martha	10/24/1840
WALKER, John M.	RICE, Polly	10/17/1828
WALKER, Jones H.	SUMMERS, Catherine	10/23/1854
WALKER, Joseph	ZACHARY, Priscilla	03/17/1800
WALKER, Landay	LOVELESS, Matilda J.	04/17/1855
WALKER, Mitchell	DAVIS, Martha P.	11/24/1846
WALKER, Monroe	BRIGGS, Minerva	10/08/1866
WALKER, Nash	WILLIAMSON, Hannah	12/22/1865
WALKER, Nicholas L.	HART, Emily F.	11/20/1849
WALKER, Phillip	MARTIN, Frances	12/27/1833
WALKER, Robert T.	MONTGOMERY, Mary	01/17/1858
WALKER, Samuel	MASON, Jean	12/16/1820
WALKER, Samuel	WALKER, Barbara	05/19/1834
WALKER, Thomas	SWAN, Peggy	10/28/1811
WALKER, Thomas J.	SOMERS, Mary	08/19/1845
WALKER, Washington	SMITHEY, Nicy	09/28/1846
WALKER, William	FORD, Levicy	10/22/1834
WALKER, William	WALKER, Jane	10/28/1830
WALKER, William A.	PARKS, Sarah T.	11/14/1843
WALKER, William F.	BOSWELL, Phebe	03/16/1850
WALKER, William L.	SIMMONS, Salina	09/14/1850
WALKER, William T.	RUDD, Celestia F.	12/28/1865
WALL, Byrd	MUIRHEAD, Elizabeth	12/04/1782
WALL, George W.	STRADOR, Delilah A. J.	09/12/1846
WALL, Robert	WALL, Catherine	02/15/1830
WALL, William D.	HIGHTOWER, Mary C.	11/28/1854
WALLAS, Benjamin	SARGENT, Sarah	06/05/1782
WALLER, John	WOODY, Frances	01/06/1819

MARRIAGE RECORDS OF CASWELL COUNTY, NORTH CAROLINA

GROOM	BRIDE	DATE
WALLER, John S.	WALTERS, Ann E.	03/21/1839
WALLERS, Robert H.	WADDELL, Nancy	10/20/1817
WALLES, William	SHEARMAN, Tempy	06/26/1795
WALLIS, Allen	SARGANT, Ann	07/05/1826
WALLIS, James	ROBINSON, Polly	09/21/1796
WALLIS, James	HALL, Eddy	12/30/1786
WALLIS, James J.	DAVIS, Elvira R.	12/22/1853
WALLIS, John	FULLAR, Elizabeth	01/07/1790
WALLIS, Major	BURTON, Susanna	04/09/1802
WALTERS, Alexander J.	VINSON, Mary F.	02/01/1840
WALTERS, Berry	SHELTON, Jane	12/28/1866
WALTERS, Davy	LINDSEY, Harriet	12/28/1866
WALTERS, Ezra	SHACKELFORD, Elizabeth	12/24/1795
WALTERS, George	WIER, Bell	05/04/1867
WALTERS, Jackson	CHANDLER, Rebecca	09/22/1852
WALTERS, John	NEWTON, Catherine	11/29/1789
WALTERS, Thomas	DODSON, Sarah	10/11/1837
WALTERS, Thomas	STOKES, Rebecca	01/05/1867
WALTERS, Thornton	BOHANNAN, Margaret P.	01/02/1816
WALTERS, William H.	INGRAM, Tally	12/26/1816
WALTON, Benjamin W.	EDWARDS, Sarah C.	02/10/1863
WALTON, John	MATLOCK, Susan	05/17/1832
WALTON, John H.	BASS, Mary A.	02/21/1860
WALTON, Lewis	RICHMOND, Fanny	03/25/1867
WALTON, Mazor	AVERETT, Betty	07/27/1867
WALTON, Thomas	JOHNSTON, Polly	12/28/1813
WALTON, William T.	ECHELS, Elizabeth D.	12/30/1858
WARD, Alfred	DEBROWER, Elizabeth	12/22/1857
WARD, George	CHATHAM, Cloey	12/08/1801
WARD, James L.	ROBERTS, Phebe	09/08/1864
WARD, John L.	ROBERTS, Mary	11/10/1867
WARD, Richard	HEDGCOCK, Lucy	05/29/1787
WARD, Richard C.	MURPHEY, Maryan	11/16/1806
WARD, T. R.	STAINBACK, Susan A.	11/02/1867
WARD, Thomas	HIGHTOWER, Permelia	03/12/1827
WARD, Thomas	PAUL, Betsy	09/03/1815
WARD, William	FOSTER, Mary A.	10/13/1845
WARE, Ansel	MATLOCK, Elizabeth	09/10/1825
WARE, James	GITTON, Rebecca	06/12/1812
WARE, James T.	GUNN, Celestia A.	06/06/1861
WARE, Jno. P.	SANDERS, Elizabeth	04/15/1818
WARE, John	TOLBERT, Nancy	09/28/1782
WARE, John	HALCOMB, Mary M.	10/09/1820
WARE, Joseph R.	CHANDLER, Susan T.	11/09/1832
WARE, Nathaniel	BOYLES, Susan	04/17/1849
WARE, Sidney G.	BURTON, Fanny	06/10/1857
WARE, Silas T.	CANNON, Sarah	09/04/1837
WARE, Silas T.	WILLIAMS, Elizabeth A.	09/19/1850
WARE, Stephen T.	SHELTON, Eliza	10/10/1837
WARE, Thomas	HOLLOWAY, Jenny	04/28/1806
WARE, Thomas	TALBERT, Sarah	10/17/1788

MARRIAGE RECORDS OF CASWELL COUNTY, NORTH CAROLINA

GROOM	BRIDE	DATE
WARE, Thomas	DURHAM, Kesiah	06/09/1805
WARE, Thomas Jr.	WARE, Nancy	08/08/1818
WARE, William	PERKINS, Frances	10/02/1781
WARE, William G.	WILLIAMS, Mildred G.	02/19/1859
WARE, William M.	HUBBARD, Nancy	09/12/1863
WARE, William M.	HUBBARD, Nancy	09/13/1863
WARF, Berry	MOORE, Nancy	06/22/1808
WARF, James	GLASPY, Sally	12/23/1801
WARF, James F.	MASON, Margaret	03/20/1836
WARF, John	LINDSAY, Julia A.	09/22/1837
WARF, Noel	BENNITT, Milly	10/29/1845
WARF, Roger	GILASPY, Betsy	01/05/1802
WARF, Tandy F.	BURNETT, Elizabeth	12/07/1847
WARF, Thomas	COX, Jane	12/08/1846
WARF, Thomas	COX, Elizabeth	02/01/1865
WARINER, Robert H.	NUNNALLY, Agness J.	11/04/1843
WARREN, Alexander	HOOPER, Elizabeth	04/13/1846
WARREN, B. H.	LEA, E. C.	02/16/1860
WARREN, Benjamin	PLEASANT, Louisa	08/12/1833
WARREN, Bozzel	MELONE, Elizabeth	12/21/1798
WARREN, Burwell	HALL, Rebecca F.	09/17/1863
WARREN, Burwell	BARNWELL, Frances C.	08/06/1852
WARREN, Drewry	TURNER, Sally	11/25/1858
WARREN, Edmund	DAMERON, Martha	10/30/1829
WARREN, Franklin L.	WELLS, Mary	04/24/1851
WARREN, Georeg N.	-----, -----	05/12/1818
WARREN, George W.	MITCHELL, Mary A.	10/03/1857
WARREN, Goodloe	VIRLOINS, Elizabeth	10/08/1816
WARREN, Granderson	TERRELL, Martha	05/08/1851
WARREN, Henry	SMITH, Elizabeth	11/25/1812
WARREN, Hiram	BROOKS, Mary	07/26/1848
WARREN, Iverson G.	MOORE, Olive	12/12/1846
WARREN, James S.	SNIPES, Teletha	01/06/1847
WARREN, Jno. G.	MELONE, Isabella	11/08/1791
WARREN, John	SMITHEY, Ann	01/26/1810
WARREN, John	HARALSON, Huldah	11/30/1850
WARREN, John D.	HUNT, Rachel	06/15/1817
WARREN, Joseph N.	KELLEY, Nancy	10/--/1814
WARREN, Madison	ROBERTS, Nancy	12/12/1842
WARREN, Martin	MILES, Ann	02/06/1836
WARREN, Mason	CAMPBELL, Naomi	10/22/1860
WARREN, Micajah	MASON, Sarag	04/19/1859
WARREN, Micajah	PLEASANT, Leatha	04/24/1859
WARREN, Samuel	FULLER, Priscilla	12/31/1799
WARREN, Samuel	HOLSONBACK, Lydia	01/05/1805
WARREN, Thomas	SMITH, Sally	01/27/1810
WARREN, Thomas	BROWNING, Ann E.	10/06/1853
WARREN, Thomas J.	SATERFIELD, Aeliade	02/10/1859
WARREN, Vinson	NEELEY, Nicey	02/15/1800
WARREN, William	LEWIS, Ann	11/28/1823
WARREN, William	WISDOM, Nancy	08/26/1809

MARRIAGE RECORDS OF CASWELL COUNTY, NORTH CAROLINA

GROOM	BRIDE	DATE
WARREN, William	RIDDLE, Polly	10/14/1807
WARREN, William H.	STADLER, Susan A.	12/20/1867
WARREN, William Jr.	TERRELL, Frances	07/05/1825
WARREN, William Jr.	HANSHAW, Catherine	03/24/1826
WARREN, Yancy G.	ELLISON, Mary C.	12/16/1842
WARREN, Yearbey	HESTER, Sarah	04/21/1828
WARRIN, Benjamin	CULBERTSON, Rachel	05/04/1791
WARRIN, Buford	YATES, Sally	02/14/1803
WARRIN, Ezekiel	WISDOM, Mary	04/15/1816
WARRIN, James	MURPHEY, Nancy	08/26/1800
WARRIN, Stuart	OLLIVER, Catherine	02/22/1791
WARRIN, Tho.	COOK, Margaret	07/04/1820
WARRIN, Timothy	TINDAL, Elizabeth	03/13/1817
WARRIN, William	MALONE, Sally	11/26/1801
WASHBERN, Joseph	CORBET, Elizabeth	09/14/1848
WASHBURN, Willis	EVANS, Nancy	05/02/1825
WASLEY, Robert	DYE, Delilah	03/22/1799
WATKINS, James	HUNT, Milly	11/18/1867
WATKINS, John	RAY, Mary	08/19/1807
WATKINS, Joseph V.B.	WATKINS, Logan S.	05/19/1857
WATKINS, King	MCGEHEE, Oney	12/23/1865
WATKINS, Martin	LEE, Mary	12/09/1865
WATKINS, Mathew W.	SHAW, Urcilla P.	04/08/1859
WATKINS, Phillip	PICKEL, Jean	12/23/1790
WATKINS, Tho. J.	GUNN, Sarah A.	08/10/1843
WATKINS, Thomas	CHAPPAL, Elizabeth	02/10/1783
WATKINS, William	TERRELL, Jane	11/06/1834
WATLINGTON, Armistad	BROOKS, Mary	04/14/1790
WATLINGTON, Armstead	WATLINGTON, Rebecca	01/02/1833
WATLINGTON, Carter	LEA, Edy	10/19/1867
WATLINGTON, David	JONES, Sally	08/31/1867
WATLINGTON, Edward	BROOKS, Jane	04/15/1820
WATLINGTON, Edward Jr.	MIMS, Mary A.	02/25/1841
WATLINGTON, Francis	HARPER, Lydia	11/04/1823
WATLINGTON, Hiram S.	BENNETT, Mary B.	11/23/1823
WATLINGTON, James	SCOTT, Jane	03/21/1825
WATLINGTON, James J. B.	WATLINGTON, Martha A.	07/08/1858
WATLINGTON, James M.	WEST, Sarah E.	03/01/1850
WATLINGTON, Jas. W.	JONES, Laura A.	03/26/1867
WATLINGTON, John	DONOHO, Betsy	09/04/1792
WATLINGTON, Jonathan B.	RICE, Dorathy C.	06/07/1823
WATLINGTON, Paul	BLACKWELL, Jane P.	02/21/1838
WATLINGTON, Reid	SINGLETON, Catherine	06/17/1828
WATLINGTON, Shepperd	KING, Celia	09/07/1867
WATLINGTON, Sidney	PAGE, Esther	12/27/1867
WATLINGTON, Thomas	BRACKIN, Dorothy B.	11/02/1824
WATLINGTON, Thompson T.	LYON, Martha W.	05/19/1849
WATLINGTON, William	MANNEN, Titia (?)	11/09/1816
WATLINGTON, William P.	SLADE, Mary J.	07/20/1850
WATSON, Anderson	MALLORY, Susan	10/29/1832
WATT, Absalom	HENDERSON, Elizabeth	12/16/1815

MARRIAGE RECORDS OF CASWELL COUNTY, NORTH CAROLINA

GROOM	BRIDE	DATE
WATT, James	BLACKWELL, Polly	11/--/1809
WATT, Jno.	PRICE, Margaret A.	04/29/1857
WATT, Russel	NEAL, Becky	11/03/1867
WATT, Samuel Jr.	BLACKWELL, Kiturah (?)	11/01/1808
WATTS, Samuel	RICE, Mary	01/25/1808
WAURRIN, John	HARNDON, Patsy	02/14/1794
WEALSH, Samuel	JEFFERS, Susanna	02/18/1789
WEATHERFORD, Barten	KING, Jane	11/30/1824
WEATHERFORD, Hiram	-----, -----	--/--/----
WEATHERFORD, Hiram	HARRELSON, Nancy	09/23/1818
WEATHERFORD, Warren	BLACKWELL, Susanna	11/27/1815
WEATHERFORD, William	HOOPER, Frances G.	02/03/1830
WEB, Anderson	SNIPES, Caroline	12/25/1866
WEBB, Daniel D.	BUCEY, Martha F.	12/19/1831
WEBB, Jonathan	MCCARVER, Grussey	02/12/1781
WEBB, Lewis	CROWDER, Mary A.	12/16/1837
WEBB, William R.	VANHOOK, Elizabeth L.	11/14/1829
WEBB, William S.	TURNER, Milly	04/04/1804
WEBSTER, Charles	STAFFORD, Betsy	05/20/1812
WEBSTER, Charles H.	STEPHENS, Mary C.	05/30/1849
WEBSTER, James	WESTBROOKS, Frances	10/29/1828
WEBSTER, John	WHITLOW, Mary	11/24/1817
WEBSTER, M. C. A.	JACKSON, Sarah	02/22/1854
WEBSTER, Micajah	HAWKINS, Nancy	02/02/1843
WEBSTER, Thomas	MORGAN, Elizabeth	03/01/1837
WEBSTER, Thomas H.	CHILDRESS, Louisa	12/08/1853
WEEKS, Henry	CROWDER, Lovey	11/11/1822
WEEKS, Richard	KIERSEY, Nancy	02/27/1826
WEIFORD, Perry W.	KELLY, Rebecca J.	06/17/1855
WEIR, David P.	HUMESTON, Hannah L.	11/20/1838
WEIR, Thomas	JOHNS, Happy	11/10/1866
WELCH, Samuel	BAXTER, Nancy	01/04/1782
WELLS, Azariah	HARRISON, Matilda	02/23/1832
WELLS, Benjamin	CRISP, Eliza	12/20/1826
WELLS, Hardy	PARKER, Elizabeth	10/20/1784
WELLS, James M.	FLORENCE, Sarah	10/24/1840
WELLS, John	SMITH, Nancy	08/22/1822
WELLS, Justian	GULIPIN, Martha	01/19/1836
WELLS, Labon C.	BARNES, Lydia A.	02/08/1861
WELLS, Miles Jr.	WELLS, Duppe (?)	03/26/1828
WELLS, Stephen H.	SNIPES, Sarah J.	11/11/1859
WELLS, Stephen N.	MITCHELL, Martha J.	12/11/1854
WELLS, Thomas	RAINEY, Polly	03/11/1809
WELLS, Thomas	FOSTER, Mary	09/26/1823
WEMPLE, Jno. D.	GWYN, Dorothy	03/17/1841
WESLEY, John	RANDAL, Nancy	01/22/1806
WEST, Benjamin C.	HATCHETT, Mary C.	02/21/1824
WEST, Cary W.	HODGES, Mary	05/10/1834
WEST, Edward	GARRETT, Ann	09/--/1866
WEST, Joseph	WILMOUTH, Nancy	10/20/1819
WEST, R. J.	BRADSHAW, Mary F.	12/21/1866

MARRIAGE RECORDS OF CASWELL COUNTY, NORTH CAROLINA

GROOM	BRIDE	DATE
WESTBROOK, John	STAFFORD, Elizabeth	12/21/1841
WESTBROOK, Paschall	SMITH, Mary	02/17/1829
WESTBROOK, Thomas	RUSSEL, Ann	10/27/1841
WESTBROOK, Yancey	COIL, Jane	12/31/1823
WESTBROOK, Yancey	CHAMBERLAIN, Jemima	01/06/1825
WESTBROOKS, Joseph B.	JOHNSON, Rosa A.	01/30/1854
WHEELER, Vincent H.	SHELTON, Louisa	03/19/1839
WHELLAN, William	FURGUSON, Ellenor	01/17/1804
WHITE, A. W.	WATLINGTON, Sally	08/01/1867
WHITE, Daniel H.	DODSON, Eliza O.	10/17/1854
WHITE, David	PONDS, Sally	11/19/1804
WHITE, Epa	WALLER, Lydia	07/24/1806
WHITE, Henry	NORMAN, Betsy	06/12/1867
WHITE, James	WARE, Nancy	08/30/1813
WHITE, James B.	REYNOLDS, Theodita	03/12/1833
WHITE, John	FUQUA, Elizabeth	01/10/1834
WHITE, John	WILLIAMSON, Elizabeth	10/26/1796
WHITE, John W.	HAMLETT, Frances M.	03/30/1854
WHITE, Paton	WILLIAMSON, Lucinda	06/22/1867
WHITE, Thomas	MITCHEL, Sally	01/12/1802
WHITE, Thomas	CARNALL, Mary	01/08/1781
WHITE, Turner D.	BRANDON, Margaret	12/21/1816
WHITE, William	GADDIS, Mary	07/14/1801
WHITE, William H.	MURRAY, Elizabeth	01/30/1830
WHITEEST, James	PARISH, Catherine	06/05/1860
WHITEFIELD, James	OWEN, Elizabeth	11/01/1817
WHITEHEAD, Andrew J.	WADE, Drucilla H.	08/08/1836
WHITEHEAD, John H.	WHITEHEAD, Lucy	05/18/1825
WHITEHEAD, Page	WRIGHT, Betsey	12/15/1809
WHITEHEART, Chrody	STAINBACK, Frances	01/20/1847
WHITEMORE, Gower	DICKINS, Patsy	03/27/1798
WHITFIELD, William	JOHNSTON, Sally	12/29/1809
WHITICE, Joseph R.	DODSON, Catherine	07/17/1844
WHITLOCK, Achilles	TERRY, Letitia W.	04/22/1833
WHITLOW, James	WHITLOW, Elizabeth	11/23/1817
WHITLOW, John	NOWEL, Eleanor	09/08/1791
WHITLOW, John	WHITLOW, Catherine	10/07/1823
WHITLOW, Josiah H.	BRADLEY, Lucy A.	04/25/1836
WHITLOW, Solomon	MOORE, Mary	12/13/1832
WHITLOW, Solomon	MCDANIEL, Nancy	11/13/1822
WHITMORE, Richard	WARREN, Nancy	06/10/1809
WHITSETT, Alfred M.	BROWN, Sarah	09/06/1833
WHITT, E. Jones	RICHMOND, Elizabeth F.	08/24/1857
WHITTAKER, John	ALLEN, Cressy	07/31/1804
WHITTED, James	NASH, Attelia	02/25/1813
WHITTED, Levi	POWELL, Emily C.	04/16/1857
WHITTEMORE, Clement W.	RYE, Nancy A.H.	08/13/1833
WHITUS, Robert	GRAVES, Almire	10/27/1866
WIER, William	BURTON, Mary	12/19/1810
WILBURN, W.H.	HART, Louisa	12/24/1855
WILDER, William	DOUGLASS, Mary	12/27/1833

MARRIAGE RECORDS OF CASWELL COUNTY, NORTH CAROLINA

GROOM	BRIDE	DATE
WILDER, William V.	PETERSON, Sarah	09/29/1836
WILES, Luke	REYNOLDS, Lucy	11/22/1814
WILES, Samuel	HOWARD, Julia	12/16/1865
WILES, Thomas	GUINN, Melvira	03/15/1860
WILES, Thomas	BANES, Fanny	04/27/1819
WILES, Thomas	BOHANNAN, Dolly	06/06/1809
WILEY, Albert G.	CHANDLER, Frances E.	08/27/1842
WILEY, Alexander	KERR, Polly	12/28/1807
WILEY, Alexander	YANCEY, Fanny	10/02/1804
WILEY, Alexander	NOWELL, Martha	03/20/1779
WILEY, Franklin A.	CURRIE, Sally L.	08/24/1851
WILEY, George	LEGANS, Letsy	04/27/1847
WILEY, Green	MURRAY, Eliza	11/30/1867
WILEY, Iverson	RUDD, Emily	09/22/1866
WILEY, John	MITCHELL, Jinny	09/06/1815
WILEY, John	MARTIN, Betty	03/30/1867
WILEY, John H.	WILEY, Adaline W.	03/27/1839
WILEY, Thomas	NOEL, Tabitha	04/12/1805
WILEY, Yancy	LEA, Annis	04/30/1855
WILEY, Yancy	THOMPSON, Ann E.	12/17/1831
WILKERSON, Jno. C.	THOMPSON, Justina L.	03/23/1852
WILKERSON, Wager	DUNCAN, Patience	05/27/1780
WILKERSON, Walter S.	BARKER, Agnes R.	09/09/1862
WILKINS, Joseph	PERRY, Eliza J.	05/21/1858
WILKINSON, Egbert S.	MCCAIN, Mary A.	01/23/1849
WILKINSON, Henry E.	HARRISON, Patsy	12/08/1819
WILKINSON, John E.	HARRISON, Mary W.	09/10/1821
WILKINSON, Robert W.	DODSON, Elizabeth F.	12/15/1865
WILKINSON, Simon T.	JENKINS, Sarah A.	07/10/1859
WILKS, Thomas U.	GRAVES, Mira L.	10/31/1837
WILLIAHSON, Charles	HILL, Mary	02/25/1866
WILLIAMS, Alexander	MITCHEL, Catherine	09/07/1867
WILLIAMS, Alfred	PERRY, Mary	12/12/1836
WILLIAMS, Craftin	YATES, Betsy	03/03/1798
WILLIAMS, Daniel	RICE, Ann	01/05/1786
WILLIAMS, Dawson M.	MANSFIELD, Lucy T.	01/03/1856
WILLIAMS, Duke	HARRISS, Edy	10/19/1790
WILLIAMS, George W.	SPAIN, Martha R.	04/15/1850
WILLIAMS, Gilbert	FOSTER, Lizzy A.	02/10/1867
WILLIAMS, Henry	GOOCH, Polly	12/31/1799
WILLIAMS, J.M.Dr.	GLASS, Mary E.	11/27/1865
WILLIAMS, James	SAWYERS, Elizabeth	06/18/1806
WILLIAMS, James M.	PURKINS, Frances	03/30/1858
WILLIAMS, John	DUNNAVANT, Fanny	11/13/1822
WILLIAMS, John A.	MILLER, Sarah E.	08/10/1835
WILLIAMS, John D.	WARE, Frances	09/09/1861
WILLIAMS, John Jr.	DIXON, Susanna	01/10/1800
WILLIAMS, John W.	ALLEN, Frances J.	01/29/1863
WILLIAMS, Maderson	WAGSTAFF, Ester	02/08/1867
WILLIAMS, Marmaduke	HARRIS, Agnes	10/26/1798
WILLIAMS, Nathaniel	STONE, -----	01/17/1832

MARRIAGE RECORDS OF CASWELL COUNTY, NORTH CAROLINA

GROOM	BRIDE	DATE
WILLIAMS, Nathaniel Jr.	DIXON, Elizabeth	06/26/1792
WILLIAMS, Nathaniel R.	SOMERS, Jemima A.	04/13/1859
WILLIAMS, Paul	DONOHO, Lucy	10/18/1791
WILLIAMS, Ralph D.	POWELL, Nanny W.	04/09/1863
WILLIAMS, Robert	ELAM, Nancy	02/06/1825
WILLIAMS, Robert H.	SLEDGE, Catherine A.	09/25/1851
WILLIAMS, Robert W.	DOTSON, Martha W.	02/20/1850
WILLIAMS, Stephen E.	MCNEILL, Emma L.	02/26/1850
WILLIAMS, Thomas N.	FULLAR, Mary	11/07/1789
WILLIAMS, Warner	LEWIS, Elizabeth M.	03/16/1813
WILLIAMS, William	PASS, Jemima	12/03/1788
WILLIAMS, William	SWANN, Peniciselia(?)	12/22/1778
WILLIAMS, Winstead	CHILDRESS, Annis	08/16/1834
WILLIAMS, Winston	PERKINS, Sarah	09/24/1842
WILLIAMS,(?) John D.	MATTOX, Sarah J.	07/06/1866
WILLIAMS,(?) John D.	MATTOX, Sarah J.	07/06/1866
WILLIAMSOIN, Mark	SLADE, Martha	08/28/1867
WILLIAMSON, Addison A.	BUTLER, Margaret E.	01/06/1849
WILLIAMSON, Anthony	LEA, Eliza K.	11/27/1818
WILLIAMSON, Anthony S.	MOORE, Sarah A.	11/12/1849
WILLIAMSON, Benjamin E.	HINTON, Eliza A.	11/15/1848
WILLIAMSON, Calvin	WILLIAMSON, Martha	03/02/1867
WILLIAMSON, Charles	HILL, Mary	02/25/1866
WILLIAMSON, Edmond	DODSON, Emeline	07/29/1866
WILLIAMSON, Elisha	SHACKELFORD, Luzeta	08/16/1867
WILLIAMSON, Emanuel	BROWN, Sophia	03/02/1867
WILLIAMSON, Felix	BUSHNELL, Mary	12/01/1866
WILLIAMSON, George	EASLY, Harriet E.	10/31/1838
WILLIAMSON, George	LEA, Rebecca S.	11/13/1815
WILLIAMSON, Green	COBB, Candice	12/24/1867
WILLIAMSON, Hall	SMITH, Nancy	10/19/1791
WILLIAMSON, Henry	LEA, Dilly A.	11/28/1867
WILLIAMSON, Jno. W.	WILLIAMSON, Virginia F.	07/30/1863
WILLIAMSON, Johnston	JOHNSTON, Maranda	02/22/1868
WILLIAMSON, Lemon	BETHEL, Louisa	04/14/1866
WILLIAMSON, Mintus	WILLIAMSON, Leatha	10/05/1867
WILLIAMSON, Monroe	CRUTCHFIELD, Minerva	04/20/1867
WILLIAMSON, Pulliam	ADKISON, Lucy	03/12/1782
WILLIAMSON, Robert H.	GUNN, Harriet E.	05/17/1865
WILLIAMSON, Simon	WATLINGTON, Victoria	12/26/1865
WILLIAMSON, Swift	LEA, Mary	12/12/1819
WILLIAMSON, Theodrick L.	SNEED, Mary	04/03/1828
WILLIAMSON, Thomas	GUNN, Ella	12/10/1865
WILLIAMSON, Thomas J.	SPENCER, Mary P.	10/19/1840
WILLIAMSON, Thompson	RICE, Harriet	01/12/1867
WILLIAMSON, Walter S.	JOHNSTON, Aderline W.	12/04/1860
WILLIAMSON, Weldon E.	JOHNSTON, Nanny N.	11/25/1856
WILLIAMSON,(? John D.	MATTOX, Sarah J.	07/06/1866
WILLIAMSON,(? John D.	MATTOX, Sarah J.	07/06/1866
WILLIASON, Simon	BETHEL, Caroline	12/13/1866
WILLINGHAM, John	BURCH, Mary	03/13/1788

MARRIAGE RECORDS OF CASWELL COUNTY, NORTH CAROLINA

GROOM	BRIDE	DATE
WILLIS, Anderson	RICE, Frances B.	05/24/1825
WILLIS, Barzilla	CANOR, Sarah	06/15/1849
WILLIS, Benjamin	CHANDLER, Susanna	11/20/1811
WILLIS, Benjamin Jr.	CAMPBELL, Lucinda	12/23/1846
WILLIS, George	SMITH, Sally J.	10/14/1841
WILLIS, George W.	STEPHENS, Malinda	01/14/1834
WILLIS, Henry	HADDOCK, Mary	05/21/1783
WILLIS, Henry	HARALSON, Darcas	02/21/1821
WILLIS, Henry Jr.	EVANS, Betsy	01/20/1830
WILLIS, James	WILLIAMS, Nancy	09/20/1834
WILLIS, James M.	BLACKWELL, Eliza	12/27/1867
WILLIS, James T.	WILLIAMS, Ann	11/19/1832
WILLIS, Jerry	PINCHBACK, Adaline	04/15/1867
WILLIS, John	WARD, Betsy	02/28/1827
WILLIS, John W.	LANDRUM, Sarah A.	10/07/1852
WILLIS, Joseph	CHANEY, Lydia	01/23/1842
WILLIS, Marshall	GRAVES, Ibby	11/24/1866
WILLIS, N.W.	WARE, C.E.	12/10/1857
WILLIS, Nicholas	TURNER, Nancy	10/29/1804
WILLIS, Peter Jr.	JONES, Rachel	12/19/1867
WILLIS, Pinkney	LEATH, Eliza	11/19/1867
WILLIS, Thomas H.	MITCHELL, Harriet R.	09/26/1844
WILLIS, Thomas J.	LEA, Sophia A.	03/01/1841
WILLIS, William	MILLER, Elizabeth	12/05/1785
WILLIS, William	MCCAIN,(?) Charlotte	08/01/1850
WILLIS, William S.	THOMPSON, Frances P.	12/06/1863
WILLSON, George M.	LEA, Polly	04/12/1810
WILLSON, James	BURGESS, Mildred	12/10/1792
WILLSON, John	BOULDING, Rebecca	11/29/1818
WILLSON, Lorenzo J.	HIX, Elizabeth	09/02/1858
WILLSON, Robert	STEPHENS, Abarilla	12/28/1782
WILLSON, Robert	BRYAN, Elizabeth M.	03/21/1797
WILLSON, Samuel	BOWS, Lucy	09/17/1860
WILLSON, Thaddus	BASS, Frances	12/28/1844
WILLSON, Wilem W.	FARLEY, Patsy	01/02/1793
WILMOTH, George	HALL, Sally	03/25/1822
WILMOTH, Miles	HALL, Adelethia	09/11/1820
WILSON, Abel	GRANT, Lucy	11/01/1800
WILSON, Abner	MORGAN, Sally	01/23/1800
WILSON, Dennis	RICE, Martha G.	08/10/1818
WILSON, George L.	PASS, Catherine	09/11/1820
WILSON, Giles	WARE, Patsy	04/24/1804
WILSON, Henry	WILSON, Betsy	01/05/1867
WILSON, Henry W.	FULLER, Nancy	04/22/1818
WILSON, Isaac	WALDEN, Mildred	08/23/1842
WILSON, James	STANBACK, Betsy	01/04/1825
WILSON, James	CRISP, Margaret	03/15/1790
WILSON, James H.	KIRBY, Ann R.	01/23/1855
WILSON, John	SMITH, Ann	12/04/1821
WILSON, John	WILLIS, Keziah W.	07/02/1833
WILSON, John W.	JACKSON, Eliza	05/16/1859

MARRIAGE RECORDS OF CASWELL COUNTY, NORTH CAROLINA

GROOM	BRIDE	DATE
WILSON, John W.	DAVIS, Abigail	02/02/1848
WILSON, Johnston	WHITLOE, Ursly	12/03/1788
WILSON, Joseph	WELLS, Sarah	07/29/1799
WILSON, Mike	MCCADEN, Juda	07/27/1867
WILSON, Robert	JOHNSTON, Elizabeth	12/28/1795
WILSON, Robert	WALKER, Polly	09/26/1831
WILSON, Rufus	JONES, Fanny	10/18/1865
WILSON, Thomas	NASH, Manerva A.	03/21/1853
WILSON, William	RUDD,(?) Nancy	01/--/1812
WILSON, William	REED,(?) Nancy	01/--/1812
WILSON, William	BERRY, Rebecca	12/29/1815
WILSON, William	CURRIE, Mary	07/02/1809
WILSON, William L.	YOUNG, Martha S.	08/26/1862
WINDSOR, Edward	POWELL, Adaline	06/19/1867
WINDSOR, Felix	BUSHNELL, Sabry	10/20/1866
WINDSOR, John Jr.	HORNBUCKLE, Susanna	09/07/1795
WINDSOR, Joseph	HARALSON, Elizabeth	10/21/1811
WINDSOR, Newman	WINDSOR, Frances	08/07/1813
WINDSOR, Thomas	HORNBUCKLE, Milly	12/31/1797
WINDSOR, William	SIMPSON, Rachel	04/13/1868
WINGFIELD, Nelson D.	FRANKLIN, Sarah A.	11/20/1833
WININGHAM Sharp	MORGAN, Polly	07/20/1793
WINNE, Obadiah	BOULTON, Ony	03/04/1786
WINNEM, Stephen	WILLIS, Mary	03/05/1789
WINSTEAD, Charles	MOORE, Sarah	06/15/1---
WINSTEAD, Stephen	HAYS, Elizabeth	11/19/1832
WINSTEAD, William	WRIGHT, Martha	12/05/1844
WINSTON, Jno. R.	LONG, Marian	11/13/1866
WINSTON, Thos.	COLEMAN, Patsy	12/29/1796
WINTER, William	BELEW, Mary	09/30/1795
WINTERS, Walter	DRAPER, Betsy	12/20/1797
WINTERS, Watson	WOMACK, Nancy	02/05/1815
WIRE, Josiah	IRBY, Mary	11/07/1829
WISDOM, Abner	FULLER, Mary	01/20/1790
WISDOM, Barzillai	DAMERON, Phebe	11/29/1827
WISDOM, John	FULLER, Sarah	02/10/1792
WISDOM, William	ROAN, Elizabeth	02/15/1830
WISEMAN, John	DOWNS, Mary A.	06/11/1842
WITCHER, Daniel P.	MILLNER, Martha A.	08/16/1852
WITHERS, Elijah	STUBBLEFIELD, Catherine	05/23/1817
WITHERS, Elijah B.	PRICE, Mary A.	03/25/1863
WITHERS, Elijah K.	LAWSON, Nancy B.	04/08/1826
WITHERS, Lewis H.	RICHARDSON, Mary A.	02/20/1844
WITHERS, Warren	BLACKWELL, Jane	07/27/1867
WOLTERS, Henry	HARGIS, Sarah	01/31/1792
WOMACK, Abraham	COBB, Louisa M.	11/29/1838
WOMACK, Algernon S.	GRAVES, Fanny W.	08/08/1855
WOMACK, Cato	HOOPER, Polly	11/20/1867
WOMACK, David	GRAVES, Delila	03/24/1800
WOMACK, Green P.	HATCHETT, Elizabeth C.	10/17/1831
WOMACK, Joseph B.	BLACKWELL, Elizabeth	12/14/1847

MARRIAGE RECORDS OF CASWELL COUNTY, NORTH CAROLINA

GROOM	BRIDE	DATE
WOMACK, Lewis P.	WILLIAMSON, Sarah F.	02/20/1846
WOMACK, Pleasant H.	HARALSON, Sarah	12/04/1828
WOMACK, Rufus Y.	STONE, Betty M.	11/23/1865
WOMACK, Thomas J.	YANCEY, Ann E.	07/09/1855
WOMACK, William P.	OLIVER, Matilda	01/27/1841
WOMBLE, James	BOULDIN, Catherine	12/01/1823
WOOD, John	FULLER, Margaret	10/22/1829
WOOD, John	ANDERSON, Polly	03/11/1797
WOODEY, John	WALTERS, Nancy	12/27/1845
WOODING, John E.	OWEN, Lucy A.	02/29/1834
WOODS, A.S.G.	LAFTIS, Martha A.	04/04/1849
WOODS, Archy S.G.	RICHMOND, Frances	11/20/1838
WOODS, J.G.	BOLTON, Mary W.	08/10/1841
WOODS, James	BERRY, Martha	12/10/1822
WOODS, John	FARLEY, Catherine	11/09/1801
WOODS, Lewis	JAMES, Jane	05/15/1867
WOODS, William	WATLINGTON, Letitia	10/21/1845
WOODS, William	FARLEY, Mary	12/20/1800
WOODY, Frank	LONG, Franky	07/04/1866
WOODY, James	FERGERSON, Sarah	09/04/1842
WOODY, John	ROBERTS, Betsy	08/05/1801
WOODY, Thomas	CARTER, Sally	03/25/1808
WOOLLEN, Minor	HATCHETT, Margaret	01/03/1867
WORD, Fleming	MCCAIN, Mary C.	01/31/1851
WORKMAN, Isaac	SULLIVANT, Susanna	10/11/1799
WORSHAM, Beary	WEST, Elizabeth	01/26/1809
WORSHAM, Ludwell	BENNATT, Nancy	07/03/1813
WORSHAM, Ludwell	COX, Elizabeth	09/03/1807
WORSHAM, Robert W.	BUCEY, Sarah	08/17/1833
WORSHAM, Thomas J.	BLACKWELL, Julia A.	11/22/1850
WORSHAM, William R.	DURHAM, Frances	12/12/1836
WOSHAM, Robert	PISTOLE, Patsy	06/10/1---
WRAY, Thomas	POWELL, Amy	02/26/1825
WRAY, Thomas Jr.	FOWLER, Rebecca	11/04/1790
WRAY, William	ADAMS, Sally	10/30/1801
WRENN, Hillmon W.	MITCHELL, Sina E.	12/10/1866
WRENN, John F.	STRATTON, Lenora H.	11/29/1858
WRIGHT, Abraham	LEA, Nancy	01/09/1826
WRIGHT, Abram M.	CHANDLER, Adeline W.	06/25/1850
WRIGHT, Caleb	THOMAS, Betsy	12/31/1792
WRIGHT, Edward	LAWSON, Sina B.	12/07/1821
WRIGHT, Elisha	POUND, Nancy	05/28/1812
WRIGHT, George W.	HOLCOMB, Sarah A.	01/05/1847
WRIGHT, Hiram A.	LAWSEN, Jane B.	10/06/1828
WRIGHT, Isaac	MCCUBBINS, Dolly	04/28/1833
WRIGHT, Isaac	SOMERS, Abajah	01/12/1804
WRIGHT, Jacob Jr.	WARREN, Nancy	11/08/1815
WRIGHT, Jacob Jr.	DONOHO, Polly	01/14/1794
WRIGHT, James B.	HAWKINS, Mary E.	09/09/1867
WRIGHT, John C.	MEACHUM, Paulina F.	10/25/1863
WRIGHT, John L.	WITHERS, Alice	10/02/1863

MARRIAGE RECORDS OF CASWELL COUNTY, NORTH CAROLINA

GROOM	BRIDE	DATE
WRIGHT, Sidney R.	LOCKARD, Sarah T.	09/05/1858
WRIGHT, William B.	KING, A.E.	09/19/1865
WRIGHT, William G.	MURPHEY, Nancy	11/01/1841
WRIGHT, Zacharias	HAYES, Polly	12/24/1793
WRIGHT, Zera	SANDERS, Lyda	10/29/1839
WYATT, Royal	JONES, Sarah	05/03/1828
WYNN, Robert S.	FEIGUS, Julia F.	07/25/1865
WYNN, Stith	RAMEY, Margaret L.	09/29/1847
WYNNE, William B.	HENDERSON, Elizabeth A.	05/10/1865
YANCEY, Algernon S.	GRAVES, Henrietta W.	05/21/1838
YANCEY, Felix	ROBERTSON, Pathena	11/16/1865
YANCEY, James	JOHNSTON, Zelpha	06/24/1811
YANCEY, James	KERR, Lucy	01/14/1794
YANCEY, Nathan	GLASS, Fanny	01/26/1867
YANCEY, Ransom	FOSTER, Henrietta	12/23/1867
YANCEY, Spivy	TAYLOR, Fanny	06/17/1849
YANCEY, Thomas	TAIT, Elizabeth	02/10/1802
YANCEY, Thomas	SIMMONS, Kesiah	02/24/1789
YANCEY, William	OLIVER, Damaris R.	12/16/1839
YANCEY, Willy	RICE, Susanna	05/12/1804
YANCY, Bartlett	GRAVES, Nancy	12/20/1808
YANCY, John	MOORE, Elizabeth L.	02/24/1789
YARBOROUGH, Samuel	WINSTED, Ailse	11/10/1787
YARBROUGH, Augustine J.	ROBERTS, Sally A.	11/02/1856
YARBROUGH, David	YARBROUGH, Miranda	07/07/1866
YARBROUGH, Joseph	HERRING, Mary	08/20/1825
YARBROUGH, Richard L.	PASS, Rachel M.	08/24/1858
YARBROUGH, Thomas S.	TERRY, Elizabeth A.	02/12/1850
YATES, Alexander	BAYES, Betsy	05/18/1850
YATES, George	DURHAM, Priscilla	05/20/1822
YATES, George W.	BAYS, Mary C.	01/29/1853
YATES, Grief	LOVELESS, Harriet A.	04/19/1860
YATES, Jackson	DURHAM, Ann	10/30/1844
YATES, James	GILLGORE, Lydia	07/21/1784
YATES, John M.	DURHAM, Harriet	08/07/1848
YATES, John M.Jr.	GATEWOOD, Louisa F.	11/19/1866
YATES, Joseph M.	HODNETT, Lucinda A.	05/06/1849
YEALOCK, Lewis	MATHEWS, Sally L.	11/13/1815
YEALOCK, Robert	HODGE, Catherine	10/22/1824
YEARBY, Charles	LAY, Patsy	10/12/1808
YEATS, John	ROPPER, Jemima	03/08/1779
YEATS, John	CALDWELL, Catherine	10/13/1780
YELOCK, James	PITTARD, Ann	10/26/1813
YOUNG, Jesse C.	BENNETT, Sarah	04/30/1857
YOUNG, Smith	HARRISON, Ann E.	05/11/1824
YOUNGER, John C.	BAUGH, Emma	08/21/1866
ZACHARY, Bartholomew	BRUCE, Polly	05/22/1797
ZACHARY, William	LEA, Nancy	11/21/1780
ZIMMERMAN, George J.	KIMBROUGH, Susan S.	01/24/1853

ALPHABETICAL LISTING
OF BRIDES

MARRIAGE RECORDS OF CASWELL COUNTY, NORTH CAROLINA

BRIDE	GROOM	DATE
-----, -----	ALEXANDER, Benjamin	08/24/1819
-----, -----	ATWELL, John	12/20/1807
-----, -----	BAGLEY, George	05/11/1808
-----, -----	BARKER, Burnley	04/25/1809
-----, -----	BAYES, Thompson	10/09/1850
-----, -----	BRINSFIELD, Dennard	10/13/1806
-----, -----	CORBETT, Burel	--/--/----
-----, -----	GRAVES, Geo.	09/20/1866
-----, -----	JAY, James	01/24/1798
-----, -----	HOWARD, Alexis	12/01/1842
-----, -----	LEA, Alexander	--/--/----
-----, -----	LEA, James	04/11/1821
-----, -----	MORTON, Alexander B.	06/16/1837
-----, -----	PHAROAH, John	10/21/1789
-----, -----	BURTON, Richd.	--/--/1787
-----, -----	CASH, Moses	06/16/----
-----, -----	RICE, John	12/23/1806
-----, -----	SARGENT, Demsy	--/--/1815
-----, -----	THOMAS, John	12/31/1811
-----, -----	WARREN, Georeg N.	05/12/1818
-----, -----	WEATHERFORD, Hiram	--/--/----
-----, Ann	EVERETT, Danl.	07/04/1843
ABLES, Sally	HODGE, John	11/10/1822
ADAMS, Amanda	TANKERSLEY, James M.	12/13/1866
ADAMS, Eliza A.	HOLYCROSS, Robert	02/18/1841
ADAMS, Elizabeth	ROLAND, Fendul	01/16/1815
ADAMS, Martha A.	BURCH, Peter L.	04/29/1842
ADAMS, Mary	BARLOW, Caloway	01/27/1845
ADAMS, Mary	KNIGHT, Evans	12/27/1841
ADAMS, Mary J.	BRIGHTWELL, Wm. C.	09/02/1859
ADAMS, Sally	WRAY, William	10/30/1801
ADAMS, Sarah J.	ROGERS, William A.	04/29/1842
ADKENS, Betsy	PAGE, James	02/22/1802
ADKERSON, Susannah	COE, William	02/05/1828
ADKINS, Ann R.	PAGE, Milton	10/12/1839
ADKINS, Caroline	SNOW, Richard	08/11/1845
ADKINS, Mary E.	PATTILLO, Anderson H. W.	09/13/1866
ADKINS, Polley	FOSTER, Jesse	11/03/1817
ADKINS, Susan	GRAVES, Morris	10/28/1866
ADKINS, Susanna	BROOKES, Thomas	12/24/1816
ADKISON, Lucy	WILLIAMSON, Pulliam	03/12/1782
AKELS, Elizabeth	RAINEY, William	01/22/1782
AKIN, Betsey	BOHANNAN, Nathaniel	05/07/1802
AKIN, Polly	FERGUSON, John	04/10/1816
ALBERT, Frances	MCCROREY, David	01/02/1838
ALBRIDGE, Jane	BURKE, William A.	01/04/1845
ALDERIDGE, Nancy	PUCKETT, James	12/27/1833
ALDRIDG, Susanna	MELTON, David	12/30/1816
ALDRIDGE, Artila	STADLER, William B.	10/20/1840
ALDRIDGE, Hannah	ALLRED, William B.	11/17/1845
ALDRIDGE, Martha	HERNDON, George	01/18/1866

MARRIAGE RECORDS OF CASWELL COUNTY, NORTH CAROLINA

BRIDE	GROOM	DATE
ALDRIDGE, Nancy	CHANDLER, Rufus W.	11/08/1843
ALDRIDGE, Susan	VAUGHAN, William	10/03/1851
ALFORD, Susanna	HOOPPER, Samuel	01/07/1817
ALISON, Mary	HOLT, Dibden	04/03/1787
ALLEN, Amanda S.	GREEN, Joseph G.	10/12/1836
ALLEN, Arenia M.	ROBERTS, Geo. W.	01/02/1840
ALLEN, Cressy	WHITTAKER, John	07/31/1804
ALLEN, Elizabeth	LAWSON, John Jr.	03/25/1790
ALLEN, Elizabeth	MARSHALL, Charles	04/17/1833
ALLEN, Frances J.	WILLIAMS, John W.	01/29/1863
ALLEN, Martha A.	MOORE, Albert	08/07/1827
ALLEN, Mary	BUCKINGHAM, Bird	08/10/1866
ALLEN, Sally	SAWYERS, John	12/31/1825
ALLEN, Sarah	BROWNING, Edmond	02/13/1790
ALLEN, Sarah A.	MCMULLIN, James M.M.	08/06/1852
ALLEN, Sarah P.	EDWARDS, Gustavus A.	02/22/1830
ALLEN, Sarah P.	OGLESBY, John S.	10/07/1834
ALLEN, Sarah S.	ROBERTSON, George W.B.	08/02/1826
ALLEN, Susannah	HUSTON, William	01/26/1785
ALLIN, Elizabeth	BROWNING, Thomas	09/19/1795
ALLIN, Elizabeth	SATTERFIELD, Jesse	05/16/1789
ALLIN, Sarah	REDMUN, William	12/27/1791
ALLREN, Nancy	RAVENS, James	10/19/1791
ALRED, Louisa E.	RUDD, Thomas H.	01/16/1866
ALVERSON, Martha G.	MCKINNEY, Robert	06/15/1852
ALVERSON, Mary A.	KENNON, James	12/01/1821
ALVERSON, Nelly	GUNN, Thomas	10/24/1797
ANDERSON, Ann	MITCHELL, David Jr.	06/24/1782
ANDERSON, Ann P.	LAND, Williamson H.	09/29/1858
ANDERSON, Caty	ECTOR, Joseph	10/15/1804
ANDERSON, Jenny	ECTOR, James	03/10/1808
ANDERSON, Minerva M.	GANT, Jesse	06/20/1840
ANDERSON, Patsey	BRIGMAN, James	03/08/1816
ANDERSON, Polly	MITCHELL, John	01/02/1796
ANDERSON, Polly	WOOD, John	03/11/1797
ANDERSON, Rachel	KERBY, Richard	01/21/1802
ANDERSON, Sarah	MUZZALL, William A.	09/04/1838
ANDERSON, Susan B.	SIMPSON, Joseph	12/12/1843
ANGLES, Sophia	NEWBY, Asa R.	05/11/1859
ANGLIN, Catherine	BROWNING, William	08/24/1797
ANGLIN, Sally	SMITH, Richard	10/26/1804
ANNMONETT, Rose E.	ROBENHISER, Robert R.	07/04/1866
ANTHONEY, Jane	CORDER, Joel	11/15/1784
ANTHONY, Elizabeth	GOOCH, Thomas	08/12/1799
ANTHONY, Pembrook	PAUL, Asa	08/27/1803
ANTHONY, V. E.	HARRIS, James L.	02/04/1852
APPLE, Mary F.	SMITH, Peter	03/08/1865
APPLE, Mary J. E.	MCCAIN, Alfred P.	09/07/1864
ARCHDEACON, Alsey	FULCHER, William	09/04/1787
ARNETT, Margaret	RUARK, Edward	11/03/1802
ARNETT, Mary L.	FURGERSON, Samuel	08/12/1822

MARRIAGE RECORDS OF CASWELL COUNTY, NORTH CAROLINA

BRIDE	GROOM	DATE
ARNETT, Nancy	PRICE, Peter	09/01/1804
ARNETT, Sally	HUGLE, John	06/20/1814
ARNOLD, Lydia F.	STADLER, Robert D.	12/03/1838
ARNOLD, Mary	TURNER, Isham	11/02/1832
ARNOLD, Nancy	STADLER, John	12/13/1812
ARRINGTON, Adeline	TURNER, James B.	06/10/1862
ARVIN, Patsey	KING, James	01/27/1817
ASHFORD, Sally	PILES, James	10/23/1802
ASHLEY, Nancy	OAKLEY, William	12/04/1790
ASLUM, Betsey	DEACON, Henry	04/09/1857
ASTIN, Margaret	BUCEY, Isaac F.	10/25/1830
ATKINS, Jenny	PAGE, Whitehead	12/23/1795
ATKINS, Mildred	SMITH, Thomas	11/27/1804
ATKINS, Zilly	THOMAS, Daniel	01/12/1808
ATKINSON, Avey	PARKS, Solomon	12/20/1782
ATKINSON, Lucey Ann	BAUGH, John J.	06/20/1857
ATKINSON, Mary F.	HARRISON, Thomas P.	11/04/1852
ATKINSON, Phebe R.	EVERETT, John	02/18/1813
ATKINSON, Polly	TURNER, John	11/22/1796
ATKINSON, Susan W.	FLIPPIN, Joseph W.	06/04/1856
ATWELL, Peggy	SWANN, William	12/24/1807
AUSTIN, Elizabeth	TERRELL, Harrison A.	10/20/1843
AUSTIN, Fannie	ARNOLD, Wiett	01/06/1836
AUSTIN, Martha	TAYLOR, Napolean B.	09/07/1845
AUSTIN, Mary F.	GILLASPIE, Edward R.	07/13/1855
AUSTIN, Sally	VANHOOK, Loyd Jr.	11/09/1804
AUSTIN, Sarah V.	TARPLEY, James A.	11/16/1840
AUSTON, Mary	DAVIS, Jonarthon	04/17/1781
AVERETT, Betty	WALTON, Mazor	07/27/1867
BADGET, Recey H.	HESTER, Hamilton	03/27/1837
BADGET, Salley	KING, Robert J.	12/24/1821
BADGETT, Drusilla	KING, Samuel J.	06/28/1834
BADGETT, Elizabeth	VASS, Thomas Jr.	11/19/1838
BADGETT, Eunice	MITCHELL, Alfred	07/12/1836
BADGETT, Mary M.	MCALPIN, Alexander	01/19/1841
BADGETT, Mary W.	GATEWOOD, William D.	02/13/1856
BADGETT, Pocahontas A.	LAW, James T.	02/24/1859
BAGGETT, Rachel	MELEAR, John	01/12/1801
BAILEY, Glasshey(?)	ROBERTSON, John	12/25/1794
BAINES, Martha	ABBOTT, Richard M.	04/09/1867
BAINS, Elizabeth	BOHANNAN, J. M.	10/08/1856
BAIRDING, Seeley	GOING, Jesse	06/09/1784
BAIRDING, Seeley	GOING, John	06/09/1784
BALDEN, Delila	STRATEN, William	01/31/1825
BALDIN, Mary	KEEN, John	10/17/1800
BALDWIN, A. C.	GARBER, A. M. Jr.	03/16/1864
BALDWIN, Frances	MILLER, William D.	12/06/1845
BALDWIN, Frances	WALKER, David	03/17/1827
BALDWIN, Nancey	BEUSEY, John	07/03/1822
BALDWIN, Salley	EUDALEY, David	12/29/1817
BALDWIN, Sarah A.	KIMBRO, William N.	09/28/1847

MARRIAGE RECORDS OF CASWELL COUNTY, NORTH CAROLINA

BRIDE	GROOM	DATE
BALL, Cary	CONNALY, William J.	03/23/1816
BALL, Helen M.	OLIVER, Bivin D.	12/02/1867
BALL, Mary M.	MCCAIN, John W.	11/08/1849
BALL, Nancy	RUDD, James	03/27/1812
BALL, Polly	CONNALLY, George O.	01/17/1811
BALLAD, Priscilla	SANDERS, James	11/19/1822
BALLARD, Betsy	MARTIN, Robert	01/02/1798
BALLARD, Mary	COTTON, Henry	08/28/1838
BALLARD, Nancy	REED, John	06/26/1807
BALLARD, Patsy	BROWN, Richard	09/11/1810
BALLARD, Silvy	JEFFRES, Walton	08/08/1818
BANE, Anne	INGRAHAM, T. E.	11/05/1851
BANES, Fanny	WILES, Thomas	04/27/1819
BARGE, Fanny	PALMER, Dabney	12/30/1848
BARKER, Agnes R.	WILKERSON, Walter S.	09/09/1862
BARKER, Ann E.	HUGHES, James	01/15/1856
BARKER, Elizabeth	SIMPSON, George	12/11/1830
BARKER, Louisa	COBB, James	12/04/1846
BARKER, Martha A.	PIKE, Samuel R.	01/01/1852
BARKER, Mary	BROWN, John	04/09/1814
BARKER, Sarah J.	CORLEY, Charles S.	12/20/1865
BARKER, Susannah	KIMBRO, William	11/09/1797
BARNARD, Sarah F.	MAY, W. H.	02/19/1850
BARNES, Fanny M.	SMITH, William P.	11/07/1865
BARNES, Lydia A.	WELLS, Labon C.	02/08/1861
BARNET, Mary	DIXSON, Robert	09/09/1779
BARNETT, Ann	STANFIELD, Joseph M.	05/26/1836
BARNETT, Elizabeth	NORMAN, Wesley	05/24/1816
BARNETT, Elizabeth	ROWARK, Elisha	09/18/1804
BARNETT, Rebeccah	DEWESE, Isaiah	12/06/1788
BARNHILL, Mary	BATMAN, Bird H.	11/14/1833
BARNWELL, Eliza	MORRIS, James	11/10/1841
BARNWELL, Frances C.	WARREN, Burwell	08/06/1852
BARNWELL, Peggy	MCCORD, William	03/03/1801
BARNWELL, Temperance A.	MCCORD, William	09/25/1824
BARRICKS, Mary J.	BARRICKS, David G.	02/14/1843
BARSDALE, Kesiah	DUNAWAY, Samuel	02/29/1792
BARTLETT, Ann	TURNER, William	12/04/1802
BARTLETT, Elizabeth	HIGHTOWER, William	05/04/1824
BARTLETT, Patsy	THOMAS, Christopher	11/19/1808
BARTON, Ann	SIMMONS, George	12/16/1797
BARTON, Kezia	BARKER, John	11/19/1806
BARTON, Margaret E.	FREELAND, Charles J.	08/30/1853
BARTON, Polly	DENNY, Simon	04/26/1796
BARTON, Sally	SIMMONS, Abraham	03/06/1813
BASDALL, Francis	BLACK, Hardy	02/06/1821
BASDELL, Mary	BUCKINGHAM, James	11/16/1819
BASS, Frances	WILLSON, Thaddus	12/28/1844
BASS, Mahala	PILES, Albert	10/08/1855
BASS, Margaret	PHILIPS, Frederick	01/14/1846
BASS, Mary A.	WALTON, John H.	02/21/1860

MARRIAGE RECORDS OF CASWELL COUNTY, NORTH CAROLINA

BRIDE	GROOM	DATE
BASTIN, Ann W.	CARVER, Benjamin F.	05/15/1830
BASTIN, Margarett	JOHNSON, John Jr.	10/26/1830
BASTINE, Hannah	NUNN, William	10/26/1830
BASWELL, Lucinda	PATTILLO, Lewis A.	01/22/1839
BATEMAN, Martha B.	COLEMAN, Alexander	10/29/1855
BATEMAN, Mary	JONES, Zalman	10/20/1846
BATEMAN, Susan	DAMERON, Samuel	03/03/1828
BATEMAN, V. W.	MALONE, James T.	09/20/1857
BATEMAN,(?) Barsheba	DAMERON, James K.	11/28/1829
BATTON, Jane	TALLEY, Peyton S.	12/04/1850
BATTON, Mary M.	GUNN, James M.	03/13/1843
BATTON, Sarah M.	CRISP, William H.	06/09/1848
BAUGH, Emma	YOUNGER, John C.	08/21/1866
BAUGH, Louisa F.	CLAPSADDLE, John H.	09/24/1863
BAULDIN, Catherine	FISHER, Tressy	01/12/1801
BAWLDIN, Delia	STRATEN, William	12/23/1823
BAXDALE, Nancy	STOCKES, Moore	10/22/1817
BAXTER, Catherine	BULLOCK, John	03/23/1791
BAXTER, Delilah	CARROL, Edward	01/09/1827
BAXTER, Frances	QUINE, William	11/12/1808
BAXTER, Maryann	STROTHER, Peter	06/11/1788
BAXTER, Nancy	WELCH, Samuel	01/04/1782
BAYES, Betsy	YATES, Alexander	05/18/1850
BAYES, Lavina J.	TRUE, Lewis J.	04/12/1864
BAYNES, Isabella	DODSON, John F.	07/04/1817
BAYNES, Jane	BURTON, Francis A.	02/02/1856
BAYNES, Nancy	BOHANNON, Maynard	09/23/1841
BAYNES, Perthena	WALKER, Freeman	11/25/1842
BAYNES, Polly	DAVIS, William	06/08/1812
BAYNES, Sally	BURTON, Drury	04/07/1864
BAYS, Lucy	FORGERSON, Garrett	08/05/1841
BAYS, Mary C.	YATES, George W.	01/29/1853
BAYS, Nancy	NORMAN, William	12/01/1858
BAZWELL, Fanny	ROBESON, John	10/12/1784
BAZWELL, Mary	MCFARLAND, Daniel	09/10/1789
BAZWELL, Susanna	SMITH, Amasa	04/02/1811
BEADLES, Elizabeth	STANFIELD, William	12/14/1789
BEAUCEY, Polley	FEGUSON, Thomas	12/15/1810
BEAVER, Ann	GOMER, John	02/20/1810
BEAVER, Betsy	WALKER, John	12/18/1813
BEAVER, Catherine	STOWERS, John	01/29/1810
BEAVER, Delila	SANDERS, Ranson P.	03/08/1832
BEAVER, Frances	SARTIN, Anslum	10/22/1834
BEAVER, Jemima	LOVELACE, Henry R.	04/08/1858
BEAVER, Judith	GOMER, Barzillai	09/29/1814
BEAVER, Mary	SCOTT, John	12/22/1789
BEAVERS, Mildred	SOMERS, John	11/11/1843
BEAVOR, Nancy	MAYO, Richard	12/23/1795
BELEW, Jamima	HARVELL, Pati	09/17/1788
BELEW, Jamima	HARVELL, Peyton	09/17/1788
BELEW, Mary	WINTER, William	09/30/1795

MARRIAGE RECORDS OF CASWELL COUNTY, NORTH CAROLINA

BRIDE	GROOM	DATE
BELL, Sarah	BRINTLE, Solomon	05/29/1810
BENNATT, Lucy	SAWYER, William	10/08/1804
BENNATT, Nancey	HENDERSON, William	01/05/1807
BENNATT, Nancy	SHRYER, Jacob	01/13/1810
BENNATT, Nancy	WORSHAM, Ludwell	07/03/1813
BENNATT, Polley	GRAVES, Thomas	05/05/1801
BENNATT, Polley	HOOPER, Thomas	05/28/1814
BENNETT, Adeline	CARTER, John	02/24/1849
BENNETT, America	SCOTT, Allen	03/30/1823
BENNETT, Betsy	BYSOR, Peter	02/22/1800
BENNETT, Elizabeth	HOOPER, Henry	09/23/1854
BENNETT, Frances N.	HALL, Lambert W.	03/25/1858
BENNETT, Julia	BENNETT, John N.	11/11/1857
BENNETT, Martha T.	GATEWOOD, Thomas L.	05/31/1853
BENNETT, Mary B.	WATLINGTON, Hiram S.	11/23/1823
BENNETT, Polly	GOWIN, Richard	07/04/1807
BENNETT, Sarah	YOUNG, Jesse C.	04/30/1857
BENNETT, Susan	HENDRICK, William H.	03/19/1841
BENNITT, Milly	WARF, Noel	10/29/1845
BENTON, Cary	SINGLETON, Jerry	04/11/1801
BENTON, Deborah	STACY, Thomas	07/30/1816
BENTON, Lucinda	LYNN, Bayless	10/10/1820
BENTON, Mary	DOUGLASS, David	11/05/1817
BENTON, Polly	ROBERTS, John	01/19/1846
BERREY, Nancy	SOMERS, Zeary	07/20/1844
BERRY, Frances	NANCE, Clemmons	12/08/1819
BERRY, Jane	KIRK, Samuel	06/17/1822
BERRY, Martha	WOODS, James	12/10/1822
BERRY, Mary	PIKE, Lewis	01/10/1787
BERRY, Nancy	SERTAIN, Johnston	07/20/1830
BERRY, Polly	NANCE, Frederick	01/09/1809
BERRY, Rebecca	ANTHONY, Jonathan	11/07/1781
BERRY, Rebecca	WILSON, William	12/29/1815
BETHEL, Caroline	WILLIASON, Simon	12/13/1866
BETHEL, Louisa	WILLIAMSON, Lemon	04/14/1866
BETHEL, Louisa N.	SNEED, William M.	06/28/1842
BETHELL, Agnes G.	TORIAN, Thomas	06/17/1836
BETHELL, Ann	MULLINS, Jerry	01/19/1867
BETTS, Eliza	HOWARD, Henry	03/20/1820
BETTS, Maria H.	FITZGERALD, Banister R.	01/05/1829
BEUSEY, Nancy	MASON, Willey	10/17/1809
BEVIELL, Thursey	LUNCEFORD, William	05/27/1833
BEVILL, Lucy	BARNWELL, Edward	02/21/1804
BEWSEY, Eliza	HARRISON, Jesse	06/13/1822
BIGELOW, Harriet	BIGELOW, Willis	12/30/1866
BIGELOW, Mary	TURNER, James C.	12/17/1823
BINGHAM, Permela	DOLTON, Isam	06/03/1833
BIRCH, Delany	PASS, John	05/28/1820
BIRCH, Sarah	COLLEY, Bannister	11/19/1848
BIRD, Caty	BROUGHTON, Jeremiah	09/21/1805
BIRD, Eliza Ann	BOSWELL, Thomas	09/28/1861

MARRIAGE RECORDS OF CASWELL COUNTY, NORTH CAROLINA

BRIDE	GROOM	DATE
BIRD, Elizabeth A.	FLORENCE, Bennett	10/18/1837
BIRD, Lucinda	BOSWELL, Calvin G.	01/15/1844
BIRD, Mary	BURKE, Johnson	12/17/1837
BIRD, Mary E.	ADAMS, Hannible A. H.	04/13/1862
BIRD, Sarah	TATE, R.T.	09/25/1821
BIRK, Mildred	COX, Thomas	01/09/1823
BIRKE, Frances	SIMMONS, Elisha	11/25/1845
BIZWELL, Betsy	MCKEEN, Alexander	12/12/1799
BIZWELL, Sally	PRIDE, Burton	10/29/1780
BLACK, Elizabeth	HARALSON, Major	07/16/1793
BLACK, Sarah	TURNER, Abraham R.	10/20/1784
BLACKSTOCK, Lucy S.	MCHANEY, William R.	12/26/1860
BLACKWELL, Betsy	MALONE, Lewis	12/02/1811
BLACKWELL, Catharine	GOMER, Wiley	09/28/1846
BLACKWELL, Eliza	WILLIS, James M.	12/27/1867
BLACKWELL, Elizabeth	WOMACK, Joseph B.	12/14/1847
BLACKWELL, Elizabeth S.	HOWARD, Cary A.	02/25/1828
BLACKWELL, Huldah B.	GLASS, Saml.	04/28/1866
BLACKWELL, Jane	WITHERS, Warren	07/27/1867
BLACKWELL, Jane P.	WATLINGTON, Paul	02/21/1838
BLACKWELL, Julia A.	WORSHAM, Thomas J.	11/22/1850
BLACKWELL, Kiturah (?)	WATT, Samuel Jr.	11/01/1808
BLACKWELL, Martha	GARRETT, John W.	02/02/1835
BLACKWELL, Martha	MITCHELL, Charles G.	09/23/1843
BLACKWELL, Martha	ROBERTS, George	03/01/1827
BLACKWELL, Martha A.	JONES, Richard H.	02/26/1843
BLACKWELL, Mary B.	PALMER, Clem	09/16/1867
BLACKWELL, Matilda	JONES, Edward M.	12/23/1817
BLACKWELL, Nancy	FOSTER, Madison P.	01/17/1842
BLACKWELL, Nancy	MALONE, Lewis	10/18/1792
BLACKWELL, Polly	WATT, James	11/--/1809
BLACKWELL, Susanna	WEATHERFORD, Warren	11/27/1815
BLACKWELL, Zilla	PARRISH, James	05/29/1861
BLAIR, Polly	RUSSEL, Edward	01/09/1808
BLAIR, Sallie	FOWLER, Harrison,	01/21/1866
BLARTLETT, Caroline	MORRIS, Richard A.	09/25/1836
BOHAN, Katey	JONES, Phillip	12/05/1815
BOHANNAN, Dolly	WILES, Thomas	06/06/1809
BOHANNAN, Margaret P.	WALTERS, Thornton	01/02/1816
BOHANNAN, Rutha	JAMES, John	04/22/1867
BOHANNON, Rebecca	RUSSELL, John	01/05/1815
BOLDIN, Elizabeth	BIRD, Thomas	04/13/1824
BOLEY, A. M. F. P.	SIMPSON, Silas	05/08/1844
BOLEY, Elvira B.	EDWARDS, James	01/15/1829
BOLOCK, Nancy	LINTHICUM, Henry	11/24/1827
BOLTON, Amanda	CURRIE, Young	12/23/1867
BOLTON, Candis	STEWART, Mack	12/26/1866
BOLTON, Leony	SMITH, Green D.	09/01/1819
BOLTON, Lydia	PRICE, Thomas L.	09/21/1830
BOLTON, Mary W.	WOODS, J.G.	08/10/1841
BOLTON, Susan	HARRISON, James R.	02/03/1852

MARRIAGE RECORDS OF CASWELL COUNTY, NORTH CAROLINA

BRIDE	GROOM	DATE
BOMAN, Betsy	RICHMOND, James	11/10/1802
BOMAN, Nancy	NOEL, Ephraim	12/13/1803
BOMAR, Ann W.	COMER, William G.	04/04/1836
BORAN, Phebe	MCBRIDE, Andrew	10/11/1784
BOSWELL, Caroline	DONOHO, Charles D.	05/08/1861
BOSWELL, Eliza	CORNWELL, Samuel	12/26/1839
BOSWELL, Eliza	FIELDER, Leonard L.	09/12/1829
BOSWELL, Eliza	FLORANCE, Empson	12/07/1846
BOSWELL, Elizabeth	MASSEY, Pleasant C.	01/06/1853
BOSWELL, Elizabeth	PICKREL, Henry	10/06/1854
BOSWELL, Elizabeth	CANNADAY, John	12/16/1828
BOSWELL, Elizabeth	CHANDLER, George W.	11/05/1857
BOSWELL, Ella	BROWN, Madison	12/02/1866
BOSWELL, Eunice	HURDLE, Jacob O.	09/27/1836
BOSWELL, Francis	BRANNOCK, Samuel T.	12/21/1850
BOSWELL, Judy	CHANDLER, Hosea A.	12/08/1847
BOSWELL, Margaret	GIBSON, Thomas	12/28/1819
BOSWELL, Margaret	PAGE, James P.	12/16/1837
BOSWELL, Martha	HIGHTOWER, Francis	09/28/1850
BOSWELL, Martha C.	THOMPSON, Andrus J.	11/16/1859
BOSWELL, Mary	HERNDON, Edmund	08/26/1851
BOSWELL, Mary	COBB, Jesse	12/05/1817
BOSWELL, Maryann	BOWLS, John	10/21/1850
BOSWELL, Nancy	BOSWELL, Bedford A.	11/71/1842
BOSWELL, Nancy	BURKE, William T.	05/04/1858
BOSWELL, Phebe	WALKER, William F.	03/16/1850
BOSWELL, Rebecca	THOMAS, William	12/29/1865
BOSWELL, Sarah	MASSEY, Levi P.	12/12/1861
BOSWELL, Sarah A.	FRANKLIN, Zeary	05/07/1850
BOSWELL, Sinthy	BROOKES, Robert H.	12/06/1842
BOSWELL, Susan	JONES, Reuben	01/02/1843
BOULAND, Elizabeth	SANDERS, William	10/24/1863
BOULDEN, Jane	SIMPSON, Dennis	08/18/1866
BOULDIN, Catherine	WOMBLE, James	12/01/1823
BOULDIN, Julia	BLACKWELL, George	12/13/1866
BOULDIN, Mary	BYRD, Albert G.	01/23/1838
BOULDIN, Mary J.	MATKINS, John C.	02/28/1861
BOULDIN, Sarah S.	FLORENCE, James	09/21/1854
BOULDIN, Susan	MCMENAMY, James	01/09/1832
BOULDIN, Susan	MATKINS, Silas	07/10/1862
BOULDING, Rebecca	WILLSON, John	11/29/1818
BOULTON, Emily F.	MCCAIN, Jospeh N.	05/15/1858
BOULTON, Judith	THOMAS, Phillip	06/13/1781
BOULTON, Lucy	LEWIS, Charles	01/08/1795
BOULTON, Nancy	DIXON, Henry	03/08/1809
BOULTON, Ony	WINNE, Obadiah	03/04/1786
BOULTON, Sarah W.	DIXON, Levi	09/14/1823
BOWE, Cilla	LONG, Edmond	05/19/1866
BOWE, Elizabeth J.	FEATHERSTON, George A.	12/15/1858
BOWE, Harriet A.	EVANS, Samuel W.	10/12/1862
BOWE, Lilly	PAGE, William	11/19/1866

MARRIAGE RECORDS OF CASWELL COUNTY, NORTH CAROLINA

BRIDE	GROOM	DATE
BOWE, Sarah V.	HARRELSON, William E.	04/20/1853
BOWE, Susan	JONES, Mintus	01/26/1867
BOWERS, Henrietta	HOOD, Stephen	09/10/1823
BOWES, Frances	BROWN, Cicero	09/12/1866
BOWLES, Nancy	MORRIS, John R.	02/15/1830
BOWLS, Sarah	SUIT, John	12/22/1789
BOWLS, Selia	HENSLEY, Sidney	05/03/1855
BOWS, Lucy	WILLSON, Samuel	09/17/1860
BOYLES, Mahala A.	ROBERTSON, Jesse	06/10/1867
BOYLES, Susan	WARE, Nathaniel	04/17/1849
BOZWELL, Frances	BERRY, Elisha	01/03/1826
BOZWELL, Jenney	GOOCH, Nathaniel	01/23/1816
BOZWELL, Kitty F.	ROE, Robert	05/08/1822
BOZWELL, Sally	CHANDLER, William	05/14/1806
BRACHER, Nama	NELSON, Ambrose	09/09/1817
BRACKIN, Agripina	FRENCH, John	03/30/1833
BRACKIN, Arkey(?)	MITCHELL, Richard	12/18/1821
BRACKIN, Dorothy B.	WATLINGTON, Thomas	11/02/1824
BRACKIN, Elizabeth	HOWARD, Hugh	11/03/1815
BRACKIN, Isabella	BLACKWELL, Carter	04/28/1797
BRACKIN, Jane	COBB, John Jr.	12/18/1786
BRACKIN, Patcey	HARRELSON, Jeremiah	11/29/1803
BRACKIN, Sarah H.	MILLS, Thomas J.	05/29/1841
BRACKIN, Sina	CORBET, Pleasant	05/24/1839
BRACKIN, Sinah	DIXON, RObert	12/17/1823
BRADLEY, Betsy	LAWSON, Moses	12/06/1788
BRADLEY, Elizabeth	LEA, John	04/23/1780
BRADLEY, Lucy A.	WHITLOW, Josiah H.	04/25/1836
BRADLEY, Mary	MCADEN, Henry	11/06/1792
BRADLEY, Susan	SHELTON, John	05/13/1780
BRADSHAW, Mary F.	WEST, R. J.	12/21/1866
BRADSHEAR, Mattie E.	BRADSHER, W. G.	07/08/1865
BRADSHER, Frances	NELSON, Ambrose	07/10/1822
BRADSHER, Frances C.	STANFIELD, David V.	08/01/1850
BRADSHER, Martha A.	RIGGS, Thomas	12/20/1838
BRADSHER, Martha B.	GARROTT, Stephen	01/18/1823
BRADSHER, Nancey	HENDRIX, William	12/23/1786
BRADSHER, Nancy E.	BURTON, Thomas W.	06/25/1845
BRADSHER, Sally B.	TAYLOR, William W.	11/22/1856
BRADY, Eliza	GOULD, Benajmin	11/10/1838
BRANDON, Amanda	CLARK, Joseph	12/26/1867
BRANDON, Catherine A.	BUCKNER, Thomas S.	09/17/1854
BRANDON, Eliza H.	GUNN, Daniel B.	10/19/1839
BRANDON, Elizabeth	FOSTER, John	01/29/1820
BRANDON, Elizabeth	TAYLOR, Septimus(?)	02/13/1786
BRANDON, Frances	MONROE, Frederick	08/02/1867
BRANDON, Isabella	DANIEL, Alexander A.	11/06/1866
BRANDON, Jenny	BURTON, Thomas	12/28/1802
BRANDON, Judith	SNEAD, Micajah	10/24/1792
BRANDON, Margaret	WHITE, Turner D.	12/21/1816
BRANDON, Margret	HOSLER, Richard	04/02/1782

MARRIAGE RECORDS OF CASWELL COUNTY, NORTH CAROLINA

BRIDE	GROOM	DATE
BRANDON, Mary	HUDSON, Shadrach	09/25/1784
BRANDON, Mary	STEPHENS, Benjamin A.	12/--/1858
BRANDON, Mary E.	CONNALLY, William T.	11/01/1858
BRANDON, Rebecca	PRESTON, David	08/20/1787
BRANNOCK, Julia	BOSWELL, James M.	04/03/1849
BRANNUM, Emily	PILES, Henry	05/27/1861
BRATCHER, Dicey	JOHNSTON, John	01/31/1792
BRAUGHTON, Missouri S.	COMBES, Orrison G.	01/16/1837
BREEZE, Jane	BARNETT, William	02/18/1795
BRGG, Manerva	HARDY, Robert	08/17/1854
BRIGGS, J.	PHILLIPS, Ben	12/12/1860
BRIGGS, Minerva	WALKER, Monroe	10/08/1866
BRIGHTWELL, Martha S.	JENNINGS, Byrd T.	10/09/1839
BRINCEFIELD, Isabella	LAMBERT, Clayton	04/14/1854
BRINCEFIELD, Letitia	TERRELL, John H.	06/29/1861
BRINCEFIELD, Nancy	UNDERWOOD, Jonathan B.	12/21/1860
BRINCKLE, Nancey	BARKER, William	01/11/1820
BRINSFIELD, Betsey	COX, Henry	09/06/1845
BRINSFIELD, Patsey	HALL, Alexander	03/25/1828
BRINSFIELD, Sarah	SMITH, Starkey	12/19/1814
BRINTLE, Amy	PAGE, Joseph F.	02/03/1832
BRINTLE, Betsy	BUSH, Bennet	08/14/1809
BRINTLE, Nancey	DICKINS, William	--/--/----
BRINTLE, Parthena	BROWN, Robert	02/23/1818
BRINTLE, Polly	ROBERTS, Roland	04/06/1829
BRINTLE, Rainey	JACKSON, Spencer	12/20/1815
BROACH, Jenney	BROCHE, George	03/19/1803
BROADNAX, Chainy	HUNT, Steven	06/15/1867
BROOKES, Mary	BYRD, John	07/21/1795
BROOKES, Mary G.	BOSWELL, James	12/03/1832
BROOKS, Barbara	LEA, William	05/12/1848
BROOKS, Elizabeth	HOLDERNESS, Robert	02/20/1819
BROOKS, Frances	HORNBUCKLE, Franklin	01/15/1825
BROOKS, Frances	SHAPPARD, James	08/30/1797
BROOKS, Henrietta	BRUCE, Levi L.	01/29/1841
BROOKS, Jane	WATLINGTON, Edward	04/15/1820
BROOKS, Jenney	DIXON, Robert	11/22/1796
BROOKS, Mary	WARREN, Hiram	07/26/1848
BROOKS, Mary	WATLINGTON, Armistad	04/14/1790
BROOKS, Mary A.	MURREY, William J.	08/25/1867
BROOKS, Patsy	BUSH, Zenas	11/27/1805
BROOKS, Polley	ADKINS, James	04/02/1814
BROOKS, Polly	RICE, Ibzan	12/08/1818
BROOKS, Sarah	BLACKWELL, Garland	02/22/1839
BROOKS, Susanna	RICE, William	12/20/1784
BROOKS, Susanna W.	MIMS, Martin M.	01/29/1824
BROOKS, Ursley	RICE, Ibzan	05/05/1824
BROUGHTON, Hobsey A.	HENDRICK, James	12/20/1836
BROUGHTON, Luzella M.	HAGIE, Thomas	10/19/1841
BROUGHTON, Parthena	OAKLEY, Alexander	02/19/1833
BROWN, Ann	PETERSON, Thomas	--/--/----

MARRIAGE RECORDS OF CASWELL COUNTY, NORTH CAROLINA

BRIDE	GROOM	DATE
BROWN, China	ANDERSON, Nelson	12/22/1865
BROWN, Constant	SMITH, Mace	08/12/1782
BROWN, Edy H.	REID, William B.	11/15/1825
BROWN, Elioner	GOODMAN, Joseph	03/15/1781
BROWN, Elizabeth	ARCHER, Richard F.	05/19/1819
BROWN, Elizabeth	SWIFT, Anthony	08/19/1784
BROWN, Emily	STUBLEFIELD, Barnett	11/27/1866
BROWN, Frances	HOLLIS, Jesse	09/27/1798
BROWN, Gerly G.	FERGUSSON, John J.	10/30/1853
BROWN, Margaret	BEVIL, Peter	09/23/1866
BROWN, Martha	FOULKES, Edward M.	12/16/1811
BROWN, Martha	RICE, Edmund	11/30/1814
BROWN, Mary	COMER, John	10/26/1824
BROWN, Mary	KENNON, Thomas	03/02/1839
BROWN, Mary	MASSEY, Nathan	09/10/1828
BROWN, Mary	PRICE, John	01/15/1781
BROWN, Mary	BROWNING, Simeon	12/23/1819
BROWN, Matilda	GRAVES, Lucien	10/27/1865
BROWN, Nancey	JOHNSON, William	12/18/1838
BROWN, Nancy	EPPS, Lewis	05/20/1867
BROWN, Nancy	LAWSON, Robert W.	11/20/1827
BROWN, Polly	BURCH, Thomas	09/26/1798
BROWN, Rebecca	TAYLOR, James	11/27/1802
BROWN, Salley	BRINTLE, Oliver	02/24/1816
BROWN, Salley	HASKINS, John	10/26/1799
BROWN, Sally	CARTER, Jesse	12/17/1809
BROWN, Sarah	MARTIN, Richard	03/16/1816
BROWN, Sarah	WHITSETT, Alfred M.	09/06/1833
BROWN, Sarah C.	TAYLOR, Samuel	01/30/1841
BROWN, Sarah F.	WALKER, John H.	02/26/1862
BROWN, Sophia	WILLIAMSON, Emanuel	03/02/1867
BROWN, Susanna	BROWN, James	02/04/1808
BROWN, Tabitha J.	STANELY, James	05/31/1852
BROWN, Usley	TOMSON, Robert	09/28/1781
BROWNING, Ann	BYRD, Thomas	10/11/1784
BROWNING, Ann	ROBERTSON, Aaron P.	11/15/1838
BROWNING, Ann E.	WARREN, Thomas	10/06/1853
BROWNING, Annise(?)	RUDD, Pleasant	02/21/1822
BROWNING, Ava P.	SMITH, John C.	04/26/1845
BROWNING, Clary	CULBERSON, David	02/22/1782
BROWNING, Delila	LANNOM, Joseph	09/21/1799
BROWNING, Elizabeth	ROBERTS, Humphrey	01/23/1793
BROWNING, Fanny	RICE, Ziba	05/17/1805
BROWNING, Frances	LOVE, Snelson	12/18/1823
BROWNING, Frances	SMITH, Samuel	11/13/1826
BROWNING, Hannah	BROWNING, Robert	01/28/1786
BROWNING, Manerva E.	CAMPBELL, Allen C.	06/11/1855
BROWNING, Mary	CULBERSON, William	05/28/1800
BROWNING, Maryan	CUNNINGHAM, Thomas	06/22/1808
BROWNING, Nancey	BEAVER, Solomon	02/24/1809
BROWNING, Nancy	MARTIN, Robert	03/21/1812

MARRIAGE RECORDS OF CASWELL COUNTY, NORTH CAROLINA

BRIDE	GROOM	DATE
BROWNING, Nancy M.	STADLER, Robert D.	08/10/1862
BROWNING, Nelly	BRUCE, John	12/28/1796
BROWNING, Sarah F.	DAMERON, William M.	12/02/1852
BROWNING, Tabitha	MURRIE, James	09/26/1818
BRUCE, Betsy	TULLOCH, David	03/26/1796
BRUCE, Elizabeth	HENSLEE, Benjamin	01/04/1812
BRUCE, Martha	JONES, Richard	12/25/1792
BRUCE, Mary	HADDOCK, Henry	02/17/1844
BRUCE, Nancy	HAYES, James	12/30/1788
BRUCE, Nancy	RICE, James	11/03/1825
BRUCE, Polly	ZACHARY, Bartholomew	05/22/1797
BRUCE, Sarah	CARROL, James	11/29/1790
BRUER, Nancy	KELLEY, George	08/12/1805
BRYAN, Elizabeth M.	WILLSON, Robert	03/21/1797
BRYANT, Eleanor	MURRY, Walter	07/18/1797
BRYANT, Eliza A.	HORTON, Thomas J.	08/21/1859
BRYANT, Mary	CHRISMUS, John	09/12/1783
BRYANT, Sarah	CARRAL, William	01/05/1782
BUCEY, Martha F.	WEBB, Daniel D.	12/19/1831
BUCEY, Sarah	WORSHAM, Robert W.	08/17/1833
BUCHANAN, Keziah	REID, John	03/20/1784
BUCKINGHAM, Elizabeth	BENNATT, Richard	01/15/1830
BUCKINGHAM, Martha	TAYLOR, James A.	12/11/1845
BUCKNER, Elizabeth	KERSEY, Alexander Jr.	06/23/1828
BUCKNER, Frances	PASS, Nathaniel W.	02/22/1821
BUCKNER, Judith	PASS, John A.	01/07/1823
BULL, Fanny	KING, Joseph	05/19/1815
BULLARD, Darkus	JONES, Thomas	10/16/1819
BUMPASS, Lucy	COLEMAN, Daniel	12/22/1789
BURCH, Amy	RHOADES, John	06/18/1822
BURCH, Elizabeth	BARTON, Rice	10/31/1826
BURCH, Elizabeth	CHISSONBURY, John	11/24/1791
BURCH, Frances	BARTON, Thomas	01/20/1813
BURCH, Frances	CRISP, Thomas	10/14/1799
BURCH, Jane	MASSEY, William	11/17/1818
BURCH, Janney	CRISP, John	04/12/1791
BURCH, Jenney	BROCHE, George	03/19/1803
BURCH, Laney	BURTON, Isaac	08/08/1838
BURCH, Lucinda	HAITHCOCK, Allen F.	02/28/1821
BURCH, Lucinda	TERRELL, William E.	11/16/1852
BURCH, Lucretia	DAMERRON, Azariah	04/04/1848
BURCH, Mary	BARTON, Abraham	06/20/1826
BURCH, Mary	JACKSON, J.R.	06/16/1860
BURCH, Mary	BURCH, James	01/26/1829
BURCH, Mary	WILLINGHAM, John	03/13/1788
BURCH, Nancy	LEE, James	08/17/1795
BURCH, Parthenia	SMITH, Green	01/08/1820
BURCH, Polly	CHAMBERLIN, John	09/16/1819
BURCH, Rita	ROAN, James	07/01/1809
BURCH, Sarah	NICHOLS, Wright	01/11/1791
BURCH, Sarah	SHEARMAN, Thomas	12/11/1800

MARRIAGE RECORDS OF CASWELL COUNTY, NORTH CAROLINA

BRIDE	GROOM	DATE
BURFORD, Judith	SWAYNEY, James	10/02/1780
BURGES, Elizabeth A.	SANDERS, James	09/23/1860
BURGESS, Eleanor	ROBERTS, Step	01/22/1814
BURGESS, Mildred	WILLSON, James	12/10/1792
BURK, Milly	REDDIN, William	11/25/1812
BURK, Nancy	ROBERTSON, John M.	11/29/1866
BURK, Polley	EGMON, Lott	10/24/1812
BURKE, Elizabeth	MASSEY, Nathan T.	09/25/1866
BURKE, Fanny G.	RIGGS, George W.	08/19/1862
BURNETT, Ann	SCOTT, John W.	05/01/1855
BURNETT, Elizabeth	WARF, Tandy F.	12/07/1847
BURNETT, Polly	DIXON, Henry	05/28/1802
BURNETTE, Martha J.	SMITH, Thomas H.	01/20/1841
BURNS, Eveline	STRADER, Christian	02/20/1844
BURNS, J. F.	HARRINGTON, J. B.	11/22/1860
BURNS, Julia F.	TERRY, Christopher G.	05/20/1844
BURNS, Lenora E.	STRATTON, John C.	06/27/1855
BURNS, Louisa G.	TERRY, Christopher G.	06/08/1840
BURNS, Martha A.	MIMS, John W.Jr.	06/11/1852
BURNS, Mary	MORROW, William	07/10/1793
BURNS, Sarah A.	STONE, Eli C.	05/30/1840
BURROUGHS, Salley	KIRK, William	01/25/1816
BURT, Nancy	COMPTON, John L.	10/24/1840
BURT, Rebecca	COMPTON, Samuel W.	12/02/1833
BURTON, Aderlaid V.	HENDRICK, Thomas W.	12/13/1859
BURTON, Ann	BINION, John	01/17/1785
BURTON, Betsey	FORREST, Thomas	12/02/1809
BURTON, Betsy	MORTON, Jesse	10/28/1802
BURTON, Diana	VANHOOK, Kindal	05/22/1813
BURTON, Dianah	KIMBRO, Miles	11/20/1822
BURTON, Dorrithy	BRADLEY, James	09/18/1788
BURTON, Elizabeth	KNIGHT, Robert	09/15/1832
BURTON, Elizabeth C.	COBB, Samuel B.	11/11/1851
BURTON, Fanny	WARE, Sidney G.	06/10/1857
BURTON, Harriet H.	PAXTON, William C.	05/19/1852
BURTON, Jane	BINION, William	11/19/1784
BURTON, Jennie Hennie	GUNN, Geo. W. Dr.	10/21/1860
BURTON, Jenny	HARRISON, Thomas Jr.	03/09/1798
BURTON, Judith	PAUL, Samuel	01/14/1784
BURTON, Louisa	BURTON, Hutchens	12/22/1828
BURTON, Lucy	MARTIN, John	11/19/1796
BURTON, Lucy	MATHEWS, Luke	10/21/1822
BURTON, Lucy A.	HOLT, James G.	02/04/1840
BURTON, Martha	FARLEY, Isehiah	11/28/1785
BURTON, Martha W.	JONES, Allen	06/26/1833
BURTON, Mary	ATKINSON, Jessee T.	02/13/1827
BURTON, Mary	DAMERON, Joseph	04/02/1790
BURTON, Mary	TEAGUE, Josiah	05/22/1867
BURTON, Mary	WIER, William	12/19/1810
BURTON, Mary A.	TRAVIS, John W. P.	04/11/1854
BURTON, Mary E.	FRANKLIN, William C.	11/10/1859

MARRIAGE RECORDS OF CASWELL COUNTY, NORTH CAROLINA

BRIDE	GROOM	DATE
BURTON, Mary J.	MATLOCK, John	11/05/1860
BURTON, Nancy	GUNN, Daniel	10/19/1818
BURTON, Nancy J.	BURTON, David S.	12/14/1842
BURTON, Polly	RICHARDSON, William	08/28/1802
BURTON, Priscilla	PAUL, Robert	05/28/1781
BURTON, Sally	KNIGHT, Evans	12/17/1800
BURTON, Sarah	KING, James P.	10/27/1830
BURTON, Sarah J.	GOODSON, George T.	10/09/1852
BURTON, Sarah J.	MOORE, Stephen J.	08/13/1859
BURTON, Susan	JAMES, Henry	06/14/1866
BURTON, Susan	RICHMOND, Thomas B.	11/18/1833
BURTON, Susanna	WALLIS, Major	04/09/1802
BURTON, Virginia	MILUM, James L.	02/21/1867
BUSEY, Eliza	DURHAM, Nathaniel	11/05/1822
BUSEY, Sally	TRIGG, William B.	12/31/1822
BUSH, Anne	HARALSON, Thomas	11/18/1787
BUSH, Avicey	SIMMONS, James	03/08/1812
BUSH, Dilley	BALLARD, Mourning	02/08/1802
BUSH, Frances	HARRELSON, Forbes	11/24/1790
BUSH, Lois	HENSLEE, Thomas	11/18/1805
BUSH, Mary	KENNON, Elijah	06/11/1813
BUSH, Mira	INGRAM, Stephen	12/10/1808
BUSH, Rhody	SIMMONS, John	11/15/1809
BUSH, Susanna	CHILDRESS, Solomon	09/--/1807
BUSH, Zibba(?)	RICE, Archibald	02/02/1803
BUSHNELL, Margaret	PEALE, Jonathan	10/07/1845
BUSHNELL, Mary	WILLIAMSON, Felix	12/01/1866
BUSHNELL, Sabry	WINDSOR, Felix	10/20/1866
BUSHNELL, Sarah J.	PEALE, Anderson N,	04/28/1857
BUTLER, Eliza	BROWN, Jonathan	01/01/1844
BUTLER, Emeline D.	NANCE, Joseph W.	06/04/1853
BUTLER, Frances	SOMMERS, William	01/11/1853
BUTLER, Malvina F.	COBB, Mastin H.	02/04/1850
BUTLER, Margaret E.	WILLIAMSON, Addison A.	01/06/1849
BUTLER, Polley	GROOM, Carter	10/27/1819
BUTLER, Rithy	HALL, Anthony	12/23/1794
BUTLER, Susanna	RICE, Nathaniel	01/29/1781
BUTTERY, Elizabeth	BREWER, James	04/28/1816
BYRD, Mary	LYNCH, Thomas	12/10/1827
CADAL, Margret	ANDERSON, James	07/09/1782
CADDEL, Phebe	GREEN, Burwell	07/04/1789
CADDELL, Elizabeth	GREEN, Lewis	12/26/1789
CAHAL, Louisa S.	NORMAN, Henry J.	03/11/1852
CAHAL, Martha E.	NORMAN, James B.	03/11/1852
CALDNOND, Susan A.	STADLER, John J.	10/28/1860
CALDWELL, Appy	GEARY, Benjamin	08/11/1817
CALDWELL, Catherine	YEATS, John	10/13/1780
CALLOWAY, Belverderrie F.	SNEED, William H.	10/17/1832
CALLUM, Mary A.	TOWLES, James M.	02/19/1838
CAMERON, Patsey	HARDICREE, Jonathan	07/05/1797
CAMMICHAL, Mary	INGRAM, Vench	03/18/1805

MARRIAGE RECORDS OF CASWELL COUNTY, NORTH CAROLINA

BRIDE	GROOM	DATE
CAMPBELL, Ann	MCCORMACK, Aaron F.	08/16/1849
CAMPBELL, Delilah	KING, Henry	12/08/1840
CAMPBELL, Elizabeth	TAYLOR, Robert	12/15/1857
CAMPBELL, Emily A.	PHILIPS, John	10/08/1840
CAMPBELL, Evelina	PHILLIPS, Franklin	01/04/1841
CAMPBELL, Evelina B.	KERR, John Jr.	12/23/1835
CAMPBELL, Letecia	COTHRAN, Elijah	02/19/1822
CAMPBELL, Lucinda	WILLIS, Benjamin Jr.	12/23/1846
CAMPBELL, Lucitta A.	LUNSFROD, Walter H.	12/01/1836
CAMPBELL, Margaret	CASCRT, Wylie	04/19/1847
CAMPBELL, Meranda	FULLINGTON, James G.	11/22/1856
CAMPBELL, Naomi	WARREN, Mason	10/22/1860
CAMPBELL, Rusalinda	LUNSFORD, Warner J.	02/02/1850
CAMRON, Martha A.	DAMERON, Christopher	04/02/1851
CANADAY, Eliza A.	PASCHAL, Jesse D.	03/06/1861
CANNADY, Rebecca F.	COBB, Archy	07/20/1865
CANNON, Darcas	SCOTT, Daniel	12/21/1811
CANNON, Jemima	SIMPSON, Charles	07/15/1841
CANNON, Sarah	WARE, Silas T.	09/04/1837
CANNON, Susan	OXFORD, Jonathan	12/12/1784
CANOR, Sarah	WILLIS, Barzilla	06/15/1849
CANTREL, Catherine	GARRISON, Hall	05/20/1809
CANTREL, Hannah	ANTHONY, Joseph	02/17/1802
CANTREL, Polley	KERR, Barzillai	03/22/1806
CANTREL, Rachel	MARTIN, Goerge	10/26/1813
CANTREL, Sophia	BROWNING, Richard	03/12/1816
CANTREL, Sophia	ROBERTS, Thomas	01/01/1859
CANTRELL, Elizabeth	BRINTLE, William	06/30/1854
CANTRELL, Sarah	MARTIN, James	02/05/1816
CANTRIL, Henrietta	MORTON, Alexander B.	11/04/1819
CANTRILL, Jemima	MASSEY, Nathan	10/20/1826
CANTRILL, Nancey	MARTIN, James	03/08/1827
CANTRILLE, Sally	MARTIN, Elijah	04/19/1815
CARLEN, Sarah	APPLE, William	02/14/1840
CARLOSS, Betsey	BOMAN, Samuel	06/30/1798
CARLOSS, Dolly G.	RICE, Ibzan	02/27/1796
CARLOSS, Nancy	BADGETT, Ransom	01/15/1803
CARMAN, Mary	STAFFORD, Samuel	08/02/1796
CARMICAL, Elizabeth C.	LEWIS, Wade W.	04/16/1860
CARMON, Abagail	CORAM, William	04/10/1782
CARMON, Hannah	JOHNSTON, Thomas	09/10/1783
CARNALL, Mary	WHITE, Thomas	01/08/1781
CARNEY, Rachel	JACKSON, Robert Jr.	06/01/1811
CARNY, Delphy	SARGENT, Daniel	01/03/1780
CARREL, Tabitha T.	RUSSELL, William F.	11/24/1825
CARRELL, Nancy	ROBERTS, Levin	11/14/1798
CARRELL, Sally	BRYAN, James	01/22/1783
CARROL, Betsy	ELAM, Robert	03/14/1804
CARROL, Betsy	TERRY, John	04/14/1804
CARROL, Hannah	KENNON, John	11/01/1812
CARROL, Patsy	POWELL, Peter	08/31/1802

MARRIAGE RECORDS OF CASWELL COUNTY, NORTH CAROLINA

BRIDE	GROOM	DATE
CARROL, Rebechah	HAMLETT, James	02/09/1793
CARROLL, Polly	BEAVER, Joshua	10/05/1793
CARROW, Julia A.	MORSE, Edward G.	06/01/1860
CARTER, Bettie	MCKINNEY, Isaac	12/25/1867
CARTER, Carnelia A.	DANIEL, John M.	07/06/1836
CARTER, Elizabeth	SIMPSON, Enoch	12/29/1818
CARTER, Elizabeth B.	BROWN, John E.	04/20/1827
CARTER, Elizabeth E.	VOSS, Okelly	12/05/1825
CARTER, Elizabeth J.	VANHOOK, Francis M.	01/18/1860
CARTER, Isabella	TURNER, George W.	12/16/1866
CARTER, Isabella P.	MURRAY, William J.	04/18/1861
CARTER, Martha	SMITH, Henry	12/13/1818
CARTER, Martha B.	LEA, William A.	02/13/1862
CARTER, Martha M.	STANFIELD, Mark M.	04/24/1849
CARTER, Mary	HANNER, James	02/03/1817
CARTER, Mary	SOUTHARD, William	02/08/1848
CARTER, Mary A.C.	BROWN, James W.	07/30/1818
CARTER, Mary J.	RAINEY, William T.	12/25/1851
CARTER, Mary P.	SAWYER, John	02/08/1799
CARTER, Mary W.	POWELL, Thomas B.	04/22/1866
CARTER, Missouri A.	SAUNDERS, Robert D.	08/17/1841
CARTER, Rebecca	SANDERS, Romulus M.	12/21/1812
CARTER, Sally	WOODY, Thomas	03/25/1808
CARTER, Sarah Frances	COURTS, William James	01/04/1858
CARTER, Sinai	CARTER, Benjamin	08/10/1867
CARTER, Susan	POWELL, Giles	02/24/1853
CARVER, Minerva J.	GREENWOOD, Thomas	11/04/1843
CARVER, Nancy	LOVELACE, John	01/09/1826
CARVER, Suffy	WALKER, David	12/24/1825
CATE, Elizabeth	COCHRON, Will	10/24/1789
CATE, Margery	DAY, Henry	03/28/1788
CATE, Nancey	BENTON, Robert	10/25/1790
CATES, Caroline	LEA, Westley	10/29/1842
CATES, Martha E.	CHEEK, Robert H.	01/27/1867
CATES, Mary	BENTON, Titus	01/09/1789
CATES, Nancy	SINGLETON, William A.	03/26/1855
CATES, Rebecca	LEA, Lemuel	11/14/1839
CAVANIS, Nancy	ROBINSON, John	10/08/1816
CEARNEY, Agness	LEWIS, Hiram	03/03/1806
CHAMBERLAIN, Catharine	JOHNSTON, William	12/10/1819
CHAMBERLAIN, Jemima	WESTBROOK, Yancey	01/06/1825
CHAMBERLIN, Jane	BATES, Lemuel	12/30/1840
CHAMBERS, Ann	STEPHENS, Andrew W.	02/27/1840
CHAMBERS, Arabella C.	RUDD, Lorenzo D.	02/03/1854
CHAMBERS, Elizabeth	PASS, William H.	11/29/1847
CHAMBERS, Harriet A.	PASS, James M.	08/30/1851
CHAMBERS, Jane N.	MCDANIEL, Joel A.	10/10/1854
CHAMBERS, Judith	BULL, Jacob	05/06/1781
CHAMBERS, Mary A.	POWELL, James	08/17/1864
CHAMBERS, Permintia	HOW, William	12/29/1835
CHAMBERS, Sally	PATTOSON, David	03/27/1781

MARRIAGE RECORDS OF CASWELL COUNTY, NORTH CAROLINA

BRIDE	GROOM	DATE
CHAMERS, Nancy	CHAMBERS, James	04/08/1787
CHANCY, Rebecca	EARP, Smith L.	03/13/1845
CHANDLER, Adeline W.	WRIGHT, Abram M.	06/25/1850
CHANDLER, Betsy	PAYNE, John	11/10/1811
CHANDLER, Elizabeth	JONES, James M.	08/30/1848
CHANDLER, Frances E.	WILEY, Albert G.	08/27/1842
CHANDLER, Frances G.	GROOM, John	08/03/1848
CHANDLER, Francis G.	HIGHTOWER, Joshua	11/17/1843
CHANDLER, Judith	CURRIE, George	09/09/1829
CHANDLER, Judith	MCKINEY, Thomas W.	01/02/1814
CHANDLER, Margarett	CURRIE, Jesse	09/29/1830
CHANDLER, Maria	JONES, Robert	12/26/1866
CHANDLER, Mary	ADKINS, William	06/03/1828
CHANDLER, Mary F.	NEWMAN, A.B.	05/01/1867
CHANDLER, Mary J.	SANDERS, Richard P.	01/30/1847
CHANDLER, Nancy	MALONE, Bennet	12/10/1817
CHANDLER, Nanny J.	DABBS, Lemuel J.	11/05/1856
CHANDLER, Polly C.	SMITH, Henderson	11/24/1828
CHANDLER, Rebecca	WALTERS, Jackson	09/22/1852
CHANDLER, Sally	MITCHELL, William	10/23/1803
CHANDLER, Sally	THOMAS, Henry	01/03/1803
CHANDLER, Susan T.	WARE, Joseph R.	11/09/1832
CHANDLER, Susanna	WILLIS, Benjamin	11/20/1811
CHANEY, Eliza E.	MOREFIELD, Paul H.	05/24/1860
CHANEY, Lydia	WILLIS, Joseph	01/23/1842
CHAPMAN, Ann	STRADER, Jeremiah	01/30/1845
CHAPMAN, Elizabeth	COOK, Henry	12/23/1851
CHAPMAN, Nancy	SUTHEN, Zachariah	12/18/1847
CHAPPAL, Elizabeth	WATKINS, Thomas	02/10/1783
CHATHAM, Cloey	WARD, George	12/08/1801
CHATTIN, Elizabeth	HODGES, Coleman	05/16/1837
CHAVOS, Charlotte	MITCHELL, John	08/22/1857
CHEATWOOD, Betsy	TENNISON, John	03/03/1798
CHEEK, Cornelia A.	RUDD, John S.	12/25/1866
CHEEK, Mary	LEA, William M.	11/11/1851
CHELES, Nancy C.	RAINEY, Dabney	05/05/1821
CHILDERS, Nancy	PYRON, Charles	09/22/1836
CHILDES, Mary M.	HAYMES, Richard W.	11/06/1827
CHILDIRS, Isabella H.	LEWIS, Anderson	01/26/1830
CHILDRES, Jane	DRAKE, James M.	12/22/1828
CHILDRESS, Annis	WILLIAMS, Winstead	08/16/1834
CHILDRESS, Louisa	WEBSTER, Thomas H.	12/08/1853
CHILDRESS, Martha	LEWIS, Pleasant	01/29/1848
CHILDRESS, Nancy	SWIFT, William	04/11/1813
CHILDRESS, Sarah	KEENER, Jackson	05/13/1843
CHILDRESS, Susan J.	PAMPLIN, James	12/20/1866
CHILDS, Betsy	MATTHIS, Thomas	11/29/1810
CHILDS, Salley	BEVILL, John	10/29/1815
CHILTON, Mary A.	DAVIDSON, John A.	12/20/1828
CHILTON, Rachel	TRAVIS, William	11/18/1816
CHITTELTON, Agnes	CULBERSON, Joseph	12/24/1787

MARRIAGE RECORDS OF CASWELL COUNTY, NORTH CAROLINA

BRIDE	GROOM	DATE
CHITTINGTON, Nancy	DOLLARHIDE, John	11/03/1784
CHOUNAN, Ester	RICE, William	12/21/1793
CHRISTENBERY, Polly	POTEET, William	03/03/1796
CHRISTENBURY, Elizabeth	FERRALL, John	11/09/1781
CIRLS, Betsy	VAUGHAN, John	01/15/1825
CLAIBORNE, Sarah Ann	DILLARD, William	11/10/1866
CLALYTON, Susannah	FULLER, John	12/09/1778
CLARK Sarah	MOORE, Spencer	12/18/1856
CLARK, Elizabeth	NANCE, Thomas	12/20/1853
CLARK, Francis L.	BALL, David	07/20/1819
CLARK, Martha M.	BLANKS, Joseph	02/06/1857
CLARK, Minerva	GARLAND, Eustace	04/21/1867
CLARK, Minerva	HARRAWAY, Richard	10/04/1867
CLAY, America F.	FOWLER, William L.	02/12/1853
CLAY, Anna	GARLAND, Peter	12/06/1866
CLAY, Elizabeth	SLEDGE, John P.	11/17/1823
CLAY, Sarah	ROGERS, Bird	02/04/1785
CLAYTON, Rebecca	CLAYTON, Daniel	01/15/1789
CLEMPSON, Magara	KNIGHT, Joseph D.	04/28/1830
CLEMPSON, Rachel	CHANDLER, Charles G.	10/14/1837
CLENDENING, Mary	FITCH, James	03/13/1830
CLETON, Nancy	BURTON, Allen	01/19/1791
CLIFT, Lettie	MERRITT, James	11/17/1795
CLIMPSON, Nancey	GAFFARD, William	10/30/1821
COATS, Sally	BEVINS, Grief	08/03/1816
COBB, Almedia A.	CARTER, Benjamin H.	05/18/1859
COBB, Ann E.	BLACKWELL, Nathaniel L.	10/16/1847
COBB, Bell	HARRISON, Martin	11/02/1867
COBB, Bell	JONES, Simon	09/14/1867
COBB, Candice	WILLIAMSON, Green	12/24/1867
COBB, Celia	HUMPHREYS, Thomas	01/25/1826
COBB, Cinthia	SCOTT, James M.	12/07/1840
COBB, Deborah	GRANT, John W.	07/16/1812
COBB, Elizabeth	JOHNSTON, George	10/11/1830
COBB, Elizabeth	KEEN, William	02/23/1811
COBB, Elizabeth	COBB, Jesse E.	12/26/1838
COBB, Emeline	SLADE, Thomas T.	05/09/1849
COBB, Frances	GIBSON, Ivoson	02/03/1841
COBB, Henrietta	MANLEY, Samuel	02/01/1821
COBB, Jamima	THAXTON, Thomas	02/04/1782
COBB, Jane	HORSFORD, John C.	02/17/1832
COBB, Jemima	CHANDLER, Pleasant	10/28/1852
COBB, Jennett	JONES, Henry	10/18/1866
COBB, Louisa M.	WOMACK, Abraham	11/29/1838
COBB, Malina S.	MANLY, Thomas M.	12/20/1860
COBB, Malinda G.	HUBBARD, Archibald D.	11/26/1837
COBB, Mariah L.	GUERRANT, Peter M. C.	01/19/1855
COBB, Martha	MADDING, Robert	10/09/1818
COBB, Martha	PAGE, Zenith	03/20/1837
COBB, Martha A.	COBB, Neptha	09/13/1840
COBB, Martha H.	GARDNER, Nathaniel W.	09/10/1832

MARRIAGE RECORDS OF CASWELL COUNTY, NORTH CAROLINA

BRIDE	GROOM	DATE
COBB, Mary	ELMORE, Benjamin	01/23/1811
COBB, Mary	RICE, John	11/19/1844
COBB, Peggy	BRUCE, James	10/07/1808
COBB, Rebecca	CREWS, Abediah	11/10/1835
COBB, Sarah	SMITH, Clement	01/11/1850
COBB,(?) Nancy	PAGE, William	12/31/1796
COBBS, Rhoda	KNIGHT, Jesse	08/10/1867
COCHRAN, Judith	HINTON, Richard	12/07/1791
COCHRAN, Polley	BARTON, Elisha	01/09/1799
COCHRAN, Sarah	BARKER, David	04/20/1790
COCHRAN, Tabitha	BRUCE, Robert	02/02/1789
COCK, Addeline	OLVIS, John	05/20/1833
COCK, Betsey	ARNOLD, Richard	09/30/1814
COE, Fanny	LEA, Henry	03/21/1846
COIL, Jane	WESTBROOK, Yancey	12/31/1823
COILE, Sarah	OVERBY, Samuel	10/11/1830
COLE, Frances	CORUM, William J.	04/30/1857
COLE, Leaner	EDWELL, Harrison	11/09/1847
COLE, Mary W.	SMITH, Robert	08/06/1783
COLE, Sarah F.	SMITH, Lea A.	08/10/1866
COLEMAN, Elizabeth	GRAVES, John	11/28/1808
COLEMAN, Elizabeth B.	TRAVIS, John	01/14/1836
COLEMAN, Judith	HUDSON, Ezekiel	11/27/1811
COLEMAN, Minerva	FULTON, William J.	01/28/1842
COLEMAN, Patsy	WINSTON, Thos.	12/29/1796
COLEMAN, Polly	MILLER, James	05/17/1814
COLEMAN, Rosy	LINDSEY, William	09/17/1800
COLEMAN, Sarah E.	RASCO, John	09/24/1859
COLEMON, Nancy	BURCH, James S.	02/17/1819
COLESTON, Ann	CUMMELL, William	03/08/1784
COLESTON, Lattis	DYE, Abraham	02/03/1787
COLESTON, Margaret	SMITH, Mace	11/18/1780
COLLEY, Elizabeth H.	HYDE Joseph	07/15/1851
COLLEY, Sally	DOCLEY, John	05/15/1806
COLLIER, Rebecca	MORTON, Williamson	12/23/1822
COLLINS, Elixena	MCADAM, David	03/02/1839
COLLINS, Euphrasia	HARRELSON, Thomas W.	01/23/1826
COLLINS, Frances	RICHMOND, Calvin J.	12/23/1837
COLLINS, Martha	HARRELSON, Thomas W.	07/29/1839
COLLINS, Mary	HESTER, Robert H.	01/15/1834
COLLINS, Syrena	BOLING, George	06/11/1832
COLLINS, Syrena	BONDS, George	06/11/1832
COLLINS, Syrena	BONDS, George	06/11/1832
COLLINS, Syrena	BOLING, George	06/11/1832
COLLIR, Judith	MASSEY, William	03/30/1814
COLLY, Mary F.	GILLISPIE, David A.	03/30/1852
COLMAN, Catherine	MOORE, Austin T.	04/22/1837
COLMON, Sucky	SAMMAN, John	02/11/1815
COMBS, Mary	HANKS, Abraham	01/12/1792
COMER, Amy	MCNEAL, M.	01/11/1866
COMER, Elizabeth	LONG, John	04/21/1800

MARRIAGE RECORDS OF CASWELL COUNTY, NORTH CAROLINA

BRIDE	GROOM	DATE
COMER, Elizabeth W.	GRAVES, Augustus	11/13/1849
COMER, Fanny	ROAN, John	12/14/1802
COMER, Jenett	STEPHENS, Matt	09/08/1866
COMER, Nancy	RICHMOND, Daniel	12/16/1805
COMER, Peggy	VANHOOK, Isaac	01/27/1817
COMPTON, Elizabeth	BIRK, Wiley	12/12/1826
COMPTON, Elizabeth	ROWARK, John	09/26/1817
COMPTON, Margarett	HENDERSON, Benjamin H.	11/14/1840
CONALLY, Sally	BOULDIN, James	11/24/1802
CONALLY, Sarah L.	ELLIOTT, David T.	11/05/1855
CONALLY, Susan	DANIEL, Martin T.	12/19/1854
CONLEY, Rebecca	BRANDON, David	12/15/1800
CONNALLEY, Frances	BOULDIN, John	09/20/1817
CONNALLY, Anna	RICHMOND, Joseph	02/06/1804
CONNALLY, Caroline	BYRD, James T.	02/11/1847
CONNALLY, Elizabeth	DAMERON, James B.	12/12/1829
CONNALLY, Emily	CONNALLY, Solomon	01/26/1867
CONNALLY, Kitty	MONTGOMERY, James	10/27/1807
CONNALLY, Mary A.	BRANDON, William L.	04/11/1842
CONNALLY, Priscilla H.	SMITH, John R.	12/22/1852
CONNOLLY, Anngelico	GADDIS, William	11/16/1795
CONNOLLY, Margaret A.	JONES, Thomas J.	02/01/1845
CONWAY, Emeline	MONTGOMERY, James	08/18/1867
COOK, Betsy	BRYANT, Harrison	03/17/1810
COOK, Elizabeth	DIX, Geroge W.	11/06/1834
COOK, Elizabeth L.	SEARCY, Alexander M.	06/13/1848
COOK, Fanny	MELTON, James	11/24/1818
COOK, Margaret	WARRIN, Tho.	07/04/1820
COOK, Martha	SPARKS, Milton	09/28/1847
COOK, Priciller	BOND, Balaam	01/23/1819
COOK, Priscilla	NORMOND, William	05/28/1825
COOK, Sarah	PITMAN, John	04/10/1794
COOK, Unity	VOSS, Pleasant	02/04/1829
COOPER, Eliza	OBRIANT, E. M.	12/10/1866
COOPER, Fannie	CORBETT, B.H.	08/08/1860
COOPER, Lavinia	COMPTON, Allen	02/17/1835
COOPER, Lillie J.	GRAHAM, Albert	12/19/1867
COOPER, Mary F.	WALKER, Jefferson M.	10/22/1854
COOPER, Nancey	FULLER, John H.	08/26/1836
COOPER, Salenia	COMPTON, Aquilla	02/04/1832
COOPER, Salley	BOMAN, John	04/29/1806
COOPER, Susan J.	OAKLY, Thomas P.	12/21/1856
CORAM, Clorey	JACKSON, Shadrach	10/01/1782
CORAM, Ester	QUINE, Benjamin	09/02/1780
CORAM, Jane	RALPH, Thomas	04/12/1791
CORBET, Elizabeth	WASHBERN, Joseph	09/14/1848
CORBETT, Mary F.	TATE, William S.	01/18/1857
CORBETT, Nancey	GWYN, Robert Z.	11/29/1859
CORBIN, Catherine C.	BLANKENSHIP, Archa F.	11/14/1866
CORBIN, Sallie A.	LEWIS, J. T.	03/05/1864
CORBIT, Elizabeth A.	COOPER, Warren	07/17/1851

MARRIAGE RECORDS OF CASWELL COUNTY, NORTH CAROLINA

BRIDE	GROOM	DATE
CORBITT, Emily T.	GWYN, Augustus	06/21/1854
CORDER, Elizabeth	ANTEONEY, James	02/07/1781
CORDER, Fanny	SCOTT, Richard	12/10/1797
CORDER, Hannah	PARKS, William	03/09/1798
CORDER, Polly	MURPHEY, Jno.	02/11/1803
CORDER, Winneyford	HIGETOWER, Charnel	01/17/1798
CORN, Martha	HOITH, Alex	02/09/1864
COUSINS, Susan	FARLEY, Kerr	03/17/1862
COVENTON, Betsey	GOING, Sherwood	12/31/1804
COVERINGTON, Mary T.	OLIVER, Ireson L.	11/13/1859
COVINGTON, Frances	SNEED, Archibal	12/23/1846
COVINGTON, Mary E.	POORE, Thomas S.	07/21/1852
COVINGTON, Virginia	CHANDLER, William G.	01/31/1856
COX, Agnes	SAWYER, Cary	06/26/1805
COX, Ann	DAVIS, James M.	12/15/1835
COX, Anne	HARPER, Jesse	06/09/1813
COX, Elizabeth	WARF, Thomas	02/01/1865
COX, Elizabeth	WORSHAM, Ludwell	09/03/1807
COX, Frances	COBB, James	08/08/1854
COX, Jane	WARF, Thomas	12/08/1846
COX, Lucinda	SWIFT, Thomas	08/09/1847
COX, Lucy	CRITTENTON, George	10/11/1800
COX, Malinda	CARTER, John B.	01/18/1847
COX, Martha	BOHANNON, Yancey	11/17/1823
COX, Mary	MAYHAN, William	09/18/1822
COX, Polly	BURGISS, John	03/28/1795
COX, Sally	BURNE, Thomas	02/06/1813
COX, Sally	SHREVE, Robert D.	12/19/1866
COX, Sarah	COWMAN, William	12/13/1838
COX, Sarah	HARVELL, William	06/10/1825
COX, Suckey	SHAW, Nathaniel	10/11/1800
COX, Susan	JONES, Henry	01/14/1833
COX, Tameran	NELSON, Joel H.	12/19/1842
CRAFTON, Welthy	GROOM, Thomas	12/28/1835
CRANE, Nancy T.	COLE, William T.	11/25/1866
CRANSHAW, Salley	DENNY, William	04/--/1818
CRAWFORD, Bettie A.	HAILEY, Patrick C.	07/12/1862
CRAWFORD, Mahael S.	HARTMAN, Frederig	11/09/1852
CRAWLEY, Elizabeth	GRIFFIN, John	07/21/1840
CREWS, Martha	FOROD, Elijah T.	12/22/1834
CREWS, Mary A.	JEFFERS, John	10/21/1833
CRIDER, Judith	NEWTON, John G.	10/14/1818
CRIDER, Mary	LEA, John	03/04/1786
CRISP, Betsy	BURCH, George	11/16/1789
CRISP, Eliza	WELLS, Benjamin	12/20/1826
CRISP, Elizabeth	TERRELL, James	03/19/1816
CRISP, Lucy	BURCH, Baylor	10/11/1790
CRISP, Margaret	WILSON, James	03/15/1790
CRISP, Marian	BURCH, Richard	02/23/1790
CRISTENBURY, Nancy	BOWERS, William	07/26/1817
CRITTENTON, Nancey	DIX, JOhn M.	08/15/1822

MARRIAGE RECORDS OF CASWELL COUNTY, NORTH CAROLINA

BRIDE	GROOM	DATE
CROSS, Ruth	WALKER, Jere (?)	12/02/1805
CROSSETT, Jane	PAISELY, John	04/25/1828
CROSSETT, Margret	MANN, Thomas	01/10/1800
CROSSIX, Elizabeth	OAKELEY, Thos.	11/16/1820
CROWDER, Lovey	WEEKS, Henry	11/11/1822
CROWDER, Mary A.	WEBB, Lewis	12/16/1837
CROWDER, Sally	CARDWELL, Richard M.	04/19/1817
CRUISE, Elizabeth	SMITH, Ewell	11/06/1826
CRUISE, Sarah	STUART, Edward G.	11/06/1826
CRUMP, Mary J.	GRAVES, Elijah Jr.	11/26/1849
CRUMPTON, Mary F.	MALONE, Bartlett Y.	11/15/1866
CRUMPTON, Rachal	HOOPER, Squire	09/08/1866
CRUTCHFIELD, Minerva	WILLIAMSON, Monroe	04/20/1867
CRUTCHFIELD, Nanny L.	PARK, M. A.	12/20/1866
CULBERSON, Edney	PRICE, William	01/12/1807
CULBERSON, Libby	PARKS, Jeptha	09/14/1800
CULBERSON, Mary	PRICE, Joshua	12/28/1818
CULBERSON, Sarah	SMITH, James	10/06/1778
CULBERSON, Susanna	RUDD, Joshua	02/24/1819
CULBERSON, Tabitha	RUDD, Joseph	01/19/1824
CULBERTSON, Rachel	WARRIN, Benjamin	05/04/1791
CUMBO, Sarah	MATHEWS, Ezekiel	05/07/1793
CUNINGHAM, Harriett	BRANDON, Jacob	12/22/1866
CUNINGHAM, Nancy	SANDERS, William	01/13/1795
CUNINGHAM, Sarah	CUNINGHAM, Glouster	07/27/1866
CUNNINGHAM, Betsy A.	MAURY, Philip	12/04/1793
CURLES, Sophia	BUTT, Ambrose	07/01/1803
CURLS, Sally	RANDOLPH, John	03/04/1806
CURLS, Sarah A.	KIERSEY, Franklin	11/02/1849
CURRIE, Bettie R.	HOLDEN, E. B.	10/04/1855
CURRIE, Catharine	CURRIE, Mitchell	02/11/1832
CURRIE, Catherine	WALKER, George	02/16/1811
CURRIE, Cornelia D.	BOYKIN, Drury D.	05/20/1849
CURRIE, Eugenia F.	THAXTON, Henry S.	09/05/1865
CURRIE, Frances	CURRIE, William	12/28/1867
CURRIE, Frances G.	EVANS, James	12/26/1851
CURRIE, Margaret	MCMULLEN, John	01/11/1787
CURRIE, Martha	PULLIAM, Jack	10/16/1867
CURRIE, Martha	WALKER, Empson	09/11/1825
CURRIE, Mary	PULLIAM, Thomas	01/19/1867
CURRIE, Mary	RICHMOND, John	02/15/1802
CURRIE, Mary	WADE, Robert D.	02/01/1828
CURRIE, Mary	WILSON, William	07/02/1809
CURRIE, Mary A.	PARKS, Samuel B.	06/02/1845
CURRIE, Partheana	WALKER, John G.	03/08/1824
CURRIE, Sally L.	WILEY, Franklin A.	08/24/1851
CURRIE, Sarah	LEA, Aaron V.	08/13/1830
CURTIS, Elizabeth	KEARSON, Charles R.	10/21/1841
DABBS, Ann E.	PAYNE, William	11/24/1853
DABNEY, Martha A.	LEWIS, Anderson	05/15/1852
DALTON, Annie	BARBER, N. S.	04/29/1848

MARRIAGE RECORDS OF CASWELL COUNTY, NORTH CAROLINA

BRIDE	GROOM	DATE
DALTON, Patience	FRAILEY, John	04/01/1811
DAMERON, Cathrine	DAMERON, William	12/05/1814
DAMERON, Elizabeth	JACKSON, William P.	12/24/1811
DAMERON, Elizabeth	MALONE, Thomas	09/25/1819
DAMERON, Elizabeth	MOORE, Eps	09/24/1811
DAMERON, Frances	BURTON, John	11/14/1867
DAMERON, Frances H.	FLORENCE, James	11/22/1858
DAMERON, Judith	KNIGHT, Joseph	12/08/1801
DAMERON, Martha	BURK, William A.	10/04/1842
DAMERON, Martha	WARREN, Edmund	10/30/1829
DAMERON, Martha A.	SCOGGINS, William H.	09/18/1852
DAMERON, Martha P.	DAMERON, Alexander M.	07/21/1821
DAMERON, Martha P.	DAMERON, Harrison	12/17/1822
DAMERON, Mary	GOLD, William	07/30/1806
DAMERON, Mary	SMITH, William H.	02/15/1856
DAMERON, Mildred	UPTON, William	01/20/1820
DAMERON, Nancey	HODGE, Isaac	11/17/1792
DAMERON, Nancy	SMITH, John H.	04/24/1862
DAMERON, Patience	JACKSON, Daniel	11/20/1805
DAMERON, Patsy	MCDANIEL, William	11/24/1802
DAMERON, Phebe	WISDOM, Barzillai	11/29/1827
DAMERON, Phoebe W.	EVANS, Barzallai A.	12/06/1845
DAMERON, Polley	JACKSON, Robert	09/27/1808
DAMERON, S.W.	BROWNING, John R.	12/19/1860
DAMERON, Salinda	DAMERON, Joseph C.	09/20/1820
DAMERON, Sally	MATHIS, Charles	09/21/1795
DAMERON, Sarah	DOBBINS, Hugh C.	11/02/1824
DAMERON, Sarah F.	PITTARD, Samuel	03/13/1866
DAMERON, Susan	GRAHAM, James	02/24/1853
DANERON, E. H.	ALDRIDGE, P. H.	03/07/1860
DANIEL, Catharine	MEEKS, John	08/30/1833
DANIEL, Elizabeth F.	CROXTON, William R.	06/02/1863
DANIEL, Martha	SMITH, Robert	05/29/1815
DARBY, Ann	MCNEILL, John H.	06/25/1810
DARBY, Elizabeth	SWANN, James	08/17/1816
DARBY, Margaret	ROBERTSON, Joseph	09/02/1780
DAVES, Ann Rebecca	COLLINS, Josiah Jr.	12/17/1803
DAVEY, Elisabeth	GILL, Robert	01/05/1784
DAVIS, Abigail	WILSON, John W.	02/02/1848
DAVIS, Ann	SHACKLEFORD, Francis	12/10/1819
DAVIS, Barbara E.	PINNIX, John C.	03/27/1844
DAVIS, Betsy	MORROW, John	12/23/1835
DAVIS, Caroline	DIX, Humphrey	04/12/1832
DAVIS, Cathrine	EVANS, Walter	02/04/1804
DAVIS, Elizabeth	SMITH, Vincen M.	01/01/1866
DAVIS, Elizabeth W.	THOMPSON, John	02/01/1837
DAVIS, Elvira R.	WALLIS, James J.	12/22/1853
DAVIS, Emaline	LANDRUM, James A.	07/02/1857
DAVIS, Emily	CROWDER, Thomas J.	07/29/1867
DAVIS, Frances	TURNER, Ephraim	12/04/1857
DAVIS, Jane	GIBSON, Samuel	11/11/1834

MARRIAGE RECORDS OF CASWELL COUNTY, NORTH CAROLINA

BRIDE	GROOM	DATE
DAVIS, Letitia	COLES, Willis	05/19/1867
DAVIS, Lucinda	KIMBROUGH, Wm. T.	12/31/1853
DAVIS, Lucinda	CHATHAM, John	02/07/1829
DAVIS, Lucy	MONTGOMERY, Michael Jr.	02/26/1816
DAVIS, Martha A.	CLARDY, William H.	12/06/1866
DAVIS, Martha J.	MEADOS, Samuel A.	11/19/1841
DAVIS, Martha P.	WALKER, Mitchell	11/24/1846
DAVIS, Mary	LEA, Nelson	09/01/1867
DAVIS, Mary	TERRELL, Julius B.	12/26/1818
DAVIS, Mary A.	MILLER, John	04/11/1838
DAVIS, Mary A.	RICHMOND, John L.	07/28/1839
DAVIS, Mary F.	MONTGOMERY, David G.	06/30/1840
DAVIS, Mary F.	MONTGOMERY, David G.	02/04/1842
DAVIS, Rebecca B.	ROBERTS, Elijah	11/04/1826
DAVIS, Sally E.	RULING, William T.	11/21/1867
DAVIS, Sarah	HADDOCK, Stephen	12/25/1834
DAVIS, Susan	PASCCHALL, William D.	11/17/1819
DAVIS, Susanna	SPENCER, Daniel	12/31/1804
DAWSON, Henrietta	HUDDLESTON, Rowland	10/05/1833
DAWSON, Jane	LAIN, Beverly	12/30/1843
DAWSON, Mileah	NOWLS, John	09/29/1807
DAY, Martha	DAMERON, Zachariah E.	01/18/1847
DAY, Mary	JONES, William	12/04/1848
DAY, Mary A.	CHRESFIELD, James A.	02/28/1867
DEAN, Susanna	PUTNAM, Jeremiah	04/04/1823
DEAN, Virginia C.	GRANT, James P.	05/31/1862
DEANE, Mary	SMALES, Thomas	11/06/1841
DEBOE, Lucy	BUTCHER, George	01/30/1828
DEBROWER, Elizabeth	WARD, Alfred	12/22/1857
DEENS, Mary Ann	COLLINS, Theophilus J.	09/07/1840
DELANEY, Catherine	MASON, Patrick	11/16/1836
DELGS, Polly	CLEMSON, William	02/12/1800
DELONE, Francis	BLACK, Samuel	12/24/1802
DENNEY, Rebecca	CRENSHAW, John	04/01/1818
DENNIS, Jenny	BAXTER, Thomas	03/05/1793
DENNY, America	ALLEN, Bob	01/06/1866
DENNY, Nancy	COBB, Amsa	12/18/1822
DICE, Martha A.	JONES, Thompson	01/03/1856
DICK, Martha W.	GRAVES, John L.	05/20/1824
DICKEN, Emily	DURHAM, George	09/11/1843
DICKEY, Elizabeth	THOMAS, Andrew	09/27/1825
DICKEY, Leannah	MCCRAY, James	10/11/1806
DICKEY, Nancey	BOWLES, Henry	11/13/1813
DICKINS, Elisabeth	BLAND, Richard	09/22/1790
DICKINS, Patsy	WHITEMORE, Gower	03/27/1798
DICKINS, Polly	DICKINS, William	03/30/1801
DICKINS, Rebecah	DICKINS, Jeremiah	10/12/1802
DICKINS, Rebecca	BUSH, Jeremiah	12/06/1794
DICKS, Martha	LOGAN, William	02/10/1859
DICKSON, Charlotte	SMITH, Robt. H.	03/04/1862
DILL, Hannah	STRADOR, David	05/31/1841

MARRIAGE RECORDS OF CASWELL COUNTY, NORTH CAROLINA

BRIDE	GROOM	DATE
DILL, Jane	COBB, Noah Sr.	11/23/1833
DILL, Joanna	DUDLEY, Elisha	12/14/1832
DILL, Mary A.	WALKER, Alexader J.	12/26/1832
DILL, Maryann	HARBEN, William	12/04/1780
DILLARD, Martha	CHISUM, Joseph	08/17/1853
DILLARD, Mary A.	MORGAN, George W.	07/23/1850
DILLARD, Minerva	MCNIELL, George	11/29/1823
DIX, Elizabeth	LORENTZ, Joseph	02/08/1865
DIX, Lucinda	DIX, James	04/22/1846
DIX, Lucy	HAIRSTON, Charles	12/29/1867
DIX, Polly	SANDERS, James	09/22/1809
DIXON, Elizabeth	BOMAN, Joseph	03/01/1790
DIXON, Elizabeth	CARNAL, Hubbard	01/21/1797
DIXON, Elizabeth	WILLIAMS, Nathaniel Jr.	06/26/1792
DIXON, Jenny	BRACKIN, Joseph	06/10/1802
DIXON, Martha	JONES, David	11/23/1819
DIXON, Nanny	WADE, Lawson	12/28/1866
DIXON, Polly	BOULTON, William	11/18/1799
DIXON, Polly	BYSOR, John	01/28/1799
DIXON, Susanna	WILLIAMS, John Jr.	01/10/1800
DOBBIN, Ann	VANHOOK, Kindle	11/25/1800
DOBBIN, Elisabeth	ESKRIDGE, George	11/25/1790
DOBBIN, Elizabeth	HOLT, Clabin	05/22/1786
DOBBIN, Mary	HORTON, Sally	02/09/1791
DOBBIN, Nancy	BURCH, William	10/10/1792
DOBBIN, Peggy	FARLEY, John	--/--/1806
DOBBIN, Rachel	VANHOOK, Robert	12/10/1793
DOBBINS, Lethe E.	THOMAS, Jesse H.	04/18/1821
DOBBINS, Nahcey	BURTON, Noel	06/05/1817
DOBBINS, Sarah	ESKRIDGE, Samuel	10/30/1829
DOBBS, Mary	CAPES, George	08/04/1863
DODD, Louisa	MUSTAIN, Clark	08/28/1828
DODSON, Alcy	DODSON, Carter	02/23/1818
DODSON, Catherine	WHITICE, Joseph R.	07/17/1844
DODSON, Eliza A.	PATTILLO, Albert A.	05/21/1838
DODSON, Eliza O.	WHITE, Daniel H.	10/17/1854
DODSON, Elizabeth F.	WILKINSON, Robert W.	12/15/1865
DODSON, Elizabeth W.	DYE, Benjamin B.	05/10/1823
DODSON, Emeline	WILLIAMSON, Edmond	07/29/1866
DODSON, Emily	SCOTT, David	06/09/1853
DODSON, Frances	CLARK, Benjamin	12/21/1867
DODSON, Frances A.	MOTZ, Andrew	09/23/1840
DODSON, Lucy M.	RAMSOUR, Jacob A.	10/03/1833
DODSON, Mary A. C.	LIPSCOMB, Thomas W.	01/30/1847
DODSON, Mary F.	BARKER, Josiah	11/14/1865
DODSON, Mary R.	RICHMOND, Caleb H.	09/28/1838
DODSON, Permelia	TURNER, Gideon B.	02/27/1826
DODSON, Rebeca H.	BARUTT, Jno. B.	07/07/1846
DODSON, Sarah	FINCH, Samuel	04/30/1859
DODSON, Sarah	WALTERS, Thomas	10/11/1837
DODSON, Seignara M. (?)	TURNER, William W.	06/26/1824

MARRIAGE RECORDS OF CASWELL COUNTY, NORTH CAROLINA

BRIDE	GROOM	DATE
DOLLARHIDE, Frankey	LEA, John B.	11/24/1802
DOLLARHIDE, Mary	DOLLARHIDE, William	09/28/1789
DOLLARHIDE, Sarah	GALLANGHER, William	11/26/1781
DOLLERHIDE, Ann	NEELEY, Garnett	06/07/1801
DOLLERHIDE, Nice	STEP, Joshua	02/06/1789
DOLTON, Patsy	WALKER, David	01/30/1806
DONALDSON, Sarah	JEFFREYS, Thomas Jr.	06/09/1866
DONOHO, Betsy	WATLINGTON, John	09/04/1792
DONOHO, Cornelia A.	SEEWELL, Robert W.	01/08/1838
DONOHO, Elizabeth	ALDRIDGE, William J.	02/06/1856
DONOHO, Emily	STANLEY, Alfred M.	09/18/1843
DONOHO, Fanney	JOHNSTON, John	01/04/1800
DONOHO, Lucy	WILLIAMS, Paul	10/18/1791
DONOHO, Mary A.	HUNTINGTON, Martin P.	09/29/1834
DONOHO, Polly	ELLIOTT, John	02/25/1808
DONOHO, Polly	WRIGHT, Jacob Jr.	01/14/1794
DONOHO, Susannah	BENNATT, Ambrose L.	02/18/1804
DOOLY, Martha J.	MARSHALL, D. P.	09/12/1865
DOOWNS, Fanny	CARVER, William	07/07/1835
DOSON, Phillisse B.	BURTON, James	01/30/1838
DOTSON, Elmina	FORD, Thomas	05/01/1828
DOTSON, Martha W.	WILLIAMS, Robert W.	02/20/1850
DOTSON, Paggey M.	MARKES, John	01/26/1815
DOUGLASS, Elizabeth	FAUSETT, James	11/03/1827
DOUGLASS, Jane	LEA, George	02/24/1785
DOUGLASS, Janet	MCMURRY, Charles	12/22/1789
DOUGLASS, Martha	GRAHAMS, James	01/09/1816
DOUGLASS, Mary	SMITH, Zion	12/15/1840
DOUGLASS, Mary	WILDER, William	12/27/1833
DOUGLASS, Nancy	RAGSDALE, John	10/14/1783
DOWDWELL, Betsy	MCADEN, James	12/28/1815
DOWELL, Nancy	SIMSON, William	07/17/1788
DOWNS, Margaret	COOK, Lemuel	03/10/1826
DOWNS, Mary A.	MARTIN, Henry T.	05/09/1836
DOWNS, Mary A.	WISEMAN, John	06/11/1842
DRAIN, Sarah E.	LIPSCOMB, J. H.	02/03/1857
DRAPER, Betsy	WINTERS, Walter	12/20/1797
DRAPER, Polly	GOING, Jesse	11/12/1807
DRISKILL, Laura L.	PRUETT, Nathaniel	12/30/1864
DRUMMOND, Joanna	STEPHENS, James	01/31/1817
DRUREY, Mary	MOORE, Robert	05/24/1780
DUDLEY, Ibby	DRUSKILL, Samuel	04/20/1820
DUDLEY, Rebecca	HUTCHERSON, Wm. W.	04/03/1821
DUDLY, Lucinda	ROBERSON, Pleasant	01/04/1825
DUKE, Betsey	DUNAVEN, John	07/13/1825
DUKE, Eliza J.	FEGANS, James W.	01/18/1847
DUNAVANT, Sarah	MERRITT, Solomon	09/09/1863
DUNAWAY, Lucy	SADLER, Benjamin	03/02/1811
DUNAWAY, Mary	DABBS, William J.	09/24/1847
DUNCAN, Francis	MADDIN, Champness	01/17/1792
DUNCAN, Lucy	STANLEY, Joel	03/13/1824

MARRIAGE RECORDS OF CASWELL COUNTY, NORTH CAROLINA

BRIDE	GROOM	DATE
DUNCAN, Mary	RAGSDALE, Benjamin	--/--/1792
DUNCAN, Nancy	MERRITT, Daniel	01/27/1784
DUNCAN, Patience	WILKERSON, Wager	05/27/1780
DUNERVENT, Jane	COOK, Owen	01/27/1855
DUNEVANT, Virginia	DUNEVANT, James	12/31/1866
DUNIVANT, Nancy	DUKE, Buckner	08/30/1825
DUNKLY, Lucy	FLORA, Melceger R.	11/18/1842
DUNN, Ellin	CARNAL, Wm. Jr.	01/26/1818
DUNNAVAN, Namcy	COIL, Ezariah	03/02/1826
DUNNAVANT, Fanny	WILLIAMS, John	11/13/1822
DUNNAWAY, Elizabeth	HICKS, William	02/07/1825
DUPREE, Permelia	GWYN, John	08/02/1839
DUPREY, Christina	SHIELDS, John	01/12/1820
DURHAM, Ann	WAID, Hampton	11/12/1796
DURHAM, Ann	YATES, Jackson	10/30/1844
DURHAM, Caroline N.	LEA, James W.	09/29/1858
DURHAM, Frances	HINES, Frank	05/19/1866
DURHAM, Frances	WORSHAM, William R.	12/12/1836
DURHAM, Harriet	YATES, John M.	08/07/1848
DURHAM, Jane	SIMPSON, Richard	12/19/1860
DURHAM, Kesiah	WARE, Thomas	06/09/1805
DURHAM, Martha	RAINEY, Jno. P.	01/14/1836
DURHAM, Mary	ROSE, Howel S.	11/19/1829
DURHAM, Nancey	FORGUSSON, James	10/04/1816
DURHAM, Nancy J.	DICKINS, Israel	10/30/1844
DURHAM, Peggy	NEALY, John	05/06/1819
DURHAM, Priscilla	YATES, George	05/20/1822
DURHAM, Sally	GLASS, Willison J.	04/20/1829
DURHAM, Sarah E.	PATTERSON, Turner	06/06/1866
DURHAM, Susan	SOUTHARD, William	04/14/1845
DURHAM, Susannah	HARDY, George	02/25/1850
DUTY, Amy	SEYMOUR, Robert	01/28/1784
DUTY, Ann	MITCHEL, Charles	01/05/1829
DYE, Ann	PHELPS, Larking	08/19/1796
DYE, Delilah	WASLEY, Robert	03/22/1799
DYE, Francis	BRINSFIELD, Anderson	12/13/1815
DYE, Mary	RANDOLPH, James	12/12/1781
DYE, Peggy	PHELPS, Obediah	12/28/1796
DYE, Sally	PHELPS, Ambrose	08/19/1796
DYSON, Martha	TONEY, Charles	07/02/1835
EARP, Druzey	EVANS, Willis R.	05/28/1862
EARP, Lydia B.	HALL, William J.	02/01/1864
EASLEY, Caroline	UNDERWOOD, Henry	03/26/1866
EASLY, Harriet E.	WILLIAMSON, George	10/31/1838
ECHELS, Elizabeth D.	WALTON, William T.	12/30/1858
ECHOLS, Frances T.	INGRAM, Thomas E.	11/13/1856
ECHOLS, Lucy	HICKS, Simon	12/27/1867
EDES, Betsy	DOSS, Thomas	03/06/1827
EDGAR, Martha E. A. H.	OWENS, William T.	01/09/1842
EDMONDS, Bettie	HODGES, Nathan	04/24/1867
EDWARDS, Fanny	SHAMAN, William	03/08/1791

MARRIAGE RECORDS OF CASWELL COUNTY, NORTH CAROLINA

BRIDE	GROOM	DATE
EDWARDS, Mary E.	SHACKLEFORD, William	09/21/1867
EDWARDS, Sarah C.	WALTON, Benjamin W.	02/10/1863
EDWELL, Eady	LONG, William	12/22/1807
EDWELL, Kizzia	LONG, John	12/09/1835
EDWELL, Polly	TONEY, Arthur Jr.	10/16/1833
EDWIN, Lucy	TONEY, John	12/19/1832
EDWYN, Jincey	JEFFREYS, John	03/09/1795
EDWYN, Milly	SHAMAN, (?) Charles	10/31/1794
EDWYN, Milly	SHEARMAN, (?) Charles	10/31/1794
EDWYN, Milly	SHEARMAN, (?) Charles	10/31/1794
EDWYN, Milly	SHAMAN, (?) Charles	10/31/1794
EDWYN, Polly	SHARMAN, William	08/17/1799
ELAM, Frances	BUCKINGHAM, Bird	03/24/1834
ELAM, Nancy	WILLIAMS, Robert	02/06/1825
ELAM, Patience	THOMAS, David	04/21/1807
ELAM, Verlinchey W.	SANDERS, Robert	07/06/1801
ELINGTON, F.	BROWN, Obedih	01/22/1861
ELLINGTON, Rachel T.	CORHAM, Richard F.	07/11/1865
ELLIOT, Elizabeth	WALKER, James	11/21/1781
ELLIOT, Susan	RUNNELS, William	06/17/1848
ELLIOTT, Caroline	PULLIAM, Calvin	03/10/1867
ELLIOTT, Ellen	HUGHES, George	06/10/1867
ELLIOTT, Frances	COZZENS, Lewis	01/06/1855
ELLIOTT, Polly	MCDOWEL, James	10/20/1801
ELLIS, Darky	COLLIER, Henry	12/03/1815
ELLIS, Dolly	BIRK, Matterson	10/17/1804
ELLIS, Rebeckah	JOHNSON, James	10/03/1810
ELLISON, Mary C.	WARREN, Yancy G.	12/16/1842
ELMORE, Betsy	MCCAIN, Tillotson	01/11/1825
ELMORE, Lucy Ann	ELMORE, John	03/06/1830
ELMORE, Martha	WADDILL, Branch	02/08/1834
ELMORE, Mary A.	COBB, William	12/05/1821
ELMORE, Polly	ROPER, Henry	11/09/1832
ELMORE, Polly	SWIFT, Harvy	10/09/1819
ELMORE, Rebecca	COBB, Levi	11/07/1808
ELMORE, Sally	FLIPPO, Joseph	09/28/1801
EMERSON, Martha	HARRISON, Richard B.	12/12/1866
EMONS, Hannah	COBB, Ebenezar	03/05/1806
ENNET, Nancy	PEARSON, Thomas	12/30/1815
ENOCHS, ELizabeth	BARNWELL, William	12/16/1812
ENOCHS, Susan	BURTON, Thomas	10/21/1843
ENOCK, Susan F.	BIRD, William A.	08/29/1858
ENOCKS, Delphia	JEFFREYS, Franklin	11/26/1867
ENOCKS, Nancy A.	COVINGTON, John E.	02/05/1866
ENOCKS, Sarah	PLEASANT, Rufin	02/18/1823
EPPERSON, Elizabeth C.	KENT, William S.	12/11/1855
EPPERSON, Jane	MITCHELL, William	01/03/1857
EPPYSON, Patsey	MAHON, Henery	12/16/1808
ERWIN, Rebecca	NASH, Thomas	07/06/1784
ESKERIDGE, Rebecah	LIPSCOMB, Thomas	10/13/1829
ESKRIDGE, Elizabeth	PRICE, Mathew	02/22/1796

MARRIAGE RECORDS OF CASWELL COUNTY, NORTH CAROLINA

BRIDE	GROOM	DATE
ESKRIDGE, Martha	LIPSCOMB, Thomas	04/29/1828
ESKRIDGE, Polly	STAFFORD, James	05/08/1799
ESKRIDGE, Sally	COIL, Nicholas	02/09/1796
ESTES, Jane	BROWNING, William	02/13/1837
ESTES, Mary F.	STONE, William M.	11/23/1855
ESTRIDGE, Alley	DICKINS, James	03/28/1781
EUBALEY, Sarah	BROWDER, David A.	03/06/1820
EUBANK, Betsy	BURCH, William	06/21/1805
EUBANK, Frances	ROWARK, Larkin	03/03/1816
EUBANK, Lucretia	ELLISON, David	12/24/1818
EUBANK, Mary	BOWLES, Stephen	10/16/1818
EUBANK, Nancey	MALONE, Loney	03/27/1811
EUBANK, Polly	GRAVES, Jacob M. Jr.	09/13/1827
EUBANKS, Elisabeth	EUBANK, James	12/01/1791
EUDALY, Elizabeth	CARTER, Patton	12/09/1819
EVANS, Amanda A.	ELDRIDGE, Daniel B.	02/19/1856
EVANS, Ann	STEPHENS, George	09/08/1866
EVANS, Betsey	INGRAM, James	10/18/1808
EVANS, Betsey	LEWIS, Feilding	10/06/1810
EVANS, Betsy	WILLIS, Henry Jr.	01/20/1830
EVANS, Catharine	DAMERON, John W.	11/27/1841
EVANS, Ednea	JACKSON, John	06/05/1816
EVANS, Eliza	NELSON, Azariah	12/10/1842
EVANS, Eliza O.	BRUMMITT, Anderson	11/07/1838
EVANS, Elizabeth	RICHMOND, Henry A.	04/10/1851
EVANS, Elizabeth A.	KIMBROU, Thomas R.	01/30/1835
EVANS, Fanny	ROAN, Weldon	11/05/1867
EVANS, Mariann	BOWERS, John	06/15/1803
EVANS, Mary	RUDD, Franklin G.	11/21/1838
EVANS, Mary C.	DAVIS, William F.	06/24/1854
EVANS, Mary P.	AMOS, William T.	09/27/1859
EVANS, Nancy	MILES, John Jr.	12/08/1828
EVANS, Nancy	WASHBURN, Willis	05/02/1825
EVANS, Nancy A.	MOORE, Thomas E.	10/24/1842
EVANS, Phebe	MALONE, Staples	02/16/1789
EVANS, Pherebe	EVANS, Daniel	03/06/1782
EVANS, Polley	DAMERON, Williamson	12/21/1813
EVANS, Sally A.	TURNER, William A.	11/10/1858
EVANS, Sarah A.	MORGAN, L.D.	12/22/1857
EVANS, Sarah H.	MOORE, Joseph E.	10/05/1854
EVANS, Susanna	RUDD, Jeremiah	01/02/1811
EVANS, Susannah	BATEMAN, John	11/23/1807
EVENS, Jane	STEVENS, William	07/26/1855
EVENS, Salley	GRIFFIN, Vincent	09/12/1820
EVERET, Rachel	ENOCH, David	10/03/1803
EVERETT, Lucy	TURNER, Walter	02/20/1868
EVERETT, Mildred A.	ENOCK, Walker L.	05/05/1864
FAIR, Catherihe	DURHAM, John	10/30/1848
FAIR, Esther D.	BOLEY, Parham A.	09/29/1854
FANNING, Judah	BRANDON, Irvin	01/28/1788
FANNING, Letty	BLAIR, Thomas	11/28/1791

MARRIAGE RECORDS OF CASWELL COUNTY, NORTH CAROLINA

BRIDE	GROOM	DATE
FANNING, Mary	GOOCH, William Jr.	12/05/1798
FAREBANKS, Rachel	MCCUBBINS, William	02/17/1784
FARISH, Lucy	NUNNALLY, Jas	04/18/1866
FARLER, Nancy	SAWYERS, Solomon	07/19/1823
FARLEY, Catherine	WOODS, John	11/09/1801
FARLEY, Charlotte	MCALPIN, Alexander	07/26/1818
FARLEY, Eliza M.	LANGHORNE, Maurice M.	05/15/1837
FARLEY, Elizabeth	BOULTON, Charles	10/07/1791
FARLEY, Elizabeth	POPE, Abraham	01/24/1820
FARLEY, Elizabeth	SANDERS, Obadiah	01/24/1786
FARLEY, Isabella	MURRAY, Mark S.	10/24/1849
FARLEY, Keziah	BURTON, Henry	11/20/1786
FARLEY, Martha J.	RUDDER, Edward V.	04/02/1866
FARLEY, Martha J.	STEVENS, Thomas L.	07/23/1832
FARLEY, Mary	WOODS, William	12/20/1800
FARLEY, Mary C.	BARKER, Eaton B.	10/12/1865
FARLEY, Pamilia	GATEWOOD, Thomas	09/23/1806
FARLEY, Patsy	WILLSON, Wilem W.	01/02/1793
FARLEY, Perthena	BROWN, Samuel	09/16/1813
FARLEY, Polly H.	FISHER, William	08/30/1814
FARLEY, Rachel	ROPER, Henry	10/04/1810
FARLEY, Rebecca	BRYAN, John	08/11/1797
FARLEY, Sally	LEA, Major	08/29/1790
FARLEY, Sarah	FERGUSON, Albert G.	11/23/1858
FARLY, Cathrine	DURHAM, Newman	04/07/1804
FARMER, Ann	HAWKINS, Ephrem	05/01/1788
FARMER, Catherine	MORGAN, Lafayette	01/19/1848
FARMER, Elisabeth H.	FARMER, Henry A.	12/24/1857
FARMER, Jincy	BUTLER, Hudson	03/26/1795
FARMER, Martha	STEWART, Anderson	02/26/1865
FARMER, Mary J.	SMITH, James M.	09/30/1848
FARMER, Sally	BRANDON, Joseph	12/20/1867
FAUCET, Elinor	BRADFORD, David	06/03/1806
FAUCETT, Ann	SMITH, James	02/18/1833
FAUCETT, Fanny	SAWYER, Thomas	12/26/1832
FAUCETT, Martha	SAWYER, Levi	12/14/1842
FAULKS, Lucy A.	BROWN, Robert A.	05/03/1830
FAWLING, Rebecca	PAUL, James	09/25/1797
FEAGINS, Elizabeth	ALLEN, John	01/29/1851
FEATHERSTON, Polly	LONG, Samuel	06/17/1867
FEIGUS, Julia F.	WYNN, Robert S.	07/25/1865
FEILDER, Sarah	ADAMS, Joel T.	10/16/1828
FERGASON, Lucy C.	MANSFIELD, James L.	10/10/1858
FERGERSON, Sarah	WOODY, James	09/04/1842
FERGIS, Nancy	PETERSON, Williamson	12/22/1835
FERGUSON, Elizabeth	LEE, Alexander	10/24/1797
FERGUSON, Jemima	LEWIS, Zachariah	03/03/1866
FERGUSON, Polly	GOADGE, William	07/01/1805
FERGUSON, Sarah J.	COVINGTON, John J.	12/30/1856
FERREL, Nancy	EVANS, Henry	02/28/1822
FERRELL, Arminta	PRICE, Hiram M.	04/16/1852

MARRIAGE RECORDS OF CASWELL COUNTY, NORTH CAROLINA

BRIDE	GROOM	DATE
FERRELL, Cathrine	DUNAWAY, James	12/29/1795
FERRELL, Eliza A.	HALL, James	12/29/1856
FERRELL, Elizabeth	FUQUA, William	07/10/1833
FERRELL, Louisa A.	GOOCH, Nathaniel	07/19/1852
FERRELL, Mary R.	FUQUA, Henry D.	08/03/1826
FERRELL, Piety	DODSON, Thomas	02/26/1817
FERRELL, Polly	BALLAD, Larkin	01/01/1846
FERRELL, Polly	CARROL, Edward	06/19/1826
FIELDER, Jane	EDWARDS, George R.	09/27/1834
FIELDER, Margaret	NICHOLSON, Joseph	02/03/1829
FINLEY, Abigail	HOWARD, Woodson	07/24/1824
FINLEY, Polly	KITCHEN, Stephen	12/23/1822
FISHER, Elizabeth	TURNER, Thomas	11/08/1815
FISHER, Jinsy	RAY, Charles	12/14/1804
FISHER, Nancy	PRICE, Haskin	11/18/1799
FISHER, Polly	SAMUEL, James Jr.	11/15/1803
FISHER, Susanna	TURNER, Daniel	09/23/1805
FITCH, Artelia	EVANS, Edward	04/19/1848
FITCH, Catherine	HUGEES, Willliam	09/21/1844
FITCH, Malinda	GRIFFIN, Alvis L.	02/23/1850
FITCH, Minerva	MAYHAN, William	12/02/1847
FITCH, Polly	DUTY, Joseph	07/23/1826
FITZGERALD, Ann	FERGUSON, Bethel	12/28/1867
FITZGERALD, Nancy	NUNNALLY, John	12/21/1865
FITZGERALD, Rosey	MALLORY, Thomas	10/16/1802
FLEEMING, Mary	PERYMAN, Richard	04/07/1794
FLEET, Mary A.	USSERY, James G.	10/25/1838
FLEMING, Lucy	MCREYNOLDS, James	12/02/1790
FLEMING, Nancy	FARLEY, John	02/21/1803
FLINN, Susanna	BROWN, Edward	03/31/1798
FLINTOFF, Sally A.	BASS, Alex	07/08/1866
FLINTOFF, Sarah	RICHMOND, David	10/03/1867
FLIPPING, Jane	BROOKES, Thomas Jr.	02/26/1791
FLOOD, Martha M.	ANDERSON, James	02/02/1839
FLORENCE, Delphey	SIMPSON, Moses S.	10/22/1804
FLORENCE, Elizabeth	COLEMAN, James	12/22/1832
FLORENCE, Frances H.	PLEASANT, John	12/14/1860
FLORENCE, Lettice	CANTRELL, Joseph	11/11/1814
FLORENCE, Sarah	WELLS, James M.	10/24/1840
FOARD, Martha A.	LUNSFORD, Weldon H.	05/17/1866
FOLEY, Narcissia	BUTREY, John	11/09/1812
FOLEY, Parrizetta	BRAUGHTON, Jerremiah	10/17/1809
FORD, Celia	LEWIS, Henry H.	12/28/1825
FORD, Elizabeth	CREWS, Thomas	04/23/1835
FORD, Elizabeth M.	TRAVIS, John C.	12/21/1854
FORD, Emily N.	PARRISH, John J.	07/18/1867
FORD, Levicy	WALKER, William	10/22/1834
FORD, Mary Ann	ALVERSON, Azariah J.	01/26/1849
FORD, Phebe	SMITH, William	01/27/1814
FORREST, Ann J.	ORR, Ezekiel J.	10/15/1867
FOSTER, Ann E.	PHELPS, Robt. C.	02/24/1858

MARRIAGE RECORDS OF CASWELL COUNTY, NORTH CAROLINA

BRIDE	GROOM	DATE
FOSTER, Celia	PAGE, William M.	11/05/1839
FOSTER, Elizabeth	CATES, John	09/25/1804
FOSTER, Geneva C.	TAYLOR, Alfred G.	11/28/1866
FOSTER, Hannah	MCCAIN, Alexander	01/29/1790
FOSTER, Henrietta	YANCEY, Ransom	12/23/1867
FOSTER, Julia F.	CHILES, William H.	05/01/1864
FOSTER, Lizzy A.	WILLIAMS, Gilbert	02/10/1867
FOSTER, Martha	HENDERSON, Hiram Jr.	02/18/1837
FOSTER, Mary	MOOR, Robert	12/20/1784
FOSTER, Mary	WELLS, Thomas	09/26/1823
FOSTER, Mary A.	MILES, Abner Jr.	04/13/1849
FOSTER, Mary A.	MONTGOMERY, William J.	11/25/1852
FOSTER, Mary A.	WARD, William	10/13/1845
FOSTER, Milly	HUDSON, George	01/22/1798
FOSTER, Nancey	ADKINS, William	10/10/1815
FOSTER, Nancy	CANTROLL, Alexander	12/17/1834
FOSTER, Nancy	TOTTEN, Richard W.	09/13/1826
FOSTER, Nancy J.	SAUNDERS, William F.	12/20/1855
FOSTER, Patsey	BRANN, John	01/06/1800
FOSTER, Peggy	BRANDON, John	12/20/1809
FOSTER, Polley	JONES, Richard	12/09/1811
FOSTER, Sarah	BENTON, Joseph	03/02/1798
FOSTER, Sarah	EARP, Lawson	08/04/1832
FOSTER, Sarah	HATCHETT, Rufus	12/24/1866
FOSTER, Sarah	MITCHELL, James	10/03/1826
FOSTER, Susanna	MITCHELL, William	10/02/1826
FOSTER, Susannah	GUNN, Richard	10/30/1810
FOSTER, Virginia	HOOPER, Woodlieff	01/24/1860
FOURD, Wyeney B.	BROWN, Clark H.	02/20/1834
FOWLER, Ann E.	MORRIS, Edwin S.	01/23/1856
FOWLER, Elizabeth C.	COVEY, James G.	04/27/1847
FOWLER, Maseniah	CAZORT, Squire	02/19/1833
FOWLER, Nancy	FOWLER, John	07/11/1853
FOWLER, Nancy A.	PUGH, E.L.	11/28/1861
FOWLER, Rebecca	GATES, Richard	11/12/1837
FOWLER, Rebecca	WRAY, Thomas Jr.	11/04/1790
FOWLER, Rosa	HANCOCK, John J.	10/10/1858
FOWLKS, Susan A.	HUDSON, William F.	12/13/1858
FOX, Mary	HOOD, Wiley	12/10/1823
FRANKLIN, Sarah A.	WINGFIELD, Nelson D.	11/20/1833
FRANKLIN, Sarah F.	MITCHALL, Gilliam D.	10/13/1855
FRASIER, Jane	STEPHENS, Iverson G.	08/21/1834
FRAZER, Ann	GARROTT, Mansell	07/04/1790
FREDERICK, Emily L.	MASSIE, Albert A.	04/14/1867
FREDERICK, Jane	KERSEY, Ricahrd	08/29/1829
FREEMAN, Charlotte	RICHMOND, Franklin	02/06/1867
FREEMAN, Eliza A.	PALMER, John	05/12/1862
FREEMAN, Elizabeth	DURHAM, Samuel	05/09/1836
FREEMAN, Mary A.E.	MORRIS, John H.	09/09/1832
FREEMAN, Rachel	MITCHELL, Willy	02/25/1839
FREMAN, Martha A.	CHILTON, Joshua L.	11/23/1836

MARRIAGE RECORDS OF CASWELL COUNTY, NORTH CAROLINA

BRIDE	GROOM	DATE
FRENCH, Polly	VAUGHN, Thomas	08/31/1808
FRETWELL, M.J.	FERRELL, J.H.	10/18/1866
FUGERSON, Arey A.	TRAVIS, Elzey	09/28/1841
FULKS, S. A.	PARRISH, A. P.	12/04/1860
FULLAR, Elizabeth	WALLIS, John	01/07/1790
FULLAR, Mary	WILLIAMS, Thomas N.	11/07/1789
FULLER, Amy	JACCB, Lewis	12/27/1866
FULLER, Barbara M.	TALLEY, Orren	10/15/1827
FULLER, Eliza	JONES, Richard	12/05/1866
FULLER, Frances	SCOGGIN, William D.	01/25/1830
FULLER, Hester A.	MOORE, John	01/09/1867
FULLER, Malinda	SOUTHARD, William	10/24/1840
FULLER, Margaret	WOOD, John	10/22/1829
FULLER, Mary	MORTON, Martin	03/14/1818
FULLER, Mary	SCOOGIN, Johnson	04/07/1827
FULLER, Mary	TUDER, Landon	01/21/1832
FULLER, Mary	STRADOR, Obediah	01/29/1838
FULLER, Mary	WISDOM, Abner	01/20/1790
FULLER, Mary L.	BAYNES, Sidney Y.	05/13/1855
FULLER, Nancy	BYRD, Temple	07/14/1809
FULLER, Nancy	WILSON, Henry W.	04/22/1818
FULLER, Nicey	EVANS, James	11/09/1825
FULLER, Nisey L.	BOLES, James M.	09/08/1830
FULLER, Pheby	FORD, Alexander	08/19/1806
FULLER, Polley	ADKINS, William	10/26/1815
FULLER, Polly	CARTER, Braxston	04/24/1832
FULLER, Priscilla	WARREN, Samuel	12/31/1799
FULLER, Sallie M.	GLASS, Iverson M.	10/08/1853
FULLER, Sarah	DOWELL, James	03/14/1782
FULLER, Sarah	WISDOM, John	02/10/1792
FULLING, Agness	JACKSON, Andrew P.	03/28/1821
FULLINGTON, Elizabeth	ROAN, James T.	08/31/1826
FULLINTON, Susan J.	CHILDRESS, James A.	02/22/1856
FULLOE, Frances	LEA, Tinsley	09/18/1820
FUQUA, Elizabeth	DUNNAVANT, Thomas	04/07/1866
FUQUA, Elizabeth	WHITE, John	01/10/1834
FUQUA, Margaret	LUNSFORD, Paten L.	07/31/1866
FURGERSON, Jane M.	NICHOLS, John W.	11/27/1866
FURGIS, Sarah L.	RAINEY, Sanford H.	10/19/1859
FURGUSON, Ellenor	WHELLAN, William	01/17/1804
FURGUSON, Mary E.	STONE, John F.	03/10/1853
FURY, ELizabeht	MURPHEY, Barzel	09/21/1803
FURY, Polly	KIMBROUGH, Elijah	09/05/1803
GADDIS, Mary	WHITE, William	07/14/1801
GALLION, Mary J.	BASS, John B.	04/08/1859
GAN, Frances	MERRITT, Daniel T.	05/28/1820
GARLAND, Amanda	BARNER, John	12/27/1865
GARLAND, Cornelia	JOHNSTON, Warren	12/27/1867
GARLAND, Eliza A.	STEPHENS, Peter	07/07/1846
GARLAND, Isabella	DONOHO, T.A.	04/18/1854
GARLAND, Lucinda	SHACKLEFORD, Abraham	08/25/1866

MARRIAGE RECORDS OF CASWELL COUNTY, NORTH CAROLINA

BRIDE	GROOM	DATE
GARLAND, Malissa	PITTARD, Martin	05/19/1867
GARLAND, Mary	IRVINE, John	01/01/1867
GARLAND, Meldenna	GARLAND, Nelson	06/16/1867
GARLAND, Pheby Ann	GARLAND, Oscar	05/19/1867
GARLAND, Victoria C.	NEBLETT, Colin	10/24/1855
GARNER, Catherine	BOULDIN, John	02/28/1843
GARRETT, Ann	WEST, Edward	09/---/1866
GARRETT, Nancey	CONNER, William B.	03/15/1855
GARRETT, Susan	FITZGERALD, Pleasant	10/06/1853
GARRISON, Margaret A.	MASSIE, Joseph W.	08/21/1867
GARROTT, Eliza A.	CRUTCHFIELD, George H.	07/04/1838
GARROTT, Mary	FOSTER, Samuel P.	12/04/1829
GARROTT, Susan	PRICE, John Jr.	01/04/1808
GASKINS, Eunice	IPOCK, William	10/02/1856
GATES, Obediance	RICHARDSON, Thomas	01/10/1819
GATEWOOD, Ann E.	FERRELL, Hutchings	10/11/1830
GATEWOOD, Ann E.	TRAVIS, James F.M.	10/25/1866
GATEWOOD, Elizabeth	KEESEE, Charles	07/26/1815
GATEWOOD, Frances	SHELTON, William H.	11/27/1812
GATEWOOD, Louisa F.	YATES, John M.Jr.	11/19/1866
GATEWOOD, Martha T.	POWELL, William B.	01/01/1860
GATEWOOD, Mary A.	RAWLINS, James M.	01/10/1855
GATEWOOD, Nancy	STOKES, Sylvanus	12/25/1809
GATEWOOD, Pamela	NUNNALLY, Archelaus (?)	03/04/1822
GATEWOOD, Patsey	COLQUHOUN, James	12/19/1796
GATEWOOD, Susan	CARTER, Iverson B.	11/27/1847
GATWOOD, Martha G.	SIMPSON, John C.	10/03/1849
GENNINGS, Nancy	COBB, Joseph	11/09/1812
GIBSON, Anne	EVANS, Zecheriah	01/03/1784
GIBSON, Elizabeth	DARBY, Daniel	02/09/1791
GIBSON, Elizabeth	SHAW, James	05/28/1783
GIBSON, Margaret	CANADAY, A. L.	12/19/1865
GIBSON, Mary	COOPER, John	07/31/1782
GIBSON, Sophia	SMITH, Richard	11/03/1815
GILASPY, Betsy	WARF, Roger	01/05/1802
GILASPYU, Milly	HORTON, John	11/20/1797
GILBERT, Sally	MASTERS, Enoch	04/19/1818
GILL, Elizabeth	FORD, Lewis	09/21/1841
GILL, Lucy	BLACK, Robert	02/08/1792
GILLAM, Fanny	MIZE, Thomas	12/22/1812
GILLASPEY, Viney	SOMERS, James	01/30/1806
GILLASPIE, -----	LUMPKIN, George	02/11/1815
GILLASPIE, Eliza	MANSFIELD, James	12/21/1849
GILLASPIE, Elizabeth	HARVEL, Henry	11/18/1814
GILLASPIE, Mary	JEFFREYS, Atkinson	12/29/1837
GILLASPY, Tabitha H.	NUNNALLY, James S.	01/21/1824
GILLGORE, Jane	HUBBARD, Sebulon B.	01/19/1785
GILLGORE, Lydia	YATES, James	07/21/1784
GILLISPIE, Lucinda	HART, Ellick	12/09/1849
GILLISPIE, Susan H.	POWELL, Mastin J.	06/20/1852
GILLYON, Mary	CULBERTSON, James	12/13/1785

MARRIAGE RECORDS OF CASWELL COUNTY, NORTH CAROLINA

BRIDE	GROOM	DATE
GIMBOE, Mary	SUMERS, John	07/02/1783
GIPSON, Catharine	BROOKS, William	11/17/1816
GIPSON, Elizabeth	SARTIN, Anslum E.	07/30/1855
GIPSON, Jemia A.	ADKINS, Akillis	07/21/1864
GIPSON, Mary	TURNER, James H.	02/08/1855
GITTON, Rebecca	WARE, James	06/12/1812
GIVINGS, Mildred	BENNETT, Thomas	10/26/1826
GLASCO, Harriet	CASORT, John H.	02/23/1843
GLASGOW, Eliza	FOWLER, Elias	11/08/1834
GLASPY, Sally	WARF, James	12/23/1801
GLASS, Fanny	YANCEY, Nathan	01/26/1867
GLASS, Martha S.	BADGETT, Henry	01/02/1830
GLASS, Mary E.	WILLIAMS, J.M.Dr.	11/27/1865
GLASS, Patience E.	JENNINGS, Joseph	08/27/1842
GLASS, Sarah J.	THOMPSON, Thomas	08/10/1867
GLAZE, Sarah	NIGHTON, Turner	01/02/1849
GLENN, Christinia J.	GARLAND, Jno T.	05/15/1821
GLENN, Mary	BROWN, Bedford	07/06/1816
GLIDEWELL, Mary	HAMLETT, Robert	12/27/1843
GODSON, Mildred	LYON, Noel W.	01/20/1852
GOIN, Alsey	TULLOH, William	01/03/1809
GOING, Heaty	PRYOR, William	07/19/1803
GOING, Lithe	LOUGHIN, David	11/18/1783
GOING, Patsey	MASON, Patrick	12/03/1790
GOING, Rhoda	STEPHENS, George	07/28/1806
GOING, Sally	CHAPMAN, Richard	06/21/1806
GOLD, Mary	RICHMOND, William A.	10/08/1829
GOLD, Sarah	LEA, William	11/03/1790
GOLDSBY, Elizabeth	MATTHIS, James	11/30/1791
GOMER, Amy	SMITHEY, Thomas	10/30/1838
GOMER, Ann	WALKER, Jethro J.	12/26/1839
GOMER, Dicey	GOMER, James	12/17/1816
GOMER, Jane	SLADE, Joshua	07/22/1815
GOMER, Judith	LONG, Benjamin	06/03/1830
GOMER, Mary	ROBERTS, Roland W.	12/24/1818
GOMER, Nancy	RICE, Iverson	10/23/1845
GOMER, Polly	BROWNING, Martin	02/20/1810
GOMER, Polly	SULLVENT, Jordan	12/23/1805
GOMER, Sarah	THOMASON, Fleming	12/25/1799
GOOCH, Arrena	STADLER, John T.	01/02/1844
GOOCH, Artelia	MASSEY, Nathan T.	11/09/1858
GOOCH, Cesley	HIGHTOWER, Devereux	01/13/1816
GOOCH, Cistey	BIRK, James	07/31/1802
GOOCH, Eliza	EDWARDS, Edward	10/18/1859
GOOCH, Frances	MASSEY, Eli	01/21/1833
GOOCH, Mary A.	TALLMAN, James	03/04/1835
GOOCH, Polly	WILLIAMS, Henry	12/31/1799
GOOCH, Sarah	RICE, William H.	09/07/1795
GOOCH, Susannah	BOSWELL, Howel	12/22/1813
GOOD, Betsey	FREEMAN, Moses	10/30/1811
GOOD, Harriett	COUSINS, Thomas	12/13/1859

MARRIAGE RECORDS OF CASWELL COUNTY, NORTH CAROLINA

BRIDE	GROOM	DATE
GOOD, Vilet	FREEMAN, Wesley	01/29/1862
GOODE, Amanda	HODGE, Henry L.	10/10/1867
GOODSON, Rebecca	RUDD, William	03/08/1809
GOODSON, Sarah J.	CHANDLER, John J.	12/01/1840
GOODSON, Temperance	GWYN, Zeri	12/21/1800
GOODWIN, Mary Ann	BARRY, Edward M.	01/20/1837
GORDIN, Elizabeth F.	TRAMMEL, Elisha B.	12/24/1856
GORDON, Betsy	VANHOOK, John	12/14/1807
GORDON, Cornelia A.	LONGWELL, David	10/08/1857
GORDON, Elizabeth	FARLEY, Abner B.	11/11/1848
GORDON, Jane P.	BAUGH, Peter	01/15/1821
GORDON, Mary A.	MCGRUDER, Albert	11/21/1860
GORDON, Narcissa R.	MERRITT, George H.	02/14/1850
GORDON, Nora W.	HARVEY, Charles L.	03/26/1867
GORDON, Sally	DYE, William	06/05/1799
GORDON, Sarah	GOSSET, Joel	10/17/1827
GORDON, Tabitha	NIPPER, Samuel	11/23/1816
GOSNEY, Nanny J.	BURCH, John W.	05/29/1862
GOULD, Jemima	MCMURREY, James	12/22/1787
GRAHAM, Lucinda	JOHNSTON, Moses	11/30/1867
GRANT, Artimesia B.	HUBBARD, James	01/02/1838
GRANT, Elizabet	FOSTER, Robert	09/05/1805
GRANT, Frances	KIDD, Lewis	03/26/1815
GRANT, Jane E.	PAGE, William C.	12/10/1844
GRANT, Lucy	CATES, Richard	03/26/1801
GRANT, Lucy	WILSON, Abel	11/01/1800
GRANT, Pamelia D.	COB, Maximin	02/25/1837
GRANT, Rachel	DENNIS, John	02/03/1796
GRANT, Sarah	MAAYHON, William	12/19/1781
GRANT, Sarah	LAMON, Alexander	03/11/1786
GRAVES, Almire	WHITUS, Robert	10/27/1866
GRAVES, Ann S.	MEBANE, Jno. H.	02/09/1837
GRAVES, Betsy	LEA, James jR.	04/15/1815
GRAVES, Betsy B.	LEA, William	06/24/1836
GRAVES, Caroline H.	REID, Hugh K.	05/27/1857
GRAVES, Catharine	JOHNSTON, Daniel	12/12/1865
GRAVES, Cornelia W.	TURBEVILLE, Lewis W.	09/14/1852
GRAVES, Delila	WOMACK, David	03/24/1800
GRAVES, Edy	BROWN, Ned	02/16/1867
GRAVES, Elizabeth	GRAVES, Lewis	11/12/1818
GRAVES, Elizabeth	KIMBROUGH, Thomas	03/29/1792
GRAVES, Elizabeth L.	LINDSEY, A. C.	06/14/1843
GRAVES, Evelina	GRAVES, Alfred	07/22/1867
GRAVES, Fanny	TUBERVILLE, Fountain M.	12/10/1851
GRAVES, Fanny W.	WOMACK, Algernon S.	08/08/1855
GRAVES, Frances L.	SETTLE, Joshua	06/03/1826
GRAVES, Frances M.	MCKEE, James L.	06/15/1852
GRAVES, Hannah	TERRELL, Lewis	10/31/1816
GRAVES, Hannah S.	THOMAS, William A.	10/01/1844
GRAVES, Henrietta	SETTLE, Thomas	09/18/1820
GRAVES, Henrietta W.	YANCEY, Algernon S.	05/21/1838

MARRIAGE RECORDS OF CASWELL COUNTY, NORTH CAROLINA

BRIDE	GROOM	DATE
GRAVES, Ibby	WILLIS, Marshall	11/24/1866
GRAVES, Isabell	MCNEILL, Hosea	03/16/1807
GRAVES, Isabella	SLADE, Thomas Jr.	12/12/1782
GRAVES, Isabella L.	BIRK, Archibald R.	10/18/1836
GRAVES, Isabella L.	DODSON, Thomas C.	10/23/1849
GRAVES, Isbell	GRAVES, William	11/25/1805
GRAVES, Laura A.	HENRY, James W.	10/12/1850
GRAVES, Leannah H.	HARRALSON, Paul A.	09/30/1824
GRAVES, Manilla	BOSWELL, Brown	10/15/1829
GRAVES, Margaret	LIPSCOMB, Joseph R. E.	05/29/1833
GRAVES, Margaret J.	SMITH, Jesse S.	03/15/1853
GRAVES, Martha	TAPSCOTT, Wesley	12/06/1866
GRAVES, Martha W.	DICK, John W.	05/31/1822
GRAVES, Mary	GRAVES, Thomas W.	07/17/1828
GRAVES, Mary	SLADE, Abisha	04/23/1846
GRAVES, Mary B.	ESKRIDGE, Robert W.	08/25/1849
GRAVES, Mary U.	PINNIX, George W.	09/19/1854
GRAVES, Mira L.	WILKS, Thomas U.	10/31/1837
GRAVES, Nancey	GRAVES, William	05/25/1815
GRAVES, Nancey	EUBANK, Thomas	12/16/1828
GRAVES, Nancey	JOHNSTON, Caleb A.	02/17/1866
GRAVES, Nancey S.	GRAVES, Solomon	05/21/1836
GRAVES, Nancy	MOORE, William	11/25/1799
GRAVES, Nancy	YANCY, Bartlett	12/20/1808
GRAVES, Patsey	ALDRIDGE, Joseph	12/25/1816
GRAVES, Patsey	GUNN, Thomas	09/22/1792
GRAVES, Polly	MEBANE, James	01/17/1833
GRAVES, Rebecca W.	GRAVES, Henry L.	02/02/1836
GRAVES, Sarah	MURPHEY, Alexander	09/11/1822
GRAVES, Sylvia	LAW, John	04/19/1867
GRAVES, Tabitha	VAUGHAN, John	10/30/1832
GRAVES, Virginia Y.	MCDONALD, William R.	01/13/1864
GRAVETT, Elizabeth J.	BOYD, Lindsey J.	11/24/1858
GRAVITT, Sarah	THAXTON, William	08/16/1783
GRAY, Polly	STREET, Anthony	06/18/1803
GRAY, Susannah	HORTON, George	02/03/1813
GREEN, Nancey	COX, Nathaniel	10/16/1838
GREEN, Peggy	HADDOCK, Andrew	06/21/1806
GREENHAW, Rachel	GOSSAGE, Richard	04/12/1797
GREER, Elizabeth	STOANE, Thomas	08/19/1793
GREER, Nancey	COMPTON, Thomas	05/22/1811
GREGORY, Julietta W.	JACKSON, Richard W.	10/17/1836
GREGORY, Mary	FULCHER, Henry	12/21/1786
GRIER, Margret	HORTON, George	02/08/1809
GRIFFIN, Martha	ROBERTS, John	04/30/1843
GRIFFIN, Patsey	FORD, Laban	04/08/1813
GRIFFIN, Polly	PHILLIPS, Joshua	11/01/1802
GRIFFIS, Sally	EDWEL, Jim	04/10/1845
GRIFFY, Ann	ROBINSON, Jesse	04/19/1785
GROGAN, Lucinda	BRIGGS, Silas	06/01/184_
GROOM, Betsey	BENTON, William	01/01/1820

MARRIAGE RECORDS OF CASWELL COUNTY, NORTH CAROLINA

BRIDE	GROOM	DATE
GROOM, Dolpha	COBB, William M.	01/25/1830
GROOM, Eliza	CHILTON, Alfred	12/10/1842
GROOM, Isabella	BENTON, Thomas	09/23/1828
GROOM, Martha	SMITHEY, Samuel	01/14/1841
GROOM, Nancy	MILLER, Henry	07/16/1818
GROOM, Polly	CHANDLER, Daniel	12/19/1821
GROOM, Satiry	WALKER, David	09/30/1845
GUINN, Melvira	WILES, Thomas	03/15/1860
GULIPIN, Martha	WELLS, Justian	01/19/1836
GUNN, Adaline A.	ADAMS, Sylvester P.	10/03/1846
GUNN, Amy	JACKSON, Robert	01/02/1866
GUNN, Barbara	HINTON, Samuel	12/27/1825
GUNN, Bell	SWIFT, Alex	09/23/1867
GUNN, Betsey	HARRELSON, James M.	05/23/1832
GUNN, Betsy B.	MILES, James	02/03/1807
GUNN, Celestia A.	WARE, James T.	06/06/1861
GUNN, Dorothy M.	HARVEY, John C.	03/21/1827
GUNN, Eleanor	QUINE, Jacob	11/09/1801
GUNN, Eliza A.	GRAVES, Elijah Jr.	10/21/1828
GUNN, Ella	WILLIAMSON, Thomas	12/10/1865
GUNN, Emily N.	ROPER, William F.	08/15/1836
GUNN, Harriet	LEWIS, Thomas J.	02/16/1867
GUNN, Harriet E.	WILLIAMSON, Robert H.	05/17/1865
GUNN, Hulda M.	THORNTON, Francis F.	10/22/1834
GUNN, Jinny	BROWN, Isham	07/03/1866
GUNN, Margaret	PATTILLO, William	12/29/1866
GUNN, Martha	PINNIX, John	06/10/1867
GUNN, Mary C.	HODGES, Henry E.	12/10/1842
GUNN, Mary C.	PAGE, James B.	10/15/1865
GUNN, Minerva A.	JORDAN, Thomas N.	11/23/1865
GUNN, Patsy H.	MATLOCK, James	01/13/1810
GUNN, Priscilla	PAYNE, John	09/--/1802
GUNN, Rebecca	BURTON, Benjamin	12/09/1801
GUNN, Sarah	BURTON, James	01/19/1800
GUNN, Sarah A.	WATKINS, Tho. J.	08/10/1843
GUNN, Susanna	RICE, Joshua M.	10/01/1806
GUNN, Susannah	HARRIS, James	11/01/1819
GUNNELL, Patcey	HUBBARD, Ralph	08/10/1809
GUY, Rhoda	GARLAND, Anderson	12/27/1867
GWYN, Dorothy	WEMPLE, Jno. D.	03/17/1841
GWYN, Elizabeth	LIPSCOMB, John	01/26/1807
GWYN, Elizabeth	MATKINS, John H,	04/17/1843
GWYN, Frances	MOORE, Solomon	12/27/1867
GWYN, Jane	BRINCFIELD, Bartlet Y.	12/20/1858
GWYN, Martha A.	HATCHETT, John W.	02/18/1858
GWYN, Susen Y.	BOWLES, Thomas	11/28/1853
GWYN, Zippora J.	NEAL, Philemon H.	09/05/1861
GWYNN, Huldah	MOORE, Matthew P.	02/20/1843
GWYNN, Jane	BOYD, David	12/01/1801
GWYNN, Permelia A.	RODGERS, R.S.	12/05/1865
GWYNN, Sarah	JONES, J. Riley	12/15/1865

MARRIAGE RECORDS OF CASWELL COUNTY, NORTH CAROLINA

BRIDE	GROOM	DATE
HADDOCK, Elizabeth	CINKLER, James	02/01/1798
HADDOCK, Mary	WILLIS, Henry	05/21/1783
HADDOCK, Nancy	STANSBURY, Luke	01/30/1791
HADOCK, Emiline	KEIRSEY, Wm.H.	01/06/1858
HAGEWOOD, Sarah F.	COLEMAN, George A.	01/14/1858
HAGGARD, Lydia	SWIFT, John	06/26/1792
HAILEY, Mary	FURGERSON, Alexander	10/06/1856
HAILEY, Rebecca	NOWLES, William	07/01/1812
HAILEY, Sarah	BROWN, William J.	12/11/1857
HAIRSTON, Amanda	PANTON, Scott	12/27/1867
HAITH, Sarah J.	HAITHCOCK, John	08/18/1867
HALCOMB, Elizabeth A.	CHEANEY, William H.	05/27/1846
HALCOMB, Mary M.	WARE, John	10/09/1820
HALCOMB, Nancy	SHACKLEFORD, Armstead	10/24/1786
HALL, Adelethia	WILMOTH, Miles	09/11/1820
HALL, Ann	CLARK, John	04/18/1855
HALL, Eddy	WALLIS, James	12/30/1786
HALL, Elizabeth	GOMER, James	04/22/1819
HALL, Elizabeth	EVEHS, William A./G.	11/13/1855
HALL, Elizabeth	EVENS, William G./A.	11/13/1855
HALL, Emily G.	JACKSON, Abel	09/04/1847
HALL, Fanny	MORROW, Daniel	10/08/1790
HALL, Judith B.	JONES, James B.	09/29/1814
HALL, Martha A.	SNEAD, Benjamin	02/24/1853
HALL, Marthy J.	BURKS, Joseph F.	09/21/1866
HALL, Nancey	LOVELESS, Benjamin C.	11/01/1837
HALL, Rebecca F.	WARREN, Burwell	09/17/1863
HALL, Rebecca J.	HAWKER, James W.	02/01/1864
HALL, Sally	BELEW, Daniel	11/01/1794
HALL, Sally	HOOPER, Thomas	11/08/1849
HALL, Sally	WILMOTH, George	03/25/1822
HAMBLETT, Nancy N.	RAGSDALE, Clement	11/12/1817
HAMILTON, Sally	CHILTON, John	01/31/1807
HAMLET, Elizabeth	HARRIS, James M.	12/04/1848
HAMLET, Jane	WADE, William	01/22/1864
HAMLET, Julia	ELLIOT, George	12/18/1824
HAMLETON, Polly	SHARP, George	11/25/1811
HAMLETT, Aggy	NEAL, Stephen	05/19/1866
HAMLETT, Belle	MOORE, William	09/28/1867
HAMLETT, Caroline	STEVENS, Henry	04/06/1867
HAMLETT, Elizabeth	ASHBURN, Lewis	12/05/1797
HAMLETT, Fanny M.	RAGSDALE, William	10/02/1783
HAMLETT, Frances M.	WHITE, John W.	03/30/1854
HAMLETT, Hannah	MALONE, Mark	09/04/1796
HAMLETT, Mary	RAGSDALE, Peter	12/09/1788
HAMLETT, Rebecca Ann	ALLEN, John	07/10/1864
HAMNER, Nancey	BENNETT, Henry	01/17/1828
HANCOCK, Lucy Ann	HALL, James H.	09/07/1868
HANCOCK, Susanna	CAMPBELL, James B.	07/22/1855
HANSHAW, Catherine	WARREN, William Jr.	03/24/1826
HANSHAW, Eliza	TERRELL, James	09/30/1852

MARRIAGE RECORDS OF CASWELL COUNTY, NORTH CAROLINA

BRIDE	GROOM	DATE
HARALSON, Agness	BARNETT, Andrew	09/21/1791
HARALSON, Betsy	TURNER, Thomas	10/28/1794
HARALSON, Darcas	WILLIS, Henry	02/21/1821
HARALSON, Dorcas	TOTTEN, John C.	06/05/1826
HARALSON, Dorcass	DONOHO, William	04/06/1784
HARALSON, Elizabeth	WINDSOR, Joseph	10/21/1811
HARALSON, Fanney	HENDERSON, Jacob	12/08/1807
HARALSON, Huldah	WARREN, John	11/30/1850
HARALSON, Jane	ROGERS, John Jr.	01/02/1785
HARALSON, Martha	GUNN, John A.	04/02/1839
HARALSON, Parthena	HODNETT, Philip	04/26/1827
HARALSON, Sarah	WOMACK, Pleasant H.	12/04/1828
HARDEN, Deborah	FREEMAN, John P.	02/01/1815
HARDEN, Elizabeth	RICE, Jeremiah	10/14/1816
HARDEN, Nancey	FOSTER, James	09/04/1812
HARDGEGREE, Ellenor	POND, Walter	07/28/1795
HARDIGE, Nancy	DANIEL, Thomas	12/16/1814
HARDY, Lucy	COOK, George	07/19/1844
HARGASS, Fanny	BARNETT, Thomas	06/06/1803
HARGIS, Lucy A.	LEA, William A.	10/02/1851
HARGIS, Nancy	HUDGING, Thos.	--/--/----
HARGIS, Nancy	ROBERTS, Arthur	03/25/1789
HARGIS, Sarah	WOLTERS, Henry	01/31/1792
HARGISS, Jean	BLACKARD, Jobe	01/31/1792
HARGRAVE, Betsey	DEBRULER, Charles	02/03/1816
HARGREAVE, Lucy	DEBRULER, Wesley	11/04/1816
HARNDON, Patsy	WAURRIN, John	02/14/1794
HARP, Eleanor	RANDOLPH, George	07/06/1813
HARP, Jamima	RANDOLPH, James	10/11/1813
HARP, Mary	LYON, Noel W.	12/26/1837
HARPER, Judy	FARMER, Stephen	03/17/1791
HARPER, Louisa	JEFFREYS, James	12/23/1822
HARPER, Lydia	WATLINGTON, Francis	11/04/1823
HARPER, Rebecca	SCOTT, William	06/22/1814
HARRALSON, Eliza	LIPSCOMB, Joseph R. E.	03/11/1830
HARRALSON, Henriatta	HODGES, Fielding L.	02/04/1865
HARRALSON, Nancey	GUNN, Asa	11/22/1819
HARRAWAY, Nancy W.	THOMAS, A.W.	05/24/1865
HARREL, Elizabeth	PAYNE, Daniel	01/22/1806
HARRELSON, Elizabeth	HOOPER, William Y.	01/25/1830
HARRELSON, Elizabeth J.	HENDERSON, William Jr.	10/29/1838
HARRELSON, Nancy	WEATHERFORD, Hiram	09/23/1818
HARRELSON, Polley	FOSTER, Thomas	12/22/1814
HARRELSON, Sarah	BARTON, Lewis	03/08/1827
HARRIS, Agnes	WILLIAMS, Marmaduke	10/26/1798
HARRIS, Betsy	NORMAN, William	10/09/1850
HARRIS, Elizabeth A.	SHACKLEFORD, Francis A.	09/30/1857
HARRIS, Gracie	FARISH, Joseph	12/27/1866
HARRIS, Kitty	COBB, Joseph K.	08/30/1825
HARRIS, Lydia	BROWN, Robert	12/19/1795
HARRIS, Martha	OWEN, Sharod	10/14/1815

MARRIAGE RECORDS OF CASWELL COUNTY, NORTH CAROLINA

BRIDE	GROOM	DATE
HARRIS, Mary E.	HUBBARD, James	02/26/1862
HARRIS, Sally	LONG, Robin E.	09/29/1830
HARRIS, Sarah	COBB, Samuel C.	12/07/1827
HARRIS, Susan S.	ROBERTS, Laton T.	12/17/1833
HARRIS, Temperance	SHELTON, Henry	08/02/1815
HARRIS, Tempy	MEBANE, Edward	12/04/1867
HARRISON, Agness R.	PRICE, Daniel S.	02/12/1833
HARRISON, Agness W.	COLEMAN, James E.	01/05/1850
HARRISON, Ann E.	YOUNG, Smith	05/11/1824
HARRISON, Ann S.	SHARP, William T.	11/07/1837
HARRISON, Araminta	JETER, Joseph H.	10/10/1837
HARRISON, Cintha	HALL, Charles	03/24/1852
HARRISON, Eliza J.	HARRISON, Edmond R.	09/13/1844
HARRISON, Elizabeth	MORTON, John	07/22/1846
HARRISON, Elizabeth	SMITH, Samuel Jr.	04/23/1792
HARRISON, Elizabeth J.	THOMPSON, George W.	02/20/1838
HARRISON, Euphranier	STARKES, Chesley	11/24/1846
HARRISON, Harriet	BLALOCK, Alfred	02/03/1843
HARRISON, Harriet S.	PINOX, Alexander K.	04/28/1848
HARRISON, Hulda	SWIFT, Washington	06/12/1866
HARRISON, Jane	DABNEY, Samuel	04/08/1817
HARRISON, Jane D.	OLIVER, Creed T.	01/15/1830
HARRISON, Louisa M.	FULTON, Jno K.	01/10/1852
HARRISON, Mary	BLACKARD, Aaron C.	12/19/1836
HARRISON, Mary E.	RYAN, Charles J.	07/29/1843
HARRISON, Mary W.	WILKINSON, John E.	09/10/1821
HARRISON, Matilda	WELLS, Azariah	02/23/1832
HARRISON, Mildred L.	HARRISON, Robert L.	02/19/1833
HARRISON, Nancey	HENSLEE, Micajah	12/06/1836
HARRISON, Nancey L.	BOYD, Alexander Jr.	12/09/1819
HARRISON, Nancy	MCDANIEL, William P.	07/15/1817
HARRISON, Nancy	PRENDERGRAST, Thomas	03/12/1799
HARRISON, Nancy	RICE, Jeremiah	10/20/1843
HARRISON, Patsy	WILKINSON, Henry E.	12/08/1819
HARRISON, Polly K.	SLADE, Abisha	01/05/1826
HARRISON, Sarah	SCOTT, Harry	05/23/1798
HARRISON, Susan	KNIGHT, William W.	01/08/1836
HARRISON, Virginia C.	HARRISON, Thomas D.	04/30/1844
HARRISON, Virginia S.	LEA, James W.	02/03/1858
HARRISS, Edy	WILLIAMS, Duke	10/19/1790
HARRIWAY, Kitty	BOWDEN, John	11/26/1817
HART, Betsy A.	BRUCE, William	09/04/1797
HART, Elizabeth	PETTERFORD, Levi T.	07/30/1861
HART, Emily F.	WALKER, Nicholas L.	11/20/1849
HART, Louisa	WILBURN, W.H.	12/24/1855
HART, Lucy	HILL, Lewis	05/21/1851
HART, Mildred A.	STOW, Henry C.	09/20/1855
HART, Patsey	HART, Thomas	03/21/1792
HART, Polley	HILLYER, James	11/08/1803
HART, Polly	TAYLOR, William	11/03/1808
HART, Susannah	COWAN, Joseph	06/01/1808

MARRIAGE RECORDS OF CASWELL COUNTY, NORTH CAROLINA

BRIDE	GROOM	DATE
HARTON, Basheba	JEFFREYS, William	04/24/1822
HARVEL, Jincy	MERRITT, Levi	04/21/1825
HARVELL, Elizabeth	TATE, Robert	09/09/1814
HARVELL, Levina	HARVELL, Littleton Taz.	09/11/1826
HARVELL, Winney	HALL, Anthony	09/22/1792
HARVEY, Sally	TAYLOR, Samuel	10/19/1841
HARVILLE, Eliza	STEPHENS, Isaac	04/12/1838
HARWELL, Nancey	HALL, John	10/18/1791
HASKINS, Betty	HARRAWAY, Daniel	10/04/1867
HASTEN, Amy	HENSLEE, Enoch	10/27/1806
HASTIN, Nanny	MASSEY, John	11/18/1801
HASTIN, Peggy	SMITH, Solomon	01/04/1816
HATCHER, Elizabeth	HIGHTOWER, Allen	01/27/1808
HATCHET, Harriet	KELLY, William	06/16/1866
HATCHETT, Clarender F.(?)	MOTLEY, Nathaniel C.	10/26/1853
HATCHETT, Elizabeth A.	JEFFRESS, Newton B.	03/14/1855
HATCHETT, Elizabeth C.	WOMACK, Green P.	10/17/1831
HATCHETT, Lucy W.	STOKES, William Y.	10/28/1836
HATCHETT, Margaret	WOOLLEN, Minor	01/03/1867
HATCHETT, Mary C.	WEST, Benjamin C.	02/21/1824
HATCHETT, Mary N.	GWYN, Daniel	08/30/1815
HATCHETT, Mildred R.	TURNER, Chesley	04/19/1821
HATCHETT, Sarah	HENDERSON, Jacob	12/31/1829
HATCHITT, Martha N.	MIMS, John W.Jr.	03/26/1850
HATCHITT, Nancy M.	MONTGOMERY, Abraham B.	06/16/1821
HAWKINS, Alice V.	GATTIS, W. A.	12/17/1866
HAWKINS, Elizabeth	PROCTOR, Daniel R.	08/04/1852
HAWKINS, Mary A.	LOCKETT, David S.	02/27/1864
HAWKINS, Mary E.	WRIGHT, James B.	09/09/1867
HAWKINS, Nancy	WEBSTER, Micajah	02/02/1843
HAWKINS, Nancy A.	ROBERDS, David	12/16/1858
HAWKINS, Sarah J.	SMITH, James C.	07/25/1867
HAWLY, Kissiah	JEFFREYS, Reubin	05/30/1808
HAYES, Elizabeth C.	LIGON, Richard F.	07/19/1837
HAYES, Polly	WRIGHT, Zacharias	12/24/1793
HAYS, Elizabeth	WINSTEAD, Stephen	11/19/1832
HAYS, Polly	THACKER, Charles	08/12/1808
HEARNDON, Clara	MURPHY, Gabriel Jr.	02/04/1788
HEDGCOCK, Lucy	WARD, Richard	05/29/1787
HENDERSON, Betsey	HARRELSON, Forbes	11/19/1793
HENDERSON, Elizabeth	FIELDER, Samuel C.	01/12/1833
HENDERSON, Elizabeth	LEA, Barzillia G.	12/08/1829
HENDERSON, Elizabeth	WATT, Absalom	12/16/1815
HENDERSON, Elizabeth A.	WYNNE, William B.	05/10/1865
HENDERSON, Frances A.	GUNN, James	05/07/1835
HENDERSON, Frances M.	CHALMERS, Joseph W.	09/08/1829
HENDERSON, Hannah	HOLCOMB, Samuel	12/29/1789
HENDERSON, Harriott E.	EASLEY, John	09/27/1830
HENDERSON, Julia A.	SIDEBOTTOM, James H.	07/02/1832
HENDERSON, Julia Ann	AYRES, William	10/11/1834
HENDERSON, Martha	POTEET, William	06/26/1828

MARRIAGE RECORDS OF CASWELL COUNTY, NORTH CAROLINA

BRIDE	GROOM	DATE
HENDERSON, Mary B.	ROAN, Nathaniel M.	11/18/1835
HENDERSON, Mary W.	CHALMERS, John G.	10/02/1827
HENDERSON, Minerva Ann	GUNN, Allen Jr. Doct.	10/07/1829
HENDERSON, Nancey	HOOPER, Benjamin	09/22/1800
HENDERSON, Pirzilla	HOOPER, Woodlief	04/12/1802
HENDERSON, Polley	KENNON, Ricahrd	05/08/1813
HENDERSON, Priscilla	EVENS, Samuel	12/01/1835
HENDERSON, Priscilla J.	JONES, Willie Dr.	05/05/1836
HENDERSON, Priscilla M.	STONE, Thomas R.	04/24/1849
HENDERSON, Sarah	HALCOM, George	12/25/1788
HENDERSON, Susan P.	MILNER, Jackson C.	12/20/1837
HENDRICK, Adelaide R.	SLADE, William G.	11/22/1854
HENDRICK, Crecy	DAVISE, James	12/25/1835
HENDRICK, Lucinda	LEA, Archibald	07/11/1821
HENDRICK, Sophia	RAINEY, James G.	08/20/1823
HENDRICK, Sophia J.	GILLISPIE, Joseph M.	08/30/1865
HENDRICKS, Martha	ROBERTS, James L.	10/15/1856
HENDSHAW, Francis	BURCH, Ephraim	03/15/1825
HENRICK, Virginia	PERROW, Stephen W.	05/16/1839
HENSHAW, Mary	EVANS, William	03/30/1836
HENSHAW, Sarah	TILLINGTON, Barrington	12/10/1832
HENSLE, Sally	BARTON, Aquila	01/20/1842
HENSLEE, Elizabeth	MASSEY, Raney	11/12/1850
HENSLEE, Elizabeth	PLEASANT, Beauford	10/31/1810
HENSLEE, Frankey	GEORGE, Isaac	11/04/1805
HENSLEE, Keziah	RAY, Joseph	10/24/1798
HENSLEE, Lucinda	PARKS, Robert	06/19/1825
HENSLEE, Sarah	PLEASANT, Beaufort	01/21/1822
HENSLEY, Ann	PAYNE, John	03/05/1779
HENSLEY, Artelia	CAYNOR, John H.	04/27/1847
HENSLEY, Dorithy	BARKER, James M.	11/02/1846
HENSLEY, Eleanor	RAY, James	10/28/1794
HENSLEY, Elizabeth Y.	NABERS, William J.	02/12/1867
HENSLEY, Frances	MASSEY, Benjamin	02/10/1835
HENSLEY, Mary	MASSEY, Rainey	11/02/1846
HENSLEY, Mary J.	KIMBROUGH, John T.	08/19/1866
HENSLEY, Rachel	MCKINNEY, Nathaniel	07/04/1833
HERNDON, Elizabeth	SMITH, James T.	12/21/1832
HERNDON, Frances	GARRISON, George	11/29/1847
HERNDON, Martha	BOSWELL, Amza	10/14/1846
HERNDON, Sally	PAGE, James	10/25/1855
HERRING, Mary	YARBROUGH, Joseph	08/20/1825
HESTER, Eliza	GRAVES, William	11/05/1833
HESTER, Margarett	HIGHTOWER, John W.	01/27/1836
HESTER, Mary C.	JONES, Calvin	11/09/1841
HESTER, Sarah	WARREN, Yearbey	04/21/1828
HESTER, Sarah C.	ROARK, Benjamin	05/03/1854
HESTON, Lucy	BRINTLE, William	11/15/1793
HEWBANK, Priscilla	MCDANIEL, William J.	05/23/1832
HEWELL, Elizabeth A.	RICHARDSON, Josiah	12/31/1834
HEWELT, Susannah	HESSE, Archibald U.	05/06/1818

MARRIAGE RECORDS OF CASWELL COUNTY, NORTH CAROLINA

BRIDE	GROOM	DATE
HEWS, Lydia	DICKINS, Henry	04/21/1791
HEYGOOD, Mary	MATLOCK, Benjamin L.	08/26/1850
HICKMAN, Betsey	GOIN, John	11/24/1795
HICKMAN, Mary	THOMAS, Jacob	10/16/1819
HICKS, Ellenor	MADREN, Amos	09/09/1840
HICKS, Frances	DUNNAWAY, James	05/10/1822
HICKS, Levina	OVERBY, Thomas	08/13/1827
HICKS, Rebecca C.	THOMAS, James W.	03/14/1857
HICKS, Sophia	FREDERICK, Jesse	06/11/1833
HIGGASON, Jane C.	DANIEL, John P.	04/30/1857
HIGHTOUER, Mary	LEA, Jonathan	10/16/1786
HIGHTOWER, Agniss	KIERSEY,(?) John	12/02/1794
HIGHTOWER, Agniss	CASEY,(?) John	12/02/1794
HIGHTOWER, Agniss	CASEY,(?) John	12/02/1794
HIGHTOWER, Agniss	KEIRSEY, (?) John	12/02/1794
HIGHTOWER, Betsy	SWANN, Joseph	10/20/1818
HIGHTOWER, Delilah	FITCH, Empson	11/24/1834
HIGHTOWER, Eliza	PITMON, Moses	01/13/1846
HIGHTOWER, Elizabeth	FULLER, Stephen	03/15/1825
HIGHTOWER, Elizabeth	JARNAGIN, Jeremiah	12/24/1808
HIGHTOWER, Fanny	LEA, Hearndon	06/22/1791
HIGHTOWER, Frances	STACY, John	05/19/1828
HIGHTOWER, Frances T.	JOHNSTON, William H.	11/29/1836
HIGHTOWER, Isabella	RICE, Thomas B.	02/20/1847
HIGHTOWER, Jane	HODGE, Thmas	11/04/1828
HIGHTOWER, Lettice	PAUL, James	02/13/1795
HIGHTOWER, Martha	BOHANNAN, Thomas	06/10/1867
HIGHTOWER, Martha P.	SIMPSON, Benjamin F.	10/13/1843
HIGHTOWER, Mary	NELSON, Iverson	04/12/1841
HIGHTOWER, Mary	BRUMMIT, William	11/30/1832
HIGHTOWER, Mary C.	WALL, William D.	11/28/1854
HIGHTOWER, Nancey	CULBERTSON, Hiram	12/15/1806
HIGHTOWER, Nancey	JACKSON, Epaphroditus	08/23/1834
HIGHTOWER, Nancey W.	FRAZIER, Madison M.	08/18/1832
HIGHTOWER, Nancy	LEA, James	11/15/1796
HIGHTOWER, Permelia	WARD, Thomas	03/12/1827
HIGHTOWER, Rebecca S.	LEA, Alanson M.	12/09/1834
HIGHTOWER, Sally	LEWIS, Pleasant	12/31/1816
HIGHTOWER, Sally	WALKER, Benjamin	12/09/1800
HIGHTOWER, Sarah	SMITH, William	01/04/1800
HIGHTOWER, Sarah	CHANDLER, Thomas B.	11/28/1838
HIGHTOWER, Sarah L.	ANDERSON, William	09/25/1834
HIGHTOWER, Susan	PALMER, Joyner	02/16/1850
HIGHTOWER, Susanah	CURL, John T.	08/29/1803
HILL, Elizabeth	RODDEN, Spencer	12/27/1821
HILL, Fanny M.	GALLOWAY, Robert	03/10/1852
HILL, Leanna	ROACH, William	04/26/1860
HILL, Lucinda B.	RODGERS, William M.	11/20/1856
HILL, Mary	WILLIAHSON, Charles	02/25/1866
HILL, Mary	WILLIAMSON, Charles	02/25/1866
HILL, Sarah F.	ROALING, William P.	03/22/1860

MARRIAGE RECORDS OF CASWELL COUNTY, NORTH CAROLINA

BRIDE	GROOM	DATE
HILL, Virginia C.	DAVIS, James T.	02/15/1866
HILLIARD, Lucy	BROWN, Tarlton W.	07/13/1830
HINES, Elizabeth B.	MOORE, Robert A.	05/04/1859
HINTON, Adaliade	OWENS, Andrew J.	08/23/1865
HINTON, Betsey	DOBBIN, John	02/03/1796
HINTON, Eliza A.	WILLIAMSON, Benjamin E.	11/15/1848
HINTON, Henrietta M.	TURNER, Stephen D.	03/20/1854
HINTON, Mary	COLEMAN, Alexander	02/06/1837
HINTON, Mary	RANDOLPH, William	08/21/1808
HINTON, Mary E.	ALLISON, John J.	04/13/1846
HINTON, Nancy	HUBBARD, Freeman	06/09/1803
HINTON, Polly	SMITH, Daniel	12/12/1842
HITE, Matilda	BOOZ, Henry	08/02/1820
HITOWER, A. L.	HICKS, John P.	02/07/1867
HIX, Artemesia	DUNERVANT, Abraham	08/03/1855
HIX, Elizabeth	DUNAVANT, Andy D.	10/01/1854
HIX, Elizabeth	WILLSON, Lorenzo J.	09/02/1858
HIX, Hannah	STANSBERY, Samuel	10/07/1786
HIX, Nancy	TARPLEY, James	07/03/1786
HLDER, Sarah P.	HINES, Benjamin	03/17/1834
HOBBS, Edy	PURKINS, Robert	07/26/1820
HOBBS, Kitty	BASTIN, Henry	07/10/1823
HOBBS, Lucy	FOSTER, Richard	02/28/1821
HOBSON, Rachel	HUGHES, William	05/18/1855
HODGE, Catherine	YEALOCK, Robert	10/22/1824
HODGE, Elizabeth	SARGENT, Ephraim	07/25/1792
HODGE, Hannah	DURHAM, Richard	12/06/1824
HODGE, Judath	BASTIN, Thomas	12/15/1823
HODGE, Louisa	RUSSELL, Joseph M.	04/05/1854
HODGE, Mary	LONG, Baszeley M.	07/05/1828
HODGE, Polley	BEWSEY, Charles	06/09/1817
HODGE, Sally	JOHNSTON, John	11/29/1819
HODGE, Sina	HODGE, William	11/16/1867
HODGE, Susan A.	CLENDENIN, James J.	12/15/1857
HODGES, Betty	TURNER, C. F.	10/16/1866
HODGES, Eliza	GATEWOOD, Robert A.	11/18/1842
HODGES, Ellen T.	ECTOR, William S.	12/19/1855
HODGES, Julia	ADAMS, William	11/15/1845
HODGES, Martha W.	SIMPSON, Thomas T.	11/21/1848
HODGES, Mary	GATEWOOD, William H.	11/23/1847
HODGES, Mary	WEST, Cary W.	05/10/1834
HODGES, Mary F.	BRADSHAW, James M.	01/17/1863
HODGES, Nancey M.	HAGWOOD, James	11/23/1836
HODGES, Susan M.	HARVEY, John C.	01/12/1864
HODGES, Susanna	TRAVIS, George A.	07/03/1861
HODGESX, Kesiah A.	ASTIN, Wilson J.	01/24/1846
HODNETT, Caroline	MIMMS, Pinkney	06/09/1866
HODNETT, Lucinda A.	YATES, Joseph M.	05/06/1849
HOGE, Louisa	DAVIS, Granville	11/10/1867
HOGG, Juda	GIBSON, John	06/08/1779
HOLCOLMB, Martha N.	HOLCOMB, Martha M.	11/17/1820

MARRIAGE RECORDS OF CASWELL COUNTY, NORTH CAROLINA

BRIDE	GROOM	DATE
HOLCOM, Elizabeth	EDDINGS, Joseph	07/17/1805
HOLCOMB, Mary	COX, Reuben	01/11/1792
HOLCOMB, Perry	JONES, Richard	10/30/1804
HOLCOMB, Salley	DAMERON, Samuel	01/10/1799
HOLCOMB, Sarah A.	WRIGHT, George W.	01/05/1847
HOLDBERY, Ann	HENDERSON, Rufus	08/11/1866
HOLDEN, Mary E.	TURBIVILLE, Charles P.	10/24/1853
HOLDER, Susan	HUNTINGTON, Martin P.	04/30/1822
HOLDERNESS, Martha	COVINGTON, John	06/09/1866
HOLDERNESS, Salley	BROOKS, Christopher	02/09/1810
HOLLADAY, Harriott	GARDNER, Starke	05/13/1835
HOLLAWAY, Polley	HUMPHREYS, William	12/27/1799
HOLLES, Elenore	ESTES, Samuel	12/25/1815
HOLLEWAY, Sally	CHILTON, William	10/04/1800
HOLLOWAY, Betsy	OLIVER, Alva	02/13/1792
HOLLOWAY, Jenny	WARE, Thomas	04/28/1806
HOLLOWAY, Joanna	DOSS, Clark H.	01/02/1832
HOLLOWAY, Patsy	BUSEY, William	02/06/1808
HOLLOWAY, Sally	SCOTT, German	06/08/1799
HOLMES, Malinda	RIMARE, James W.	02/19/1822
HOLOWAY, Susan	BARNARD, William	02/15/1842
HOLSONBACK, Lydia	WARREN, Samuel	01/05/1805
HOLT, Sarah	DILLARD, Richard	12/07/1796
HOLYCROSS, Sarah	TURNER, William B.	08/04/1864
HONBUCKLE, Elisabeth	HARDEN, Henry	08/14/1795
HOOD, Lotty	DISON, Thomas	09/17/1840
HOOFMAN, Sarah E.	IRWIN, James C.	03/28/1840
HOOPER, Ann L.	OLIVER, Monroe	05/24/1860
HOOPER, Barbara	EVANS, Samuel J.	10/08/1836
HOOPER, Eliza L.	HUNDLY, Henry W.	12/14/1837
HOOPER, Elizabeth	HALCOMB, Warren	01/20/1824
HOOPER, Elizabeth	SWIFT, George R.	03/18/1852
HOOPER, Elizabeth	WARREN, Alexander	04/13/1846
HOOPER, Elizabeth J.	HINTON, Alexander	07/15/1848
HOOPER, Elizabeth L.V.	DE NORDENDORF Charles Chak.	04/24/1865
HOOPER, Elizabeth L.V.	DE NORDENORF, Charles Chaky.	04/24/1865
HOOPER, Emily	GUNN, George	01/12/1867
HOOPER, Frances	HINTON, Nathaniel	06/11/1848
HOOPER, Frances G.	WEATHERFORD, William	02/03/1830
HOOPER, Manerva A.	BLAIR, William Thos.	12/01/1858
HOOPER, Martha	DUNNAWAY, Allen J.	04/12/1837
HOOPER, Martha	FITZGERALD, Richard	01/31/1822
HOOPER, Martha	MOTLEY, Hartwell	03/22/1824
HOOPER, Martha	POWELL, Joshua	06/26/1849
HOOPER, Martha A.	HENDERSON, Albert G.	02/19/1856
HOOPER, Martha J.	HAIZLIP, Haywood H.	09/25/1856
HOOPER, Martha J.	MILES, Richard	10/09/1850
HOOPER, Martha J.	NEAL, William R.	11/11/1846
HOOPER, Mary	FERGUSON, Richard	05/20/1833

MARRIAGE RECORDS OF CASWELL COUNTY, NORTH CAROLINA

BRIDE	GROOM	DATE
HOOPER, Mary	KIMBRO, Andrew J.	03/18/1858
HOOPER, Mary W.	CONNALLY, William T.	12/19/1854
HOOPER, Nancey	BRACKIN, Joseph	01/05/1841
HOOPER, Polly	ROE, Robert	01/01/1817
HOOPER, Polly	WOMACK, Cato	11/20/1867
HOOPER, Sally	CARROLL, Lemuel H.	09/11/1819
HOOPER, Sarah	HARDISON, Thomas	08/02/1845
HOOPER, Susan	CORBETT, Solomon	12/10/1844
HOOPER, Susanna	KENNON, Thomas	02/12/1814
HOOPER, Winnie	BLACKWELL, James	11/23/1867
HOPPER, Winifred	BENTON, Richard	12/28/1787
HORNBUCKLE, Frances	GWYN, John W.	09/14/1856
HORNBUCKLE, Milly	WINDSOR, Thomas	12/31/1797
HORNBUCKLE, Nancey	HORNBUCKLE, Thomas	07/22/1800
HORNBUCKLE, Susanna	WINDSOR, John Jr.	09/07/1795
HORRELSON, Martha F.	PASCHAL, Elisha	02/17/1857
HORSEFORD, Elizabeth	BURTON, James	01/01/1833
HORSLEY, Susan	MATHIS, Samuel	08/02/1784
HORTON, Elizabeth	POTEAT, John Jr.	02/08/1859
HORTON, Francis	BRINCFIELD, Colmon W.	08/24/1858
HORTON, Leanah	MILLER, James	11/29/1785
HORTON, Martha	CHANCE, Yancy	01/08/1864
HORTON, Mary	ALLEN, William	03/04/1866
HOUSE, Mary J.	ALLEN, Randolph J.	12/21/1859
HOWARD, Ann	BADGETT, Jno.	01/16/1817
HOWARD, Ann	KING, William D.	02/17/1859
HOWARD, Anne	INGRAM, Martin	11/06/1827
HOWARD, Betsy	PASCHALL, Jerry	01/06/1866
HOWARD, Caroline M.T.	NANCE, William M.	01/09/1844
HOWARD, Caty F.	LATTA, James G.	10/26/1867
HOWARD, Elizabeth	MCNEELEY, George W.	11/16/1834
HOWARD, Isabella S.	GRAVES, Azariah	03/17/1858
HOWARD, Jane S.	LATTA, Jas. C.	10/26/1867
HOWARD, Julia	WILES, Samuel	12/16/1865
HOWARD, Lucy A.	NEAL, Jno. T.	12/11/1859
HOWARD, Margaret S.	POWELL, Richard M.	12/18/1867
HOWARD, Martha E.	GARDNER, Joseph C.	09/04/1867
HOWARD, Mary	HORTON, Willis	11/13/1835
HOWARD, Nancy	HOWARD, Braodie	04/07/1813
HOWEL, Hannar	HARGIS, William	02/03/1791
HOWEL, Nancey	GLASGOW, William T.	03/20/1815
HUBARD, Virginia	SMITH, John	12/07/1854
HUBBARD, Malinda	HUNTER, Solomon G.	04/16/1835
HUBBARD, Martha	SHIELDS, Thomas R.	02/28/1867
HUBBARD, Martha J.	BRACKIN, Julius A.	12/09/1867
HUBBARD, Mary	BIRD, Joel	07/20/1867
HUBBARD, Mary	EVANS, Joel	12/23/1846
HUBBARD, Mary	HOOPER, Zachariah	05/11/1860
HUBBARD, Mary	SLADE, Ezekiel	01/17/1798
HUBBARD, Mildred	LECOUNT, John	04/06/1850
HUBBARD, Nancy	BROWNING, Martin	12/22/1852

MARRIAGE RECORDS OF CASWELL COUNTY, NORTH CAROLINA

BRIDE	GROOM	DATE
HUBBARD, Nancy	READ, Noel	04/15/1815
HUBBARD, Nancy	WARE, William M.	09/12/1863
HUBBARD, Nancy	WARE, William M.	09/13/1863
HUBBARD, Polly	RUTHERFORD, John	02/16/1782
HUBBARD, Rhody	GILLASPY, James	02/18/1799
HUBBARD, Sally	SMITH, Daniel	01/09/1810
HUBBARD, Susan	DISMUKES, John	07/13/1835
HUBBIRD, Patsy	QUINE, Goolsby	01/07/1823
HUBBIRD, Polly	CARROLL, James R.	08/10/1827
HUDGINS, Susan A.	FITTS, Marcellus G.	03/01/1865
HUDSON, Ann	COX, Armstead	03/15/1834
HUDSON, Betsy	ROBERTS, Simon	09/01/1798
HUDSON, Peggy	GOSSAGE, Danl.	01/05/1801
HUDSON, Sarah	SIDDALL, Job	08/17/1791
HUGHES, Ann T.	RODDEN, James W.	09/27/1853
HUGHES, Betsy	MASON, John	01/31/1814
HUGHES, Elizabeth	BRANDON, Isaac	11/21/1866
HUGHES, Elizabeth	PHILIPS, William	12/25/1857
HUGHES, Lucy	HUGHES, Milton T.	01/10/1853
HUGHES, Margaret	LIGGON, John	01/19/1867
HUGHES, Mary	FOSSETT, Robert	02/07/1800
HUGHS, Elizabeth A.	SHAW, Joseph M.	12/04/1857
HUGHS, Joyce	MITCHELL, David	02/20/1823
HUGHS, Joyce	MITCHELL, David	01/30/1823
HUGHS, Louisa R.	ROYESTER, Thomas	02/05/1833
HUGHS, Malinda	HADDOCK, Bedford	04/22/1829
HUGHS, Martha	EPPERSON, Branch	11/02/1842
HUGHS, Martha	TAYLOR, Hiram	12/23/1837
HUGHS, Mary	MARAIN, Thomas	10/20/1800
HUGHS, Rosetta	STEVENS, William	06/11/1859
HUGHS, Sarah	DURHAM, Charles	11/27/1862
HUGHSTON, Anna	STUART, Stephen	09/12/1812
HUGHSTON, Elizabeth	RICHMOND, Jesse	12/29/1817
HUGHSTON, Jenny	BURTON, Drury	10/04/1808
HUMESTON, Hannah L.	WEIR, David P.	11/20/1838
HUMPHREYS, Elizabeth	DUNCAN, Nathan	09/05/1818
HUMPHREYS, Margaret C.	POWELL, John	03/18/1834
HUMPHREYS, Nancy	SANDERS, Andrew	03/22/1830
HUMPHREYS, Nancy	COBB, Ebenezear	12/04/1839
HUMPHRIES, Nancy	MIDDLEBROOKS, John	01/18/1781
HUNLEY, Mary	GRAVES, Isaac	09/21/1867
HUNLY, Mary H.	ENGLISH, George C.	11/25/1856
HUNT, Ellen	MOTLEY, Booker	10/13/1867
HUNT, Emily	CARDWELL, William	07/23/1868
HUNT, Hannah	ROBERTSON, Alex	11/12/1866
HUNT, Louisa	HUNT, Charles	12/08/1866
HUNT, Lucinda	HOGE, Winston	11/09/1867
HUNT, Mary	CUNINGHAM, Charles	07/29/1866
HUNT, Mary Jane	EASELY, Charles	12/27/1866
HUNT, Milly	WATKINS, James	11/18/1867
HUNT, Precilla	HUNT, Samuel	01/12/1867

MARRIAGE RECORDS OF CASWELL COUNTY, NORTH CAROLINA

BRIDE	GROOM	DATE
HUNT, Rachel	WARREN, John D.	06/15/1817
HUNT, Salley	KELLEY, George	08/08/1820
HUNTER, Elizabeth	SIMPSON, Solomon	11/17/1813
HUNTER, Jane L.	FULTON, Mathias	01/09/1822
HUNTER, Marey	JACKSON, Thomas	12/--/1818
HUNTER, Patsy	CAMPBELL, William	04/14/1816
HUNTER, Rebecca	POTEET, Miles Jr.	07/10/1828
HURDLE, Ann	JONES, David A.	02/27/1856
HURLEY, Ann	MORROW, Robert	10/15/1782
HUSKINS, Mary	SIMPSON, Vinson	02/16/1826
HUSTON, Agness	JOHNSON, James	10/04/1813
HUSTON, Betsey	HUBBARD, Charles	01/31/1804
HUSTON, Jane	HARRALSON, Jonathan	03/12/1782
HUSTON, Rebecca	DANIEL, John	12/21/1822
INGRAM, Betsy	CHANDLER, Stephen	12/21/1805
INGRAM, Clary	GLENN, Sampson M.	02/--/1803
INGRAM, Elizabeth	ATKINSON, Johnson E.	05/05/1832
INGRAM, Elizabeth	HUBBARD, Phenias	04/05/1839
INGRAM, Mary N.	TRAVIS, Isaac	12/30/1836
INGRAM, Priscilla	ALLEN, Moses	05/02/1795
INGRAM, Priscilla	TRAVIS, Ellis	02/27/1836
INGRAM, Sarah E.	SHANNON, William R.	07/15/1858
INGRAM, Susan	PERKINS, Jesse	08/19/1795
INGRAM, Tally	WALTERS, William H.	12/26/1816
INGRAM, Tirzah	TRAVIS, Stephen	11/21/1836
INGROM, Morning	HALL, Solomon	12/24/1817
IRBY, Mary	WIRE, Josiah	11/07/1829
IRBY, Sarah	ROBERTSON, Edward	07/12/1856
IRVINE, Jennie	IRVINE, Richmond	04/20/1867
IRVINE, Mary	HARRIS, Gustin	01/19/1867
JACKSON, Agness	NUTT, David D.	04/18/1816
JACKSON, Catharine	MILES, Thomas C.	09/17/1846
JACKSON, Cloe	FANNING, Hezekiah	11/28/1796
JACKSON, Delilah	MATHEWS, Drury	07/21/1821
JACKSON, Elisha	SIMMONS, Levi	12/16/1832
JACKSON, Eliza	WILSON, John W.	05/16/1859
JACKSON, Elizabeth D.	MATHIS, John	12/03/1823
JACKSON, Frances	CHANCE, James	09/30/1848
JACKSON, Huldah	BOWE, George	03/09/1867
JACKSON, Julia W.	TATE, Samuel S.	11/19/1849
JACKSON, Margret J.	BARKER, Tolbert	07/10/1864
JACKSON, Martha	HAGWOOD, Lewis	04/07/1819
JACKSON, Mary	HIGHTOWER, John A.	11/09/1843
JACKSON, Mary E.	ECHOLS, Philip J.	01/20/1813
JACKSON, Mildred	MCCRE, William C.	04/04/1856
JACKSON, Nancey	HUGHS, John	09/12/1810
JACKSON, Nancy F.	RUDD, David	01/26/1846
JACKSON, Priscilla	BURTON, Absalom	10/02/1815
JACKSON, S.C.	TERILL, Thomas J.	01/31/1866
JACKSON, Sally	SMITH, George	08/14/1807
JACKSON, Sarah	MATHEWS, Isaac	09/19/1827

MARRIAGE RECORDS OF CASWELL COUNTY, NORTH CAROLINA

BRIDE	GROOM	DATE
JACKSON, Sarah	WEBSTER, M. C. A.	02/22/1854
JACKSON, Susan	HIGHTOWER, Joshua	10/18/1833
JACKSON, Susanah	JOHNSTON, Pleasant	08/22/1804
JACOB, Nancy	FOX, Wm.	12/28/1820
JAMES, Amy	BOWE, William B.	06/10/1858
JAMES, Jane	WOODS, Lewis	05/15/1867
JAMES, Nancy	HILL, Henry	12/29/1866
JAMES, Virginia	PIERCE, Gabriel	11/19/1865
JAY, Sally	MORROW, William	01/05/1789
JEFFERS, Isabella	LANIER, C.V.	01/14/1839
JEFFERS, Susanna	WEALSH, Samuel	02/18/1789
JEFFREYS, Betsy	TERRY, Dabney	10/13/1825
JEFFREYS, Cornelia	MCGEHEE, Paul	04/20/1867
JEFFREYS, Elizabeth Jane	FURGERSON, William G.	10/30/1848
JEFFREYS, Elizabeth M.	MCGEHEE, Thomas	12/07/1812
JEFFREYS, Harriett A.	MARTIN, Samuel F.	11/06/1857
JEFFREYS, Helen E.	PINCHBACK, John W.	07/19/1841
JEFFREYS, Isabella	HUNT, Garland	12/25/1865
JEFFREYS, Jane	BIRD, Wilie	12/08/1866
JEFFREYS, Lydia	DONALDSON, James	11/03/1866
JEFFREYS, Martha	CHANDLER, Pleasant	08/26/1816
JEFFREYS, Mary	SCOTT, John	10/28/1816
JEFFREYS, Mary	BROWN, William	03/02/1867
JEFFREYS, Mary E.	HUNT, Littleton T.	06/14/1854
JEFFREYS, Melissa	JEFFREYS, Jackson	12/14/1848
JEFFREYS, Mildred	GROOM, Thomas	10/17/1821
JEFFREYS, Mildred W.	MITCHELL, James T.	03/19/1849
JEFFREYS, Nancy	HALCOMB, William	08/16/1805
JEFFREYS, Susan	CHAVERS, Evans	12/22/1857
JEFFREYS, Virginia A.	IRVINE, William Jr.	10/31/1857
JEFFRYS, Patty	GILLASPY, William	10/26/1782
JENINGS, Mary E.	GARLAND, Wilson	07/16/1860
JENKINS, Sarah A.	WILKINSON, Simon T.	07/10/1859
JENNINGS, Elizabeth M.	HALES, Samuel	07/01/1856
JENNINGS, Emma J.	MCLEAN, Jesse R.	01/18/1859
JENNINGS, Mary	MCDONALD, Alexander	12/27/1818
JENNINGS, Samuella	LEWIS, Fielding B.	12/07/1859
JERRILL, Willie L.	COLE, Theophilus M.	11/27/1843
JOHNAGAIN, Faithey	KIMBRO, Thomas	08/18/1781
JOHNS, Elizabeth	LANIER, James	02/11/1804
JOHNS, Happy	WEIR, Thomas	11/10/1866
JOHNS, Polly	LANIER, James	10/23/1809
JOHNSON, Ann	CARTER, Joseph G.	06/25/1832
JOHNSON, Frances	MOSELEY, John R.	12/26/1866
JOHNSON, Mary P.	BROWN, Richard H.	09/25/1841
JOHNSON, Rosa A.	WESTBROOKS, Joseph B.	01/30/1854
JOHNSTON, Adaline M.	FERRELL, James A.	11/01/1859
JOHNSTON, Aderline W.	WILLIAMSON, Walter S.	12/04/1860
JOHNSTON, Ann	PERRY, William	11/19/1792
JOHNSTON, Ann	STAFFORD, John	07/29/1800
JOHNSTON, Anna	FULLINGTON, James	10/25/1825

MARRIAGE RECORDS OF CASWELL COUNTY, NORTH CAROLINA

BRIDE	GROOM	DATE
JOHNSTON, Betsy	CHAPMAN, John	07/26/1796
JOHNSTON, Catherine	JOHNSTON, Remus	03/03/1866
JOHNSTON, Charlotte	CROSET, James	02/15/1816
JOHNSTON, Eliza	CURRIE, Isaac R.	03/08/1824
JOHNSTON, Elizabeth	WILSON, Robert	12/28/1795
JOHNSTON, Fanny	SHELTON, W. N.	01/20/1863
JOHNSTON, Fanny	SMITH, Stephen	09/02/1812
JOHNSTON, Frances	MALONE, William	09/02/1829
JOHNSTON, Jane	BARBER, James	01/09/1802
JOHNSTON, Jane E.	KEESEE, Jno. D.	01/26/1854
JOHNSTON, Malinda	HICKS, Thomas D.	10/21/1837
JOHNSTON, Maranda	WILLIAMSON, Johnston	02/22/1868
JOHNSTON, Mary S.	MOTLEY, Thomas J.	09/27/1855
JOHNSTON, Mildred	HARRISON, Thomas	11/04/1807
JOHNSTON, Milissa	HATCHETT, Jack	11/03/1867
JOHNSTON, Nancy R.	ESKRIDGE, Bird B.	11/27/1821
JOHNSTON, Nanny N.	WILLIAMSON, Weldon E.	11/25/1856
JOHNSTON, Phebe	CLAY, James	10/22/1819
JOHNSTON, Polly	ALLISON, John	12/02/1799
JOHNSTON, Polly	EDDINGS, William	03/18/1807
JOHNSTON, Polly	ESKRIDGE, William	01/04/1820
JOHNSTON, Polly	WALTON, Thomas	12/28/1813
JOHNSTON, Rebeca	BRANN, Vincent	08/26/1856
JOHNSTON, Rebecca	BYRD, Thomas	10/25/1816
JOHNSTON, Rebecca L.	HENDERSON, James A.	05/23/1866
JOHNSTON, Sally	HOLDEN, James	01/17/1805
JOHNSTON, Sally	STAFFORD, William	08/15/1793
JOHNSTON, Sally	WHITFIELD, William	12/29/1809
JOHNSTON, Sarah	LONG, William	10/02/1828
JOHNSTON, Sarah P.	STANFIELD, Benjamin F.	09/05/1825
JOHNSTON, Sophia	HERNDON, Larkin	08/22/1802
JOHNSTON, Susana	BARKER, James	01/26/1779
JOHNSTON, Susannah	GORDON, Alexander	10/19/1807
JOHNSTON, Vina	HIGHTOWER, William	07/09/1847
JOHNSTON, Zelpha	YANCEY, James	06/24/1811
JONES, Agness	BELL, David	12/22/1812
JONES, Amanda	OLIVER, Charles J.	09/22/1835
JONES, Ann	VAUGHN, Maurice	09/10/1825
JONES, Ann P.	FOSTER, William A.	12/20/1860
JONES, Barbara	BRUMIT, Pleasant	01/11/1837
JONES, Betsy	LEATH, Joel	12/21/1798
JONES, Catherine L.	STAULCUP, Levi	06/12/1843
JONES, Celia	COUSINS, Alexander	03/29/1851
JONES, Cyntha	JEFFRES, Newell	08/01/1828
JONES, Elizabeth	FRANKLIN, Ambrose	03/18/1826
JONES, Elizabeth	NELSON, John H.	07/28/1848
JONES, Elizabeth	RAY, Robert	10/01/1840
JONES, Elizabeth A.	ANDERSON, William A.	01/18/1853
JONES, Ellen	JONES, Henry	11/19/1865
JONES, Ellin	DOSON, William H.	12/13/1837
JONES, Fanny	MITCHELL, James E.	02/08/1833

MARRIAGE RECORDS OF CASWELL COUNTY, NORTH CAROLINA

BRIDE	GROOM	DATE
JONES, Fanny	WILSON, Rufus	10/18/1865
JONES, Frances	HENSLEE, Masfield	09/22/1801
JONES, Frances A.	ANDERSON, Nelson S.	01/18/1853
JONES, Georgiana	HODGES, Fealding L.	02/01/1867
JONES, Hester	LEA, Louis	12/25/1866
JONES, Jane	JONES, James	12/19/1850
JONES, Jane W.	MCALPIN, Alexander	10/31/1857
JONES, Jenny	WADKINS, Isaac	02/23/1816
JONES, Jincey	CAMEL,(?) Edley	11/27/1812
JONES, Jincey	CAMPBELL,(?) Edley	11/27/1812
JONES, Julia	BARNETT, John	07/01/1866
JONES, Laura A.	WATLINGTON, Jas. W.	03/26/1867
JONES, Leana	KING, Henry	12/07/1867
JONES, Leanna	GUNN, Samuel	03/24/1866
JONES, Lucy	BAKER, General	11/11/1819
JONES, Lucy	OWEN, Peter	12/22/1842
JONES, Maria	JONES, Randolph	12/10/1828
JONES, Martha	LOVELESS, Brewis W.	05/06/1824
JONES, Martha	PRICE, Wm.	06/23/1866
JONES, Martha J.	WALKER, Abraham	12/17/1857
JONES, Mary	HOOPER, William	12/21/1854
JONES, Mary A.	GUNN, Sterling	01/14/1868
JONES, Mary A.	SHELTON, James W.	02/09/1841
JONES, Mildred	LYON, Nicholas	02/15/1853
JONES, Milly	SMITH, Gardner	11/02/1822
JONES, Nancy	SEED, Thomas	12/09/1818
JONES, Polly	ANDERSON, William R.	11/19/1860
JONES, Priscilla	SLADE, James M.	01/16/1866
JONES, Rachel	WILLIS, Peter Jr.	12/19/1867
JONES, Salley	MALLORY, James	01/16/1798
JONES, Sally	HARGESS, Shadrach	12/18/1817
JONES, Sally	BROWN, John	12/29/1786
JONES, Sally	WATLINGTON, David	08/31/1867
JONES, Sarah	WYATT, Royal	05/03/1828
JONES, Selley	STANDLEY, Allen	07/24/1838
JONES, Sidney	LINTON, Michael	06/09/1847
JONES, Suckey	CARREL, Daniel	01/05/1801
JONES, Susan	MEDLIN, Harrison	12/30/1819
JOPLING, Catherine	SMITH, Thomas	04/04/1815
JORDON, Mary	PATTILLO, Zachariah	12/10/1814
JOUETTE, Polley	DIXON, ROger	12/16/1794
JOUIT, Susanna D.	ROGERS, Armistead	06/11/1781
JOURDAN, Martha	CLOWDERS, Samuel	12/26/1829
JOVET, Nancy	RICE, Jepthah	08/19/1784
JUSTICE, Martha J.	PASKEL, John	11/20/1854
KEEN, Mary E.	HOWARD, John W.	09/08/1866
KEEN, Nancy	SHACKLEFORD, John	12/08/1815
KEEN, Polly	MCCLAIN, George	11/02/1804
KEEN, Susannah	HUMPHREYS, John H.	01/11/1817
KEER, Ann	SPENCER, John	07/26/1781
KEESEE, Louisa T.	STOKES, William Y.	12/18/1829

MARRIAGE RECORDS OF CASWELL COUNTY, NORTH CAROLINA

BRIDE	GROOM	DATE
KEESEE, Paulina Ann	ANDERSON, William	03/14/1836
KELLEY, Elisabeth	GOOCH, James	08/03/1785
KELLEY, Elizabeth	JONES, Moses	02/14/1809
KELLEY, Nancy	WARREN, Joseph N.	10/--/1814
KELLY, Margaret	SMITH, Moses	07/30/1794
KELLY, Rebecca J.	WEIFORD, Perry W.	06/17/1855
KEMP, Elizabeth	SMITH, Reuben	03/01/1818
KEMP, Matilda	HENSLEE, John Jr.	04/02/1816
KENDIRCK, Mildred	MURPHEY, William	10/07/1830
KENDRICK, Elizabeth	LEWIS, Edward	02/09/1815
KENNADAY, Joannah	CHILTON, James	01/09/1800
KENNEBREW, Elizabeth	BARTON, Aquilla	02/10/1813
KENNON, Ann	POWEL, Thomas	08/04/1820
KENNON, Anney	DAVIS, Ashley	09/08/1814
KENNON, Eveline	HUBBARD, James	09/18/1849
KENNON, Frances	COX, William	03/23/1858
KENNON, Jane	DILL, James	05/20/1843
KENNON, Janey	KANON, Bartlet	01/20/1794
KENNON, Polly	STRATEN, William	01/21/1824
KENNON, Sally	MURPHEY, Jospeh	10/27/1800
KENNON, Thursday Ann	BOMAN, Thomas P.	12/23/1856
KENT, Ann	PIPER, Robert P.	10/13/1858
KENT, Sally	TAYLOR, Dorman	03/21/1808
KERMICHAEL, Leminah	CLIMER, Thomas	11/05/1799
KERMICHAEL, Sarah	SMITHEY, John	11/18/1798
KERNAL, Mary	BURTON, John J.	11/13/1839
KERNALL, Milly	OLIVER, Douglas	03/18/1783
KERR, Betsy	PINNIX, Joseph	01/22/1816
KERR, Fanny L.	MEBANE, Benjamin F.	09/08/1857
KERR, Frances A.	GRAVES, James L.	11/07/1849
KERR, Frankey	BARKER, George	10/18/1783
KERR, Isbel	BROOKES, Christopher W.	11/28/1812
KERR, Lucy	YANCEY, James	01/14/1794
KERR, Martha	SLADE, William	12/22/1786
KERR, Mary P.	LEA, Jeremiah	11/09/1830
KERR, Nancy	LEA, Alvis	03/29/1832
KERR, Nancy	LEA, Benjamin	02/09/1796
KERR, Polly	LEA, Jeremiah	12/20/1797
KERR, Polly	WILEY, Alexander	12/28/1807
KERSEY, Juliann	BROWN, James	08/11/1866
KERSEY, Ursley	PARKER, William	10/20/1798
KEY, Phoebe	COVINGTON, Bird	05/25/1826
KEY, Sarah	HARRISON, James	01/13/1825
KIERSEY, Lucy	STEPHENS, Armstead	12/24/1835
KIERSEY, Nancy	WEEKS, Richard	02/27/1825
KIERSEY, Polley	JONES, Allen	07/29/1813
KIERSEY, Ritta	MCFARLAND, William	04/19/1832
KILE, Betcey	HODGE, David	11/29/1819
KIMBRO, Hannah	ADKINS, Green	10/20/1866
KIMBRO, Isbel	COLLIER, Joseph	09/17/1805
KIMBRO, Margaret	TURNER, James H.	04/10/1847

MARRIAGE RECORDS OF CASWELL COUNTY, NORTH CAROLINA

BRIDE	GROOM	DATE
KIMBRO, Mary J.	CHANDLER, John	12/16/1822
KIMBRO, Sarah	TURNER, John	02/14/1787
KIMBRO, Susannah	KIMBRO, James B.	01/09/1823
KIMBROUGH, Charity	ADKINS, Henry	03/08/1867
KIMBROUGH, Elizabeth J.	DAVIS, James M.	09/01/1847
KIMBROUGH, Mary	PRENDERGRAST, George W.	09/14/1841
KIMBROUGH, Nancey G.	EVANS, Goodwin	01/05/1814
KIMBROUGH, Nancy	KIMBROUGH, William C.	08/26/1852
KIMBROUGH, Nancy	RASCOE, Ethelbert	10/20/1840
KIMBROUGH, Patsey	COLLIER, William	03/13/1814
KIMBROUGH, Patsy	THOMAS, David	04/14/1799
KIMBROUGH, Rebecca	TATE, Joseph	01/11/1828
KIMBROUGH, Salley	COLLIER, James	09/05/1810
KIMBROUGH, Susan S.	ZIMMERMAN, George J.	01/24/1853
KIMBROUGH, Tabitha	HOOPER, Henry Jr.	12/13/1830
KIMBROUGH, Tabitha	SNIPES, Nathaniel	06/16/1801
KINDRICK, Sally	MORRIS, Samuel	01/10/1807
KING, A.E.	WRIGHT, William B.	09/19/1865
KING, Alicey	GOOCH, Francis	12/30/1837
KING, Betsey	FOSTER, Colby	06/16/1808
KING, Celia	WATLINGTON, Shepperd	09/07/1867
KING, Elisabeth	ENOCHS, Andrew	03/11/1787
KING, Elizabeth E.	COBB, John W.	12/14/1852
KING, Elvira J.	HENDERSON, John N.	01/18/1839
KING, Frances	BLACKWELL, Samuel	03/07/1868
KING, Jane	WEATHERFORD, Barten	11/30/1824
KING, Lucy	KING, Newton	12/25/1866
KING, Minerva	HASTIN, James	05/25/1830
KING, Nancey	FOSTER, Ezariah	06/30/1828
KING, Nancy	GOOCH, Nathaniel	03/20/1864
KING, Polly	RICE, Nathan	01/19/1825
KING, Rachel	PAGE, Whitehead	03/20/1815
KING, Rebecca J.	COLEMAN, James E.	10/14/1866
KING, Sarah	HARALSON, William	11/07/1837
KINSEY, Salley	ALVERSON, Jesse	09/02/1818
KIRBY, Ann R.	WILSON, James H.	01/23/1855
KIRBY, Fanny H.	ANDERSON, Albert J. B.	08/06/1860
KIRK, Pamela	BURRIS, Rawzel	01/16/1810
KIRKPATRICK, M. E.	NORFLEET, M. W.	12/15/1864
KIRSEY, Dicy	JONES, Wilie	05/27/1797
KITCHEN, Elizabeth	SAWYERS, William	01/11/1814
KITCHEN, Elizabeth	SINGLETON, Joseph	12/23/1824
KITCHEN, Ester	LANGLEY, Thomas	10/25/1813
KITCHEN, Salley	BENTON, Richard	04/20/1819
KNIGHT, L.	PRICE, Robert M.	12/12/1860
KNIGHT, Margaret	HODGES, Henry E.	01/14/1863
KNIGHT, Margaret E.	TOWLER, H.A.	05/07/1858
KNIGHT, Martha	HOLDERBY, James D.	06/30/1832
KNIGHT, Sarah E.	FARRAR, Richard J.	09/14/1856
KNIGHTEN, Mary	HOBBS, Isaac	09/02/1823
KURSEY, Sarah	BUCKNER, John	04/15/1830

MARRIAGE RECORDS OF CASWELL COUNTY, NORTH CAROLINA

BRIDE	GROOM	DATE
KYLE, Jane	KERR, William	01/19/1824
LACKSON, Sarah	MATHIS, William	12/03/1823
LAFTIS, Martha A.	WOODS, A.S.G.	04/04/1849
LAMB, Martha	COILE, Theopolas	05/29/1828
LAMKIN, Susan	VAUGHN, William	08/18/1820
LAMPKIN, Nancey	GRAVES, Thomas	07/26/1821
LAMPKIN, Sarah	GILL, Richard D.	11/18/1822
LAMPKIN, Sophia W.	MATTHEWS, Albert M.	07/17/1833
LAND, Sophia A.	FITZGERALD, Jno. B.	11/15/1867
LANDERS, Nancey	CRESWELL, John	03/30/1810
LANDERS, Rachel	JONES, William	11/20/1816
LANDRUM, Elgy	PERKINS, Logan	02/01/1845
LANDRUM, Sarah A.	WILLIS, John W.	10/07/1852
LANE, Mary E.	DOWNS, Rolling L.	09/09/1842
LANGELY, Alcy	TANNER, Matthew	01/20/1800
LANGHORN, Elizabeth	SNEED, John	04/26/1841
LANGLEY, Mary	BRANDON, William	01/12/1796
LANIER, Jane B.	CABELL, P. B.	09/03/1857
LANNOM, Tabitha	POE, Jonathan	--/--/1804
LANSDOWN, Elizabeth H.	BOLTON, Lewis	09/18/1826
LASHLY, Harriet J.	CAPE, Thomas R.	03/18/1865
LAUGHINGHOUSE Melinda	SIMPKINS, Meldon	02/07/1856
LAWSEN, Jane B.	WRIGHT, Hiram A.	10/06/1828
LAWSON, Elisabeth	HARRIS, Robert	10/18/1791
LAWSON, Kate	SMITH, Sam P.	10/22/1860
LAWSON, Nancy	NEAL, John	01/22/1788
LAWSON, Nancy B.	WITHERS, Elijah K.	04/08/1826
LAWSON, Sally	STUBBLEFIELD, George W.	08/12/1817
LAWSON, Silvey	FERGUSON, Joseph	11/17/1866
LAWSON, Sina B.	WRIGHT, Edward	12/07/1821
LAY, Patsy	YEARBY, Charles	10/12/1808
LAY, Polly	BROWNING, Thomas	11/09/1801
LAY, Sarah	VAUGHON, Gidon	02/09/1780
LEA, Anna R.	GRAVES, William G.	12/11/1865
LEA, Annis	WILEY, Yancy	04/30/1855
LEA, Annis(?)	RICHMOND, Leonidas	04/04/1859
LEA, Anniss	MCNIEL, John	09/08/1780
LEA, Arrimenta	GUNN, Wiley	04/03/1867
LEA, Barbara	HAYES, Richard H.	11/04/1813
LEA, Betsey	FARLEY, James	09/05/1793
LEA, Betsey	MALONE, Daniel Jr.	12/11/1801
LEA, Betty	CARTER, John	09/15/1784
LEA, Caroline	RICHMOND, Bethel	12/27/1866
LEA, Celestia	BALL, Rufus	02/18/1866
LEA, Cornelia K.	STALCUP, William	07/06/1847
LEA, Delila	THOMPSON, James H.	03/17/1822
LEA, Delilah	GRAVES, Jeremiah	03/14/1816
LEA, Dicey	MCFARLAND, Jno.	07/15/1779
LEA, Dilly A.	WILLIAMSON, Henry	11/28/1867
LEA, E. C.	WARREN, B. H.	02/16/1860
LEA, Edy	WATLINGTON, Carter	10/19/1867

MARRIAGE RECORDS OF CASWELL COUNTY, NORTH CAROLINA

BRIDE	GROOM	DATE
LEA, Elisabeth	EVANS, Elisha	03/03/1789
LEA, Eliza G.	BROWN, Stephen E.	11/02/1846
LEA, Eliza K.	WILLIAMSON, Anthony	11/27/1818
LEA, Elizabeth	GRAVES, Calvin	06/02/1830
LEA, Elizabeth	LUNSFURD, Colley W.	09/17/1839
LEA, Elizabeth	PAUL, Samuel	03/22/1819
LEA, Enicey	HIGHTOWER, Joshua	03/31/1800
LEA, Frances	MCFARLAND, John	02/24/1804
LEA, Henrietta	THOMAS, Marcus C.	06/15/1858
LEA, Judith	OLIVER, Yancy	12/22/1826
LEA, Maggie R.	GRAVE, Charles I.	11/08/1862
LEA, Marianne	ELMORE, John	11/27/1798
LEA, Martha A.	WALKER, James M.	03/30/1835
LEA, Mary	WILLIAMSON, Swift	12/12/1819
LEA, Mary H.	BROWN, Michael	02/11/1840
LEA, Mary J.	CURRIE, Joseph M.	01/19/1858
LEA, Matilda	ESKRIDGE, Walker	08/04/1827
LEA, Matilda	OLIVER, Durrett	11/02/1811
LEA, Nancy	OLIVER, Reuben	01/17/1824
LEA, Nancy	ZACHARY, William	11/21/1780
LEA, Nancy	THOMPSON, John	02/19/1823
LEA, Nancy	WRIGHT, Abraham	01/09/1826
LEA, Nicey	DONOHO, William	11/08/1797
LEA, Phebe	BOWERS, Lemual	01/11/1810
LEA, Phebe	VANHOOK, John C.	11/24/1819
LEA, Pheby	KILLGORE, Thomas	01/02/1786
LEA, Polly	MORTON, Elijah	11/05/1811
LEA, Polly	WILLSON, George M.	04/12/1810
LEA, Prudence	TAYLOR, William	01/07/1791
LEA, Rebecca S.	WILLIAMSON, George	11/13/1815
LEA, Rebecca V.	FUQUA, John	11/29/1851
LEA, Rosannah	JEAN, Sherwood	02/20/1785
LEA, Sally	LEA, Thomas	10/13/1801
LEA, Sally	STAFFORD, James	12/30/1817
LEA, Sarah	ATKINSON, John	09/15/1782
LEA, Sarah	BAYNES, John	09/10/1845
LEA, Sarah	RICHMOND, John	12/21/1799
LEA, Sarah H.	GRAVES, William B.	07/17/1863
LEA, Sophia A.	WILLIS, Thomas J.	03/01/1841
LEA, Susan C. V.	VERTRES, James C.	07/28/1849
LEA, Susan J.	LEA, William G.	03/19/1848
LEA, Unice	KILLGORE, Charles	09/24/1796
LEA, Virginia	HUBBARD, Rufis	06/29/1857
LEA, Virginia E.	HICKS, William T.	09/06/1865
LEACHMOND, Elizabeth	BLAKE, Ellis G.	02/19/1830
LEATH, Eliza	WILLIS, Pinkney	11/19/1867
LEATH, Frances	NUTT, Absalom	08/04/1820
LEATH, Rebecah	JOHNSON, John	09/16/1796
LEATH, Sarah	PYRON, John	11/26/1799
LEATH, Susan	BOULDIN, George T.	05/12/1840
LEATH, mary E.	KERNODLE, Richard	08/11/1843

MARRIAGE RECORDS OF CASWELL COUNTY, NORTH CAROLINA

BRIDE	GROOM	DATE
LEDFORD, Catherine	BUCHANAN, John	02/27/1799
LEE, Ann	ROWLAND, Micajah	11/19/1812
LEE, Mary	WATKINS, Martin	12/09/1865
LEE, Polly	MATLOCK, Benjamin	01/21/1806
LEGANS, Letsy	WILEY, George	04/27/1847
LEGRAND, Mary	STEPHENS, Thomas	09/07/1838
LEGRAND, Nancy	KING, Edmund	08/11/1800
LEMORNS, Anne	FADDIS, John	01/31/1822
LENOX, Elizabeth	LEWIS, Shadras	10/10/1826
LEONARD, Elizabeth	VANHOOK, Aaron	--/--/----
LESTER, Mary C.	PLATS, Frank	04/21/1864
LEVY, Caroline E.	CALDWELL, Jno. M. M.	06/07/1844
LEWIS, Ann	WARREN, William	11/28/1823
LEWIS, Eliza	BROOKS, Christopher	09/16/1858
LEWIS, Elizabeth	JACKSON, William	11/15/1828
LEWIS, Elizabeth	LEWIS, Charles A.	12/15/1853
LEWIS, Elizabeth M.	WILLIAMS, Warner	03/16/1813
LEWIS, Ellen	CLAY, Henry	12/27/1867
LEWIS, Henrietta	TAYLOR, Harrison	01/16/1867
LEWIS, Lucy M.	WALKER, Ajax J.	05/18/1820
LEWIS, Mary A.	IRVINE, William C.	08/14/1843
LEWIS, Milly	STAMPS, James	05/18/1867
LEWIS, Nancy	ROPER, David	07/13/1801
LEWIS, Pheby A.	KELLY, Aaron	08/24/1867
LEWIS, Sally	TAYLOR, Phillip	08/06/1780
LINDSAY, Julia A.	WARF, John	09/22/1837
LINDSEY, Dorcas	STAMPS, William	12/27/1867
LINDSEY, Harriet	WALTERS, Davy	12/28/1866
LINDSEY, Mollie E.	LEA, J.A.	02/15/1867
LINK, Betsey	KIMBROUGH, John	09/06/1804
LIPSCOMB, Charlotte T.	COBB, Joseph P.	11/02/1860
LIPSCOMB, Mary	FARQUHAR, Abraham M.	03/25/1823
LIPSCOMBE, Mary C.	TOWNS, William M.	08/06/1851
LISBERGER, Lucinda	MCGEHEE, Jeremaih	01/11/1868
LOAFMAN, Ann	SAWYERS, Absalom	02/08/1808
LOAFMAN, Jincey	BALLARD, Larkin	01/02/1812
LOCKARD, Mary J.	CRAFT, Andrew J.	09/28/1859
LOCKARD, Sarah T.	WRIGHT, Sidney R.	09/05/1853
LOCKET, Caroline	FRETWELL, William A.	05/23/1842
LOCKET, Margaret	REED, James W.	10/10/1844
LOCKETT, Isabella R.	DUNN, Jarrett	05/22/1852
LOCKETT, Laura A.	HOLT, Robert T.	07/25/1858
LOCKHART, Julia C.	MCCAIN, James A.	11/20/1866
LOCKHART, Nancy	JONES, Thomas	01/24/1829
LOGAN, Cathrine	FARLEY, Daniel S.	10/13/1785
LOGAN, Mecay	DAVIS, John	01/18/1859
LONDON, Sarah	NICHOLLS, Isaac	10/27/1825
LONG, Agness	MAXWELL, Bezl	06/30/1798
LONG, Elizabeth G.	ROAN, Justin	10/26/1836
LONG, Fanny	SARGENT, Stephen	11/11/1786
LONG, Franky	WOODY, Frank	07/04/1866

MARRIAGE RECORDS OF CASWELL COUNTY, NORTH CAROLINA

BRIDE	GROOM	DATE
LONG, Hannah	STEPHENS, Alfred	11/10/1866
LONG, Jane	UPTON, Edward	12/19/1781
LONG, Leah	LEA, William	08/31/1816
LONG, Margaret	PARRETT, Thomas	01/10/1860
LONG, Marian	WINSTON, Jno. R.	11/13/1866
LONG, Mary	RIGGS, Drusis	02/04/1812
LONG, Nancy	CLYFT, John	10/27/1780
LONG, Sally	HODGE, John	03/28/1812
LONG, Sally	LONG, John	02/16/1866
LOOT, Mary	GRESHAM, Henry	01/05/1788
LOVE, Dicy	RUDD, Bethel	01/31/1867
LOVE, Elizabeth	MCKISSACK, John	08/23/1830
LOVE, Elizabeth	MATHEWS, Christopher	01/20/1814
LOVE, Ester	MITCHEL, Robert	02/04/1787
LOVE, Jane	BURTON, William	11/17/1818
LOVE, Jane	SARGENT, James	10/02/1792
LOVE, Kitty	MARTIN, Zenes	12/11/1816
LOVE, Margaret	MORROW, Benjamin	01/29/1828
LOVE, Martha	MITCHEL, David	01/30/1788
LOVE, Mary	HOOPER, Zachariah Jr.	08/12/1825
LOVE, Mary	LOVE, Samuel Jr.	07/18/1828
LOVE, Mary	MABE, William P.	07/17/1856
LOVE, Nancey	DAMERON, John	01/22/1828
LOVE, Nancey	HEGGIE, Archibald	09/24/1835
LOVE, Rebeccah	BARNWELL, Robert	05/28/1796
LOVE, Salley	KIMBROUGH, M.Duke	11/30/1818
LOVE, Zilphah	BURTON, Francis H.	12/17/1810
LOVELACE, Jemima A. P.	PRUIT, Griffin P.	05/21/1867
LOVELACE, Libba	LOVELACE, William	12/15/1828
LOVELACE, Lucind	JONES, Erasmus K.	09/13/1827
LOVELACE, Lucinda	STRADOR, Christian Jr.	09/19/1827
LOVELACE, Mary	COTHRAN, James H.	01/11/1841
LOVELACE, Mary	COBB, Henry Sr.	06/14/1826
LOVELACE, Matilda	LOVELACE, Joseph	07/02/1850
LOVELACE, Matilda	LOVELACE, Nicholas	12/26/1822
LOVELACE, Nancy	MURPHEY, Thomas	02/--/1852
LOVELACE, Nancy F.	SNOW, Stephen T.	02/15/1866
LOVELACE, Nelly	SOUTHARD, John	12/22/1840
LOVELACE, Phebe	COBB, Noah	01/29/1820
LOVELACE, Sarah	MURPHEY, James	03/02/1843
LOVELASS, Cloey A.	PERKINS, Nathan	10/05/1832
LOVELASS, Louisa	MEACHAN, Banks	11/24/1829
LOVELESS, Harriet A.	YATES, Grief	04/19/1860
LOVELESS, Matilda J.	WALKER, Landay	04/17/1855
LOWELL, Margarett	HIGHTOWER, Robert	04/24/1830
LOWNS, Isabella C.	SWIFT, Joseph M.	11/18/1856
LOYD, Elizabeth	RASCO, Henry T.	01/19/1855
LOYD, Elizabeth	TRASCO, Henry	01/21/1855
LOYED, Margaret	WALKER, John	11/23/1858
LUMKIN, Nancy	PARKER, Powel	12/24/1787
LUMPKIN, Nancy	BENNETT, Mumford	02/17/1821

MARRIAGE RECORDS OF CASWELL COUNTY, NORTH CAROLINA

BRIDE	GROOM	DATE
LUMPKINS, Elizabeth	COX, William	12/17/1853
LUNSFORD, Martha	MILES, John	12/30/1840
LUNSFORD, Mary	MILES, Elijah H.	01/14/1840
LUNSFORD, Sarah E.	PLEASANT, Stephen N.	01/13/1868
LUNSFORDM Mary A.	INGRAM, James J.	01/22/1858
LYDNAR, Ailcey	BARKSDALE, Armistead	05/26/1824
LYIN, July	HOWARD, Horac	03/20/1841
LYNCH, Celia	RICE, Zadok	02/27/1821
LYNCH, Cynthia	FERRILL, George W.	11/10/1835
LYON, Elizabeth F.	ROBERTS, James L.	08/19/1857
LYON, Frances	BROWN, William V.	11/20/1812
LYON, Frances	CHANCE, David	06/24/1853
LYON, Francis	BENSON, John	12/24/1841
LYON, Margarett	HINTON, James N.	09/09/1866
LYON, Martha W.	WATLINGTON, Thompson T.	05/19/1849
LYON, Mary	MIDDLEBROOKS, John	07/16/1781
LYON, Mary E.	FARLEY, John E.	02/10/1867
LYON, Polley	HAILEY, Henry B.	07/22/1812
LYON, Rebeccah	KNIGHT, William	03/30/1809
LYON, Tempy	POTEET, James	11/11/1801
MABREY, Mary	STUBBLEFIELD, William	12/18/1778
MADANIEL, Louisa M.	HARRISON, Samuel S.	09/11/1838
MADDING, Jane E.	GWYN, Augustus	06/02/1838
MAHAN, Mary	JOHNSTON, Joseph	05/28/1831
MALLARY, Diana	CARTER, Theoderick	04/16/1793
MALLERY, Ann	CARTER, Joseph	12/18/1790
MALLORY, Nancey	DAVIS, Thomas	08/23/1805
MALLORY, Rebeccah	JONES, Ezekiel	01/10/1799
MALLORY, Sally	PIKE, Joshua	03/01/1805
MALLORY, Sally	SAWYER, William	01/02/1805
MALLORY, Susan	WATSON, Anderson	10/29/1832
MALLORY, Zebba	BUCKLEY, Peyton	08/23/1811
MALONE, Chloe	RAINEY, William	09/28/1789
MALONE, Dicey	EUBANK, George	09/03/1799
MALONE, ELiza	BROOKS, John K.	06/28/1847
MALONE, Eliza B.	BURTON, Hutchens	11/02/1813
MALONE, Frances	LOVE, Samuel	05/03/1791
MALONE, Henrietta	VAUGHAN, James	12/--/1803
MALONE, Margaret	COVINGTON, Henry	03/02/1867
MALONE, Margaret J.	HAWKINS, John	12/13/1854
MALONE, Mary	DAMERON, William	08/26/1820
MALONE, Mary	MUZZALL, William	08/22/1789
MALONE, Mary J.	FALKNER, Franklin	11/09/1867
MALONE, Minerva	MITCHELL, William M.	01/29/1842
MALONE, Nancy	MURPHEY, Stephen	11/05/1827
MALONE, Polly	MILES, Henry	05/06/1830
MALONE, Rebeccah	DAMERON, Bartholomew	08/27/1798
MALONE, Sally	STEPHENS, Benjamin	06/19/1822
MALONE, Sally	WARRIN, William	11/26/1801
MALONE, Senia	SCOTT, Jesse M.	07/25/1833
MALONE, Tempy	SMITH, William	09/07/1819

MARRIAGE RECORDS OF CASWELL COUNTY, NORTH CAROLINA

BRIDE	GROOM	DATE
MALORY, Nancy	SAWYER, John	04/30/1820
MAN, Jenny	HICKMAN, William	12/07/1796
MANGRAM, Eliza	PRIOR, Joseph	06/17/1859
MANGUM, Margarett	BARTS, James H.	01/13/1861
MANGUM, Martha	DANIEL, John	02/05/1860
MANLEY, Elacy	GUTRY, John D.	12/15/1838
MANLEY, Henrietta	HEYDON, Leachman	02/01/1825
MANLEY, Ibba	FOSTER, Franklin	10/07/1841
MANLEY, Ibby	HARRELSON, James C.	02/10/1858
MANLEY, Lucy	FOSTER, Franklin	01/28/1864
MANLEY, Mary	PAGE, William	12/09/1854
MANLY, Matilda	MORTON, John	07/04/1843
MANLY, Polly	PYRON, Westley	07/02/1839
MANN, Elizabeth	BUSBY, James	06/01/1863
MANNEN, Susanah	GILLESPIE, William	06/13/1805
MANNEN, Titia (?)	WATLINGTON, William	11/09/1816
MANNING, Susanna	RUDD, William	06/10/1805
MANSFIELD, Amy J.	CLARK, Richard H.	01/06/1853
MANSFIELD, Lucy T.	WILLIAMS, Dawson M.	01/03/1856
MARABLE, Fannie	HUNT, James	03/23/1867
MARLER, Sally	SWANN, James	04/08/1820
MARLOW, Nancy	SWAN, Daniel W.	12/14/1826
MARR, Elizabeth	NELSON, John B.	12/20/1852
MARR, Lucy T.	FARMER, Evans	05/01/1859
MARR, Margaret	PRIOR, Pinkny C.	02/19/1859
MARR, Priscilla	DOWNS, William	03/09/1853
MARRIABLE, Elizabeth	BOHANNAN, Ambrose	07/09/1810
MARSHALL, Elizabeth	RANSOM, Charles	01/03/1867
MARSHALL, Mary A.	PURKINS, Wm. N.	10/24/1857
MARSHALL, Rebeccah	FENN, Gabriel	01/05/1796
MARTIN, Betty	WILEY, John	03/30/1867
MARTIN, Elizabeth	GROOM, Calvin	11/08/1859
MARTIN, Frances	GOOCH, Thomas	10/06/1834
MARTIN, Frances	SAUNDERS, William	01/15/1825
MARTIN, Frances	WALKER, Phillip	12/27/1833
MARTIN, Hetta C.	MORTON, Azariah G.	06/08/1837
MARTIN, Lucinda S.	DOWNEY, John A.	08/08/1846
MARTIN, Lucy F.	TATE, A.J.	02/19/1868
MARTIN, Malinda	SCOTT, John H.	07/08/1836
MARTIN, Martha	BRADSHER, Wilson A.	02/11/1858
MARTIN, Martha C.	SHELTON, James W.	04/04/1848
MARTIN, Mary	BOSWELL, Moses	12/01/1866
MARTIN, Mary	VINCENT, James	08/14/1841
MARTIN, Nancy	LOYD, Alexander G.	11/02/1825
MARTIN, Nancy	OWEN, John	11/05/1788
MARTIN, Polly	EVANS, Ellis	04/25/1797
MARTIN, Polly	OWIN, David	09/21/1798
MARTIN, Sarah J.	JEFFREYS, Adkinson	02/03/1862
MARTIN, Sue F.	RICHMOND, William D.	05/15/1862
MASON, Ann	WALKER, James	12/16/1820
MASON, Betsy	SCOTT, William	05/02/1827

MARRIAGE RECORDS OF CASWELL COUNTY, NORTH CAROLINA

BRIDE	GROOM	DATE
MASON, Elizabeth	SCOTT, William	11/08/1824
MASON, Jean	WALKER, Samuel	12/16/1820
MASON, Margaret	WARF, James F.	03/20/1836
MASON, Patsy	MATHEWS, Joel	04/24/1822
MASON, Salley	GOMER, Thomas	08/17/1829
MASON, Sarag	WARREN, Micajah	04/19/1859
MASSEY, Margaret	MASSEY, Thomas	08/29/1832
MASSEY, Mary A.	RUDD, James C.	02/12/1857
MASSEY, Nancey	ASHFORD, Willis	05/09/1812
MASSEY, Nancy	BIRK, Tompson	08/09/1805
MASSY, Aggy	BRINTLE, William	05/13/1802
MATCH, Nancy	DURRUM, Isaac	08/25/1789
MATHEWS, Matilda	DAMERON, Benjamin	11/20/1820
MATHEWS, Sally L.	YEALOCK, Lewis	11/13/1815
MATHEWS, Susan L.	TERRELL, Jonathan H.	12/11/1851
MATHIS, Patience	FULINGTON, John R.	11/17/1827
MATHIS, Susanna	UPTON, William	11/03/1823
MATHISON, Christian	BRODIE, Thomas	05/13/1779
MATKINS, Martha E.	BRINCEFIELD, A. J.	11/01/1865
MATLOCK, Agness	HIGHTOWER, John	03/22/1790
MATLOCK, Barbara	CRUTCHFIELD, William B.	05/08/1837
MATLOCK, Betsey	DYAR, Samuel	08/18/1796
MATLOCK, Elizabeth	WARE, Ansel	09/10/1825
MATLOCK, Frances	EVANS, Madison	10/07/1865
MATLOCK, Judah	MORGAN, William M.	07/14/1847
MATLOCK, Leathy	SMITH, Robert	11/17/1846
MATLOCK, Lucy	MONTGOMERY, Alexander	12/03/1801
MATLOCK, Mary	EVANS, Bird	12/23/1840
MATLOCK, Mary	KERSEY, Samuel	12/23/1790
MATLOCK, Nancy	LEWIS, William	01/31/1805
MATLOCK, Sarah	MONTGOMERY, William	02/28/1804
MATLOCK, Susan	WALTON, John	05/17/1832
MATTHEWS, Ann M.	JACKSON, James	12/31/1824
MATTHEWS, Betsey	GOING, Goodrich	09/06/1791
MATTHEWS, Martha	DAVIS, John	10/11/1817
MATTOX, Sarah J.	WILLIAMS,(?) John D.	07/06/1866
MATTOX, Sarah J.	WILLIAMSON,(? John D.	07/06/1866
MATTOX, Sarah J.	WILLIAMSON,(? John D.	07/06/1866
MATTOX, Sarah J.	WILLIAMS,(?) John D.	07/06/1866
MAUGHAN, Jane	LLOYD, Thomas	08/23/1804
MAYO, Dorothy C.	MOORE, Thomas J.	08/22/1837
MAYO, Hannah	MASON, David	12/--/1800
MCADEN, Caroline	ROAN, James	04/22/1867
MCADEN, Cathrine	FARLEY, Danl. S.	06/16/1800
MCADEN, Cynthia	HALL, Pleasant	02/10/1807
MCADEN, Mary	HOWARD, Henry	12/19/1787
MCADEN, Nancey G.	DISMUKES, James M.	04/11/1838
MCADEN, Sally M.	ROSE, Duncan Jr.	08/19/1799
MCADEN, Sarah G.	JOHNSTON, Thomas D.	02/23/1825
MCADIN, Mary J.	BRANDON, David G.	04/14/1821
MCALPIN, C.A.	TOTTEN, Joseph S.	09/24/1840

MARRIAGE RECORDS OF CASWELL COUNTY, NORTH CAROLINA

BRIDE	GROOM	DATE
MCALPIN, Caroline	LOCKHART, William	05/12/1841
MCALPIN, Mary J.	PATTON, John D.	12/27/1853
MCALPIN, Narcissa G.	VALENTINE, Thos. J.	12/24/1842
MCCADEN, Juda	WILSON, Mike	07/27/1867
MCCAIN, America L.	ROBSON, William G.	09/14/1865
MCCAIN, Betty A.	SLADE, John R.	05/27/1863
MCCAIN, Elizabeth	POORE, Thomas S.	11/21/1842
MCCAIN, Elizabeth S.	JONES, Jno. G.	12/10/1834
MCCAIN, Mary	SHELTON, Samuel E.	08/04/1846
MCCAIN, Mary A.	WILKINSON, Egbert S.	01/23/1849
MCCAIN, Mary C.	WORD, Fleming	01/31/1851
MCCAIN, Matilda	THOMAS, William	01/17/1867
MCCAIN, Nancy	CONALLY, William J.	07/23/1857
MCCAIN, Nancy	ROBSON, William	08/25/1817
MCCAIN, Sarah A.	MURRAY, David R.	07/06/1847
MCCAIN,(?) Charlotte	WILLIS, William	08/01/1850
MCCALIN, Rachel	PASCHALL, Elisha	12/22/1819
MCCALIPS, Jane	KELLEY, James	01/23/1802
MCCALRNEY, Polly	VAUGHAN, Bailey	12/18/1827
MCCAMPBELL, Nancy J.	CLYCE, James T.	01/13/1850
MCCARVER, Grussey	WEBB, Jonathan	02/12/1781
MCCLARY, Polly	PARKS, Robert G.	02/26/1803
MCCLENEHAN, Lucy J.	TOSH, Thomas	04/06/1833
MCCORMICK, Catherine	FINCH, George A.	05/19/1862
MCCOY, Unity	COLE, Thomas	09/21/1780
MCCUBBINS, Dolly	WRIGHT, Isaac	04/28/1833
MCCULLEY, Nancy	SPARKS, Thomas	07/08/1817
MCCULLOCH, Narsissus	PITTS, James S.	01/26/1859
MCDANIEL, Elisabeth	DARBY, John	09/15/1794
MCDANIEL, Elvira A.	HODGES, Henry E.	01/19/1853
MCDANIEL, Mary	LEIGH, William	09/01/1814
MCDANIEL, Nancy	WHITLOW, Solomon	11/13/1822
MCDANIEL, Sally	HALRESON, Calvin	02/16/1867
MCDANIEL, Sarah	PRICE, Meredith	04/13/1819
MCDANIEL, Susan W.	PRICE, Robert M.	11/10/1851
MCDANIEL, Susannah	FULLER, Levi	02/03/1810
MCDANIELS, Jane	HOOPER, N. C.	02/25/1867
MCFARLAND, Fanny	RAGGAN, John C.	01/24/1861
MCFARLAND, Frances	REAGIN, John C.	03/27/1861
MCFARLAND, Margurete	BARNET, Hugh	01/26/1784
MCFARLAND, Nancy	TAITE, Robert J.	03/31/1859
MCFARLAND, Polly	KIERSEY, Drury	02/09/1826
MCFARLIN, Julia	RAGIN, William T.	12/31/1858
MCGEHEE, Elizabeth	MOORE, Robert	08/24/1784
MCGEHEE, Oney	WATKINS, King	12/23/1865
MCGHEE, Martha	MORTON, George	02/18/1788
MCGHEE, Sarah	STANDFIELD, Harrison	03/31/1789
MCGILL, A. B.	PENICK, Giles	02/21/1866
MCGINNIS, Betsy	MORRIS, William	03/12/1786
MCHANEY, Julia A.	FARIS, Thomas D.	03/10/1860
MCKEE, Mary	KEMP, Barnett	02/23/1810

MARRIAGE RECORDS OF CASWELL COUNTY, NORTH CAROLINA

BRIDE	GROOM	DATE
MCKEE, Polly	BURCH, Richard	01/02/1815
MCKENNEY, Eliz.	PAYNE, Robert	09/14/1807
MCKINNEY, Elizabeth	DENNEY, Azariah	09/26/1823
MCKINNEY, Lucy	ROBERSON, Pinckney	01/31/1839
MCKINNEY, Martha	WALKER, John M.	10/24/1840
MCKINNEY, Martha J.	SCOTT, John J.	07/05/1860
MCKINNEY, Mary	ALVERSON, William L.	01/20/1853
MCKINNEY, Mary F.	STANLEY, Alpheus	11/18/1858
MCKINNEY, Mary J.	ROBERTSON, Green	09/30/1857
MCKINNEY, Patsy	TURNER, Henry	11/23/1826
MCKINNEY, Sarah	MOORE, William W.	10/28/1826
MCKINNEY, Susan	SCOTT, Pleasant	06/05/1851
MCKINNY, Martha A.	MASSEY, William H.	01/09/1844
MCKINNY, Milly D.	PAGE, Franklin B.	08/04/1859
MCKINNY, Susan	POWELL, J. C.	11/12/1866
MCKISSOCK, Priscilla	LOCARD, Hiram	04/--/1819
MCKNIGHT, Mary	CRUMMELL, Charles	03/19/1785
MCLAUGHLAN, Sally H.	ADAMS, John W.	11/21/1867
MCMENEMY, Sally	BYRD, Temple	05/28/1809
MCMINAMY, Sarah	MOTHERAL, Samuel	12/26/1782
MCMULLEN, Jane	GREEN, Thomas C.	05/13/1844
MCMULLIN, Elizabeth	VANHOOK, Isaac D.	12/02/1817
MCMULLIN, Margaret	SNIPES, James L.	12/20/1837
MCMULLIN, Margret	HATLER, James R.	02/05/1825
MCMULLIN, Polley	HESTER, Elijah	11/30/1813
MCMULLIN, Rebeccah	BREEZE, James	11/01/1797
MCNAB, Phebe	FARROW, John	12/20/1813
MCNEEL, Mary E.	MOORE, William J.	12/21/1840
MCNEEL, Ursula G.	NORFLEET, James S.	02/11/1826
MCNEELEY, Polley	JONES, Allen	08/09/1811
MCNEELY, Rachel	FORD, Mumford	10/07/1806
MCNEIL, Margaret J.	MOORE, Leonadas B.	10/21/1844
MCNEIL, Millisa V.	TURNER, Marcus A.	09/25/1851
MCNEIL, Nancy	VIRMILLION, Wilson	07/18/1778
MCNEILL, Emma L.	WILLIAMS, Stephen E.	02/26/1850
MCNEILL, Julia A.	POTEAT, James	11/17/1855
MCNEILL, Lois	DUTY, Richard	07/21/1791
MCNEILL, Patty H.	LEA, Carter	02/26/1782
MCNIEL, Elizabeth	RICHMOND, David	12/09/1834
MCNIEL, Frances	KERR, James	09/29/1835
MCNUTT, Elizabeth L.	SIMMONS, Joseph B.	10/16/1854
MEACHUM, Paulina F.	WRIGHT, John C.	10/25/1863
MEADOWS, Betty	STOKES, Jesse	11/12/1866
MEANS, Poly	SHANKS, Thomas	01/09/1799
MEBANE, Emma C.	MEBANE, William G.	12/14/1865
MEBANE, Harriet	MCCAIN, Edmund	01/13/1867
MEBANE, Henrietta V.	ROBERTSON, John E.	06/12/1867
MEBANE, Jane	THOMAS, Hurt	06/16/1866
MEBANE, Sarah	DOLL, Archer	09/28/1866
MEDLIN, Sidney	RHODES, Noah	04/06/1827
MEELEY, Nelly	RAINEY, John	09/14/1798

MARRIAGE RECORDS OF CASWELL COUNTY, NORTH CAROLINA

BRIDE	GROOM	DATE
MELONE, Elizabeth	WARREN, Bozzel	12/21/1798
MELONE, Isabella	WARREN, Jno. G.	11/08/1791
MELONE, Mary A.	STEPHENS, John Q.	12/13/1837
MELONE, Sarah	REANY, Isaac	03/06/1786
MELTON, Mary	ARNOLD, Richard	03/24/1818
MELTON, Patsey	ALDRIDGE, Andrew	04/17/1834
MENDRICK, Rhody	FREEMAN, John	01/10/1856
MEREDITH, Elisabeth	HOWARD, John	11/28/1785
MERONY, Mary	BOSWELL, James	10/21/1819
MERRICKS, Polly	HILL, Levi	01/18/1817
MERRITT, Freelove	HALCOM, George	10/02/1786
MERRITT, Mary	LEGRAND, Herbert W.	04/04/1836
MERRITT, Susanna	SMITH, John	01/02/1824
MESSER, Mime	GATLEY, John	01/30/1787
MICHEL, Nancy	SAWYER, John	12/15/1807
MIDKIFF, Mary J.	COLLIER, James H.	12/26/1866
MIDLETON, Mary	CARLEN, Richard	11/18/1780
MILAM, Elizabeth	MOOREFIELD, John H.	03/02/1865
MILES, Ann	WARREN, Martin	02/06/1836
MILES, Bidsey	COCK, George	12/09/1822
MILES, Dolly	VAUGHN, Warren T.	10/06/1859
MILES, Elizabeth	KIMBROU, William	12/09/1799
MILES, Elizabeth	PLEASANT, Pinkey J.	10/06/1849
MILES, Elizabeth	VAUGHAN, John	11/18/1847
MILES, Elizabeth J.	BOSWELL, John A.	01/24/1867
MILES, Fanny	ROBERSON, Thomas	11/20/1832
MILES, Hulda	MINOR, Richard	09/01/1844
MILES, Leah	VAUGHAN, John Jr.	03/20/1827
MILES, Lucy	CARNEY, Joshua	12/26/1786
MILES, Martha E.	PLEASANT, John J.	09/05/1838
MILES, Martha R.	JONES, Yancey	07/20/1850
MILES, Nancy	SMITH, William B.	12/22/1859
MILES, Nancy R.	DONOHO, William C.	03/19/1833
MILES, Patcey	GUNN, Thomas	09/20/1802
MILES, Peggy	TAIT, James M.	10/29/1834
MILES, Polly	ROBERSON, Christopher	04/15/1830
MILES, Rody	SCOTT, Miles	06/08/1808
MILES, Sally	PINNIX, Frank	07/05/1867
MILES, Susan	CORBETT, Burel	12/16/1839
MILLER, Elizabeth	WILLIS, William	12/05/1785
MILLER, Sarah E.	WILLIAMS, John A.	08/10/1835
MILLNER, Martha A.	WITCHER, Daniel P.	08/16/1852
MILLS, Ann	LOCKETT, Zachariah	07/11/1825
MILS, Caroline	VAUGHN, A. B.	12/21/1860
MILTON, Elizabeth B.	HENSLEY, Thomas	03/16/1842
MILTON, Nancy	KING, Daniel	10/19/1820
MIMMS, Fanny	RICHARDSON, George	02/12/1866
MIMS, Charlotte	DANIEL, Martin	08/11/1834
MIMS, Frances	HENDERSON, William	09/18/1844
MIMS, Martha J.	JONES, James W.	09/24/1844
MIMS, Mary A.	SIDEBOTTOM, James H.	10/04/1832

MARRIAGE RECORDS OF CASWELL COUNTY, NORTH CAROLINA

BRIDE	GROOM	DATE
MIMS, Mary A.	WATLINGTON, Edward Jr.	02/25/1841
MIMS, Mary J.	PARK, Jno. S.	12/04/1856
MIMS, Matilda B.	MULLINS, Thomas	10/10/1836
MIMS, Sarah F.	SOMERS, Alfred	05/05/1858
MITCHEL, Catherine	WILLIAMS, Alexander	09/07/1867
MITCHEL, Cisily	FOSTER, Lewis,	09/02/1797
MITCHEL, Eleanor	ROBERTS, Stephen	08/13/1791
MITCHEL, Jenny	POWELL, Edmund	11/09/1865
MITCHEL, Lavina	GUY, Alvis	12/24/1867
MITCHEL, Sally	WHITE, Thomas	01/12/1802
MITCHELL, Betsy	POWELL, James M.	01/10/1809
MITCHELL, Betty A.	CRISP, David H.	08/31/1856
MITCHELL, Catherine	HEYDON, John H.	09/16/1825
MITCHELL, Caty	STUBLEFIELD, Solomon	12/25/1867
MITCHELL, Cornelia	HUGHES, Thomas H.	01/20/1844
MITCHELL, Elizabeth	GOMER, James J.	08/12/1845
MITCHELL, Elizabeth	ECTOR, Hugh	10/19/1821
MITCHELL, Elizabeth A.	CURRIE, James	10/15/1822
MITCHELL, Frances	MEBANE, Alexander	09/26/1818
MITCHELL, Harriet R.	WILLIS, Thomas H.	09/26/1844
MITCHELL, Huldath	BROOKES, Thomas	05/28/1823
MITCHELL, Jane	KENT, S.S.	--/--/1843
MITCHELL, Jinny	WILEY, John	09/06/1815
MITCHELL, Julia Ann	CURRIE, James	02/24/1837
MITCHELL, Lucinda	HOLT, Washington	06/05/1858
MITCHELL, Lucy A.	HARRALSON, Sidney	04/09/1866
MITCHELL, Martha	MITCHELL, Jefferson	07/20/1867
MITCHELL, Martha J.	WELLS, Stephen N.	12/11/1854
MITCHELL, Mary	RICE, Zeri	09/03/1782
MITCHELL, Mary A.	FOSTER, Thomas T.	11/12/1850
MITCHELL, Mary A.	WARREN, George W.	10/03/1857
MITCHELL, Mirine(?)	SAWYERS, William	12/06/1824
MITCHELL, Nancey	BLACKWELL, Milton	12/27/1820
MITCHELL, Nancy	BLACKWELL, Milton	04/26/1823
MITCHELL, Nancy S.	SOWELL, Thomas L.	06/01/1830
MITCHELL, Penny	MILLER, Charles	04/07/1826
MITCHELL, Polly	SPENCER, Thomas	02/21/1796
MITCHELL, Sarah	LACKEY, Robert	02/14/1795
MITCHELL, Sina E.	WRENN, Hillmon W.	12/10/1866
MITCHELL, Susannah	HASTIN, Eldridge	01/02/1802
MITCHELL, Vilet	GUDE, William Jr.	11/03/1850
MONTGOMERY, Anne	GUNN, Thomas Junr.	01/22/1811
MONTGOMERY, Eliza C.	MITCHELL, John B.	12/18/1856
MONTGOMERY, Elizabeth	CHUMBLY, Larkin	12/23/1835
MONTGOMERY, Elvira	RUDD, Thomas	11/19/1844
MONTGOMERY, Harriett E.	HATCHETT, William H.	12/04/1866
MONTGOMERY, Jane	DAVIS, David	03/23/1808
MONTGOMERY, Mary	WALKER, Robert T.	01/17/1858
MONTGOMERY, Mary M.	LONG, Alexander M.	07/19/1824
MONTGOMERY, Polly	HOWARD, Francis	11/11/1801
MONTGOMERY, Rebecca	GATTIS, William	03/18/1820

MARRIAGE RECORDS OF CASWELL COUNTY, NORTH CAROLINA

BRIDE	GROOM	DATE
MONTGOMERY, Rebecca	MURRAY, Thomas	03/12/1850
MONTGOMERY, Sally	FOSTER, Williamson P.	01/27/1845
MONTGOMERY, Sarah L.	BOULDIN, William J.	05/12/1837
MONTGOMRY, Elizabeth	KITCHEN, John	12/23/1820
MOOR, Frances	MURPHEY, James	08/11/1825
MOOR, Maria	CARVER, Lemuel	01/02/1838
MOORE, Adeline S.J.	DAVIDSON, Leroy	03/14/1828
MOORE, Alcey	LESTER, Robert	05/02/1832
MOORE, Amanda	HOOPER, Charles H.	12/10/1851
MOORE, Ann	ROBERTS, David	07/20/1790
MOORE, Betsy	DURRETT, Francis	11/31/1807
MOORE, Betsy	PRICE, Abraham	07/18/1808
MOORE, Blanche A.	SMITH, Richard S.	12/26/1866
MOORE, Delpha	FANNING, Midelton	12/13/1787
MOORE, Elizabeth	MCNIEL, Benjamin	12/18/1787
MOORE, Elizabeth E.	NEWMAN, Anderson B.	12/17/1851
MOORE, Elizabeth L.	YANCY, John	02/24/1789
MOORE, Emily	TURNER, Lewis P.	09/21/1855
MOORE, Frances	DICKINS, Jesse	11/07/1791
MOORE, Isbella G.	ALDRIGE, James	10/27/1824
MOORE, Jamima	TAYLOR, Shadrach	04/24/1841
MOORE, Judith	TRAVISE, David	02/04/1782
MOORE, Louisa A. E.	NOBLE, Andrew	12/04/1857
MOORE, Lucy	CAMPBELL, John	01/26/1785
MOORE, Malinda	DARBY, Archibald L.	02/10/1830
MOORE, Manerva	MITCHELL, John	06/09/1858
MOORE, Margaret	MAYNARD, Richard	10/23/1844
MOORE, Martha	RICHMOND, George T.	03/15/1840
MOORE, Martha	TURNER, Moses	02/22/1780
MOORE, Martha F.	STAMPS, Rufus	06/17/1845
MOORE, Mary	EVANS, David H.	10/08/1851
MOORE, Mary	BURCH, A. J.	03/05/1853
MOORE, Mary	ROBERTSON, John	04/03/1782
MOORE, Mary	WHITLOW, Solomon	12/13/1832
MOORE, Mary A.	CLARK, Peter F.	10/15/1856
MOORE, Mary R.	ALLEN, James M.	11/10/1854
MOORE, Matilda	COMER, John	01/04/1827
MOORE, Melesia	BROOKS, Christopher	05/09/1848
MOORE, Mildred	TURNER, John	08/27/1854
MOORE, Nancy	BURCH, Jesse	01/08/1834
MOORE, Nancy	WARF, Berry	06/22/1808
MOORE, Olive	WARREN, Iverson G.	12/12/1846
MOORE, Olive Ann	DAMARON, James K.	11/30/1840
MOORE, Pennelope	FOULKES, Thomas C.	04/06/1811
MOORE, Polly	MCCAULEY, John	09/14/1796
MOORE, Polly	RICHARDS, Durritt	07/12/1802
MOORE, Polly	TAYLOR, James	02/18/1807
MOORE, Rachel	LONG, Benjamin	05/24/1780
MOORE, Rebecca H.	MANLY, William S.	12/16/1858
MOORE, Roxey	MCCAIN, Louis	12/20/1867
MOORE, Sally	RICE, William H.	11/11/1852

MARRIAGE RECORDS OF CASWELL COUNTY, NORTH CAROLINA

BRIDE	GROOM	DATE
MOORE, Sarah	LOVE, Robert	12/12/1833
MOORE, Sarah	BURCH, Squire	01/28/1826
MOORE, Sarah	WINSTEAD, Charles	06/15/1---
MOORE, Sarah A.	WILLIAMSON, Anthony S.	11/12/1849
MOORE, Scecily	CONOLEY, John	05/23/1788
MOORE, Sophronia	FULLER, Jesse	11/24/1846
MOORE, Susan	BARTLETT, Thompson M.	06/19/1826
MOORE, Tabitha	HIX, William	03/09/1784
MORGAN, Elizabeth	LEA, James	12/20/1819
MORGAN, Elizabeth	WEBSTER, Thomas	03/01/1837
MORGAN, Louisa J.	OYLER, James T.	10/24/1867
MORGAN, Mary	POTEAT, Alex	01/25/1867
MORGAN, Nancy	MCCAIN, John	12/20/1842
MORGAN, Nancy	STAFFORD, Eli	12/26/1807
MORGAN, Polly	WININGHAM Sharp	07/20/1793
MORGAN, Sally	WILSON, Abner	01/23/1800
MORGAN, Susan	RIGGS, Aderson	11/25/----
MORRIS, Eliza	MELTON, Albert	03/04/1841
MORRIS, Mary	MANSFIELD, Thomas	01/04/1853
MORRIS, Susannah	DODSON, Hugh H.	12/26/1816
MORRISON, Malinda A.	POWELL, Thomas J.	10/14/1863
MORTON, Avey	LINK, Byrd	03/12/1799
MORTON, Barbary	BAYNES, Archibald	02/22/1840
MORTON, Betsey	LINK, John	01/12/1802
MORTON, Elizabeth	BOMAN, Siar	05/03/1793
MORTON, Elizabeth	CRITTENDEN, Richard	06/29/1850
MORTON, Ellen	PRICE, O. D.	01/20/1864
MORTON, Maranda R.	LOVE, John C.	05/15/1839
MORTON, Martha	KENNON, Abel K.	01/28/1843
MORTON, Mary	BROWNING, Francis	12/22/1838
MORTON, Mary F.	HARRALSON, Henderson	03/31/1853
MORTON, Nancy	RICHMOND, John	12/21/1805
MORTON, Polley	MARTIN, Lewis	01/02/1811
MORTON, Polly	MEADOWS, Gabriel	05/14/1818
MORTON, Vina	THOMPSON, James	09/15/1866
MOSELEY, Agnes	LIPFORD, John J.	11/01/1855
MOSS, Catherine	SWIFT, Richard	11/02/1787
MOSS, Nancey	JEFFREYS, John	11/29/1823
MOSS, Polly	MANN, Henry	01/11/1826
MOSS, Susanah	GRAVETT, Lodwick	12/07/1789
MOTHERAL, Margret	DONALDSON, William	09/05/1793
MOTHERAL, Mary	DONELSON, Andrew	07/18/1791
MOTLEY, Virginia	TOTTON, Sidney	05/15/1866
MOTON, Pheby	ESTERS, Daniel	03/03/1825
MOTT, Phebe M.	SWIFT, John	05/04/1815
MUCHMORE, Hannah	GIBBS, John	01/18/1783
MUIRHEAD, Elizabeth	WALL, Byrd	12/04/1782
MULLENS, Rilla	BROWNING, Nathan	12/26/1810
MUNNALLY, Martha E.	NEAL, James M.	05/18/1846
MURPHEY, Betsey	BAULDWIN, John	09/24/1808
MURPHEY, Betsey	MCADEN, John	11/30/1797

MARRIAGE RECORDS OF CASWELL COUNTY, NORTH CAROLINA

BRIDE	GROOM	DATE
MURPHEY, Elizabeth	HOPPER, Samuel	03/24/1801
MURPHEY, Elizabeth	COBB, Hugh	09/20/1811
MURPHEY, Elizabeth F.	MCDADE, John M.	12/08/1853
MURPHEY, Frances	BAULDWIN, John	04/11/1825
MURPHEY, Harriet A.	RICHMOND, Yancey	07/08/1866
MURPHEY, Jane	CHAPMAN, Nelson	01/31/1849
MURPHEY, Lilla	EVANS, David H.	11/23/1860
MURPHEY, Lucy	DANIEL, Jno.	07/25/1805
MURPHEY, Margaret	MITCHELL, James E.	11/18/1819
MURPHEY, Marian	BROWNING, Edmund	09/09/1800
MURPHEY, Mary	AKIN, James	07/09/1779
MURPHEY, Mary	HARALSON, Herndon	10/04/1791
MURPHEY, Mary	MARTIN, George Jr.	12/27/1824
MURPHEY, Mary M.	BUCHANAN, Washington	01/08/1857
MURPHEY, Maryan	WARD, Richard C.	11/16/1806
MURPHEY, Matilda A.	CHATMAN, James	04/13/1866
MURPHEY, Nancy	MCINTOSH, Nimrod	12/15/1788
MURPHEY, Nancy	RUDD, Aldridge	08/28/1824
MURPHEY, Nancy	WARRIN, James	08/26/1800
MURPHEY, Nancy	WRIGHT, William G.	11/01/1841
MURPHEY, Nancy S.	THOMPSON, Thomas A.	11/03/1820
MURPHEY, Permilia A.	MURPHEY, John C.	05/15/1851
MURPHEY, Sena	SHELTON, Peter	06/05/1838
MURPHY, Elizabeth	LEWIS. Charles	04/02/1865
MURPHY, Lucinda	SMITH, Andrew H.	12/19/1846
MURPHY, Susan	SANDERS, Robert	12/23/1861
MURRAY, Eliza	MILES, John S.	01/25/1849
MURRAY, Eliza	WILEY, Green	11/30/1867
MURRAY, Elizabeth	WHITE, William H.	01/30/1830
MURRAY, Frances T.	MURRAY, Hector	01/07/1843
MURRAY, Mary Ann	HARRISON, John L.	12/15/1846
MURRAY, Mary F.	PETERSON, James O.	05/30/1858
MURRAY, Nancy	PLEASANT, Micajah Jr.	05/07/1827
MURRY, Franky	ST JOHN, Abraham	09/26/1806
MURRY, Martha M.	DAMERON, Willias A.	12/22/1853
MURRY, Sarah C.	MILES, John K.	12/23/1858
MUSE, Frances E.	ROBBINS, Thomas J.	04/19/1850
MUSICK, Pheby	ESTES, Bartlett	12/28/1790
MUSTING, Rachel	HENSLEY, Addison	11/25/1847
MUSTION, Sinai(?)	STEPHENS, Isaac	02/22/1849
MUZE, Sarah	BARNWELL, John	12/31/1792
MUZLE, Frances	LEA, Absalom	04/30/1794
MUZZAL, Frances	SOWELL, Thomas L.	01/21/1819
MUZZALL, Elizabeth	BARTLETT, Edward	02/24/1814
MUZZALL, Nancy	MITCHELL, David Jr.	02/12/1817
MUZZLE, Jane	MALONE, Thomas	10/20/1789
NANCE, Elizabeth	FITZGERALD, William	06/27/1848
NANCE, Isabella G.	BAYES, Robert J.	06/06/1866
NASH, Attelia	WHITTED, James	02/25/1813
NASH, Cornelia	FITCH, William W.	11/20/1866
NASH, Eliza	MCKNIGHT, Andrew	01/07/1783

MARRIAGE RECORDS OF CASWELL COUNTY, NORTH CAROLINA

BRIDE	GROOM	DATE
NASH, Eliza E.	MEUX, Thomas W.	10/01/1819
NASH, Farmesia	GRAHAM, William P.	09/28/1819
NASH, Manerva A.	WILSON, Thomas	03/21/1853
NASH, Nancy	ERWIN, James	10/10/1786
NASH, Viny	TOLLER, John	07/11/1854
NEAL, Becky	WATT, Russel	11/03/1867
NEAL, Cynthia A.	RUSSELL, William	03/29/1859
NEAL, Elizabeth	GRAVES, Azariah Jr.	06/20/1846
NEAL, Emeline	HENDERSON, Bryon	09/08/1866
NEAL, Harret A. E.	INGRAM, William R.	11/10/1857
NEAL, Mary A.	MITCHELL, John	11/18/1850
NEAL, Mary P.	SLEDGE, Crawford D.	02/03/1868
NEAL, Rebecca M.	LYNCH, William B.	04/04/1861
NEAL, Virginia E.	LYNN, Patrick H.	03/08/1857
NEELEY, Nicey	WARREN, Vinson	02/15/1800
NELLSON, Phebe	BRADSHER, Richard	10/31/1817
NELSON, Harriet	STEGALL, Durell	12/18/1850
NELSON, Martha B.	MOORE, William G.	10/29/1842
NELSON, Mary A.	HINTON, Allen	11/28/1843
NELSON, Mary C. V.	BARNWELL, William H.	09/21/1844
NELSON, Nancy	LANDERS, Abraham	11/08/1809
NELSON, Permelia	BROWNING, William	11/12/1823
NELSON, Polly	PARKS, Alfred	03/11/1806
NELSON, Rebecca	OWEN, Henry S.	09/28/1842
NELSON, Sally	THOMAS, John	08/15/1803
NELSON, Willy	CASE, John L.	06/22/1841
NEW, Susan	WALKER, John H.	08/24/1838
NEWBELL, Martha	HUGHES, B. G.	01/13/1851
NEWBELL, Parthena E.	SLATE, Richard J.	11/03/1841
NEWTON, Catherine	WALTERS, John	11/29/1789
NEWTON, Rachel	DINWIDDIE, John	11/01/1791
NICHOLS, Betsey	MASSEY, Joseph	11/30/1815
NICHOLS, Chainey	BARNETT, Clifton R.	06/28/1851
NICHOLS, Nancy J.	REEVES, Asa	10/09/1867
NICHOLS, Polly	KING, Harvey	04/25/1822
NICHOLSON, Martha	SHAPARD, Louisa	11/22/1796
NICHOLSON, Nancy D.	BOMAN, James W.	01/07/1860
NICKELS, Sarah	LYON, Richard	10/13/1791
NICKLESON, Betsy	CALDWELL, Alexander	02/13/1811
NIPPER, Eliza	GORDEN, William	05/11/1802
NOEL, Tabitha	WILEY, Thomas	04/12/1805
NORFLEET, Jean	MUZZALL, Joseph W.	05/02/1815
NORFLET, Julia A.	DANIEL, Robert	08/27/1842
NORFLETT, Fannie P.	BRANDON, Henry F.	10/22/1856
NORMAN, Ann	NICKOLS, Isaac	12/25/1818
NORMAN, Betsy	WHITE, Henry	06/12/1867
NORMAN, Maria	HOWARD, Baalam	02/29/1868
NORMAN, Mary S.	NORMAN, Charles H.	02/26/1856
NORMAN, Nancey	HUMPHREYS, Henry A.	07/19/1841
NORRIS, Catherine J.	POLLARD, Joseph B.	11/17/1865
NORTH, Polly	COBB, Mathew	02/03/1809

MARRIAGE RECORDS OF CASWELL COUNTY, NORTH CAROLINA

BRIDE	GROOM	DATE
NORTON, Elizabeth	PARR, William	12/26/1788
NORTON, Marguret	BRADY, Thomas	12/21/1791
NORWOOD, Parthena	KENNON, Richard	09/18/1850
NOWEL, Eleanor	WHITLOW, John	09/08/1791
NOWEL, Mary	STEVENS, William	01/04/1789
NOWELL, Elizabeth	HOWELL, Leroy	12/29/1795
NOWELL, Martha	WILEY, Alexander	03/20/1779
NOWLES, Holly	DRAPER, Joshua	04/01/1796
NOWLES, Nancy	REED, Blewford(?)	06/25/1793
NOWLES, Patsy	PETERSON, William	01/20/1814
NOWLIN, Frances A.	HODNETT, James M.	11/23/1841
NUNN, Ary	MURPHEY, James	12/14/1824
NUNN, Martha	MANLY, William	01/20/1830
NUNN, Mary	BENTON, Zachariah	01/11/1843
NUNN, Mary J.	TALLEY, William S.	01/02/1867
NUNN, Nancey	HARPER, Thomas	12/25/1824
NUNN, Nancy	LONDON, Joseph	08/11/1835
NUNNALLY, Agness J.	WARINER, Robert H.	11/04/1843
NUNNALLY, Elmira J.	BLACKWELL, Robert	05/19/1838
NUNNALLY, Hesteran	LINDSAY, Isaac N.	11/15/1865
NUNNALLY, Mary P.	STUBBLEFIELD, Peyton T.	10/27/1832
NUNNALY, Martha	COBB, Henry	12/07/1818
NUNNARY, Polly	BEAVER, Johnston	07/03/1792
NUTT, Cornelia A.	LEATH, John F.	04/03/1847
OAKLEY, Arrena	MOORE, Lawrence H.	10/30/1865
OAKLEY, Cornelia F.	MOORE, Lawrence H.	04/01/1854
OAKLEY, Jeen	DAY, Isaac	02/26/1791
OAKLEY, Sarah	BROWNING, Sanders	10/15/1857
OBRIAN, Mary Ann	COOK, Edmund	02/15/1830
OBRION, Hannah	TYREE, David	04/06/1830
OLDHAM, Amy	BURTON, Samuel	05/19/1784
OLIVER, Ann C.	HOUSE, Henderson	11/13/1839
OLIVER, Caroline	WAGSTAFF, John F.	01/25/1851
OLIVER, Damaris R.	YANCEY, William	12/16/1839
OLIVER, Frances	ADKINS, Henry F.	12/09/1847
OLIVER, Lovina	LEA, Jack	12/21/1867
OLIVER, Mary E.	GARLINGTON, John L.	05/30/1857
OLIVER, Matilda	WOMACK, William P.	01/27/1841
OLIVER, Nancy	MURRAY, Eli	07/28/1845
OLIVER, Patsy	POSEY, Alexander	08/09/1816
OLLIVER, Catherine	WARRIN, Stuart	02/22/1791
OLRIDG, Sally	CUTLER, Joshua	07/18/1816
ONEILL, Mary	ROPER, James	03/27/1792
ORR, Betsy	LOVELACE, Barnett	05/23/1821
ORR, Nancy	RAY, David	12/09/1820
ORR, Nellet	HUMPHRY, Colmore	02/28/1809
ORRIH, Lucy A.	LOCHER, Henry S.	07/28/1852
OVERBY, Elizabith	HINTON, Christopher	09/01/1830
OVERBY, Frances	DUNNAVANT, Jesse	10/25/1827
OVERBY, Nancy	HULGIN, John R.	01/02/1856
OVERBY, Rebecca	HINTON, James	05/09/1833

MARRIAGE RECORDS OF CASWELL COUNTY, NORTH CAROLINA

BRIDE	GROOM	DATE
OVERBY, Saluda	LOWERY, Henry	10/21/1850
OVERBY, Susanah	DUNAVENT, Edward	10/19/1818
OVERBY, Virginia	DUNEVANT, John H.	10/02/1866
OVERSTREET, Mary	OVERSTREET, John	04/01/1779
OWEN, Adeline A.	EVANS, Allen W.	09/30/1850
OWEN, Ann	FARELY, Abner B.	09/15/1835
OWEN, Caroline	CONNALLY, George R.	10/05/1854
OWEN, Elizabeth	WHITEFIELD, James	11/01/1817
OWEN, Lucy	HALL, Beverly	08/21/1854
OWEN, Lucy A.	WOODING, John E.	02/29/1834
OWEN, Martha	OWEN, John	01/25/1825
OWEN, Martha	REID, Anthony	03/09/1833
OWEN, Martha A.	EVANS, Samuel J.W.	12/05/1866
OWEN, Mary	HALL, Berry	03/28/1856
OWEN, Mary A.F.	NEAL, Abram T.	09/16/1865
OWEN, Mary P.	HUDSON, David P.	01/15/1833
OWEN, Nannie W.	LEWIS, George W.	12/08/1863
OWEN, Sally K.	NORRIS, William	10/01/1840
OWEN, Susanna	TERREL, William	10/31/1814
OWEN, Tabitha	REED, Anthony	11/30/1824
OWENS, Margaret	NELSON, Barzillai	08/26/1822
OWENS, Parthena	MCMURRY, Samuel	11/07/1818
PAGE, Betsy	VAUGHAN, James Jr.	02/14/1826
PAGE, Deborah	SCOTT, Azariah	05/03/1837
PAGE, Delila	PAGE, Samuel	12/21/1819
PAGE, Elizabeth	PAGE, Daniel J.	01/26/1860
PAGE, Esther	WATLINGTON, Sidney	12/27/1867
PAGE, Frances	RUDD, Rufus A.	06/15/1846
PAGE, Henrietta	PAGE, Josiah	04/05/1827
PAGE, Jane	RICE, John H.	12/30/1845
PAGE, Lucinda	BOSWELL, William	12/19/1837
PAGE, Lucy	MANLEY, John	11/14/1815
PAGE, Martha	FERRELL, William	04/16/1825
PAGE, Mary	BARTON, Chesley L.	05/15/1855
PAGE, Mary	MANLY, George W.	03/25/1852
PAGE, Mary	PAGE, Zenith	04/06/1858
PAGE, Mary C.	SARTIN, Moses R.	10/11/1865
PAGE, Milley	FULLINGTON, William	01/03/1825
PAGE, Nancey	EVANS, Berry	12/01/1830
PAGE, Pamelia F.	KING, Joseph	06/26/1850
PAGE, Rachael J.	FERRELL, John O.	02/03/1859
PAGE, Rachel	DRAKE, Thomas	06/27/1829
PAGE, Salley	LOVELESS, Pryor	08/29/1809
PAGE, Sally A.	FERRELL, Henry W.	04/01/1858
PAGE, Sarah A.	KERSEY, Clark A.	12/12/1860
PAGE, Susan	FITCH, Anderson N.	10/20/1860
PAGE, Susan M.	ESTIS, Richard B.	01/04/1855
PALMER, Elizabeth	GUNN, John Jr.	07/05/1827
PALMER, Hettie	GRAVES, Peter	11/19/1867
PALMER, Lucy A.	SAWYER, John	05/12/1845
PALMER, Lucy L.	MILES, Thomas H.	11/18/1863

MARRIAGE RECORDS OF CASWELL COUNTY, NORTH CAROLINA

BRIDE	GROOM	DATE
PALMER, Mary	PRICE, George	09/26/1823
PALMER, Sarah	VANHOOK, Thomas	06/21/1779
PAMPLIN, Virginia H.	OLIVER, John M.	11/15/1865
PANE, Polly	MILLER, Tho.	05/12/----
PANTON, Isabella	FERRELL, Moses	12/27/1867
PARISH, Catherine	WHITEEST, James	06/05/1860
PARISH, Harriet	RICE, Thomas	12/22/1828
PARISH, Mary J.	ROBERTS, John R.L.	12/07/1849
PARKER, Ann	MCNEELEY, Addom	12/20/1791
PARKER, Edey	TYLER, Zachariah	04/08/1822
PARKER, Elizabeth	COOPER, Martin	01/20/1790
PARKER, Elizabeth	WELLS, Hardy	10/20/1784
PARKES, Susanna	DAVIS, James	04/02/1822
PARKS, Artilia	HENSLEY, John	12/24/1840
PARKS, Celey	MALONE, Stephen	10/01/1804
PARKS, Celia	SMITH, Joseph	11/08/1827
PARKS, Drady	BROWNING, James S.	11/12/1826
PARKS, Eliza	HENSLEE, Addison	09/15/1843
PARKS, Elizabeth	POE, John	01/12/1793
PARKS, Hariet	BOULDIN, Edward	07/03/1838
PARKS, Mary	LANDERS, John	10/15/1833
PARKS, Milly	WALKER, James	11/22/1843
PARKS, Nancy	COUSINS, James	08/12/1820
PARKS, Rachel	BROWNING, Nimord	08/21/1789
PARKS, Sarah T.	WALKER, William A.	11/14/1843
PARRISH, Eliza E.	PASCHAL, Ezekiel D.	10/09/1850
PARRISH, Elizabeth	SAWYER, Stephen	01/09/1816
PARRISH, Martha	NICHOLS, James E.	07/18/1867
PARRISH, Polley	GOMER, John	03/11/1816
PARRISH, S.T.	ELIOTT, George C.	03/17/1860
PARSCHALL, Sarah	SMITHY, John	02/05/1842
PARSONS, Mary	SLAYTON, James	10/20/1849
PARTEE, Marshaw	JONES, Beverly	06/17/1817
PASCHAEL, Frances	SERTAIN, Elisha	12/08/1840
PASCHAEL, Nancy	PASHAEL, William	01/14/1840
PASCHAEL, Susan	BUTLER, Thomars	03/27/1839
PASCHAL, Rebecca H.	BROOKES, Iverson I. W.	02/05/1861
PASCHAL, Sally	GANNAWAY, G. T. F.	02/12/1868
PASCHALL, Catherine	ORR, William	11/09/1804
PASCHALL, Eliza	SUMERS, Pharo	11/05/1841
PASCHALL, Mary Ann	DUNAWAY, Allen	12/05/1841
PASCHALL, Nancy	POYNOR, Jesse	01/03/1818
PASCHALL, Polly	SMITHEY, Thomas	08/03/1837
PASCHALL, Slema	LOVELACE, William	01/24/1842
PASCHALL, Susanna	HUMPHREYS, Henry	09/24/1824
PASCHELL, Hannah	DUNCAN, Jessee	07/14/1780
PASCHELL, Reliance	MORGAN, William	01/17/1806
PASKELL, Sarah	SOMERS, Zera	02/22/1837
PASKILL, Nancy	HUMFRES, Alfred	01/11/1825
PASS, Catherine	WILSON, George L.	09/11/1820
PASS, Elizabeth	RICHARDSON, James	04/04/1803

MARRIAGE RECORDS OF CASWELL COUNTY, NORTH CAROLINA

BRIDE	GROOM	DATE
PASS, Ellis	TAYLOR, George	12/22/1795
PASS, Fanny	TAYLOR, Abel	12/22/1795
PASS, Jane	FULLER, Henry	07/21/1867
PASS, Jemima	WILLIAMS, William	12/03/1788
PASS, Lucy	RAMEY, George	12/30/1866
PASS, Martha	GILLASPY, Gidel	11/24/1817
PASS, Mary	PHELPS, Thomas	12/17/1791
PASS, Rachel M.	YARBROUGH, Richard L.	08/24/1858
PASS, Rebeccah	GANN, William	03/03/1798
PASS, Sally	MOORE, Jesse	01/07/1785
PASS, Sarah	PHELPS, Hiram	10/06/1818
PATELLOR, Frances H.	CURRIE, William	12/28/1842
PATILLO, Elizabeth B.	BAYNES, Thornton Y.	05/10/1854
PATITE, Adaline	HOOPER, Z.	06/07/1854
PATTERSON, Cassandra	SWANN, William W.	10/20/1843
PATTERSON, Cassindia Carol	GREGORY, Thomas	04/04/1825
PATTERSON, Elizabeth	MERIDETH, James	10/31/1780
PATTERSON, Fanny	SWANN, Joseph	01/17/1811
PATTERSON, Jane	DIX, William	01/28/1836
PATTERSON, Martha A.	ROBERTSON, Thompson G.	11/09/1854
PATTERSON, Mary	BRAGG, Cicero	03/07/1855
PATTERSON, Pelina	ADAMS, William A.	09/02/1858
PATTILLO, Ann E.	KIMBELL, Thomas M.	11/19/1837
PATTILLO, M. V.	PAYLOR, James H.	03/14/1865
PAUL, Betsy	WARD, Thomas	09/03/1815
PAUL, Charlotte	PHIPPS, James	04/28/1848
PAUL, Elizabeth	DENSON, Richard	08/28/1828
PAUL, Patsey	BENNETT, Jesse	11/25/1788
PAUL, Rachael	COE, Joshua	10/26/1784
PAYLOR, Manda	PULLIAM, James	12/19/1867
PAYNE, Ann V.	MCGEHEE, Albert G.	10/17/1834
PAYNE, Betsy	SMITHEY, John	08/13/1805
PAYNE, Caty	ROBERSON, Christopher	12/17/1835
PAYNE, Caty	RUSSEL, Joseph	04/07/1815
PAYNE, Clary	COCK, Augustin	01/20/1789
PAYNE, Elizabeth B.	GRAVES, Iverson	10/02/1828
PAYNE, Elizabeth C.	STOKES, Joel A.	10/07/1836
PAYNE, Lucinda	DENTON, John	07/08/1842
PAYNE, Martha	SMITH, Stephen	10/16/1827
PAYNE, Mary	FORD, Levi	01/04/1814
PAYNE, Missouri F.	LEMMON, H.S.	07/26/1846
PAYNE, Polly	HARRIS, Christopher	01/12/1801
PAYNE, Priscilla	BURTON, Noel	04/08/1822
PAYNES, Frances	NOBLE, John	04/06/1807
PAYNOR, Eleanor	SANDERS, Zepheniah	08/25/1822
PEARCE, Delilah	ELMORE, William	08/02/1819
PEARCE, Philadelphia	BULLES, John	04/30/1794
PENDERGRASS, Mary	SHAW, James	01/09/1786
PENICK, Barbara J.	MAYNARD, Wagstaff	12/04/1841
PENICK, Elizabeth A.	LONG, John D.	02/08/1854

MARRIAGE RECORDS OF CASWELL COUNTY, NORTH CAROLINA

BRIDE	GROOM	DATE
PENIX, Prudence	DODSON, Matthew	12/20/1819
PENNIX, Sallie A.P.O.	MCKINSEY, John A.	02/22/1864
PEOPLES, Ursley D.	OLDHAM, Richard	10/20/1786
PERKINS, Betsy	PAGE, John	11/10/1806
PERKINS, Disey	COLEMAN, Archibald	02/13/1795
PERKINS, Elizabeth	FOSTER, John	07/29/1816
PERKINS, Elizabeth	HUBBARD, William	03/18/1852
PERKINS, Frances	WARE, William	10/02/1781
PERKINS, Lucy	GRANT, Neely	09/23/1793
PERKINS, Lucy A.	CASE, Luther A.	02/13/1856
PERKINS, Malinda C.	NEW, John D.	11/13/1866
PERKINS, Mary A.	RICE, Jeremiah	06/03/1851
PERKINS, Nancey	LAOFMAN, Benjamin	09/07/1813
PERKINS, Polley	KING, William	10/30/1804
PERKINS, Rachel	KING, Isaac	11/07/1808
PERKINS, Salley	FOSTER, Anthony	10/01/1811
PERKINS, Salley	LOAFMAN, Edward	07/24/1810
PERKINS, Sarah	WILLIAMS, Winston	09/24/1842
PERRY, Eliza J.	WILKINS, Joseph	05/21/1858
PERRY, Jenny	BRUCE, Thomas	07/07/1792
PERRY, Mary	WILLIAMS, Alfred	12/12/1836
PERSONS, Helena	SMITH, John	10/07/1826
PETERSON, Blanche	HALL, David	03/07/1825
PETERSON, Delilah	BENNETT, James	11/14/1833
PETERSON, Martha	SATTERFIELD, Anthony	12/27/1825
PETERSON, Nancy	STAFFORD, Adam	09/07/1790
PETERSON, Nicy L.	TANKERSLEY, Pleasant	08/05/1852
PETERSON, Polly	BLACKLOCK, John	12/15/1818
PETERSON, Polly	PETERSON, Vincent	05/19/1821
PETERSON, Sarah	WILDER, William V.	09/29/1836
PETERSON, Susan	PAGE, Noah	01/10/1820
PETERSON, Susanna	MORTON, Edward Z.	07/03/1825
PETTIFOOT, Eliza	MASON, Henry	08/06/1859
PETTIFORD, Frances	CRAWFORD, John	02/20/1868
PETTY, Mariah A.	HUBBARD, John S.	12/11/1838
PHELPS, Betty W.	BENNETT, James W.	02/20/1866
PHELPS, Delphia	ROAN, George	03/29/1788
PHELPS, Frances	BUCKNER, James	02/03/1849
PHELPS, Lucy	SMITH, Willis B.	11/11/1794
PHELPS, Nancy	ROAN, Thomas	11/14/1782
PHELPS, Nicey N.	OLIVER, Josiah	12/ 2/1834
PHELPS, Rachel	SARGENT, James	08/04/1791
PHELPS, Rebeckah	HICKS, Larkin W.	10/08/1818
PHILIPS, Adeline	GOODWIN, James H.	05/09/1837
PHILIPS, Frances	POWELL, Peter Jr.	09/19/1832
PHILIPS, Mahala	KENNON, John	02/02/1826
PHILIPS, Mar	MCLAUGHLAN, Rawley	10/16/1847
PHILIPS, Mildred A.	NORVELL, Braxton	12/28/1830
PHILIPS, Nancy	COZENS, Tazwell	04/21/1851
PHILIPS, Polly	TONEY, Nat	11/23/1837
PHILIPS, Susan	LONG, Joseph	05/31/1838

MARRIAGE RECORDS OF CASWELL COUNTY, NORTH CAROLINA

BRIDE	GROOM	DATE
PHILIPS, Susan	PILES, Henry	07/01/1858
PHILLIPS, Ann	RIGGS, John	04/01/1840
PHILLIPS, Celly	JONES, Andrew	11/30/1843
PHILLIPS, Eliza	GUNN, John	04/04/1866
PHILLIPS, Mary	BOWE, George	12/26/1866
PICKEL, Jean	WATKINS, Phillip	12/23/1790
PIERCE, Nancey	GROOM, William	03/24/1813
PIERSON, Jane	MCKINNEY, William	02/20/1820
PIKE, Nancy	MCALISTER, John	01/26/1801
PILES, Eliza	ROBERTS, Henry	12/22/1836
PILES, Jane	COOPER, Plumer	03/24/1867
PILES, Jane	FREEMAN, Willis W.	05/06/1848
PINCHBACK, Adaline	WILLIS, Jerry	04/15/1867
PINDEXTER, Nancy	BADGETT, Peter	09/16/1820
PINICK, Jane M.	TRAVIS, Thomas	08/20/1830
PINIX, Judeth	BURTON, William	12/11/1827
PINIX, Sarah	STAMPS, William	11/20/1825
PINIX, Tabitha F.	MONTGOMERY, Edward	02/22/1825
PINNICK, Sarah B.	BALDWIN, John C.	12/27/1866
PINNIX, Jane	NUNNALLY, Hartwell	11/09/1867
PINNIX, Margaret	OUTLAW, Samuel	05/16/1867
PINNIX, Martha	PINNIX, Robert	09/02/1866
PINNIX, Mary A.	DICKEY, Jacob	12/17/1839
PINNIX, Mary E.	TUNSTALL, Green	06/07/1867
PINNIX, Mary J.	BROCKES, William 1.	02/03/1864
PINSON, Elizabeth	GROOM, Robert	12/04/1824
PINSON, Frances	PAGE, Zacharian	10/01/1867
PINSON, Rebecca	PINSON, Isaac	12/15/1810
PINSON, Rhody	CAMPBELL, Banister	12/09/1815
PINSON, Susannah	COLLIER, Thomas	12/21/1822
PIPER, Catherine	TERRELL, Joseph J.	09/18/1860
PIRANT, Rebecca	BENNATT, Richard	02/18/1836
PIRKINS, Nancy	FOSTER, John	12/22/1783
PISTOLE, Patsy	WOSHAM, Robert	06/10/1---
PITMAN, Emsey H.	MCFARLING, Zechariah	12/10/1835
PITTARD, Ann	YELCCK, James	10/26/1813
PITTARD, Frances	MASCN, Stephen	05/02/1820
PITTARD, Nancey	HADCOCK, Stephen	10/30/1820
PITTARD, Rebecca	MALCNE, John	11/05/1816
PITTS, Susan	BROWNING, Edmund E.	10/13/1841
PLEASANT, Artesia	MURPHEY, William	02/06/1839
PLEASANT, Dolly	MILES, William	09/10/1821
PLEASANT, Elizabeth	GRAVES, James	11/18/1824
PLEASANT, Elizabeth	DISHOUGH, Lewis	04/01/1845
PLEASANT, Harriet	RASCO, William	07/05/1815
PLEASANT, Leatha	WARREN, Micajah	04/24/1859
PLEASANT, Louisa	WARREN, Benjamin	08/12/1833
PLEASANT, Lucy	ALDRIDGE, Richard	01/21/1822
PLEASANT, Lucy	GRIFFIN, William	04/13/1812
PLEASANT, Lucy	TURKER, James	08/05/1793
PLEASANT, Martha	RASCOE, John	12/05/1816

MARRIAGE RECORDS OF CASWELL COUNTY, NORTH CAROLINA

BRIDE	GROOM	DATE
PLEASANT, Martha A.	PAGE, William C.	12/28/1848
PLEASANT, Mary M.	FLINTOFF, John F.	05/11/1850
PLEASANT, Mary Milberey	HENSLEE, William	01/23/1811
PLEASANT, Nancey	BENSON, John	02/25/1828
PLEASANT, Patcey	FLORENCE, William	11/06/1808
PLEASANT, Patty	BENSON, Alexander	02/10/1802
PLEASANT, Polly	VAUGHAN, Nicholas	03/06/1804
PLEASANT, Sarah A.	UNDERWOOD, William	12/05/1843
PLEASANTS, Artelia S.	MADDEN, Samuel Q.	10/08/1861
PLEASENT, Betsy	STALLCUP, Austin	09/24/1802
PLEASENT, Sylvia	STALLCUP, John	01/30/1801
PLERRA, Susan	NIPPER, James	08/05/1809
POGUE, Fanny	ROSSON, Abner	02/20/1790
POGUE, Hannar	FARMER, William	12/30/1790
POINDEXTER, Eliza	BULLOCK, John C.	12/20/1815
POINOR, Sally	MASON, Stephen	07/29/1794
POLSTON, Elizabeth	SMITH, Daniel	12/08/1804
PONDS, Betsy	CARMAN, Elihjah	07/11/1797
PONDS, Sally	WHITE, David	11/19/1804
PONSONBY, Elizabeth	VERSER, Daniel	09/30/1837
POOL, Anniss	MATLOCK, William	11/20/1848
POOL, Matilda M.	FAULKNER, Joseph T.	10/16/1859
POORE, Betty	FARLEY, William T.	08/29/1866
POPE, Mary R.	RUCKER, George G.	12/30/1850
PORTER, Polley	BIRK, James Jr.	04/08/1809
PORTER, Sally	GOOCH, James	11/29/1801
POSTON, Betsy	SMITH, William	06/28/1800
POSTON, Priscilla	DICKINS, William	05/06/1794
POSTON, Rebeccah	JOHNSON, James	06/19/1781
POTEAT, Liley A.	SMITH, James M.	08/07/1859
POTEAT, Martha	BRADSHER, Henderson	12/07/1867
POTEAT, Nancy	SANDERS, James M.	11/23/1865
POTEAT, Sallie E.	LINDSEY, George R.	02/05/1861
POTEAT, Sarah	HALL, John	07/03/1859
POTEAT, Tempa	MCCLAIN, Joseph	03/17/1806
POTEAT, V. E.	BRYANT, W. W. R.	02/12/1867
POTEATE, Cindy	POOL, Isaac	01/12/1867
POTEATE, Elizabeth	MERRITT, Solomon	12/10/1789
POTEET, Betsy	POWELL, Barzilai	12/17/1825
POTEET, Nancy	MORTON, John	01/03/1820
POTEET, Nancy	POWELL, Henry	07/14/1826
POUND, Nancy	WRIGHT, Elisha	05/28/1812
POWEL, Eliza A.	HORTON, John	01/28/1835
POWELL, Adaline	WINDSOR, Edward	06/19/1867
POWELL, Amy	WRAY, Thomas	02/26/1825
POWELL, Ann Catharin	FULLER, Albert G.	10/11/1847
POWELL, Anna	CARTER, Thomas	02/27/1816
POWELL, Ary W.	DEVINEY, Madison	04/02/1838
POWELL, Elizabeth	PADGETT, Tinsly	01/14/1833
POWELL, Elizabeth A.	HENSLEY, Henry T.	02/22/1866
POWELL, Emily C.	WHITTED, Levi	04/16/1857

MARRIAGE RECORDS OF CASWELL COUNTY, NORTH CAROLINA

BRIDE	GROOM	DATE
POWELL, Fanny	ADAMS, Philip	06/24/1800
POWELL, Hannah	ANGLIN, Caleb	11/09/1809
POWELL, Harriet E.	TURNER, Green	12/27/1849
POWELL, Jemima	COBB, Andrew J.	01/22/1846
POWELL, Kesiah	PRITCHETT, Edward	06/09/1805
POWELL, Leah	PATTERSON, William B.	05/19/1843
POWELL, M. E.	GOODSON, George T.	09/24/1865
POWELL, Margaret E.	GLASS, John D.	02/14/1854
POWELL, Maria A.	SAWYERS, Henry	02/22/1843
POWELL, Mary A.	PERKINS, John	02/10/1846
POWELL, Mary C.	HORTON, William J.	01/26/1862
POWELL, Mary C.	PHILLIPS, Paul C.	10/17/1863
POWELL, Mary G.	EDWARDS, Christopher B.	11/16/1865
POWELL, Mary J.	SMITH, Henry	03/17/1840
POWELL, Matilda	COBB, Samuel M.	01/05/1854
POWELL, Nancy M.	CHAMBERS, Joshua	02/17/1832
POWELL, Nanny W.	WILLIAMS, Ralph D.	04/09/1863
POWELL, Polly	HARRELSON, James	01/06/1834
POWELL, Polly	MOORFIELD, James	09/13/1816
POWELL, Rebecca F.	GILLISPIE, David A.	09/30/1848
POWELL, Susan	SOMERS, Henry	10/21/1866
POWELL, Virginia V.	FORBES, William	05/09/1867
POYNER, Sally	RICE, Nathan Jr.	12/23/1801
POYNER, Sarah	BUCKLEY, Nathan	01/04/1792
PRATHER, Elizabeth W.	HAMLETON, Joseph	12/18/1831
PRATHER, Margarett	CORNWELL, Joseph	12/31/1833
PRATHER, Martha A.	ATKINSON, James H.	11/14/1836
PRATHER, Mary W.	FARISH, Adam T.	03/16/1836
PRENDERGAST, Caroline	BARNWELL, Carter	08/02/1837
PRENDERGAST, Elizabeth	LASHLEY, Powell	09/21/1844
PRENDERGAST, Harriet	NELSON, Samuel	11/14/1820
PRENDERGAST, Nancy	CHANDLER, Stephen J.	12/28/1829
PRICE, Ann W.	PRICE, John P.	11/10/1851
PRICE, Elizabeth	BURGESS, William	08/20/1816
PRICE, Fannie	BENTON, Daniel	09/06/1867
PRICE, Jenny	VENABLE, Joseph	02/22/1866
PRICE, Louisa	PRICE, Grinville	05/27/1866
PRICE, Margaret A.	WATT, Jno.	04/29/1857
PRICE, Martha A.	DEJARRATTE, James P.	12/13/1856
PRICE, Mary	TULLOH, William	03/05/1800
PRICE, Mary A.	WITHERS, Elijah B.	03/25/1863
PRICE, Mary J.	CHAMBERS, William P.	07/19/1843
PRICE, Mary M.	MCDANIEL, John	04/08/1828
PRICE, Mary S.	BETHELL, William P.	06/15/1865
PRICE, Matilda	PRICE, William	12/18/1866
PRICE, Nancy	NUNNALLY, William H.	05/06/1823
PRICE, Nancy	PASCHELL, Thomas	02/11/1789
PRICE, Sarepta W.	HODGES, Washington T.	07/27/1858
PRICE, Susan C.	CHANDLER, James C.	07/11/1852
PRICE, Susana B.	HARRISON, Charles P.	10/12/1820
PRUETT, Frances	PASS, Fantelleroy	03/10/1837

MARRIAGE RECORDS OF CASWELL COUNTY, NORTH CAROLINA

BRIDE	GROOM	DATE
PRUITT, Emily	TRUE, Benjamin H.	01/19/1853
PRYOR, Elizabeth W.	LAYN, Garret C.	12/11/1834
PRYOR, Tabitha	WAITE, William	12/11/1778
PRYRANT, Subrina	POTEAT, William	03/23/1856
PUCKET, Agnes	TURNER, Thomas	12/18/1856
PUCKETT, Polly	SCOTT, William	09/30/1826
PUGH, Martha	ALLEN, Thomas T.	10/25/1837
PUGH, Mary E.	PUGH, Alfred M.	03/01/1857
PULHIM, Agniss	FOSTER, John	12/31/1786
PULLHAM, Jane Allin	BRANDON, Thomas Jr.	01/08/1785
PULLIAM, Ann	ELLIOTT, Granderson	04/15/1867
PULLIAM, Susannah	HOLLOWAY, James	01/19/1796
PURKINS, Frances	WILLIAMS, James M.	03/30/1858
PURKINS, Julia A.	BROWN, John T.	01/07/1861
PURKINS, Mary J.	HUBBARD, Thomas	09/13/1856
PUTTERY, Sally	BURCH, Larkin	01/22/1812
PYRANT, Mary	TURNER, Thomas	11/17/1862
PYRANT, Nelly	GOSSETT, Thomas	01/04/1808
PYRON, Elenor	CRITINTON, Deveraux	07/03/1832
PYRON, Frances	KENNON, John	08/28/1840
PYRON, Jane	HARGIS, John	06/03/1778
PYRON, Margery	ESTES, Micajah	07/08/1801
QUARLES, Nancey	HUBBARD, William	09/14/1807
QUINE, Betsy	STAFFORD, John	06/13/1791
QUINE, Nelly	DAVIS, James	10/23/1816
QUINE, Sarah	CARMAN, William	03/27/1792
RAGLAND, Ann W.	THOMAS, Richard W.	06/30/1832
RAGLAND, Martha S.	FARMER, James M.	11/25/1849
RAGLAND, Orphie	RAYNER, Willie	08/11/1850
RAGSDALE, Elizabeth	GATTY, Joseph	12/22/1789
RAGSDALE, Leander	BRADSHER, Henry	09/27/1867
RAGSDALE, Martha A.	HILL, Anderson G.	11/07/1853
RAGSDALE, Mary E.	DIX, William	01/26/1862
RAIMEY, Catharine	HARRIS, Reubin	01/16/1837
RAIMEY, Delilah L.	HOOPER, William	11/07/1833
RAIMEY, Elizabeth	HOOPER, Zachariah Sr.	05/16/1825
RAIMEY, Sally	BURROUGHS, Bennett	02/16/1820
RAIMEY, Susan H.	DONOHO, Alexander	08/06/1832
RAINEY, Ann S.	RICHHOND, Caleb H.	04/11/1830
RAINEY, Elizabeth	JOHNSTON, William	03/20/1783
RAINEY, Elizabeth H.	JONES, Edward D.	10/10/1811
RAINEY, Elizabeth S.	DISHOUGH, Reddick	12/12/1817
RAINEY, Jane	DUNCAN, Nathaniel	11/06/1782
RAINEY, Polly	WELLS, Thomas	03/11/1809
RAINEY, Sarah A.	GROOM, John	04/04/1858
RAINY, Fannie	HOOPER, George J. N.	11/30/1857
RAMEY, Margaret L.	WYNN, Stith	09/29/1847
RAMEY, Susan	RAMEY, Edward	12/05/1846
RANDAL, Nancy	WESLEY, John	01/22/1806
RANDOLPH, Betsey	HUTSON, Moses	10/09/1784
RANKIN, Vottory	VANHOOK, Laurence Sr.	11/01/1787

MARRIAGE RECORDS OF CASWELL COUNTY, NORTH CAROLINA

BRIDE	GROOM	DATE
RANSOM, Betsey	BAILEY, Noah	09/05/1809
RAON, Nancey	HOOD, Martin	12/25/1821
RASBERRY, Betsey	HICKS, Luke	05/14/1810
RASCO, Mrs. Nancy	RASCO, W.M.	10/19/1867
RAWLINS, Martha A.	FERGUSON, Samuel D.	01/06/1858
RAY, Mary	BALDWIN, Henry S.	10/22/1824
RAY, Mary	WATKINS, John	08/19/1807
RAY, Rachel	PRUIT, John A.	10/10/1850
RAY, Sarah	BRADLEY, Samuel	12/26/1837
RAY, Susanna	SLEDGE, Littleton	11/24/1821
RAYNOLDS, Lelia S.	TAYLOR, John W.	05/29/1861
REA, Sarah	MOORE, John	04/11/1821
READ, Mary	STANFIELD, William A.	05/04/1854
REAR, Lucy R.	HAWKS, Randal	12/24/1827
REASE, Elizabeth	ESTES, Bartlet	12/06/1819
REASON, Mary	FLETCHER, James	11/28/1781
REAVES, Mary E.	GARROD, John C.	04/11/1867
REDDEN, Catherine	MASSEY, William Sr.	06/09/1835
REED, Clarissa H.	SMITH, Maurice	04/27/1830
REED, Haley	BALLARD, Andrew	12/23/1809
REED, Lucy	TAYLOR, John	11/01/1802
REED, Nancy	GOWING, Vincent	12/30/1806
REED, Rebecah	BRACKIN, Samuel	10/29/1799
REED, (?) Nancy	WILSON, William	01/--/1812
REID, Eliza W.	RIGGS, Thomas	11/26/1849
REID, Frances	THOMAS, Woodliff	11/08/1834
REID, Isabella V.	MCKINNEY, William T.	12/15/1858
REID, Laura	PAYLOR, Moses	02/14/1867
REID, Letetia J.	DAVIS, Henry J.	12/15/1852
REID, Mary	PUCKET, Goselin	01/25/1808
REID, Mary	RAY, Darling	11/12/1794
REID, Mary Ann	GRAVES, Benjiman	02/25/1867
REID, Mary E.	INGRAM, James	05/13/1858
REID, Milly	BRUCE, Scott	11/02/1867
REID, Sarah	SLADE, William	12/23/1856
REID, Silvey	ROBERTSON, William	04/20/1867
REND, Mary J.	FOX, Nathan	11/06/1848
RENNETT, Ruth	GOING, Sherwood	04/30/1793
REW, Nannie	GUINN, James	12/27/1866
REYNOLDS, Lucy	WILES, Luke	11/22/1814
REYNOLDS, Sarah	HACKNEY, Samuel	09/23/1791
REYNOLDS, Theodita	WHITE, James B.	03/12/1833
RHOADES, Mary	RUARK, Samuel	08/03/1815
RICE, Ann	OLDHAM, John	02/26/1783
RICE, Ann	WILLIAMS, Daniel	01/05/1786
RICE, Betsy	SIMPSON, Oliver	03/10/1810
RICE, Betsy	CHUNING, Richard	03/26/1802
RICE, Delphia	BUZWELL, John	03/19/1799
RICE, Dorathy C.	WATLINGTON, Jonathan B.	06/07/1823
RICE, Eliza	STUBBLEFIELD, Richard C.	06/08/1832
RICE, Elizabeth	LEA, James	03/09/1841

MARRIAGE RECORDS OF CASWELL COUNTY, NORTH CAROLINA

BRIDE	GROOM	DATE
RICE, Elizabeth	VERNON, Robert T.	12/21/1854
RICE, Elizabeth B.	GWYN, Rice	03/01/1842
RICE, Frances B.	WILLIS, Anderson	05/24/1825
RICE, Harriet	WILLIAMSON, Thompson	01/12/1867
RICE, Henrietta	RICE, Edmond	12/05/1795
RICE, Henrietta	RICE, Nathaniel L.	12/23/1812
RICE, Julia A.	MAYNARD, Wagstaff	04/21/1859
RICE, Kerin Happuch	ANGLIN, William	11/15/1789
RICE, Kerin Happuch	ANGLIN, Wright	11/15/1789
RICE, Liddey	BUSH, Ezenus	06/14/1797
RICE, Martha G.	WILSON, Dennis	08/10/1818
RICE, Marthy E.	HAYMES, John B.	07/12/1865
RICE, Mary	WATTS, Samuel	01/25/1808
RICE, Mary F.	THACKER, Isaac	08/29/1849
RICE, Milly	CHALLES, John	11/25/1786
RICE, Minerva J.	ANDERSON, Jno. Q.	12/16/1863
RICE, Nancy	BIRK, Anderson	11/20/1804
RICE, Nancy	MILES, Jacob Jr.	10/07/1783
RICE, Nancy E.	BEAVER, James P.	08/23/1859
RICE, Patsy	SCOGGIN, William	06/20/1804
RICE, Polly	SCOTT, James	07/02/1806
RICE, Polly	WALKER, John M.	10/17/1828
RICE, Rebecca	NEAL, Zachariah	12/16/1811
RICE, Sally	BLACKWELL, Whitson G.	04/07/1853
RICE, Sally	LANE, Joseph	10/10/1809
RICE, Sarah	COBB, Hugh E.	12/22/1832
RICE, Sarah M.	ARNOLD, James W.	01/06/1840
RICE, Susan	WALKER, Benjamin	03/01/1833
RICE, Susanna	YANCEY, Willy	05/12/1804
RICE, Willy	FIELDER, John	09/28/1842
RICE, Zilpah	JUDKINS, Edmund	11/19/1832
RICH, Nancy V.	SIMPSON, Alvis	12/20/1859
RICHARDSON Nancy P.	SERGANT, Stephen	01/01/1828
RICHARDSON, Elizabeth	COOK, Philip	06/09/1792
RICHARDSON, Elizabeth	GLASS, Joshua S.	11/24/1846
RICHARDSON, Frances	HUBBARD, Ralph	03/06/1821
RICHARDSON, Harriet M.	FURGUSON, Robert F.	09/14/1854
RICHARDSON, Louisa	RIGGS, George W.	12/03/1846
RICHARDSON, Lucy	GATES, John	03/10/1821
RICHARDSON, Lucy	JAMES, David	07/18/1848
RICHARDSON, Mary	BEAVER, Jesse	02/13/1786
RICHARDSON, Mary	PRICE, John S.	12/22/1824
RICHARDSON, Mary A.	WITHERS, Lewis H.	02/20/1844
RICHARDSON, Mary S.	SNEAD, Wm. L.	12/08/1849
RICHARDSON, Prudence	HARRISON, Calloway J.	02/16/1839
RICHARDSON, Rachel	MANN, Forgis	02/21/1797
RICHARDSON, Susan	MARTIN, Robert	11/30/1781
RICHARDSON, Susan	STEVENS, George	08/19/1830
RICHARDSON, Susanna	MCKINNEY, Drury	09/19/1820
RICHARDSON, Unity	COOKE, William	07/08/1793
RICHMON, Susan	NEWMAN, Aaron	08/02/1866

MARRIAGE RECORDS OF CASWELL COUNTY, NORTH CAROLINA

BRIDE	GROOM	DATE
RICHMOND, Agness S.	PITTARD, Benjamin S.	01/07/1839
RICHMOND, Agness S.	BURTON, James M.	10/20/1848
RICHMOND, Ann	MCCADEN, Atkinson	06/30/1866
RICHMOND, Anne	MATLOCK, B. L.	01/18/1843
RICHMOND, Catherine A.	MARTIN, Thomas	10/17/1842
RICHMOND, Elizabeth	DONALDSON, Robert	01/16/1799
RICHMOND, Elizabeth	RAINEY, John P.Jr.	05/12/1855
RICHMOND, Elizabeth F.	WHITT, E. Jones	08/24/1857
RICHMOND, Ellen	RAMSEUR, S.Dodson	10/27/1863
RICHMOND, Fanny	POTEAT, George	01/26/1867
RICHMOND, Fanny	WALTON, Lewis	03/25/1867
RICHMOND, Frances	WOODS, Archy S.G.	11/20/1838
RICHMOND, Hulday A.	SMITH, Thomas B.	06/02/1860
RICHMOND, Jane	DAMERON, John	08/14/1834
RICHMOND, Jane	DODSON, Woodson	12/26/1867
RICHMOND, Maranda	RICHMOND, Willis M.	10/06/1846
RICHMOND, Margarett C.	MALONE, Lewis	03/11/1836
RICHMOND, Martha W.	REID, Jno. W.	11/21/1865
RICHMOND, Mary	BOULTON, George	01/28/1867
RICHMOND, Mary	MORGAN, Addison	12/02/1839
RICHMOND, Mary A.	BROWN, Green W.	03/15/1857
RICHMOND, Mary A.	VANHOOK, Solomon	04/29/1839
RICHMOND, Mary D.	HARDING, Ephraim H.	01/18/1859
RICHMOND, Minerva	OODS, Andy M.	07/18/1834
RICHMOND, Nancy	MORTON, Step(?)	01/02/1809
RICHMOND, Peggy	BURTON, Drury	12/03/1816
RICHMOND, Phebe	LIPSCOMB, John	12/14/1808
RICHMOND, Polly	CARNEY, Rhobartis	10/29/1799
RICHMOND, Sally J.	REED, A.	08/21/1860
RICHMOND, Sally L.	SIMS, William B.	05/20/1858
RICHMOND, Sarah	JOHNSTON, Thomas M.	11/20/1839
RICHMOND, Sarah	MURPHEY, Wiley	10/14/1866
RICHMOND, Sarah	NEWMAN, Remus	01/14/1866
RICHMOND, Sarah	RICE, Archibald	07/22/1813
RICHMOND, Sarah	CHANDLER, Thomas W.	10/24/1843
RICHMOND, Sina	VINSON, Henry	01/17/1867
RICHMOND, Susan A.	PITTARD, Benjamin S.	11/05/1859
RICHMOND, Susan T.	RICHMOND, James D.	06/01/1865
RICHMOND, Violet	RICHMOND, Tinsley	01/12/1866
RICHMOND, Virginia C.	FEATHERSTON, Thomas W.	11/14/1867
RICKETTES, Nancy D.	SAWYARS, Isaac O.	11/20/1839
RICKMAN, Agnes	RICKMAN, John	11/13/1794
RIDDLE, Polly	WARREN, William	10/14/1807
RIFFETOE, Lavinia E.	RAMEY, Albert W.	04/11/1848
RIGGS, Elizabeth	AUSTIN, John H.	12/16/1863
RIGGS, Polly	RIGGS, Thomas	12/22/1812
RIGHT, Eliza A.	BLAIR, William	08/16/1834
RIGNEY, Talitha J.	ADKIN, William D.	09/08/1865
RINES, Jane	LAME, John	12/23/1829
ROAN, Anness	GRIFFIS, Alexander	09/12/1809
ROAN, Asanath	STUART, John	07/15/1815

MARRIAGE RECORDS OF CASWELL COUNTY, NORTH CAROLINA

BRIDE	GROOM	DATE
ROAN, Eliza	HOLDERNESS, John	12/27/1865
ROAN, Elizabeth	WISDOM, William	02/15/1830
ROAN, Fanny	THOMAS, Jacob	01/29/1805
ROAN, Margaret A.	OWEN, Eliza W.	05/01/1847
ROAN, Martha J.	JONES, Lawson	10/11/1842
ROAN, Mary	NORFLEET, Marmaduke	12/05/1833
ROAN, Mourning	LEA, Barnett	12/21/1782
ROAN, Nancy	STEWART, Barzillai	11/04/1833
ROAN, Patsy	MOORE, William	09/10/1828
ROAN, Sarah	DAMERON, Joseph C.	04/14/1841
ROAN, Sarah	ROAN, James P.	08/27/1825
ROAN, Virginia	LEA, Henry	12/26/1866
ROARK, Dolly	HAWKINS, Thomas	12/21/1852
ROBARDS, Susan	TONEY, Monroe	12/26/1865
ROBERSON, Hannah	SHANKS, Thomas Jr.	08/02/1828
ROBERSON, Mary	SHANKS, Joseph	01/18/1832
ROBERTS Mary A.	LEWIS, James H.	12/17/1857
ROBERTS, Barshaba	SCOTT, Bartlett	01/14/1824
ROBERTS, Betsy	WOODY, John	08/05/1801
ROBERTS, Bettie	KERSEY, James L.	05/20/1866
ROBERTS, Comfort	STANSBURY, Luke	05/16/1788
ROBERTS, Eliza	FAUKNER, Osmund B.	12/24/1832
ROBERTS, Eliza F.	SALMAN, William T.	12/24/1865
ROBERTS, Elizabeth	HERRING, James A.	12/07/1833
ROBERTS, Elizabeth M.	LANE, William N.	12/24/1834
ROBERTS, Faithey	JONES, Benjamin	11/30/1788
ROBERTS, Frances	STARKEY, Thomas	01/22/1829
ROBERTS, Hannah	CLARKE, Robert	05/26/1799
ROBERTS, Henrietta	KING, James	11/17/1849
ROBERTS, Isabella G.	POTEAT, James	10/14/1837
ROBERTS, Jamima	POWELL, George	03/08/1793
ROBERTS, Jane	LEWIS, James	12/19/1853
ROBERTS, Judith	BARNWELL, David	12/19/1804
ROBERTS, Kitty	SINGLETON, Robert	12/11/1816
ROBERTS, Lucinda	TURNER, James R.	10/21/1854
ROBERTS, Lucinda	TURNER, James R.	10/13/1854
ROBERTS, Lucy	READ, Thomas	01/22/1823
ROBERTS, Lucy A.	SANDERS, Leroy	10/25/1858
ROBERTS, Martha J.	HAWKINS, Stephen	01/07/1857
ROBERTS, Mary	HODGE, Samuel	05/19/1790
ROBERTS, Mary	WARD, John L.	11/10/1867
ROBERTS, Nancy	WARREN, Madison	12/12/1842
ROBERTS, Phebe	RICHMOND, Joshua	01/04/1800
ROBERTS, Phebe	WARD, James L.	09/08/1864
ROBERTS, Polly	SMITHEY, Reuben	05/19/1802
ROBERTS, Polly	STEPHENS, Benjamin	01/25/1803
ROBERTS, Salley	HADDOCK, David	05/13/1802
ROBERTS, Sally A.	YARBROUGH, Augustine J.	11/02/1856
ROBERTS, Sarah	MARSHALL, Willis L.	12/23/1859
ROBERTS, Sarah	UNDERWOOD, John	10/06/1841
ROBERTS, Stacy	SIMMONS, James	09/05/1791

MARRIAGE RECORDS OF CASWELL COUNTY, NORTH CAROLINA

BRIDE	GROOM	DATE
ROBERTSON, Amy	JONES, Calvin	06/10/1867
ROBERTSON, Ann S.	DURHAM, George	03/15/1841
ROBERTSON, Dilly	COLLIER, Thomas	12/20/1804
ROBERTSON, Dolly	LAWSON, John	12/28/1866
ROBERTSON, Eady	PAGE, James H.	12/23/1860
ROBERTSON, Eleanor	CROWDER, Robert A.	06/23/1826
ROBERTSON, Emily	TATE, James	09/01/1842
ROBERTSON, Maria	VANHOOK, Reuben	04/20/1867
ROBERTSON, Mary R.	ALEXANDER, Wallace H.	10/21/1850
ROBERTSON, Pathena	YANCEY, Felix	11/16/1865
ROBINSON, Chany	TERRY, Matthew	04/07/1800
ROBINSON, Ester	GIBES, Shadrach	05/11/1785
ROBINSON, Kiziah	PASS, Holoway	12/21/1785
ROBINSON, Nelly	CAMPBELL, Hugh	06/27/1812
ROBINSON, Patsy	STANFIELD, Jno.	03/24/1800
ROBINSON, Peninah	HALL, William	11/18/1783
ROBINSON, Polly	BROWNING, Reubin	02/09/1802
ROBINSON, Polly	WALLIS, James	09/21/1796
RODD, Irena	MILES, Uriah	09/11/1834
RODENHIZER, Martha E.	CORBIN, Thomas J.	03/21/1866
RODENHIZER, R. C.	BAUGH, John J.	01/23/1867
ROE, Sally P.	SAUNDERS, John	10/23/1820
ROE, Susanna	GRIFFITH, James	01/31/1822
ROE, Susanna	SANDRES, Zephaniah	12/28/1821
ROLAND, Susan H.	SARTIN, Ellis	08/30/1864
ROLEN, Lucrasey F.	ELLIS, John H.	12/16/1856
ROLLEY, Martha	STRADOR, John	12/23/1822
RONE, Anne	DARBY, James	10/12/1802
ROPER, Alice W.	BURTON, John A.	10/22/1865
ROPER, Ann	BUCKLEY, Randolph	11/15/1803
ROPER, Ann E.	ELMORE, John A.	02/27/1833
ROPER, Arreminta	JONES, Benjamin B.	11/09/1827
ROPER, Frances C.	BRANDON, Thomas S. Jr.	12/16/1846
ROPER, Isabella C.	HUDSON, William F.	12/11/1865
ROPER, Jane F.	SAMUELL, Harnden	11/04/1815
ROPER, Jane N.	PASS, Thomas C.	12/19/1837
ROPER, Mary L.	BOYLES, Abel	11/06/1848
ROPER, Mary M.	REED, Thomas	11/06/1838
ROPER, Patsy	MCCAIN, Tollotson	11/19/1839
ROPER, Rachel R.	BENNETT, Richard	01/21/1845
ROPER, Sarah	CONNALLY, John Spencer	11/28/1844
ROPPER, Jemima	YEATS, John	03/08/1779
ROSE, Elizabeth A.	RICHMOND, John Jr.	10/10/1827
ROSE, Jane	GRAY, Yancey	03/25/1828
ROSE, Martha Stout	GRAHAM, Travees	02/13/1786
ROSE, Polly	CARMAN, Archibald	02/11/1795
ROSEBROUGH, Jane	FULLAR, Peter	04/23/1781
ROWARK, Polly	OWEN, William	11/11/1794
ROWE, Mary	SMITH, Jeremiah	11/13/1835
ROWELL, Arminta A.	MCCAIN, Samuel D.	09/25/1865
ROWLAND, Mary	COMBS, James	08/23/1859

MARRIAGE RECORDS OF CASWELL COUNTY, NORTH CAROLINA

BRIDE	GROOM	DATE
ROWLAND, Mary R.	SLAYDON, William W.	12/02/1833
ROWLETT, Saludia(?)	MILES, James Jr.	11/20/1834
ROYAL, Betsey	HILL, Richard	10/15/1799
ROYESTER, Lou F.	REAGAN, John C.	11/09/1865
ROYSTER, Elizabeth	JOHNSON, Hampton	08/25/1866
RUARK, Polley	LONGWELL, Timothy	11/27/1811
RUCKER, Amelia Ann	ADAMS, Richard	03/30/1833
RUCKS, Virginia M.	GILLIAM, R. C.	11/30/1863
RUDD, Betsey	FAULKS, Abel	04/13/1815
RUDD, Boza	STAFFORD, Adam	12/25/1809
RUDD, Celestia F.	WALKER, William T.	12/28/1865
RUDD, Elizabeth	SWIFT, George A.	12/14/1847
RUDD, Elizabeth F.	MCKINNEY, D.W.	10/31/1860
RUDD, Emily	WILEY, Iverson	09/22/1866
RUDD, Frances	FORD, Amos	09/24/1811
RUDD, Frances A.	OAKLEY, F. L.	10/25/1866
RUDD, Judy	RUDD, Jesse	08/18/1866
RUDD, Julia	TURNER, Dennis	08/26/1866
RUDD, Lizzie	GRAVES, Cato	10/20/1866
RUDD, Malinda	MILES, James Jr.	12/10/1834
RUDD, Margaret	ROBERTSON, Green	01/02/1849
RUDD, Martha	POTEAT, Thomas	12/22/1834
RUDD, Mary A.	SMITH, Jerry	12/27/1855
RUDD, Patience	FOULKS, Oliver	10/11/1825
RUDD, Polly	TURNER, Charles	04/10/1805
RUDD, Sabine	BAINES, Willis	01/12/1867
RUDD, Sarah J.	ROBERTSON, Albert G.	07/01/1866
RUDD, Susan A.	CHEEK, John W.	11/14/1866
RUDD, Vienna	BENNETT, Ambrose L.	11/30/1836
RUDD,(?) Nancy	WILSON, William	01/--/1812
RUDDER, Mildred	ROBERTTSON, Christopher	02/05/1830
RUDDER, Sally	PASS, Thomas Y.	11/26/1826
RUNNALDS, Patsey	HOLLAND, John	05/04/1805
RUNNELLS, Sally	POUNDS, Shack	08/09/1847
RUSH, Betsey	FLEMMING, Pleasant	07/25/1798
RUSSEL, Ann	WESTBROOK, Thomas	10/27/1841
RUSSEL, Elizabeth	DORIS, John	04/12/1804
RUSSEL, Judiah	CORBETT, Solomon	04/20/1842
RUSSEL, Mary N.	HESTER, J. R.	02/22/1866
RUSSELL, Eliza J.	FURGUSON, James T.	02/15/1866
RUSSELL, Elizabeth	BURKE, John	03/05/1842
RUSSELL, Emily T.	CORBET, John	08/04/1840
RUSSELL, Judy	BURTON, John	01/20/1867
RUSSELL, Martha J.	CARDWELL, William W.	01/07/1868
RUSSELL, Rebecca	SLAYTON, Richard	12/10/1853
RUSSELL, Sarah E.	DAMREON, Henry W.	01/13/1856
RYE, Nancy A.H.	WHITTEMORE, Clement W.	08/13/1833
SADDLER, Martha L.	DIX, Tandy	02/17/1836
SADLER, Mary	DICKENS, Joseph W.	09/27/1850
SADLER, Sally	KENT, Smith F.	02/21/1807
SAILES, Permela F.	FLOYD, Samuel B.	07/21/1833

MARRIAGE RECORDS OF CASWELL COUNTY, NORTH CAROLINA

BRIDE	GROOM	DATE
SAMUEL, Ann	STANFIELD, Marmaduke	08/26/1795
SAMUEL, Anne	CROWDER, Richardson	03/13/1821
SAMUEL, Betsey Pain	ATKINSON, Thomas	08/14/1822
SAMUEL, Elizabeth	PITTARD, Samuel	12/21/1790
SAMUEL, Jenny	RAINEY, Thomas	09/17/1792
SAMUEL, Letty	MORTON, Anderson	12/09/1803
SAMUEL, Lucy	SAMUEL, Walker	12/29/1829
SAMUEL, Mary	SAMUELL, Archibald	03/13/1782
SAMUEL, Milly	MORTON, William	05/31/1803
SAMUEL, Patsy	ROGERS, John C.	03/09/1810
SAMUEL, Sally	SAMUEL, Jeremiah	12/30/1782
SAMUEL, Susanna	SATTERFIELD, Amos	02/04/1805
SAMUELL, Fanney	DAMERON, Samuel	07/11/1801
SAMUELL, Judith	SAMUELL, Walker	01/10/1811
SAMUELL, Nancey	FINLEY, George	02/07/1816
SAMUELS, Nancy	PASS, Thomas C.	11/03/1859
SANDERS, Aggy	SAMUELL, Benjamin	01/24/1785
SANDERS, Ann	SMITH, Nicholas C.	11/02/1832
SANDERS, Ann P.	SAMUELL, Josiah	02/27/1804
SANDERS, Anne	GOMER, James J.	12/18/1838
SANDERS, Betsey	BARNETT, William	10/27/1798
SANDERS, Delpha	ESTES, Richard	05/18/1822
SANDERS, Elizabeth	DILL, Joseph	01/09/1858
SANDERS, Elizabeth	MARTIN, William	07/18/1814
SANDERS, Elizabeth	WARE, Jno. P.	04/15/1818
SANDERS, Ida V.	GRAVES, David S.	09/26/1862
SANDERS, Jemima	BEAVER, Humphrey	11/24/1835
SANDERS, Lyda	WRIGHT, Zera	10/29/1839
SANDERS, Manerva	MCKINNEY, Henry	10/13/1829
SANDERS, Mary	CHEEK, Robert H.	07/24/1864
SANDERS, Omah(?)	SANDERS, Jesse	01/13/1838
SANDERS, Patsy	MONTGOMERY, Frank	10/11/1866
SANDERS, Patsy	PASCHALL, Isiah	01/13/1813
SANDERS, Polly	SANDERS, Leroy	09/05/1832
SANDERS, Susan	COMBES, James	05/01/1849
SANDERS, Susan	SANDERS, Alves	11/04/1856
SARGANT, Ann	WALLIS, Allen	07/05/1826
SARGANT, Sarah	SKEEN, Peter	10/15/1782
SARGENT, Dready	WADE, Charles D.	04/18/1816
SARGENT, Elizabeth	DOYLE, Simon	08/26/1791
SARGENT, Elizabeth	PARKER, Byrd G.	08/06/1807
SARGENT, Elizabeth	SKEEN, Jonathan	01/14/1792
SARGENT, Mary	FULLER, Abraham	02/06/1786
SARGENT, Phebe	LEA, Lawrence	09/23/1793
SARGENT, Rachel	VANHOOK, Laurance Jr.	09/17/1785
SARGENT, Ruth	DOYLE, Edward	04/17/1782
SARGENT, Sarah	WALLAS, Benjamin	06/05/1782
SARTIN, Ann	NUNN, Admiral N.	01/26/1836
SARTIN, Elizabeth	MCKINNEY, Brooks	02/04/1843
SARTIN, Emma C.	MCKINNEY, George C.	01/22/1866
SARTIN, Mary	RUDD, Hezekiah	07/25/1848

MARRIAGE RECORDS OF CASWELL COUNTY, NORTH CAROLINA

BRIDE	GROOM	DATE
SARTIN, Mary A.	SOMERS, William	11/12/1852
SARTIN, Matilda P.	GARRISON, Daniel	08/21/1867
SARTIN, Nancy A.	TOTTEN, Joseph H.	10/20/1859
SATERFIELD, Aeliade	WARREN, Thomas J.	02/10/1859
SATERFIELD, Nancy	CARTER, Martin	08/12/1863
SAUNDERS, Ann	CHATHAM, John C.	06/15/1866
SAUNDERS, Susan	DILL, John H.	06/10/1841
SAWYER, Dicy	PERKINS, Martin	08/21/1787
SAWYER, Elizabeth	PERKINS, Martin	12/02/1833
SAWYER, Elizabeth	UNDERWOOD, James	12/14/1816
SAWYER, Martha Ann	GRIFFIN, Ander J.	09/20/1851
SAWYER, Mary	DISHOUGH, George F.	01/10/1835
SAWYER, Mary	BRUCE, William	10/18/1806
SAWYER, Nancey	IRVIN, Robert	04/04/1822
SAWYER, Nancy	COOPER, Hiram	01/15/1805
SAWYER, Sally	UNDERWOOD, James	09/13/1851
SAWYER, Zibby	RUDD, Alexander	08/31/1842
SAWYERS, Anthony	PARISH, James	10/12/1826
SAWYERS, Betsy	SMITH, Garnett	04/20/1810
SAWYERS, Elizabeth	WILLIAMS, James	06/18/1806
SAWYERS, Jane	ISELEY, Asa	12/18/1849
SAWYERS, Martha	MIMMS, Drury A.	07/18/1836
SAWYERS, Nancy	STARKEY, John	09/27/1790
SAWYERS, Polly	HOOD, Jesse	05/18/1807
SAWYERS, Sarah	RUDD, Jeremiah Jr.	07/10/1837
SCARLET, Mary A.	STRADER, John	06/04/1863
SCARLETT, Jane	PAGE, Benjamin	04/10/1832
SCHAVERS, Sally	MAYHOE, Vernell W.	06/07/1858
SCOGGINS, Ann	MOORE, Thomas	08/06/1850
SCOGGINS, Rachel	ANDERSON, Moses G.	12/26/1867
SCOTT, Amanda	READ, Jackson	04/30/1845
SCOTT, Betsey	HOLLOWAY, Robert	08/06/1799
SCOTT, Delila	STANLEY, James	06/09/1840
SCOTT, Fanny	MITCHELL, John	05/14/1800
SCOTT, Frances	GROOM, Samuel	07/20/1824
SCOTT, Frances	HALL, Robert	12/11/1800
SCOTT, Frances	STEPHENS, Peter	03/18/1850
SCOTT, Jane	WATLINGTON, James	03/21/1826
SCOTT, Lucey	AUSTIN, Ransom B.	04/18/1854
SCOTT, Martha F.	DILL, Reubin H.	03/09/1868
SCOTT, Martha R.	EVANS, Ellis	08/07/1838
SCOTT, Mary	FORD, George	05/27/1852
SCOTT, Mary	HUBBARD, Freeman	06/08/1844
SCOTT, Nancy	CUNNINGHAM, Moses	10/05/1867
SCOTT, Nanny	POTEAT, Thomas	12/17/1855
SCOTT, Polly	BLACKWELL, Garland	12/02/1811
SCOTT, Polly	STRADER, Henry	03/16/1784
SCOTT, Rachel	SCOTT, William	03/11/1786
SCOTT, Rebecah	BRANDON, William	08/15/1785
SCOTT, Sarah	BRANDON, Francis	02/13/1786
SCOTT, Silvia	COCHRAN, Robert	08/25/1800

MARRIAGE RECORDS OF CASWELL COUNTY, NORTH CAROLINA

BRIDE	GROOM	DATE
SCOTT, Susanna	ROBIRSON, John H.	12/30/1853
SEAL, Rebecca	NEWBELL, John	09/19/1828
SEAMORE, Susan	SEAMORE, Singleton	01/27/1820
SEATES, Harriett F.	FACKLER, Abraham	10/23/1858
SELF, Sarah J.	TALLEY, William S.	01/20/1858
SERGANT, Polly	BADGETT, William	11/14/1801
SERGENT, Margaret D.	LEA, James K	12/16/1848
SETTLE, Elizabeth G.	HOWARD, Henry A.	05/22/1847
SEWELL, Polley	ARNOLD, Thomas	12/16/1812
SHACFORD, Elizabeth	BAYNS, Eaton	07/26/1810
SHACKELFORD, Ann A.	BENETT, Warren E.	12/28/1855
SHACKELFORD, Elizabeth	WALTERS, Ezra	12/24/1795
SHACKELFORD, Luzeta	WILLIAMSON, Elisha	08/16/1867
SHACKLEFORD, Mary H.	BENNETT, William D.	12/29/1854
SHACKLEFORD, Mildred	COX, William	01/13/1821
SHACKLEFORD, Nancey	COX, Henry	08/21/1827
SHACKLEFORD, Salley	BROWN, James	01/12/1815
SHACKLFORD, Anna	COX, Gabriel	12/10/1810
SHACKLFORD, Anne	BENNETT, Thomas	02/06/1813
SHALTON, Patsy	SCOTT, Asa	12/--/1812
SHANKES, Sophia	GODWIN, George W.	11/13/1818
SHANKS, Elizabeth	DICKIE, Samuel	12/11/1787
SHARPE, Matilda H.	HARRISON, Andrew W.	09/30/1836
SHAW, Letta	SHANON, Marcus	01/02/1837
SHAW, Nancy	REESE, Josias	06/19/1779
SHAW, Urcilla P.	WATKINS, Mathew W.	04/08/1859
SHEARMAN, Heathy	BRYANT, John	10/31/1783
SHEARMAN, Tempy	WALLES, William	06/26/1795
SHEARMON, Elizabeth	BURCH, John	04/12/1791
SHELTON, Caroline M.	MCCAIN, Benjamin C.	04/29/1842
SHELTON, Drucilla	MOSS, John P.	09/12/1827
SHELTON, Eliza	WARE, Stephen T.	10/10/1837
SHELTON, Eliza M.	BENNETT, John	12/24/1839
SHELTON, Elizabeth	GLAZE, Ralph	11.06.1823
SHELTON, Elizbeth	LEWIS, William	08/06/1847
SHELTON, Jane	WALTERS, Berry	12/28/1866
SHELTON, Louisa	WHEELER, Vincent H.	03/19/1839
SHELTON, Margaret	RICE, Henry	12/20/1798
SHELTON, Martha	CARROL, Jackson	04/12/1838
SHELTON, Mary	BRINSFIELD, Calvin	07/02/1847
SHELTON, Mary A. M.	SHELTON, James F.	04/24/1843
SHELTON, Sally	HARRISON, Headley	12/10/1803
SHELTON, Sally	MUSTAIN, James W.	03/11/1814
SHELTON, Susan	DICKIN, Beverly	12/05/1840
SHELTON, Susan S.	HOWARD, Alanson	12/10/1833
SHELTON, Susannah	CROWDER, Godfrey	02/23/1802
SHEMCY, Catherine	TOWLERMAN, Phillip	08/15/1820
SHEON, Misura E.	ASEWELL, William A.	02/18/1857
SHEPARD, Elizabeth	PAGE, Stephen	01/11/1832
SHEPARD, Susanna	BIRKS, James A.	01/22/1852
SHEPERD, Sally	MONROE, John	02/08/1787

MARRIAGE RECORDS OF CASWELL COUNTY, NORTH CAROLINA

BRIDE	GROOM	DATE
SHEPHERD, Martha	MILAM, John	04/20/1854
SHEPPARD, Elisabeth	GUTTEPY, William	10/02/1782
SHEPPARD, Joanna	CAMPBELL, Archibald	09/22/1846
SHEPPARD, Mary	POWELL, Henry A.	01/09/1840
SHEPPARD, Susan W.	BURKE, James A.	01/20/1852
SHIELDS, Sally A.	TALLY, D.H.	01/27/1868
SHIELDS, Susan P.	HILL, Joseph W.	04/20/1835
SHIRLY, Susanna P.	DURHAM, Archibald	09/29/1830
SHOCKLEE, Polly	PAYNE, Thomas W.	09/16/1821
SHORT, Mavel	BOYD, Thomas	01/11/1813
SHUEMAKER, Ann	AYNCEY, James M.	06/05/1833
SHY, Marthy	EVERET, Samuel	05/01/1786
SHY, Nancey	ENOCH, John	06/30/1798
SHY, Polly	VISAGE, Thomas	10/01/1792
SHY, Sally	ENOCH, Benjamin	10/08/1796
SIDDEL, Sarah	NOWEL, Ephraim	12/27/1787
SIDDLE, Cloe	COBB, James N.	05/25/1830
SIDDLE, Martha E.	BLACKWELL, N. L.	06/22/1859
SIDDLE, Mary	BOSWELL, Antiochus	11/08/1836
SIDDLE, Nancy	SWIFT, Robert	12/17/1825
SIDDLE, Parthena	STAINBACK, William H.	08/20/1841
SIDDLE, Sarah	SCARLETT, William	09/07/1829
SIKES, Mary	SHIELDS, Johnson	10/10/1826
SIMMONS, Hannah	LEATH, Colman	03/14/1808
SIMMONS, Kesiah	YANCEY, Thomas	02/24/1789
SIMMONS, Levina	DENNY, Lewis	04/19/1830
SIMMONS, Lydia	SIMKINS, Nathan	08/13/1807
SIMMONS, Margaret	RICE, Edmond B.	10/19/1844
SIMMONS, Martha	LEAK, William Jr.	03/24/1782
SIMMONS, Nancy	SIMMONS, John	12/15/1840
SIMMONS, Priscilla	TAYLOR, Joshua	09/06/1785
SIMMONS, Rebeca H.	HEYDON, Samuel F.	06/06/1840
SIMMONS, Rita	THOMAS, Henry Jr.	12/10/1839
SIMMONS, Salina	WALKER, William L.	09/14/1850
SIMMS, Alletha	SAWYER, Robert	01/23/1798
SIMMS, Frances	MALLERY, Thomas	12/29/1789
SIMMS, Henrietta	BROWN, Hudson	04/16/1796
SIMMS, Zuriah(?)	RICE, Williamson	01/09/1797
SIMONS, Sally	ANTHONY, William	07/30/1794
SIMPSON, Almeda	PINNIX, Benjamin	02/12/1840
SIMPSON, Anice	VAUGHN, Wiatt	03/28/1868
SIMPSON, Annie	HENDERSON, Ludolphus B.	08/10/1862
SIMPSON, Celenis B.	BROOKS, John K.	11/03/1845
SIMPSON, Citty	BOSWELL, John	10/05/1805
SIMPSON, Delilah	COOPER, James	08/31/1811
SIMPSON, Delphia	HIX, Reubin	05/21/1792
SIMPSON, Elizabeth	HENDERSON, William	12/19/1829
SIMPSON, Hannah Ann	BOULDIN, James O.	02/07/1860
SIMPSON, J. T.	BOULDIN, W. L.	02/15/1866
SIMPSON, Louisa	MATKINS, Joseph	01/14/1834
SIMPSON, Martha A.	VERNON, Thomas	01/05/1855

MARRIAGE RECORDS OF CASWELL COUNTY, NORTH CAROLINA

BRIDE	GROOM	DATE
SIMPSON, Martha G.	RAWLINS, James M.	05/03/1865
SIMPSON, Mary W.	MITCHELL, Milton P.	11/20/1856
SIMPSON, Matilda	BLACKWELL, Robert	01/11/1813
SIMPSON, Nancey	BROWN, Green L.	01/01/1802
SIMPSON, Nancy	NEAL, Philemon	12/08/1804
SIMPSON, Nanny	BOSWELL, James	12/11/1823
SIMPSON, Nanny L.	PAGE, Albert M.	--/--/1867
SIMPSON, Penelope	GRAVES, Azariah	05/16/1809
SIMPSON, Polley	HAMBLETT, Bird	01/04/1806
SIMPSON, Priscilla	SIMPSON, Fracis L.	12/16/1815
SIMPSON, Rachel	WINDSOR, William	04/13/1868
SIMPSON, Susan	SIMPSON, Richard Jr.	02/02/1807
SIMPSON, Susan B.	GRAVES, John S.	04/04/1858
SIMPSON, Susanna	BURTON, David	02/07/1780
SIMS, Mary	BOSWELL, Thomas	11/27/1802
SIMS, Nancy	MASON, Wiley	12/16/1825
SIMS, Zilpah	ELLIOTT, John	08/20/1785
SINGLETON, Ann	TULLOCH, James M.	02/29/1808
SINGLETON, Catherine	WATLINGTON, Reid	06/17/1828
SISSON, Mary	GREGORY, John H.	05/22/1841
SKEEN, Hannah	LONG, William	11/05/1788
SLADE, Adeline H.	HARRISON, Thomas S.	08/23/1863
SLADE, Delitah	HIGHTOWER, Joshua	11/24/1792
SLADE, Elizabeth	COBB, John Jr.	12/09/1826
SLADE, Hannah	LEA, John	01/22/1793
SLADE, Hannah M.	HENDERSON, James S.	11/26/1832
SLADE, Harriet	HARRELSON, Madison	10/29/1866
SLADE, Isabella	RUSSELL, William	05/29/1828
SLADE, Josephine	PRICE, Brunswick	05/20/1867
SLADE, Lucinda	MOORE, Rufus	06/02/1866
SLADE, Margaret	SLADE, Robert	11/30/1867
SLADE, Martha	WILLIAMSOIN, Mark	08/28/1867
SLADE, Martha L.	EDWARDS, Joseph M.	01/01/1854
SLADE, Mary A.	TURNER, Edmund	10/12/1824
SLADE, Mary C.	CRUMPTON, Robert T.	03/23/1858
SLADE, Mary J.	WATLINGTON, William P.	07/20/1850
SLADE, Nancy	STAMPS, Jno.	01/13/1808
SLADE, Nancy	STEPHENS, William	12/01/1866
SLADE, Nancy G.	BURTON, Henry A.	12/21/1823
SLADE, Polley	GRAVES, James	04/15/1800
SLADE, Virginia E.	HODGES, John T.	11/18/1867
SLATEN, Eliza F.	HILL, John R.	01/09/1866
SLAYDEN, Frances K.	BEADLES, John W.	03/27/1828
SLAYTON, Judith T.	ELLIOTT, James	10/09/1862
SLAYTON, Martha J.	BARKER, Stephen Y.	12/08/1864
SLAYTON, Mary	BOWLER, Ellis G.	10/14/1850
SLEDGE, Catherine A.	WILLIAMS, Robert H.	09/25/1851
SMITH, Alemdia	BARTS, Allen	05/26/1866
SMITH, Amanda	ROBERTSON, James	07/27/1854
SMITH, Ann	WILSON, John	12/04/1821
SMITH, Ann R.	THORP, Richard	10/30/1838

MARRIAGE RECORDS OF CASWELL COUNTY, NORTH CAROLINA

BRIDE	GROOM	DATE
SMITH, Arrela S.	THOMPSON, Thomas M.	11/02/1857
SMITH, Beney	ATWELL, John	12/08/1810
SMITH, Betsey	ELLMORE, Thomas	05/11/1801
SMITH, Betsey	ENOCH, Samuel	08/13/1804
SMITH, Betsey	EVANS, Bird	12/11/1815
SMITH, Betsy	ROBERTS, Zephanieh(?)	08/29/1822
SMITH, Betsy	SLADE, Lemuel	04/02/1867
SMITH, Catherine	BURGE, John	10/08/1787
SMITH, E. M.	HENDRICK, C. M.	10/15/1866
SMITH, Elisabeth	HORNBUCKLE, Richard	01/09/1792
SMITH, Eliza A.	BRINTLE, Zachariah	01/01/1866
SMITH, Elizabeth	COX, Gabriel	11/21/1846
SMITH, Elizabeth	WALKER, Abraham	11/02/1833
SMITH, Elizabeth	WARREN, Henry	11/25/1812
SMITH, Elizabeth A.	BENNETT, John A.	01/26/1854
SMITH, Elizabeth M.	BALL, Alfred L.	02/05/1852
SMITH, Ellen	MILLER, Jn.	10/15/1823
SMITH, Ellen	MILLS, Samuel	05/15/1847
SMITH, F. E.	BURTON, George M.	09/29/1866
SMITH, Frances	POTEAT, Charles	12/27/1866
SMITH, Frances	CHANDLER, Stephen J.(?)	10/26/1827
SMITH, Frances	CHANDLER, James D.(?)	10/26/1827
SMITH, Francis	ESKRIDGE, John	11/22/1811
SMITH, Isabella	ESTES, Nathaniel	11/16/1830
SMITH, Isabella	POTEAT, Allen	08/30/1866
SMITH, Isabella	SMITH, William A.	02/06/1833
SMITH, Jane	DAY, Philip	02/07/1815
SMITH, Jane	SIMPSON, Moses	11/04/1833
SMITH, Jenney	JACKSON, Thomas	12/05/1798
SMITH, Jirilla (?)	OAKLEY, Archibald	03/13/1847
SMITH, Joannah	HUSTON, Jonathan	10/21/1817
SMITH, Kiziah	CONNALLY, Charles	05/13/1794
SMITH, Malissa	MEBANE, Giles	12/16/1865
SMITH, Manerva	SUMMERS, George	09/12/1855
SMITH, Martha	MOORE, Charles W.	10/30/1858
SMITH, Martha	MOORE, Charles W.	11/21/1854
SMITH, Martha A.	SIMPSON, James H.	05/25/1858
SMITH, Mary	BROWNING, John K.	04/06/1825
SMITH, Mary	READ, Thomas	10/11/1841
SMITH, Mary	WESTBROOK, Paschall	02/17/1829
SMITH, Mary F.	BARNWELL, Robert S.	02/26/1850
SMITH, Mary K.	CRISP, John H.	08/31/1836
SMITH, Mary W.	JONES, Keen	08/13/1862
SMITH, Mimi	RUARK, John	07/22/1811
SMITH, Nancey	BEVILL, Robert	11/28/1810
SMITH, Nancy	CONNALLY, Charls.	03/02/1793
SMITH, Nancy	HIGHTOWER, James	12/14/1812
SMITH, Nancy	THOMAS, Daniel C.	08/06/1827
SMITH, Nancy	WELLS, John	08/22/1822
SMITH, Nancy	WILLIAMSON, Hall	10/19/1791
SMITH, Nancy B.	GATES, James M.	02/10/1824

MARRIAGE RECORDS OF CASWELL COUNTY, NORTH CAROLINA

BRIDE	GROOM	DATE
SMITH, Patsey	BLACKWELL, Levi	02/16/1799
SMITH, Patsy	PINSON, Thomas	02/19/1823
SMITH, Polley	ATWELL, Lock	12/05/1807
SMITH, Polley	MALONE, Alfred	12/08/1813
SMITH, Polly	INMAN, Henry	12/16/1836
SMITH, Polly	PARKS, Alfred	10/16/1825
SMITH, Polly	MURPHEY, Alexander	08/29/1815
SMITH, Polly	SIDDALL, Ira	11/02/1802
SMITH, S----	NORTHERN, T. H.	06/29/1854
SMITH, Sally	GUNNELL, John	01/04/1838
SMITH, Sally	CARMIKEL, William	10/25/1799
SMITH, Sally	WARREN, Thomas	01/27/1810
SMITH, Sally J.	WILLIS, George	10/14/1841
SMITH, Sarah	ESTES, Jonathan	03/26/1834
SMITH, Sarah	MITCHELL, Charles	12/08/1803
SMITH, Sarah Frances	COLE, Tilman	10/22/1851
SMITH, Sarah J.	MILES, Abner	04/10/1856
SMITH, Susan	COLE, Green W.	11/18/1851
SMITH, Susan	PINSON, Drury	10/18/1816
SMITH, Susan A.L.	MURPHY, William H.	10/12/1858
SMITH, Susan F.	THORNTON, Robert B.	11/02/1833
SMITH, Susanna	CLARK, Martin	10/04/1805
SMITH, Teby	RUDD, David	12/25/1853
SMITH, Virginia	HINTON, William	11/20/1867
SMITH, Virginia	PERKINS, John	11/29/1862
SMITHER, Julia C.	FARLEY, William A.	03/28/1849
SMITHEY, Ann	WARREN, John	01/26/1810
SMITHEY, Elizabeth	ALDRESS, William	10/14/1799
SMITHEY, Elizabeth	SOMERS, James	12/17/1846
SMITHEY, Nicy	WALKER, Washington	09/28/1846
SMITHY, Martha E.	SOMERS, Reuben T.	04/08/1867
SMITHY, Nancy	DICKIE, John	10/10/1796
SMITHY, Sarah Jane	BEEVERS, William T.	11/06/1854
SNEED, Annis	ATKINSON, Le Roy	03/02/1835
SNEED, Catherine	LAWRENCE, James	12/29/1836
SNEED, Elizabeth	CUNNINGHAM, Nathaniel	09/24/1790
SNEED, Frances N.	CROCKETT, John H.	12/07/1834
SNEED, Mary	WILLIAMSON, Theodrick L.	04/03/1828
SNEED, Sarah	LITTLE, David	03/02/1789
SNIPES, Caroline	WEB, Anderson	12/25/1866
SNIPES, Cornelia	NASH, Alfred M.	03/30/1841
SNIPES, Elizabeth L.	SIMPSON, John H.	11/08/1853
SNIPES, Frances	PINNIX, James	02/01/1868
SNIPES, Nancey	HESTER, Elijah Col.	09/06/1828
SNIPES, Nici	HEISLEEP, F. C.	07/03/1865
SNIPES, Sarah J.	WELLS, Stephen H.	11/11/1859
SNIPES, Teletha	WARREN, James S.	01/06/1847
SNODY, Elizabeth	BRYANT, Fleming B.	12/21/1837
SOMERS, Abajah	WRIGHT, Isaac	01/12/1804
SOMERS, Catherine	LEMMON, Alexander	09/12/1808
SOMERS, Frances J.	ALLEN, Thomas H.	03/13/1862

MARRIAGE RECORDS OF CASWELL COUNTY, NORTH CAROLINA

BRIDE	GROOM	DATE
SOMERS, Jemima A.	WILLIAMS, Nathaniel R.	04/13/1859
SOMERS, Mary	WALKER, Thomas J.	08/19/1845
SOMERS, Mary Ann	APPLE, Samuel	10/22/1851
SOMERS, Nancy	BOMAN, John	12/28/1807
SOMERS, Sarah	MAYS, Samuel	09/30/1837
SOMERS, Susan	SANDERS, Alves	01/06/1845
SOMMS, Lornah	MALLORY, Stephen	12/18/1790
SOTHERLAND, Susan	PUCKET, Thomas	12/24/1832
SOURTHERD, Matilda	CHATMAN, William	01/01/1840
SOUTHARD, Lithy	LOVELACE, Pickney	02/11/1840
SOUTHARD, Mary	MURPHEY, William M.	12/28/1852
SOUTHARD, Nancy M.	FORD, Pleasant	10/19/1833
SOUTHARLAND, Patsy	LAW, Butler	12/28/1812
SPAIN, Elizabeth	MOORE, William D.	11/22/1851
SPAIN, Martha R.	WILLIAMS, George W.	04/15/1850
SPARROW, C.G.	STRICKLAND, Edwin C.	10/19/1856
SPARROW, Eliza C.	INGRUM, Jordan L.	02/06/1860
SPARROW, Nancey	LUNSFURD, Rushea H.	01/12/1835
SPARROW, Willy	POWELL, Barzilai	01/02/1834
SPENCE, Caroline	NUNNALLY, Archelaus (?)	09/14/1835
SPENCER, Barbara	PINNIX, John	12/08/1780
SPENCER, Elizabeth	STACEY, Eli	12/23/1789
SPENCER, Francis	JACKSON, George	10/10/1785
SPENCER, Mary	STACE, Malon	04/09/1787
SPENCER, Mary P.	WILLIAMSON, Thomas J.	10/19/1840
SPRATTEN, Elizabeth	BOHANAN, Ludwell	11/25/1816
SQUIRE, Sina	HUGHS, Henry	03/26/1828
SREPHENS, Elizabeth	LYON, Robert	12/30/1821
STACEY, Henrietta	OLDHAM, George	01/06/1807
STACY, Fannie E.	CRENSHAW, Thomas E.	05/03/1864
STACY,(?) Elizabeth	BROWN, Henry	11/27/1815
STADLER, Elizabeth	BROWN, William	03/19/1803
STADLER, Lidia	FITZ, William	02/16/1805
STADLER, Martha F.	MCKINNEY, James A.	01/12/1854
STADLER, Mary S.	BROWNING, Elijah C.	02/13/1859
STADLER, Nancy A.	ALBART, William B.	11/21/1840
STADLER, Polley	MAUGHAN, James	07/29/1809
STADLER, Polly	MASSEY, Levi	08/23/1836
STADLER, Susan A.	WARREN, William H.	12/20/1867
STADLER, Susannah	ARNOLD, Luke	02/21/1810
STADOR, Zeporiah	FORD, Eli	12/22/1827
STAFFORD, Betsey	HARLEY, Hiram	12/27/1815
STAFFORD, Betsy	WEBSTER, Charles	05/20/1812
STAFFORD, Cinthia	PETERSON, Joseph Jr.	09/07/1790
STAFFORD, Cynthia	BRADSHER, John Jun.	03/13/1830
STAFFORD, Delilah	COOK, Johnston	07/25/1796
STAFFORD, Elizabeth	WESTBROOK, John	12/21/1841
STAFFORD, Nelley	FORSHEE, Joseph	02/15/1784
STAFFORD, Phoebe	ESKRIDGE, Thomas	11/26/1827
STAFFRD, Sarh	ASPIN, Thomas	03/14/1782
STAINBACK, Frances	WHITEHEART, Chrody	01/20/1847

MARRIAGE RECORDS OF CASWELL COUNTY, NORTH CAROLINA

BRIDE	GROOM	DATE
STAINBACK, Mary	BOSWELL, Abner	11/22/1838
STAINBACK, Susan A.	WARD, T. R.	11/02/1867
STAMPS, Anna	HOWARD, George Jr.	12/03/1861
STAMPS, Jane	NELSON, James	08/18/1867
STAMPS, Jane	CLAIBORNE, William	12/20/1866
STAMPS, July	BRANDON, Reubin	11/18/1867
STAMPS, Lucinda	HENSLEE, Bedford W.	02/12/1833
STAMPS, Lucinda	LINDSEY, Henry	04/20/1867
STAMPS, Mary	HIGHTOWER, William	12/16/1844
STAMPS, Mary E.	PRICE, Robert M.	12/13/1854
STAMPS, Milly	THOMPSON, George	12/19/1867
STANBACK, Betsy	WILSON, James	01/04/1825
STANBACK, Martha	NUNN, Carlton	01/25/1820
STANBACK, Mary F.	BURKE, Wyly M.	03/31/1832
STANDBURY, Elizabeth	POND, James	01/16/1786
STANDFIELD, Elizabeth A.	RICHARDSON, James N.	04/01/1856
STANDFIELD, Martha T.	BRANN, Peter D.	01/20/1859
STANDSBURY, Rachel	CARMAN, Elijah	09/19/1896
STANFIELD, Ann M.	SIBLEY, James W.	05/28/1862
STANFIELD, Anna	IRVINE, John Sr,	04/11/1811
STANFIELD, Frances	DAVIS, Thomas W.	09/02/1848
STANFIELD, Mary L.	PITTARD, Jno.	12/19/1851
STANFIELD, Nanny	CHAMBERS, Josias	06/20/1780
STANFIELD, Sarah J.	GUERRANT, T. D. F.	10/25/1858
STANFIELD, Sarah J.	RUSSELL, John A.	09/21/1844
STANFIELD, Susan	MCGEHEE, Henderson	12/29/1865
STANLEY, Martha J.	TRAVIS, James J.	10/23/1844
STANLEY, Mary F.	BROWN, Thomas M.	12/18/1847
STANLEY, Nancy	STEPHENS, John	04/22/1830
STARKEY, Elisabeth	DELPS, Michael	01/29/1782
STARKEY, Elizabeth	RICE, John	12/21/1805
STARKEY, Judith	GRIFFITH, Richard H.	12/10/1820
STARKY, Rebecca	SMITH, John	11/09/1803
STAULCUP, Silvia	PAGE, William A.	12/09/1833
STEEL, Nancy E.	COVINGTON, Elisha J.	11/04/1866
STEGALL, Rebecca A.	FLEMING, Jasper	01/22/1861
STENSON, Nancy	MORGAN, John	09/27/1796
STEPHEN, Nancy	FOARD, Francis	03/29/1798
STEPHENS, Abarilla	WILLSON, Robert	12/28/1782
STEPHENS, Ann	LUSTER, Jacob W.	07/14/1842
STEPHENS, Barbara	STEPHENS, Williamson M.	11/16/1844
STEPHENS, Betsey	COMBS, Jesse	11/02/1799
STEPHENS, Betsy	JEFFREYS, Washington	02/03/1830
STEPHENS, Betsy	RICHMOND, John C.	07/31/1821
STEPHENS, Catey	HIGHTOWER, Daniel	10/14/1806
STEPHENS, Catharine	HAGWOOD, John	10/24/1839
STEPHENS, Elizabeth	HAGWOOD, John	01/08/1835
STEPHENS, Malinda	LEA, Isaac	11/10/1866
STEPHENS, Malinda	WILLIS, George W.	01/14/1834
STEPHENS, Mary	LEA, John	12/30/1786
STEPHENS, Mary C.	WEBSTER, Charles H.	05/30/1849

MARRIAGE RECORDS OF CASWELL COUNTY, NORTH CAROLINA

BRIDE	GROOM	DATE
STEPHENS, Nancey	HUBBARD, Charles	09/27/1819
STEPHENS, Nancy	ROBERTS, Joshua	01/29/1820
STEPHENS, Patsey	LYON, John	02/23/1813
STEPHENS, Polley	KITCHEN, Moses	10/09/1815
STEPHENS, Rebecca	RIGGS, John	12/19/1866
STEPHENS, Rebeccca	MARTIN, John	05/28/1809
STEPHENS, Sarah	RUDD, Luther	06/21/1855
STEVENS, Marth J.	SCOGGINS, Milton G.	01/11/1837
STEVENS, Matilda	LUSTER, Robert	10/28/1860
STEVENS, Temperance	PHELPS, James L.	11/19/1866
STEWARD, Betsy	STEWARD, Littleton	12/11/1838
STEWARD, Elizabeth	EVANS, George	05/16/1859
STEWARD, Mildred C.	FARMER, Joseph	10/01/1865
STEWART, Adeline T.	NEWMAN, Robert	11/16/1849
STEWART, Frances A.	TAYLOR, William W.	06/08/1846
STEWART, Jane	DANIEL, James	08/13/1830
STEWART, Lydia A.	FARMER, Samuel	12/26/1866
STEWART, Mary R.	MOORE, Thomas A.	09/18/1851
STEWART, Rachel	HOLLOWAY, Richard	02/13/1792
STINSON, Lucy P.	BROWER, Lewis S.	03/25/1846
STOKES, Betsy	BOZWELL, Kindall	01/09/1817
STOKES, Eliza F.	PRICE, Daniel S.	12/14/1842
STOKES, Elizabeth	GRAY, James	11/29/1780
STOKES, Martha	HARRISON, Charles K.	05/05/1818
STOKES, Mary	STOKES, Allen	02/23/1829
STOKES, Nancy	PERRYMAN, William	01.16.1782
STOKES, Nancy	SWIFT, William B.	10/01/1821
STOKES, Nanny	ROBERTSON, John	12/25/1866
STOKES, Peggy	BURCH, Samuel	08/24/1802
STOKES, Rebecca	WALTERS, Thomas	01/05/1867
STOKES, Salley	GATEWOOD, Lewis	02/01/1811
STOKES, Susan B.	PRICE, William W.	09/24/1814
STONE, -----	WILLIAMS, Nathaniel	01/17/1832
STONE, Ann	STRADER, James	05/27/1849
STONE, Betty M.	WOMACK, Rufus Y.	11/23/1865
STONE, Ellen J.	ELLIOTT, James A.	08/07/1858
STONE, Lucy	FORRELL, Enoch	11/03/1784
STONE, Lucy	DURHAM, Martin	01/08/1847
STONE, Mary L.	VOSS, Milton	12/14/1858
STONE, Nancey	BAXTER, James	07/03/1804
STONE, Priscilla	MERRITT, Solomon	08/30/186-
STONE, Sarah	DURHAM, RIchard	10/11/1844
STONE, Sarah A.	ESTES, Marcus E.	06/23/1846
STONE, Susan A.C.	STOKES, John Y.	04/05/1866
STONER, Polly	HENDRIX, John	11/11/1785
STORKS, Salley	HARVEY, David	11/14/1809
STRADER, Celia	WALKER, Archibald J.	10/13/1859
STRADER, Lydia M.	ROBERSON, William	12/29/1824
STRADER, Mary	GOMER, Pinckney	10/02/1847
STRADER, Mary Ann	DURHAM, John	12/05/1861
STRADER, Sarah J.	PEARCE, James S.	02/07/1867

MARRIAGE RECORDS OF CASWELL COUNTY, NORTH CAROLINA

BRIDE	GROOM	DATE
STRADER, Susan	DOVE, William J.	03/25/1853
STRADOR, Betsey	BLACKWELL, Marshal	08/25/1818
STRADOR, Delilah A. J.	WALL, George W.	09/12/1846
STRADOR, Esther	FORD, John N.	12/22/1827
STRADOR, Jane	DURHAM, James	12/14/1842
STRADOR, Mahala	FRENCH, James	05/14/1818
STRADOR, Martha	DURHAM, Richard	11/02/1838
STRADOR, Seluda	BRAGG, John	11/19/1866
STRADOR, Susanna	TURNER, Berry	11/18/1828
STRATTON, Lenora H.	WRENN, John F.	11/29/1858
STREET, Martha	HAGUE, James	10/09/1784
STREET, Polly	BROWNING, Richard	10/16/1798
STREET, Sally	SHANKS, Charles	01/05/1798
STRINGER, Maryann	REECE, John	07/29/1780
STUART, Aggy	BURCH, Henry	12/21/1807
STUART, Hannah	JUSTICE, Julas	--/--/178-
STUBBLEFIELD, Allice	BLACKWELL, Robert A.	10/12/1865
STUBBLEFIELD, Nancy	PEMBERTON, William B.	07/01/1819
STUBBLEFIELD, Rebecca H.	MILES, William	03/10/1859
STUBBLEFIELD, Susanna	BOAZ, David R.	12/03/1816
STUBLEFIELD, Patsy	MULLINS, Thomas	07/26/1797
SUBBLEFIELD, Catherine	WITHERS, Elijah	05/23/1817
SULLIVANT, Susanna	WORKMAN, Isaac	10/11/1799
SUMMERS, Catherine	WALKER, Jones H.	10/23/1854
SUMMERS, Elizabeth	BUTLER, Moses M.	02/18/1855
SUMMERS, Elizabeth	SHREVE, Robert	02/14/1854
SUTHARD, Elizabeth	COBB, Milton	10/25/1825
SUTHERLAND, Philena	PRICE, Christopher M.	05/10/1827
SWAIN, Martha A.	MARTIN, Claiborn R.	08/12/1867
SWAINEY, Margaret	BUCKLEY, John	11/26/1780
SWAN, Arree	CARTER, Richard T.	03/22/1854
SWAN, Mahaley	VOSS, Paschall	12/16/1833
SWAN, Milly	PONDS, Benjamin	01/19/1807
SWAN, Peggy	WALKER, Thomas	10/28/1811
SWAN, Sarah W.	COLEMAN, George J.	01/11/1847
SWANN, Adaline	SWANN, Geo.	11/08/1866
SWANN, Betsy	VOSS, Greenbery	10/30/1793
SWANN, Elizabeth F.	FITZGERALD, James W.	04/23/1847
SWANN, Huldah	MARR, George W.	02/03/1834
SWANN, Louisa A.	SCALES, Joseph A.	01/07/1850
SWANN, Lucrecia	ALLEN, Robert	01/11/1867
SWANN, Lucy	CHAMBERS, Anthony	04/13/1867
SWANN, Matilda J.	ALVERSON, Claiborn W.	11/30/1850
SWANN, Peggy	ROBERTS, Thomas	10/14/1812
SWANN, Peniciselia(?)	WILLIAMS, William	12/22/1778
SWANN, Pensey	COX, Whitaker	11/04/1799
SWANN, Sarah C.	TRAVIS, Alfred R.	08/10/1851
SWANN, Susan B.	NUNN, Miller	10/10/1859
SWIFT, Betsy	SHELTON, William	12/25/1809
SWIFT, Caroline	LEA, Jake	11/25/1865
SWIFT, Emeline	SNIPES, James C.	05/27/1847

MARRIAGE RECORDS OF CASWELL COUNTY, NORTH CAROLINA

BRIDE	GROOM	DATE
SWIFT, Frances	JEFFREYS, Isaac	10/10/1827
SWIFT, Frances	ORR, Robert	01/02/1811
SWIFT, Frances M.	JONES, Richard Jr.	12/08/1844
SWIFT, Frances T.	TAPSCOTT, John	01/29/1827
SWIFT, Margaret	HIGHTOWER, William S.	09/25/1848
SWIFT, Mary	MARTIN, George W.	10/21/1845
SWIFT, Mary H.	SUMMERS, Andrew	03/18/1833
SWIFT, Nancey	EVINS, John	03/15/1836
SWIFT, Nancy	ORR, Samuel	03/16/1813
SWIFT, Nancy	SELLEARS, William	08/19/1836
SWIFT, Polly	LEA, John	03/30/1816
SWIFT, Polly	TATE, Caswell	12/29/1806
SWIFT, Sally	POOL, Lea	06/09/1866
SWIFT, Sarah	RUDD, James	04/30/1845
SWIFT, Sarah S.	RICE, Solomon	11/18/1826
SWIFT, Susanah	HARRIS, Tyree	04/18/1785
SWIFT, Susanna W.	FIELDER, Benjamin T.	10/02/1810
TABER, Elizabeth	SLADE, Thomas	01/30/1823
TABER, Polly	HARRELSON, Nathaniel	08/09/1821
TAIT, Edy	POSTON, William	01/29/1803
TAIT, Elizabeth	YANCEY, Thomas	02/10/1802
TAIT, Fanny	FLACK, Elijah	05/08/1801
TAIT, Huldah	COLLINS, Brice	12/17/1808
TAIT, Isabell	FIELDER, Alfred T.	11/28/1832
TAIT, Jenny	SMITH, George	12/20/1800
TAIT, Lydia	BROWN, John	11/02/1801
TAIT, Mary S.	PRATHER, Leonard D.	01/01/1833
TAIT, Polly	KERR, William	07/14/1800
TAITE, Mary A.	ANDERSON, Quintin A.	03/06/1862
TALBERT, Sarah	WARE, Thomas	10/17/1788
TALLAW, Joicy	BUCKINGHAM, George	11/26/1833
TALLY, Eliza E.	SHIELDS, Doctor P.	08/29/1864
TALLY, Mary C.	MARSHALL, G. W.	05/25/1867
TANNER, Mary J.	RAILEY, C.H.	11/09/1849
TANNER, Patsey A.	DIX, John M.	12/13/1816
TAPLEY, Milly	PASS, Nathaniel Jr.	07/09/1794
TAPLEY, Sally	ROBERTS, John	12/28/1802
TAPLEY, Sarah M.	FARMER, Daniel	08/07/1781
TAPLEY, Susan	POTEET, Miles	05/12/1796
TAPP, Sophia	JEFFREYS, Washington	08/17/1866
TAPSCOTT, Lucinda	WALKER, James	12/21/1820
TARPLEY, Janey	GOMER, Benjamin	11/04/1789
TATE, Adeline	PETTIGRUE, Charles L.	12/28/1855
TATE, Elizabeth	PASS, Seth W.	10/07/1840
TATE, Hannah	JOUETT, Thomas	01/26/1801
TATE, Lucinda	HUGHES, Andrew	01/26/1818
TATE, Patsey	GOOCH, Nathnl.	11/30/1797
TATE, Sarah	JACKSON, Williams	03/25/1786
TATE, Susannah	GIBSON, Benj.	10/20/1795
TAYLOR, Fanny	YANCEY, Spivy	06/17/1849
TAYLOR, Frances	HANCOCK, Farmer	12/18/1852

MARRIAGE RECORDS OF CASWELL COUNTY, NORTH CAROLINA

BRIDE	GROOM	DATE
TAYLOR, Jane	TULLOCH, Thomas	04/30/1822
TAYLOR, Joyce	DRAPER, Solomon	07/04/1790
TAYLOR, Leathy	BENNETT, Ambrose L. Jr.	02/23/1830
TAYLOR, Lucinda	FOSTER, William L.	07/28/1846
TAYLOR, Margaret C.	MCDOWELL, Joseph M.	10/24/1854
TAYLOR, Margarett	BALL, G. S.	09/27/1864
TAYLOR, Martha	HOPE, George N.	08/18/1846
TAYLOR, Martha	NICHOLS, David A.	12/13/1849
TAYLOR, Mary A.	PATERSON, John	07/26/1838
TAYLOR, Mary M.	PHELPS, Reuben	05/16/1848
TAYLOR, Mary W.	JEFFREYS, Archible W.	05/12/1858
TAYLOR, Nancey	BARKER, James	12/14/1807
TAYLOR, Patsey	HAMLETT, James	10/07/1822
TAYLOR, Peggy	INGRAM, Elisha	--/--/1808
TAYLOR, Polly	ELMORE, John	01/06/1829
TAYLOR, Ruth	JEFFREYS, John	12/18/1843
TAYLOR, Salley	JEFFREYS, Osborn	06/03/1778
TAYLOR, Sarah L.	TAYLOR, Nathaniel M.	03/25/1843
TENNESSON, Creasy	SHORT, James	12/25/1800
TENNESSON, Elizabeth	FORD, George	12/13/1800
TENNESSON, Sarah	ARTWELL, Richard	12/08/1803
TENNISSON, Celia	PATTERSON, Turner	07/25/1808
TERREL, Lucy	MURPHEY, William	03/02/1798
TERREL, Mercy	NELSON, James	02/01/1816
TERRELL, Ann	MOORE, Terrell	04/02/1834
TERRELL, Betsey	BROOKS, David	10/06/1816
TERRELL, Frances	WARREN, William Jr.	07/05/1825
TERRELL, Jane	WATKINS, William	11/06/1834
TERRELL, Lucy	ELLIS, Andrew	09/22/1819
TERRELL, Lucy	PAGE, Bently	09/29/1843
TERRELL, Lucy	PITTARD, Davis	11/30/1840
TERRELL, Margaret	MITCHELL, Randolph	10/04/1819
TERRELL, Martha	WARREN, Granderson	05/08/1851
TERRELL, Patsy	MURPHEY, James	03/21/1795
TERRELL, Salley	MANSFIELD, John	03/16/1814
TERRELL, Sarah	MURPHEY, John	04/10/1804
TERRELL, Tabitha	CHEEK, Robert	12/06/1838
TERRILL, Elizabeth	HERNDON, Larkin	02/13/1790
TERRY, Elizabeth A.	YARBROUGH, Thomas S.	02/12/1850
TERRY, Harriet	FITZGERALD, Joseph M.	12/07/1843
TERRY, Julia A.	MELLETT, J.Y.Dr.	03/27/1865
TERRY, Letitia W.	WHITLOCK, Achilles	04/22/1833
TERRY, Lettice W.	INGRAM Yancey W,	07/28/1834
TERRY, Martha	JOHNSON, Thomas	11/06/1827
TERRY, Mary A/	MARR, David J.	04/04/1862
TERRY, Narcesia B.	POWELL, James B.	10/06/1840
TERRY, Sarah A.	FAUCETT, David L.	04/07/1849
TERY, Milly	THORP, John	07/03/1802
THACKER, Martha A.	MANLY, Rufus	02/05/1849
THARP, Patsey	GREGORY, Samuel	12/05/1807
THAXTON, Amanda	THOMPSON, Robert	12/13/1866

MARRIAGE RECORDS OF CASWELL COUNTY, NORTH CAROLINA

BRIDE	GROOM	DATE
THOMAS, Allice	GARLAND, Jacob	04/21/1867
THOMAS, Betsy	WRIGHT, Caleb	12/31/1792
THOMAS, Catharine	HAMLETT, Andrew J.	05/11/1867
THOMAS, Celia A.	EDWEL, Harrison	01/29/1842
THOMAS, Diana	STEPHENS, Anthony Jr.	09/22/1837
THOMAS, Dicy	STEPHENS, Henry	08/03/1835
THOMAS, Elisabeth	BROOKES, Jeremiah	03/18/1795
THOMAS, Frances	SMITH, Elijah R.	12/14/1854
THOMAS, Jinsy	POGUE, Joshua	07/13/1804
THOMAS, Margaret	JONES, Matt	02/24/1846
THOMAS, Margaret	THOMAS, Thomas	06/29/1857
THOMAS, Martha	SIMMONS, John	12/19/1835
THOMAS, Martha A. E.	SHELTON, F. L. R.	11/17/1849
THOMAS, Martha J.	CARTER, Robert H.	04/26/1843
THOMAS, Mildred	OWEN, Thomas W.	01/28/1834
THOMAS, Nancey	KERSEY, William	12/07/1816
THOMAS, Polley	EVANS, William	12/17/1817
THOMAS, Polley	HIGHTOWER, Thomas	11/23/1803
THOMAS, Sally	DAMERON, James H.	08/15/1846
THOMAS, Sarah	HALCOMB, William	01/05/1824
THOMAS, Susan B.	READ, James W.	05/10/1839
THOMAS, Susan V.	JONES, James	02/17/1867
THOMPSON, Ann E.	BOSWELL, Howell Jr.	08/13/1856
THOMPSON, Ann E.	WILEY, Yancy	12/17/1831
THOMPSON, Betsey	FLETCHER, Reubin	12/22/1802
THOMPSON, Eveline	THORNTON, Presly L.W.	10/07/1859
THOMPSON, Frances P.	WILLIS, William S.	12/06/1863
THOMPSON, Justina L.	WILKERSON, Jno. C.	03/23/1852
THOMPSON, Mary	BELLSIRE, Thomas	08/25/1807
THOMPSON, Nancey	DOWELL, Walker	12/29/1806
THOMPSON, Nanny	BURTON, Noel	11/26/1857
THOMPSON, Sarah S.	LEWIS, A. S.	12/08/1846
THOMPSON, Susan C.	ENOCH, Rees H.	01/06/1859
THORN, Kitty C.	BENNATT, William T.	07/16/1814
THORNTON, Adaline	HOOD, Thomas	06/19/1867
THORNTON, D. R.	GRAVES, Jeremiah Jr.	06/13/1860
THORNTON, Fanny	SMITH, Green	09/22/1866
THORNTON, Sallie F.	JEFFRESS, Wm. C.	06/11/1866
THORNTON, Susan E.	FORD, John R.	09/04/1851
THORNTON, Susan J.	HUNT, L. J.	12/11/1856
THORP, Louisa	MURPHY, Lewis	09/10/1866
TINDAL, Elizabeth	WARRIN, Timothy	03/13/1817
TIRPIN, Susan R.	DANIEL, Elias J.	04/05/1843
TODD, Elizabeth	STUBBLEFIELD, Nathan	11/06/1794
TODD, Priscilla	LONG, James	02/16/1782
TOLBERT, Elizabeth	MILES, Thomas	12/15/1784
TOLBERT, Martha	BASS, William	05/31/1841
TOLBERT, Nancy	WARE, John	09/28/1782
TOLER, Mary	DUNNAVENT, Thomas	08/26/1840
TOLLOH, Frances	ROBERTSON, William A.	05/05/1821
TOMSON, Sally	POGUE, Daniel	08/10/1814

MARRIAGE RECORDS OF CASWELL COUNTY, NORTH CAROLINA

BRIDE	GROOM	DATE
TONEY, Mary	GURNES, Richard	02/19/1855
TONEY, Nancy	LONG, William	01/26/1842
TONEY, Sarah	MASON, John	10/16/1843
TORIAN, Mandy	RUSSELL, James	12/19/1866
TOTTEN, Emeline	RICE, Ibzan	12/13/1849
TOTTEN, Mary A.	PARISH, William T.	10/28/1856
TOTTEN, Parthena A.	PASCHAL, John H.	10/18/1860
TOTTON, Nancy W.	VANHOOK, Jacob T.	07/19/1865
TRACEY, Jenny M.	SIMPSON, Moses	11/23/1809
TRAMMEL, Elizabeth	TURNER, John P.	04/11/1867
TRAMMELL, Crosha	GORDON, Robert	12/11/1845
TRAVIS, Alcey S.	DAMERON, William J.	09/28/1841
TRAVIS, Eliza A.	STANDLEY, Will R.	07/04/1844
TRAVIS, Maryann	MORTON, Bedford B.	05/30/1848
TRAVIS, Polley	JONES, William	06/20/1820
TRAVIS, Purlina	KNIGHTEN, James	08/09/1841
TRAYLOR, Elisabeth	BROOKS, James	12/26/1782
TRICKY, Anness	DUEST, Hezekiah	08/09/1784
TRIGG, Betsy	BUSEY, Samuel	12/26/1823
TRIGG, Teletha	ARNETT, Stephen	04/17/1837
TRIM, Frances	DOBBINS, Azariah	05/31/1828
TRU, Nancy	HARDY, Samuel	01/11/1851
TRYWIG, Jane	LYON, James N.	11/21/1866
TUCK, Louisania C.	SMITH, Samuel R. Jr.	10/20/1836
TUCKER, Perlina	OWEN, Alfred	06/25/1860
TUCKER, Sally P.	OLD, William B.	04/21/1867
TUNKS, Frances	DEBO, Benjamin	07/27/1790
TURNER, Elizabeth	LIPSCOMB, Thomas	10/14/1799
TURNER, Elizabeth	SLADE, Elias	04/11/1825
TURNER, Elizabeth F.	SATTERFIELD, R.A.	08/17/1859
TURNER, Elizabeth T.	FARISH, G. James	11/22/1841
TURNER, Fanney	LEWIS, Burrell G.	08/24/1813
TURNER, Frances	MARTIN, Richard	10/25/1783
TURNER, Frances A.	NEAL, Stephen	12/26/1838
TURNER, Lottie	BRUCE, Robert	12/29/1801
TURNER, Louisa	SAUNERS, Drewry W.	12/22/1864
TURNER, Martha M.	VAUGHAN, Drury M.	03/11/1830
TURNER, Mary	GOOCH, William	06/10/1866
TURNER, Mary	SLADE, William	11/22/1820
TURNER, Mary A.	ALLEN, George W.	12/26/1866
TURNER, Mary A.	TURNER, Stephen H.	01/01/1850
TURNER, Mary F.	ELLIOTT, Allen W.	12/10/1855
TURNER, Matilda	TURNER, Jordon	05/06/1867
TURNER, Milly	WEBB, William S.	04/04/1804
TURNER, Nancey	ELLIOTT, Martin S.	10/12/1814
TURNER, Nancey	FISHER, Anthony	09/06/1825
TURNER, Nancey	KIMBRO, James	12/27/1787
TURNER, Nancy	KIMBROUGH, John M.	05/05/1825
TURNER, Nancy	VAUGHN, Richard	09/28/1803
TURNER, Nancy	WILLIS, Nicholas	10/29/1804
TURNER, S. E.	FORSTER, F. K.	10/14/1848

MARRIAGE RECORDS OF CASWELL COUNTY, NORTH CAROLINA

BRIDE	GROOM	DATE
TURNER, Salley	FRENCH, Benjamen	11/10/1784
TURNER, Sally	MOORE, Armistead	12/14/1795
TURNER, Sally	WARREN, Drewry	11/25/1858
TURNER, Sarah	BOSWELL, John	12/11/1826
TURNER, Susannah	DONOHO, James	04/22/1802
TYRE, Martha	DUNCAN, Nathan	03/02/1827
TYREE, Mary	MCCLARNEY, Holt	12/30/1830
TYRRELL, Isabell	MOORE, Brittain	01/02/1808
UNDERWOOD, Annis	HENSLEE, Buford B.	11/10/1853
UNDERWOOD, Artelia	CHATHAM, Joseph	01/30/1847
UNDERWOOD, Margaret	CHRISMAS, Thomas	04/13/1811
UNDERWOOD, Sarah E.	SAUNDERS, Charles W.	12/27/1866
VADEN, Amanda	MEADERS, Major	11/05/1841
VADEN, Patsey	ADAMS, Edmon	06/18/1818
VANHOCK, Bridget	HARGIS, Thomas	06/03/1778
VANHOOK, Araminta D.	MORRIS, Edward J.	07/18/1842
VANHOOK, Betsey	DARBY, George	11/12/1800
VANHOOK, Elizabeth L.	WEBB, William R.	11/14/1829
VANHOOK, Penelope M.	OWEN, Thomas W.	10/28/1845
VANHOOK, Polly	ROSE, Alexander Jr.	04/03/1805
VANHOOK, Sally	CARNAL, Richard	12/22/1789
VANHOOK, Susannah	JONES, Reuben	06/11/1801
VARSHEAR, Ammy	HARRELSON, Benatt	08/14/1815
VAUGHAN, Betsey	KITCHEN, Joseph	11/08/1815
VAUGHAN, Elizabeth	KING, J.W.	10/15/1849
VAUGHAN, Elizabeth	LEA, John	05/08/1809
VAUGHAN, Frances	HENSLEY, Azariah	10/17/1824
VAUGHAN, Lucy	LOVE, Lewis H.	01/21/1851
VAUGHAN, Nancy	BIRK, Benjamin	09/28/1800
VAUGHAN, Nancy	SHAW, John W.	11/16/1847
VAUGHAN, Nancy	REED, John	07/01/1825
VAUGHN, Eddy	JONES, James	08/31/1783
VAUGHN, Eliza	FARLEY, John B.	12/26/1816
VAUGHN, Lucy	PARKS, Hiram	01/02/1799
VAUGHN, Nancy	PAGE, Thomas	02/19/1800
VAUGHN, Patsy	SCOTT, Robert	02/15/1800
VAUGHN, Sarah J.	MILES, William W.	07/05/1859
VAUGHN, Susan	SHELTON, David	06/03/1784
VERMILLION, Mary J.	PADGETT, Joseph M.	10/08/1841
VERMILLION, Nancy	BLACKARD, Charles	07/18/1780
VERNON, Edith A.	DENNIS, Franklin J.	04/07/1857
VERNON, Marinda C.	PAGE, Levi C.	07/21/1841
VERNON, Mary J.	GRIFFITH, Jesse C.	01/15/1845
VERNON, Narcissa	SWEPSON, Elijah	02/24/1866
VERSER, Martha	HARRISON, William K.	10/21/1839
VINCENT, Ann	STREET, John	12/15/1798
VINCENT, Sarah J.	BOULDIN, Lewis P.	10/08/1846
VINSON, Mary F.	WALTERS, Alexander J.	02/01/1840
VIRLOINS, Elizabeth	WARREN, Goodloe	10/08/1816
VOSS, Kitty	HENDERSON, Thomas	07/05/1813
VOSS, Sarah E.	SWANN, John M.	02/22/1852

MARRIAGE RECORDS OF CASWELL COUNTY, NORTH CAROLINA

BRIDE	GROOM	DATE
VOWELL, Susan	SCOTT, Robert	01/25/1832
WADDELL, Nancy	WALLERS, Robert H.	10/20/1817
WADDELL, Patience	AKIN, John	08/03/1816
WADE, Ann	WADE, Robert Jr.	09/16/1788
WADE, Ann R.	HUDSON, Shelton	11/08/1843
WADE, Drucilla H.	WHITEHEAD, Andrew J.	08/08/1836
WADE, Elizabeth	MUIRHEAD, Claud	06/13/1781
WADE, Elizabeth D.	SMITH, John W.	02/21/1866
WADLETON, Sina	MOORE, T.Jefferson	10/20/1860
WADLINGTON, Frances	PRICE, Charles	02/20/1792
WAGSTAFF, Ester	WILLIAMS, Maderson	02/08/1867
WAID, Betsey	HILL, Garland	09/14/1801
WALDEN, Mildred	WILSON, Isaac	08/23/1842
WALDROPE, Ann	JONES, Jeremiah	06/03/1806
WALF, Lucy A.E.	STRADER, David	12/14/1856
WALKER, Barbara	WALKER, Samuel	05/19/1834
WALKER, Barbary	GUNN, James	04/21/1808
WALKER, Catharine	GUNN, Penny	12/24/1867
WALKER, Celie	LOVELACE, Nicholas	08/17/1864
WALKER, Eliza	RICE, William H.	11/23/1841
WALKER, Eliza A.	DURHAM, William F.	12/24/1866
WALKER, Eliza A.	STAMPS, Thomas	03/16/1842
WALKER, Elizabeth	BULL, Jacob	07/12/1784
WALKER, Elizabeth	SMITH, William	10/20/1816
WALKER, Elizabeth	SMITHEY, Reuben	02/04/1840
WALKER, Frances	LAMBETH, John	09/11/1828
WALKER, Frances	MCCAULY, John	01/10/1843
WALKER, Jane	BIRD, John	12/05/1867
WALKER, Jane	RUARK, Henry	02/24/1816
WALKER, Jane	SNIPES, Cato	01/30/1867
WALKER, Jane	WALKER, Azariah	12/18/1837
WALKER, Jane	WALKER, William	10/28/1830
WALKER, Jane E.	LAMBETH, John J.	12/16/1855
WALKER, Jemima	CHAMBERS, Abner	01/08/1789
WALKER, Jemima	SUMERS, John	09/02/1824
WALKER, Leticia	NEWMAN, Washington	12/05/1838
WALKER, Lucinda	WALKER, Garrison	10/12/1840
WALKER, M. C.	HURDLE, B. F.	12/23/1866
WALKER, Malinda	HURDLE, James M.	01/22/1856
WALKER, Malinda	PARKS, James N.	10/20/1843
WALKER, Margaret	CONNALLY, John S.	05/27/1826
WALKER, Margaret F.	HURDLE, James M.	12/09/1858
WALKER, Martha	GILLAM, Robert	04/24/1837
WALKER, Martha	LOVELESS, Joseph	11/26/1857
WALKER, Martha	CARTER, Thomas	04/18/1846
WALKER, Martha F.	TALLY, P.F.	01/23/1866
WALKER, Martha F.	COBB, Achy	11/17/1863
WALKER, Mary	MURPHEY, Abraham	03/07/1839
WALKER, Mary	BROWN, Nathan	11/03/1842
WALKER, Mary	BURTON, James	10/17/1861
WALKER, Mary	WALKER, George	12/17/1822

MARRIAGE RECORDS OF CASWELL COUNTY, NORTH CAROLINA

BRIDE	GROOM	DATE
WALKER, Mary A.	GARRETT, R. J.	02/27/1855
WALKER, Mary C.	MILES, Richard	12/18/1860
WALKER, Mary E.	WALKER, Charles H.	04/29/1867
WALKER, Milly	WALKER, Daniel	06/23/1866
WALKER, Nancey	JOHNSTON, Peter	12/21/1835
WALKER, Nancy	ENOCH, John	12/03/1832
WALKER, Nancy	LOYD, John	03/10/1823
WALKER, Nancy	MCCULLOCH, Joseph	04/09/1814
WALKER, Nancy	COBB, Noah	10/23/1812
WALKER, Nancy J.	MCCAULEY, John W.	12/20/1845
WALKER, Peggy	NIGHTIN, James	01/07/1814
WALKER, Polly	SWANN, John	11/25/1803
WALKER, Polly	WILSON, Robert	09/26/1831
WALKER, Priscilla	PINNIX, Jerry	0/11/1867
WALKER, Rachel	ROLAND, Fendul	01/18/1790
WALKER, Rachiel	CRAWFORD, William	03/25/1833
WALKER, Rebecca J.	MATKINS, Dennis	01/29/1867
WALKER, Sarah	GILLAM, Joseph	01/21/1839
WALKER, Sarah	SHAW, Samuel	09/23/1867
WALKER, Sarah A.	MATKINS, William	12/18/1866
WALKER, Virginia A.	ANDERSON, Quinton T.	02/14/1866
WALL, Catherine	WALL, Robert	02/15/1830
WALL, Jincy	HIGHTOWER, Joshua	04/15/1817
WALL, Nancy	HODGE, David	02/07/1801
WALLACE, Nancey	HORN, Abel	11/07/1803
WALLACE, Parthena	PEARCE, Obediah	01/21/1829
WALLACE, Sarah	HUSTON, William	11/18/1826
WALLER, Lydia	WHITE, Epa	07/24/1806
WALLIS, Elizabeth	BRADSHER, Moses	01/11/1825
WALLIS, Elizabeth	FULLER, William	03/09/1796
WALLIS, Rachel	LESLEY, John	05/15/1799
WALTERS, Ann E.	WALLER, John S.	03/21/1839
WALTERS, Cloe	JEFFREYS, Joshua	07/31/1804
WALTERS, Elizabeth	GORDON, James	11/19/1845
WALTERS, Elizabeth	FILLIPS, Joseph	12/21/1812
WALTERS, Julia	ALDERSON, James A.	11/23/1867
WALTERS, Leathy M.	PHELPS, Levi	07/25/1866
WALTERS, Louisanna	CHANDLER, Thomas J.	08/31/1852
WALTERS, Lucy	DANIEL, John	03/29/1844
WALTERS, Martha	MCKINSEY, John W.	03/24/1841
WALTERS, Martha A.	SLADE, John T.	05/26/1866
WALTERS, Martha B.	CHANDLER, William	11/23/1857
WALTERS, Mary F.	GILLISPIE, William O.	12/02/1851
WALTERS, Mary J.	HARAWAY, William	01/29/1866
WALTERS, Matilda	CARTER, James	12/09/1832
WALTERS, Nancy	WOODEY, John	12/27/1845
WALTERS, Polley	GOOCH, John	08/25/1807
WALTERS, Sally	EVANS, Francis	11/24/1842
WALTON, Candis J.	BUTLER, J. H.	09/23/1857
WAMACK, Lucy	INGRAM, Charton	11/02/1778
WARD, Betsy	WILLIS, John	02/28/1827

MARRIAGE RECORDS OF CASWELL COUNTY, NORTH CAROLINA

BRIDE	GROOM	DATE
WARD, Elizabeth J.	ROBERTS, William R.	05/19/1852
WARD, Letitia	BARROW, Henry	11/09/1835
WARD, Louisa	MASSEY, Mark	06/28/1838
WARD, Nancy	RILEY, Thomas W.	12/27/1855
WARD, Salley	JACKSON, Daniel	08/31/1807
WARD, Susanna	HUGINS, Jacob	10/28/1817
WARE, Aryann	HODGES, Harrison L.	11/15/1845
WARE, C.E.	WILLIS, N.W.	12/10/1857
WARE, Celia	TURNER, Thomas	10/21/1819
WARE, Charlotte	MCCAIN, Robert	03/15/1842
WARE, Elizabeth	HUBBARD, Henry	10/17/1842
WARE, Frances	WILLIAMS, John D.	09/09/1861
WARE, Francis	DICKINS, Israel	03/04/1842
WARE, Hannah	ONEILL, John	12/20/1790
WARE, Harriet	BURTON, Franklin	10/22/1847
WARE, Huldy	GUNN, John	01/28/1807
WARE, Louisa	HOOPER. Zachariah Jr.	06/12/1836
WARE, Martha	BAXTER, John Jr.	08/15/1825
WARE, Martha	GOSNE, Benjamin H.	09/19/1825
WARE, Martha	MCCALLAM, William	11/02/1787
WARE, Mary	LEA, Thomas A.	10/11/1843
WARE, Nancy	TRAVIS, James	07/19/1814
WARE, Nancy	WARE, Thomas Jr.	08/08/1818
WARE, Nancy	WHITE, James	08/30/1813
WARE, Patsy	WILSON, Giles	04/24/1804
WARE, Rody	HENDERSON, Samuel	12/03/1804
WARE, Salley	DAMERON, Christopher	06/06/1815
WAREN, Fanny	ATKINSON, John	03/06/1816
WARF, Elizabeth	DAVIS, Alfred	02/26/1840
WARF, Kezziah	DAVIS, Lewis	12/18/1832
WARNER, Mary	RAY, Robert	01/24/1843
WARREN, Agness	BURK, Granderson	03/26/1840
WARREN, Ann	HANCOCK, Stephen	07/03/1839
WARREN, Betsey	MANN, James	01/08/1810
WARREN, Betsy	ROBERTS, George	01/13/1811
WARREN, Catharine A.	KELLEY, George	11/05/1823
WARREN, Fanney	COOPER, Allin	08/04/1800
WARREN, Frances	JONES, Eli	09/25/1837
WARREN, Leatha	BROWNING, Sanders	10/15/1823
WARREN, Lucy	MANN, William Jr.	04/19/1800
WARREN, Lucy	STANFIELD, Durret	12/18/1797
WARREN, Mary A.	COOPER, William	02/06/1847
WARREN, Mary A.	BURCH, William	10/10/1850
WARREN, Mary C.	JONES, Robert	12/13/1857
WARREN, Mehala	SMITH, James T.	05/23/1850
WARREN, Nancey	CORBITT, William	02/25/1830
WARREN, Nancy	MURPHEY, Bazel	12/23/1846
WARREN, Nancy	WHITMORE, Richard	06/10/1809
WARREN, Nancy	WRIGHT, Jacob Jr.	11/08/1815
WARREN, Pemelia	HESTER, Wilson	01/07/1833
WARREN, Rachel	DUTY, William	02/13/1783

MARRIAGE RECORDS OF CASWELL COUNTY, NORTH CAROLINA

BRIDE	GROOM	DATE
WARREN, Sarah	CRISP, Chesley	01/02/1827
WARREN, Sarah	THOMAS, Nelson	05/13/1834
WARREN, Viney(?)	MILES, William	09/29/1818
WARRICK, Nancy	DAVIS, Elijah	06/16/1823
WARRIN, Anness	CARNAL, Patrick	12/17/1790
WARRIN, Betsey	HOBSON, William	06/10/1788
WARRIN, Elizabeth	MCCAIN, John	06/23/1790
WARRIN, Frances	MURRAY, Walter	03/04/1825
WARRIN, Frankey	CARNAL, Flemman	10/22/1804
WARRIN, Jane	PHELPS, William	01/10/1786
WARRIN, Nancy	SMYTHE, Samuel	03/17/1787
WARSHAM, Mary	TRAYNHAM, David	12/28/1825
WARSON, Elizabeth	POSTON, Jeremiah	05/03/1779
WARWICK, Elizabeth	STEPHENS, Thomas	02/04/1788
WARWICK, Margaret	THOMAS, Robert	12/26/1787
WARWICK, Polley	KIMBROUGH, John	10/19/1809
WARY, Sally	BALLARD, Lewis	12/23/1812
WASHBURN, Recey	GRIDER, Jacob	04/22/1797
WASHINGTON, Lucy	BARKEDALE, Squire	09/29/1867
WATERFIELD, Elizabeth	MORGAN, John C.	06/27/1827
WATERS, Anna	SAMUEL, Anthony	12/25/1786
WATERS, Mary J.	NUNN, James	12/27/1860
WATKINS, Anna S.	HUNT, Eustance	09/30/1863
WATKINS, Jane	HICKS, Maryland	09/12/1842
WATKINS, Logan S.	WATKINS, Joseph V.B.	05/19/1857
WATKINS, Mollie	HOWARD, Daniel	01/12/1867
WATLINGTON, Ann P.	POWELL, Edward M.	01/08/1857
WATLINGTON, Elizabeth	BOLTON, Joel	02/07/1820
WATLINGTON, Frances	BENNETT, Ambrose L.	11/08/1822
WATLINGTON, KIziah B.	JEFFREYS, Thomas	10/22/1824
WATLINGTON, Letitia	WOODS, William	10/21/1845
WATLINGTON, Malissa	BOSWELL, Andrew J.	09/07/1866
WATLINGTON, Martha A.	WATLINGTON, James J. B.	07/08/1858
WATLINGTON, Mary	JONES, John E.	10/05/1847
WATLINGTON, Mary	SCOTT, John	12/17/1823
WATLINGTON, Mary A.	SCOTT, John W.	07/21/1849
WATLINGTON, Mary B.	BROOKES, John	11/17/1824
WATLINGTON, Mary C.	ROBERTS, William A.	02/01/1859
WATLINGTON, Mary E.	RICHARDSON, Robert P.	12/30/1850
WATLINGTON, Mildred	HOOPER, John J.	12/15/1825
WATLINGTON, Nancy	PRESNELL, Gilbert	07/14/1835
WATLINGTON, Penelope	VERNON, Calvin D.	03/08/1855
WATLINGTON, Phillis	GWYN, James	12/31/1866
WATLINGTON, Rebecca	WATLINGTON, Armstead	01/02/1833
WATLINGTON, Sally	WHITE, A. W.	08/01/1867
WATLINGTON, Sarah L.	TOTTEN, Thomas R.	12/21/1853
WATLINGTON, Victoria	WILLIAMSON, Simon	12/26/1865
WATSON, J. B.	GILLIAM, Wm. M.	09/01/1860
WATSON, Nancey	GOMER, William	03/11/1807
WATSON, Nancy A.	RUSSELL, John P.	08/10/1863
WATSON, Polley	HOLLAN, James	08/01/1816

MARRIAGE RECORDS OF CASWELL COUNTY, NORTH CAROLINA

BRIDE	GROOM	DATE
WATSON, Sarah	MCCUBINS, Alfred	12/05/1827
WATSON, Susan E.	RENO, John P.T.Dr.	10/27/1838
WATTERFIELD, Polly	STEPHENS, William	10/09/1816
WATTS, Martha S.	SHAPARD, John J.	02/11/1867
WATTSON, Anny	HINTON, William	08/14/1805
WEASTBROOK, Jane	LEA, William A.	11/10/1824
WEATHERFORD, Elizabeth	DALTON, Claiborn	06/30/1810
WEATHERFORD, Fannie	BLACKWELL, Henry	06/08/1866
WEATHERFORD, Mary Ann	DALTON, John	12/04/1838
WEATHERFORD, Nancy	MITCHELL, Charles	04/12/1828
WEBSTER, Mary	HAWKINS, Robert	08/10/1844
WEBSTER, Nancey	HAWKINS, Harbird	11/28/1833
WEBSTER, Sallie Ann	BOZES, Jno. Thos.	07/26/1854
WEDDING, Jereney	BROOKS, Andrew P.	06/15/1850
WEDDING, Sarah	MORGAN, William H.	10/11/1838
WEEDEN, Louisa	SAWYER, Stephen	12/01/1818
WEEDEN, Mary A.	HARDY, Green	12/03/1844
WEIRE, Betty J.	STEPHENS, C.	01/06/1866
WELDON, Marthany	SLAYTE, James H.	08/05/1829
WELLS, Duppe (?)	WELLS, Miles Jr.	03/26/1828
WELLS, Mary	WARREN, Franklin L.	04/24/1851
WELLS, Mary	CHILDRESS, Jeremiah	07/07/1821
WELLS, Prisilla	HERNDON, George	12/20/1805
WELLS, Sarah	CHAMBERLIN, Ebenezer	08/31/1819
WELLS, Sarah	WILSON, Joseph	07/29/1799
WEMPLE, Laura	HOWARD, Henry O.	12/18/1867
WEST, Ann	STRATTON, John D.	12/04/1829
WEST, Elizabeth	WORSHAM, Beary	01/26/1809
WEST, Judith	ROHR, William M.	05/26/1830
WEST, Louisa J.	BOSWELL, Romulus S.	08/25/1856
WEST, Mahaley J.	OVERBY, Thomas	02/05/1833
WEST, Margarett	HIGHTOWER, Vinson	04/22/1867
WEST, Martha A.	BURKE, William A.	09/23/1854
WEST, Martha T.	HARGIS, James O.	09/10/1825
WEST, Mary	MCKNIGHT, Anthony	03/11/1794
WEST, Mary B.	TRAVIS, John	06/26/1843
WEST, Milcey	NORMAN, William	01/14/1812
WEST, Sarah E.	WATLINGTON, James M.	03/01/1850
WESTBROOK, Peggy	LEA, Simeon	03/28/1822
WESTBROOKS, Caroline	MOORE, Thompson	09/07/1835
WESTBROOKS, Frances	WEBSTER, James	10/29/1828
WESTBROOKS, Malinda	MANSFIELD, James L.	12/19/1845
WESTLY, Elionar	DYE, Shadrach	11/16/1802
WHALEBONE, Sina	CANADAY, James	03/27/1804
WHEALER, Frances	LEA, Ambrose	08/10/1779
WHEELER, Elsey	BRECHEN, William Jr.	01/12/1807
WHEELER, Susanna	SATERFIELD, William	10/01/1791
WHITE, Celia	ALVERSON, Azariah J.	12/11/1841
WHITE, Jincy	PARKER, Jeptha	10/02/1813
WHITE, Louisa D.	KENNON, Joseph B.	02/26/1851
WHITE, Mary	TRAVIS, Ellis	04/10/1843

MARRIAGE RECORDS OF CASWELL COUNTY, NORTH CAROLINA

BRIDE	GROOM	DATE
WHITE, Mildred	NEWTON, Henry	03/23/1791
WHITE, Milly A.	SPRUCE, George	05/08/1858
WHITE, Polley	COLLIER, Joseph	07/06/1815
WHITE, Rachel	DEWEESE, Samuel	04/08/1782
WHITE, Sally	RANDOLPH, William	11/15/1783
WHITE, Sarah	HENDERSON, Rufus R.	09/06/1834
WHITED, Catherine M.	GRAVES, John A.	05/31/1848
WHITEHEAD, Lucy	WHITEHEAD, John H.	05/18/1825
WHITEHEAD,(?) Nancy	PAGE, William	12/31/1796
WHITEMORE, Eliza K.	MOTLEY, Joel	10/24/1823
WHITEMORE, Jemima J.	LAUSON, John B.	09/29/1827
WHITLOCK, Nancy	SIMMS, Buckner	10/20/1784
WHITLOE, Ursly	WILSON, Johnston	12/03/1788
WHITLOW, Catherine	WHITLOW, John	10/07/1823
WHITLOW, Caty	CARRELL, Ellis	05/14/1817
WHITLOW, Elizabeth	WHITLOW, James	11/23/1817
WHITLOW, Fanny	STAFFORD, Thomas	02/23/1791
WHITLOW, Mary	WEBSTER, John	11/24/1817
WHITLOW, Nancy	STAFFORD, Joseph	06/09/1809
WHITMORE, Sally	SMITH, James	06/08/1825
WHITTEMORE, Aniva E.	BLACKWELL, James M.	09/16/1856
WHITTROW, Susan C.	HORN, Edward M.	10/06/1855
WIER, Bell	WALTERS, George	05/04/1867
WILEY, Adaline W.	WILEY, John H.	03/27/1839
WILEY, Eleoner	DURREM, Daniel	02/22/1808
WILEY, Esther	BRANDON, William	12/14/1811
WILEY, Jincey	CURRIE, Joseph	09/01/1802
WILEY, Julia	CHANDLER, Thomas W.	10/12/1830
WILEY, Lucinda R.	GRAY, Alexander	11/10/1840
WILEY, Margaret	GRAY, John	12/16/1800
WILEY, Mary	HOOPER, Spencer	10/06/1832
WILEY, Nancy	CHANDLER, Josiah	03/23/1810
WILKERSON, Edy	TERRY, Enoch	12/07/1832
WILKERSON, Jane	MALONE, Henry	11/05/1820
WILKERSON, Marthy E.	BARKER, Minyard	11/14/1865
WILKERSON, Parthana F.	COWARDIN, Francis C.	12/08/1836
WILKERSON, Polly	MCKEE, Robert	07/23/1814
WILKERSON, Puritha	OVERBY, Owen	04/19/1825
WILKERSON, Rachel	DAVIS, Jonathan	10/--/1817
WILKERSON, Rhody	OVERSTREET, Robert	10/27/1801
WILKES, Lucy A.	CLYBORNE, George	02/02/1836
WILKINS, Patsy	TURNER, Lewis	09/27/1825
WILLIAMS, Aggy	GATES, Richard	08/06/1798
WILLIAMS, Ann	WILLIS, James T.	11/19/1832
WILLIAMS, Ann R.	COLE, Harvie J.	01/16/1844
WILLIAMS, Betsy	PARKER, William	12/15/1801
WILLIAMS, Eliza G.	COURTS, Jennings H.	07/12/1819
WILLIAMS, Elizabeth	HORTON, James G.	11/03/1826
WILLIAMS, Elizabeth	MCGINNIS, James	01/15/1790
WILLIAMS, Elizabeth	CARMICHEL, William	06/01/1818
WILLIAMS, Elizabeth A.	WARE, Silas T.	09/19/1850

MARRIAG   ASWELL COUNTY, NORTH CAROLINA

BRIDE	GROOM	DATE
WILLIAMS, Jenny	, David	12/19/1788
WILLIAMS, Judith	Ambrose R.	08/17/1837
WILLIAMS, Letitia	R, James M.	05/11/1853
WILLIAMS, Martha	RD, Freeman	12/09/1793
WILLIAMS, Mary	, Thomas Jr.	11/22/1779
WILLIAMS, Mary	S, Joel P.	12/16/1837
WILLIAMS, Mildred	William G.	02/19/1859
WILLIAMS, Nancey	LL, William	11/18/1789
WILLIAMS, Nancy	S, James	09/20/1834
WILLIAMS, Phebe C	LL, Alfred R.	04/22/1839
WILLIAMS, Sally	S, Edward	01/02/1796
WILLIAMS, Sarah	, Wm.	11/17/1866
WILLIAMS, Sarah	R, John	09/12/1818
WILLIAMS, Sophia	ON, Wm. B.	12/14/1858
WILLIAMS, Susan A	S, Archibald W.	04/03/1850
WILLIAMS, Ursly I	S, Reuben	02/01/1783
WILLIAMSON, Adal:	, William M.	08/14/1839
WILLIAMSON, Ann E	, Augustus C.	06/09/1836
WILLIAMSON, Candi	W, Calvin	06/01/1867
WILLIAMSON, Corne	Robert J.	04/15/1840
WILLIAMSON, Eliza	Samuel	09/29/1783
WILLIAMSON, Eliza	, Samuel	11/09/1812
WILLIAMSON, Eliza	, John	10/26/1796
WILLIAMSON, Emil:	, William C.	11/13/1855
WILLIAMSON, Emil:	Pleasant A.	09/09/1850
WILLIAMSON, Emil:	, Thomas	01/22/1857
WILLIAMSON, Fran:	R, Leonard	02/11/1799
WILLIAMSON, Hann:	R, Nash	12/22/1865
WILLIAMSON, Isab:	John W.	06/15/1861
WILLIAMSON, Isab:	William H.	09/02/1866
WILLIAMSON, Isabe	S, George A.	04/04/1865
WILLIAMSON, Julia	LL, William	01/12/1867
WILLIAMSON, Leath	AMSON, Mintus	10/05/1867
WILLIAMSON, Lethe	R, Henry	11/02/1866
WILLIAMSON, Litt:	TT, Archer	12/26/1867
WILLIAMSON, Loui:	, William	12/25/1866
WILLIAMSON, Lucey	Jethro	05/28/1788
WILLIAMSON, Lucir	Paton	06/22/1867
WILLIAMSON, Marga	ON, Dennis	12/25/1865
WILLIAMSON, Maria	D, Charles	07/06/1867
WILLIAMSON, Mart:	SON, Thomas	07/10/1802
WILLIAMSON, Mart:	Caswell	02/24/1819
WILLIAMSON, Mart:	AMSON, Calvin	03/02/1867
WILLIAMSON, Mary	R, John C.	11/20/1856
WILLIAMSON, Mary	James	06/13/1810
WILLIAMSON, Mary	S, Robert S.	08/31/1818
WILLIAMSON, Nancy	ON, Andrew	04/18/1785
WILLIAMSON, Peggy	ON, Roger	12/27/1808
WILLIAMSON, Polle	William	02/13/1795
WILLIAMSON, Racha	, David	08/16/1866
WILLIAMSON, Sarah	Daniel B.	08/14/1827

MARRIAGE RECORDS OF CASWELL COUNTY, NORTH CAROLINA

BRIDE	GROOM	DATE
WILLIAMSON, Sarah F.	WOMACK, Lewis P.	02/20/1846
WILLIAMSON, Silvy	OLIVER, Jerry	12/22/1866
WILLIAMSON, Virginia F.	WILLIAMSON, Jno. W.	07/30/1863
WILLIAMSON, Winny	LEWIS, Charles	06/22/1804
WILLIS, Betsy	SMITH, Francis	10/21/1802
WILLIS, Ebby	BAINS, James	12/29/1810
WILLIS, Elizabeth B.	PATTILLO, Zachariah A.	05/22/1847
WILLIS, Joicey	CREWS, Thomas	01/21/1837
WILLIS, Joicy	CHANDLER, Wilkins	11/29/1818
WILLIS, Judah F.	FURGESON, Andrew J.	11/26/1856
WILLIS, Keziah W.	WILSON, John	07/02/1833
WILLIS, Laura A.	GRAVES, Jno. K.	01/20/1844
WILLIS, Malissa	MEBANE, Henry	01/01/1867
WILLIS, Malissa Rose	BOWE, Geo.	11/14/1867
WILLIS, Margaret	HINTON, Wesley	08/11/1866
WILLIS, Martha A.	OLIVER, Linsey	05/24/1842
WILLIS, Martha A.	VALENTINE, Thomas J.	10/21/1850
WILLIS, Mary	KENNON, William	01/31/1827
WILLIS, Mary	PAGE, James	11/24/1830
WILLIS, Mary	WINNEM, Stephen	03/05/1789
WILLIS, Nancey	GRAVES, Lewis Dixon	09/20/1836
WILLIS, Nancy	SMITH, Jonathan	02/09/1822
WILLIS, Nancy E.	ROBERTS, William H.	12/17/1865
WILLIS, Polly	HERITAGE, William	12/19/1809
WILLSON, Abbarillah	EVANS, Thomas	11/26/1821
WILLSON, Agnes	SWANN, Joseph	01/03/1787
WILLSON, Betsy	MORGAN, William	09/07/1812
WILLSON, Margret	BARTON, Lewis	07/24/1804
WILLSON, Mary L.	LEA, William	10/07/1834
WILLSON, Rebecca	STUBBLEFIELD, Beverly	10/07/1826
WILMOUTH, Nancy	WEST, Joseph	10/20/1819
WILSON, Ann	JEFFREYS, Iverson	12/21/1854
WILSON, Ann E.	COBBS, James S.	10/05/1867
WILSON, Betsy	WILSON, Henry	01/05/1867
WILSON, Betsy A.	SMITH, William	06/28/1832
WILSON, Candis	GARLAND, William	10/08/1865
WILSON, Catherine	PHILLIPS, Hugh	01/22/1814
WILSON, Dafney	STAMPS, Samuel	12/01/1866
WILSON, Ellen	HUNT, Algernon	03/04/1867
WILSON, Huldah G.	DONOHO, William A.	06/30/1859
WILSON, Keziah	HINTON, John	10/05/1801
WILSON, Lucy	PHELPS, Henry J.	10/13/1867
WILSON, Martha	HAITHCOCK, Martial	12/07/1866
WILSON, Martha	HODGES, James M.	11/08/1865
WILSON, Mary	LEIGH, David G.	12/16/1822
WILSON, Pensy C.	WALKER, Fielding L.	11/28/1866
WILSON, Polly	REID, James	02/12/1800
WILSON, Polly	VAUGHAN, Lewis	08/01/1801
WILSON, Rebecca	SUIT, William	05/28/1787
WILSON, Silvia	SMITH, Edmond	12/28/1866
WIMBUS, Nancy	WADDILL, John C.	10/27/1817

MARRIAGE RECORDS OF CASWELL COUNTY, NORTH CAROLINA

BRIDE	GROOM	DATE
WINDSOR, Eliza J.	LAMBETH, Lovick L.	11/25/1848
WINDSOR, Elizabeth	FRYER, William	04/14/1815
WINDSOR, Frances	WINDSOR, Newman	08/07/1813
WINDSOR, Martha A.	FAULKS, Edwd J.R.	04/24/1843
WINDSOR, Rebeccah	BOSWELL, Craven	02/15/1812
WINDSOR, Sarah	TAPSCOTT, Edney	05/23/1797
WINDSOR, Susan	BROWN, Franklin	01/25/1866
WINN, Sarah F.	HUDSON, J. M.	01/27/1859
WINSTEAD, Dianah	LEA, Bedford	10/20/1866
WINSTED, Ailse	YARBOROUGH, Samuel	11/10/1787
WINTERS, Elizabeth	FLEMING, William	12/14/1801
WINTERS, Elizabeth	SALMON, Henry	08/23/1824
WINTERS, Mary	HIPWORTH, Jno.	02/18/1782
WINTERS, Polly	TREW, Oza	09/11/1815
WINTERS, Rachel	MCFARLAND, Thomas	03/15/1797
WISDOM, Catherine	GRIFFIN, Owen	04/17/1816
WISDOM, Mary	WARRIN, Ezekiel	04/15/1816
WISDOM, Nancy	WARREN, William	08/26/1809
WISDOM, Rachel	STUART, William	07/23/1802
WISDOM, Sally	JAY, James	02/04/1804
WISDOM, Sally	ROBERTS, James	11/02/1818
WITCHER, Julina F.	ARNN, George W.	03/26/1851
WITERS, Susan L.	NUNNALLY, John H.	06/20/1854
WITHERS, Alice	WRIGHT, John L.	10/02/1863
WITHERS, Eliza	BLACKWELL, Elias	03/26/1867
WITHERS, Elizabeth A.	DUPREY, John W.	06/12/1843
WITHERS, Jamima Jane	BARNARD, William L.	07/05/1857
WITHERS, Nancy B.	BLACKWELL, John N.	10/07/1862
WITHERS, Sytha A.	NUNNALLY, John	07/22/1817
WLKER, Catherine	HURDLE, James	10/26/1840
WOFF, Sally	TAYLOR, Reuben	08/12/1806
WOMACK, Adline	GRAVES, Nathan	12/26/1865
WOMACK, Cisley	MCFARLAND, James H.	01/22/1787
WOMACK, ELizabeth S.	JUSTICE, Benjamin W.	11/08/1824
WOMACK, Elizabeth C.	GRAVES, James L.	03/12/1840
WOMACK, Elizer A.	HATCHETT, Allen L.	03/30/1859
WOMACK, Martha	BRACKIN, John H.	12/01/1835
WOMACK, Martha J.	RUSSELL, William	07/27/1861
WOMACK, Mary A.	SAUNDERS, Reason C.	03/18/1842
WOMACK, Mary Jane	CONNALLY, George A.	05/26/1830
WOMACK, Mary P.	ADAMS, William W.	07/30/1842
WOMACK, Nancey	INGRAM, Benjamin	05/09/1786
WOMACK, Nancy	WINTERS, Watson	02/05/1815
WOMACK, Sinna	BRACKIN, Joseph	01/28/1795
WOMACK, Susan A.	SAMMONS, Branch	06/04/1842
WOMACK, Vashti	GUNN, Griffin	09/18/1837
WOMBLE, SUsannah F.	FLORENCE, George W.	09/21/1854
WOMBLE, Sarah E. F.	GATTIS, Alexander Rev.	11/24/1857
WOMMACK, Delila	MILES, Abner	11/24/1819
WOOD, Betsey	BROOKES, Samuel	11/10/1792
WOODEY, Judith	MABRY, Lewis	09/01/1784

MARRIAGE RECORDS OF CASWELL COUNTY, NORTH CAROLINA

BRIDE	GROOM	DATE
WOODING, Susan T.	PATE, Richard A.	01/07/1848
WOODS, Ann E.	ALLEN, John W.	10/03/1865
WOODS, Betsey	BIRKS, Johnson	08/24/1802
WOODS, Margaret	RICHMOND, William	10/01/1802
WOODS, Margaret A.	CEARNAL, Robert V.	12/04/1837
WOODS, Martha	SHAW, John S.	02/15/1848
WOODS, Mary	MORGAN, Warren	12/19/1838
WOODS, Mary J.	MORGAN, Benjamin F.	11/28/1848
WOODS, Nancy M.	MCDADE, John A.	08/21/1830
WOODS, Poley	HUGHES, John D.	08/14/1809
WOODS, Sarah A.E.	FITZGERALD, William	03/14/1846
WOODY, Frances	WALLER, John	01/06/1819
WOODY, Nancy	BRANDON, Louis	02/17/1867
WOOTSON, Bettie S.	DICKERSON, Benjamin G.	03/24/1864
WORD, M.C.	ROBSON, J.W.	11/13/1863
WORD, Virginia	BROOCKS, William M. Dr.	12/01/1841
WORSHAM, Emily	TOWNLEY, Alvah R.	05/26/1830
WORSHAM, Lucy	HENDRICK, James	07/23/1814
WORSHAM, Mary R.	HENDRICK, A. J.	10/15/1866
WRAY, Milly	HINTON, Henry	01/29/1801
WRAY, Salley	FORD, William	12/05/1787
WRIGHT, Adaline W.	HARDY, Robert T.	10/04/1865
WRIGHT, Ann B.	LEA, Thomas L.	04/16/1833
WRIGHT, Betsey	COLEMAN, Joshua	12/15/1809
WRIGHT, Betsey	WHITEHEAD, Page	12/15/1809
WRIGHT, Betsy	PAGE, (?) Whitehead (?)	12/15/1809
WRIGHT, Betsy	COLEMAN, (?) Joshua (?)	12/15/1809
WRIGHT, Ester J.	THORNTON, Joseph	12/25/1866
WRIGHT, Henny	ALVERSON, Jesse	07/20/1816
WRIGHT, Laura V.	LILLARD, Thomas M.	10/06/1866
WRIGHT, Martha	WINSTEAD, William	12/05/1844
WRIGHT, Martha J.	PRICE, James A.	06/26/1841
WRIGHT, Mary J.	MOTLEY, Alfred H.	07/10/1856
WRIGHT, Molly	RAINEY, William	10/01/1784
WRIGHT, Nancey	EVANS, James	08/02/1837
WRIGHT, Nancy	LEA, Edmund	10/01/1784
WRIGHT, Nancy	MORGAN, Daniel	04/15/1806
WRIGHT, Polley	FARGUSSON, John	02/01/1797
WRIGHT, Polly	SIMS, John	10/18/1791
WRIGHT, Priscilla	INGRAM, Benjamin	04/21/1814
WRIGHT, Providence	HADDOCK, Richard	07/29/1796
WRIGHT, Rebecca	SOMERS, John	07/25/1804
WRIGHT, Sarah E.	LEA, George G.	05/05/1835
WRIGHT, Susanna	LEA, John	09/10/1825
WRIGHT, Ursley	GRAVES, Barzallai	04/09/1783
WYATT, Hannah	JOHNSTON, Peter	02/21/1782
WYATT, Manerva J.	HOLT, Joseph R.	06/21/1865
WYATT, Polly	JEAN, Jessy	11/23/1789
WYNE, Carthrina	CARTER, Thornton	05/18/1814
WYNN, Jerusha	BEAVER, Jesse	06/25/1810
WYNN, Sarah C.	INGRAM, James	11/02/1841

MARRIAGE RECORDS OF CASWELL COUNTY, NORTH CAROLINA

BRIDE	GROOM	DATE
WYNNE, Charity	MURPHY, William	04/17/1832
WYNNE, Polly	GREGORY, Thomas J.	12/01/1827
YANCEY, Ann E.	GARNER, Archibald W.	01/09/1862
YANCEY, Ann E.	WOMACK, Thomas J.	07/09/1855
YANCEY, Anna	ADKINS, Byrd	04/22/1866
YANCEY, Caroline L.	MEBANE, Lemuel H.	11/01/1841
YANCEY, ELizabeth	BOZWELL, Thomas	12/22/1819
YANCEY, Elizabeth	HARRIS, John	05/28/1837
YANCEY, Elizabeth	SLADE, Nathan	06/26/1792
YANCEY, Fanny	WILEY, Alexander	10/02/1804
YANCEY, Frances W.	MCADEN, Henry	11/04/1829
YANCEY, Mary C.	MEBANE, Giles	03/08/1837
YANCEY, Mildred A.	MALONE, James	01/02/1849
YANCEY, Nancy	JOHNSON, Isaac	12/10/1795
YANCEY, Nancy	RAMSEY, Ambrose K.	10/07/1817
YANCEY, Polly	GRAVES, John Jr.	02/13/1794
YANCEY, Pricilla	HOWARD, JOhn	12/26/1814
YANCEY, Sally	RICE, Archibald	07/06/1811
YANCEY, Virginia B.	SWEPSON, George W.	11/23/1842
YANCY, Elizabeth	MABANE, David	10/28/1817
YARBOROUGH, Martha	TERRY, Dabney	06/20/1846
YARBROUGH, Mary N.	POWELL, William H.	01/05/1861
YARBROUGH, Matilda	SMITH, Abenego	04/22/1867
YARBROUGH, Miranda	YARBROUGH, David	07/07/1866
YARBROUGH, Sally B.	TERRY, Abner R.	07/04/1850
YARBROUGH, Sarah	SATERFIELD, Isaac	09/03/1782
YARBROUGH, Temperance D.	HARRISON, William	05/31/1833
YATES, Betsy	WILLIAMS, Craftin	03/03/1798
YATES, Celia	MCGONNIGIL, Samuel	12/29/1832
YATES, Dolly	SWANN, Burch	04/09/1808
YATES, Elizabeth	TERRY, Wm. E.	12/09/1867
YATES, Joyce	SWANN, Edward	04/20/1782
YATES, Keziah	ROPER, William	08/31/1781
YATES, Mary B.	MEGONEGAL, George W.	12/21/1839
YATES, Nancy	NORMAN, William	07/03/1845
YATES, Polly	MCNEELY, James	09/06/1804
YATES, Polly	PERKINS, William	12/26/1811
YATES, Sally	WARRIN, Buford	02/14/1803
YATES, Sarah	TURNER, William W.	10/09/1860
YOUNG, Martha S.	WILSON, William L.	08/26/1862
YOUNG, Mary L.	HALL, Benjamin P.	06/16/1858
YOUNG, Sally	DODSON, William T.	09/28/1812
YOUNG, Susan A.	ROBERTSON, Edward S.	12/10/1844
YUILLE, Susan S.	BURKS, Richard H. Jr.	11/28/1852
ZACHARY Prudence	BRUCE, David	08/23/1795
ZACHARY, Polly	CARR, John	03/15/1797
ZACHARY, Priscilla	WALKER, Joseph	03/17/1800
ZACHORY, Judah	MORTON, John	04/04/1804
ZIGLER, Martha Jane	EDWARDS, N.R.	03/02/1863

Heritage Books by Frances T. Ingmire:

Arkansas Confederate Veterans and Widows Pension Applications

Citizens of Missouri Territory: 1787-1810, Grants in Present Day Missouri, Arkansas and Oklahoma, Vol. 1

Citizens of Missouri Territory: 1810-1812, Grants in Present Day Missouri, Arkansas and Oklahoma, Vol. 2

Citizens of Missouri Territory to-1835, Grants in Present Day Missouri, Arkansas and Oklahoma, Vol. 3

Hunt County, Texas Archives and Pioneers, Volume 2

Hunt County, Texas Archives and Pioneers, Volume 3

North Carolina Marriage Bonds and Certificates Series: Caswell County, North Carolina, Marriage Records, 1778–1876

North Carolina Marriage Bonds and Certificates Series: Craven County, North Carolina, Marriage Records, 1780–1867

North Carolina Marriage Bonds and Certificates Series: Cumberland County, North Carolina, Marriage Records, 1803–1878

North Carolina Marriage Bonds and Certificates Series: Guilford County, North Carolina, Marriage Records, 1771–1868

North Carolina Marriage Bonds and Certificates Series: Lincoln County, North Carolina, Marriage Records, 1783–1866

North Carolina Marriage Bonds and Certificates Series: Orange County, North Carolina, Marriage Records, 1782–1868

North Carolina Marriage Bonds and Certificates Series: Randolph County, North Carolina, Marriage Records, 1785–1868

North Carolina Marriage Bonds and Certificates Series: Rowan County, North Carolina, Marriage Records, 1754–1866

North Carolina Marriage Bonds and Certificates Series: Stokes County, North Carolina, Marriage Records, 1783–1868

North Carolina Marriage Bonds and Certificates Series: Surry County, North Carolina, Marriage Records, 1783–1868

North Carolina Marriage Bonds and Certificates Series: Wake County, North Carolina, Marriage Records, 1781–1867

North Carolina Marriage Bonds and Certificates Series: Wilkes County, North Carolina, Marriage Records, 1779–1868

Texas Ranger Service Records, 1838–1846

Texas Ranger Service Records, 1847–1900, Volume 1: A-C

Texas Ranger Service Records, 1847–1900, Volume 2: D-G

Texas Ranger Service Records, 1847–1900, Volume 3: H-K

Texas Ranger Service Records, 1847–1900, Volume 4: L-N

Texas Ranger Service Records, 1847–1900, Volume 5: O-S

Texas Ranger Service Records, 1847–1900, Volume 6: T-Z

www.ingramcontent.com/pod-product-compliance
Lightning Source LLC
Chambersburg PA
CBHW080420270326
41929CB00018B/3095